Laura Elizabeth Poor

Sanskrit and its Kindred Literatures Studies in Comparative

Mythology

Laura Elizabeth Poor

Sanskrit and its Kindred Literatures Studies in Comparative Mythology

ISBN/EAN: 9783337191863

Printed in Europe, USA, Canada, Australia, Japan

Cover: Foto ©Thomas Meinert / pixelio.de

More available books at **www.hansebooks.com**

AND ITS

KINDRED LITERATURES.

Studies in Comparative Mythology.

BY

LAURA ELIZABETH POOR.

QUI LEGIT REGIT

BOSTON:
ROBERTS BROTHERS.
1880.

UNIVERSITY PRESS:
JOHN WILSON AND SON, CAMBRIDGE.

PREFACE.

———◆———

THIS is not an encyclopædia: therefore every author will not be found in it. It is an attempt, first, so to interest people in the new discoveries in literature as to induce them to study for themselves; in order to do this, only the greatest writers have been mentioned, and long extracts given from their works to illustrate the opinions stated; second, to put all literature upon that new basis which has been created by the new sciences of comparative philology and comparative mythology. For this reason the greatest space has been given to the Sanskrit literature, which caused these discoveries, contains so many elements of all literature, and is so much less familiar. Some apology is perhaps necessary for writing anything upon the Greek philosophers and historians. But I was requested to add this chapter. The chapter on modern literature formed part of the original plan. If any should consider it irrelevant to these new discoveries, I should say, on the contrary, that the whole book is but a leading-up to that; for modern literature is the most elaborate expression of those ideas whose origin and growth I have endeavored to trace.

CONTENTS.

SANSKRIT

AND ITS KINDRED LITERATURES.

---·◊·---

CHAPTER I.

THE ORIGIN OF LITERATURE.

I PROPOSE to write about the literature of different nations and different centuries. I wish to show that this literature is not many, but one; that the same leading ideas have arisen at epochs apparently far separated from each other; that each nation, however isolated it may seem, is, in reality, a link in the great chain of development of the human mind: in other words, to show the unity and continuity of literature.

This has only been possible within a few years. To the despairing school-boy of fifty years ago the histories of Phœnicians, Carthaginians, Romans, or Greeks, were so many detached pieces of information to be fixed in the memory by dreary plodding. But the moment the mind realizes the mighty truth that one nation is connected with all others, its history becomes delightful and inspiring; because we trace its method of reproducing the ideas we had met elsewhere. And it is to the Sanskrit language that we owe this entire change in our standpoint.

Our subject in this chapter is the origin of literature; but before we reach it we ought to have, therefore, a

general idea of the Sanskrit language, its enormous
importance, and its relations to modern science. Max
Müller says, " The discovery of Sanskrit is in many
respects equally important, in some even more important,
than the revival of Greek scholarship in the fifteenth
century ; " that is the Renaissance.

Formerly Greek and Latin were the boundary of
knowledge in the direction of literature. Real students
may have devoted a few thoughts to the ancient Egyptians ; but the average scholar who had conquered these
literatures felt a serene consciousness of having explored
the farthest domain of human thought in one line. Men
were even satisfied to devote a lifetime to poring over
one Greek tragedy : but within the last hundred years
a new language with its literature has become known,
which has revolutionized all preconceived ideas ; created
two new sciences, and possibly three. These are
comparative philology ; that is, the study of different
languages : comparative mythology, the study of different religions : and Sir Henry Sumner Maine thinks that
another science will soon be crystallized, called comparative jurisprudence, the study of the laws of different
nations.

A hundred years ago Sir William Jones and other
Englishmen living in India heard of a literary language
of the Hindoos called Sanskrit. The name means a " completed " or " perfected " dialect in distinction from the
Prakrit or " natural " dialect. It was a spoken language
at the time of Solomon, 1015 B. C., also of Alexander,
324 B. C., but for the last two thousand years it has been
kept alive like Latin in Europe. by grammars and diction-
aries, and an educated caste of men. They studied this

language, and were amazed to find that it contained many words resembling those of the European languages ; for example : —

English.	Sanskrit.	Zend.	Latin.	Irish Keltic.	Gothic. Teutonic.
Father	pitar	patar	pater	athair	fadar
Mother	matar	matar	mater	mathair	
Brother	bhratar	bratar	frater	brathair	brothar
Sister	svasar	quahar	soror	suir	svistar
Daughter	duhitar	dughdhar		dear	dauhtar
Door	dvar		fores	dor	daur
Two	do	du	duo		

Slavic.

Lord   vis-patar or tribe father   weizpater.

They published a grammar of the language and translations from the literature in 1785, 1787, 1789, 1794, and thus threw open Sanskrit to the European mind. Learned men of all nations eagerly studied and commented upon these books. Max Müller says, "The first who dared boldly to face both the facts and conclusions of Sanskrit scholarship was the German poet, Frederic Schlegel. He was not a great scholar, many of his statements have since been proved erroneous ; but he was a man of genius, and when a new science is to be created, the imagination of the poet is wanted even more than the accuracy of the scholar."

Many minds contributed to the great-work, and the new science of comparative philology was created. Max Müller says, "I may express my conviction that the science of language (comparative philology) will yet enable us to withstand the extreme theories of the evolutionists, and to draw a hard and fast line between spirit and matter, between man and brute." In brief these are its conclusions. First: if a word is essentially the same in several languages, it must have existed in the parent tongue from which all are descended; therefore language is the most reliable proof of relationship between nations. Second: if this be so, the whole human race may be divided into four families and languages, with four great streams. These are, —

1. The *Chinese* race : this language is the only relic of the first forms of human speech, being made up of words of one syllable, and to the student of language, the philologist, it is far more interesting and valuable than the completed tongues, such as Sanskrit, Greek, or Latin. It shows the real character of language left to develop itself in its own way. To illustrate what is meant I will just indicate in the briefest way that there are three stages of language : The first is monosyllabic, " such a deed would be like man." The second stage is agglutinative where the root remains distinct from the addition " manlike, Godlike." The third stage, is inflexional, where the root and inflexions are so interwoven as to be no longer distinguishable, " manly," " godly." The Chinese civilization was the third earliest in the world. Its earliest chronicle dates from 1500 B. C.

2. The *Turanian* races, including most of the original inhabitants of Asia; the Mongolians in India; the Mantchu Tartars in China; the Finns; the Lapps; the Samoyedes in Northern Europe; the Turks, Hungarians, Bulgarians of Southern Europe, — the Hungarians and Bulgarians being the only Turanian races who have embraced Christianity, — the Mexicans, Peruvians, In-

dians of North and Central America. Some authorities include the Pelasgi in Greece, the Etruscans in Italy, but Mommsen calls them Aryan. The Egyptians were formerly called Turanian, but now are said to have a mixed nationality. Their dialects are also very valuable to the philologist, as marking the second, agglutinative stage of language. The Turanian races are always tomb builders. These tombs are sometimes mounds, — especially in Greece, Italy, and America. From the implements found in Etruscan tombs and Peruvian mounds we know that they used gold, silver, and copper, and that they manufactured bronze. They were, indeed, more civilized than their Aryan invaders, but these latter conquered, because they knew the use of iron.

3. The *Semitic* races include the Jews, the Arabs, the Phœnicians, the Carthaginians, the Mesopotamians, — probably the native inhabitants of Nineveh, Babylon, and Assyria. Their languages are of the third stage, inflexional. They played an important part in the world while the Aryans were living quietly at home. The Chaldeans, the Moabites, the Edomites, belong to them, and perhaps partly the Egyptians. This Egyptian civilization is the oldest in the world. Menes, their king, dates back 5000 B.C., and their civilization culminated and began to decline 3000 B.C. The Chaldean civilization was the second: its earliest chronicle is 2234 B.C.

4. The conquering *Aryan* race, whose languages belong to the third stage, the inflexional. It includes the *Hindus*, with their Sanskrit language ; the *Persians*, with the Zend ; the *Greeks ;* the *Romans*, with the Latin

language and its six children, — The Provençal, French, Italian, Spanish, Portuguese, and Wallachian ; the *Kelts*, to whom belong the Gauls of ancient France ; the Britons of ancient England, and their modern languages, — the Gaelic of Scotland, the Erse of Ireland, the Kymric of Wales ; the Bas Bréton of France ; the *Teutons*, who include the ancient Goths, Franks, Anglo-Saxons : their modern languages are Icelandic, Danish, Swedish, Norwegian, German, Low Dutch, English. The *Slavs*, their name, which comes from *slowan*, to speak, was given by themselves. They considered all the rest of the world dumb, because it could not understand them ; the race includes the Russians, Servians, Montenegrins, Poles, Bohemians, Dalmatians, and all these are our kindred. The dark-skinned Hindu of to-day is as much our brother as the fair-haired Norwegian. What was the mother tongue of the Aryan families, what language they spoke before they left their native home, and separated in such widely scattered directions, we do not know ; all that precedes this period is hopelessly lost to us, but these just mentioned are sister tongues with the family likeness plainly to be seen.

It is our pride and glory to belong to that conquering Aryan race, whose beginnings have lately been made known to us. In the north-western part of Asia lived these shepherd tribes. The climate was far colder then than now ; the winters were longer ; this we know, because among the words common to all the Aryan families, and therefore in use in their original home, are none to express great heat or plants dependent upon heat. They must have lived inland, because there is no common word for ocean. Yet they must have known

something of river navigation, because all the languages
have boat, rudder, oar. They had domesticated the
animals, and surrounded themselves with oxen, sheep,
horses, dogs ; they cultivated the ground, for there are
words for flax, barley, wheat, and hemp. They used
the moon to measure time, and divided the year into
twelve months. Incredible as it may seem, they could
count up to one hundred, and they used the same numbers which we do. We find the words, father, mother,
brother, sister, husband, wife : but these at first only
expressed the occupations of the persons spoken of;
bhratar, brother, was he who helps ; *swasar*, sister, she
who consoles and pleases ; *pitar*, father, he who protects
and supports ; *duhitar*, daughter, means a milkmaid.
For the cow was even then the most valuable animal.
In Sanskrit the patriarch is called " the lord of the
cattle ; " the morning is the " calling of the cattle."
In German, the word *abend*, evening, means the " un-
binding of cattle." In Slavonic the title *hospodar*, their
title for prince, means " the protector of the cattle,"
from *gôspada*, the word *go* meaning cow. They dwelt in
well-built houses with walls around them ; they used
carriages with wheels over plainly defined roads ; they
were divided into families with a name. Those institutions for self-government, which we fondly suppose to
be the prerogative of the Teutonic family, originated
before the Aryans left their common home. At first
the family existed, entirely independent of any external authority. Each householder united with the
others to form villages, which had their own magistrates ;
these again formed a tribe, subject to a feudal lord, *vis
pitar*, the " people's father." These village communi-

ties have survived every change of dynasty in India,
and continue to this day.   It ennobles human nature
that such ideas should have arisen spontaneously.   For
family life implies affection, as law, respect, for others ; so
our ancestors were not solitary savages, but five thousand years ago they were living together in peace and
good government in happy families.   But the words of
the different Aryan languages which express wild beasts,
weapons of war and of hunting, are quite different ; and,
since a new word marks a new condition, we know that
they separated.   It has been discovered that the Khiva
desert, stretching between the Caspian Sea and the Sea
of Aral, has been formed by the shrinkage of these two
seas.   Once fertile land was there, but the desert caused
the migrations of the Aryans westward.   Each branch
went on a different path.   Wherever it paused it conquered the native Turanian tribes, the original inhabitants of the land, and amalgamated their language with
its own, until a new tongue was formed.

Such are the astonishing historical facts revealed to us
by the comparison of words with the Sanskrit words, —
facts that were undreamed of one hundred years ago,
and scoffed at when first proclaimed.   But they are as
certain as a mathematical demonstration, and universally
accepted to-day.

The inquiries awakened were pushed still further.
The gods and goddesses of the Sanskrit literature
seemed strangely like those of Greek literature.   The
mythologies of all the Aryan races were carefully compared ; the revolutionary inferences were carried on till a
result was obtained which seemed at first incredible, and
the new science of comparative mythology claimed its

place among the other sciences. It must be said that its conclusions are not universally adopted as yet, but they are fast becoming so among the most critical scholars.

When the simple-hearted Aryan saw the sun go down at night and disappear, he cried out that the sun was dead, just as in French we say " the fire is dead," *le feu est mort*, instead of " the fire has gone out." When the darkness settled down upon the earth, he said that an enemy had killed the sun. " Will the sun ever come back to us," he cried in terror. When the dawn gradually drove away this darkness, and nature and man began a new life, he thought she was a real person who awoke the world and brought back the sun. When, finally, the sun itself came up in its light and splendor, it seemed to him a being of mighty power. Its beams shone like spears, and its heat dried up the dew. So mythology is called " a disease of language," and comparative mythology teaches that the gods and goddesses of the Aryan races are only nature personified; its powers put into human form. A few simple objects were personified in as many ways as the unrestrained imagination of these child-like people could invent, and gave rise to a host of gods and goddesses. *Dyu* meant originally the bright shining sky; the heaven next it became the *Dyaus pitar*, — the heaven father, the protector. This is the first name given to a god, and we are sure that this heaven father was worshipped before the Aryans left their native home, because we find Zeus-Pater in Greek, Jupiter in Latin, Zio and Tuisco in German, Tyr in Norse. The course of the sun from his rising to his setting became the life of some god; he has a struggling infancy, early prosperity with a beloved bride ; then the bride of his youth is torn from him, and he goes forth to toils and dangers undertaken for the good of another. He serves beings meaner than himself ; finally, after a fierce battle with dark powers which obstruct him in every way, come rest and victory and death, and reconciliation with his abandoned bride. That is the sun struggles through the clouds which obstruct his rising ; leaves the dawn behind ; is covered by dark clouds which hide him at night, as he sinks out of sight and sets. The twilight darkness comes, the soft and tender bride soothes the dying hours of her husband. Again the sun loves the dawn, that is Apollo loves Daphne ; she flies before him ; he tries to overtake her, but of course the dawn must disappear before the sun, and Daphne escapes Apollo. Or else the sun dries up the dew ; that is Kephalos kills Procris ; when the sun's scorching heat parches up earth and man, he is slaying with his spears, that is his rays, and becomes the enemy of man. When drought comes, they call the dark clouds which hang near the earth, without giving out rain, a snake or dragon who is shutting up the rain in prison. When the thunder rolled, they said this hateful monster was uttering riddles. When the rain finally burst forth, and gave relief to man and beast and the earth, they said the rain had killed the serpent who was devouring everything. In Sanskrit Indra slew Vritra, the great serpent ; in Greek Apollo slew the Python ; in Norse Sigurd slew the worm Fafnir ; in the middle ages St. Michael conquered the dragon. Balder, the beautiful, the pride of the Norse pantheon, is the summer, he is light and heat killed by the cold and darkness of winter :

the myth is exactly reversed. The same incidents recur in all the different mythologies.

Each one has numerous demigods or heroes; all have invincible weapons, which none but themselves can wield; the bow of Odysseus, the club of Herakles, the sword of Sigurd. They are vulnerable only in one spot, the heel of Achilleus, the eyes in Isfendyar; or by one weapon, the firebrand of Meleagros, the thorn of Siegfried. All these heroes have fair faces and golden locks flowing over their shoulders. They all abandon the bride of their youth; they all toil and suffer for others; they are subject to strange fits of gloom and inactivity, such as the wrath of Achilleus, the anger of Rustem. In the end, they overcome this, break forth in their early cheerfulness, conquer their enemies, and die on a blazing funeral pile. It is again the sun; its rays changed into golden locks, into invincible spears or arrows. It leaves the dawn, struggles through dark clouds, and sets hidden by flame-colored clouds. These are the shirt of flame which enwrap and kill Herakles, — simply a magnificent red sun-set. It is a most amusing occupation to trace these numerous forms of the solar myth. Ixion bound upon the burning wheel is the sun. Tantalus, from whom food and drink recede, is the sun, whose beams dry up the water and the fruit. Sisyphus continuing to roll the stone up the hill from which it always rolls back, is the sun which no sooner reaches the highest point of the sky, than it is obliged to go down again.

The comparison has not only been applied to the gods of mythology, the heroes of epic poetry, but also to the popular ballad heroes of the middle ages, and even

William Tell is reduced to a solar myth; his unerring arrows to the rays of the sun, alike dangerous to friend or foe. Historical investigations have proved that he did not exist literally in the form under which we know him, and now the comparative mythologist claims him as the lineal descendant of Indra and Apollo and Odysseus: he bends the bow which none but he can wield.

Of course this is the merest sketch; I shall allude to these gods and heroes as we come to them in each literature, and fill out the outline. We may perhaps be more ready to accept the conclusions of comparative mythology when we have studied our own English poetry, or gazed upon Guido's frescoed ceiling where the dawn flies before the chariot of the sun, and the bright hours follow after in human shape. In fact it is the natural spontaneous utterance of the poetic mind in every age and country, afterwards accepted as a literal fact.

The theory has been confirmed from a despised and unexpected source. That the gods were changed into the heroes of epics, that they even descended to the popular ballads might be acknowledged. But how can we believe what is expected that even the nursery tales of the different Aryan families are but another form of the solar myth? It seemed at first too absurd, but the German scholar Grimm threw " off the yoke of classical tyranny," and asserted that the popular tale had a science of its own, and a meaning worthy to be explored. It is true that Jack the Giant Killer, the Sleeping Beauty, and Faithful John, have found a parallel in Sanskrit nursery tales told to little Hindu children; in the volumes collected from old peasants by the broth-

ers Grimm in Germany; in the Gaelic legends, still
lingering in the Highlands of Scotland; in the Norse
stories which shorten the long winter evenings in Iceland.
It is pleasant to find our beloved fairy tales taking so important a place in literature after being frowned down
by the stern guardians of our childhood.   It is poetic
justice.   The same properties are found everywhere.
The sandals of Hermes become the seven-leagued boots
of Jack the Giant Killer.   The helmet of Hades becomes
the invisible cap of Fortunatus.   The Holy Grail which
the bad cannot see or touch becomes the horse-shoe nailed
up for good luck, because the bad cannot touch it.
The lovely Sleeping Beauty, who pricks her finger with
a spindle, is the earth frozen by the sharp sudden touch
of winter.   The many dead princes who strive to reach
and awaken her are the suns which rise and set in the
first bleak days of spring.   "The fated prince with
golden locks" is the sun of summer.   With its ardent
kiss it awakens the white earth from its long winter
sleep, and she sleeps in every land and every literature.
The talisman which, for one moment, opens a mountain
or a cave and reveals marvellous treasures within, is
found in Aladdin, in Tannhaüser and the Bréton folk-
tales.   It is an arrow or a flower, or the name of some
grain; and it means the lightning which splits the rock.
Out of a vast number of illustrations I have taken these
familiar ones, but they are sufficient to explain the
theory.   And so before the Aryans left their common
home, and separated, they had in their memory these
nursery tales which have developed into the folk-lore of
different Aryan families.   It is quite impossible that
there should have been any intercourse between the

tribes, and yet the resemblances are even more striking than in mythology, epic and ballad. Folk-lore becomes a most important witness for the two sciences.

When we realize the bearing of these new ideas, and the vast change they will produce in human thought, you will agree that I have not over-estimated the importance of Sanskrit in its twofold branching, the language and the literature. The grammatical structure of the language is not connected with our subject, so I will go on at once to the delightful literature.

To India we must go for our pioneers — I had almost said our masters — in every department of literature but one, that of history. The Hindoo dreamed and speculated and argued, but he did not observe or record the events of external, every-day life. There is no literary or political history in Sanskrit, so that the chronology of every work must be judged from internal evidence alone. It is now fully recognized that a hymn to a god or gods is the earliest utterance of the human mind in every nation. Accordingly in Sanskrit the first book is a general collection of hymns; it is called a "Veda." The word means "highest knowledge," and there are in Sanskrit four Vedas. The oldest and best of them is called the Rig or praise Veda; the word *Rig* meaning praise. It contains one thousand and seventeen hymns written in poetry in stanzas of two lines called *aslokas*. The Aryan conquerors of India were the last to leave the early home. They are supposed to have entered India about 3100 B. C., and the oldest of the hymns of the Rig Veda are supposed by the best authorities to have been written 2400 B. C., the last perhaps 1500 B. C. Each Brahman was obliged to learn by heart the one thousand and seventeen hymns during the twelve years that he passed as a student. They were transmitted by repetition from father to son, — handed down as sacred heirlooms in different families. This seems a most astonishing power of memory. But even at the present day there are thousands of Brahmans in India who know the whole of the Rig Veda by heart, and can repeat it. Finally they were written down on palm-leaves about 1000 b. c. But the four Vedas themselves contain no mention of books or of writing.

The Rig Veda was sung in the Indus Valley, the country of the seven rivers, before the Aryan invaders had penetrated far into India. Therefore it is our authority for the earliest manners and customs of our ancestors as well as for their simple and childlike beliefs, and has a double value, — one to the historian and philologist, the other to the comparative mythologist. Max Müller says, "The whole history of the world would be incomplete without this first chapter in the life of Aryan humanity which has been preserved to us in Vedic literature." There are different stages of civilization distinctly marked. At first each head of a family was a warrior, a poet, and a priest. He raised a single altar of turf and kindled upon it the sacred fire, which was kept perpetually burning ever after. Before every meal it was his office to throw upon the sacred fire some portion of the food, to pour out upon the ground a part of the drink, to call upon the gods to receive his offering and grant his requests.

For what then did the Hindoo Aryans pray? Their hymns are the outcry of a child to a Father for temporal good. They are invading India and wish to settle there, so they cry out for lands and cattle, for riches and many children, for power and a long life, for a happy immortality after death, for victory over their enemies. The hymns are as simple as they are sincere. They call down curses; they shout exulting songs of victory; but they very seldom give any rules for action or any precepts of morality. · They are somewhat vague and incoherent but charming nevertheless, beautiful from their very simplicity. They are fresh, vigorous, and poetical, and uttered with absolute, unquestioning faith. " Whoever asks obtains," is the key-note to them all. In most of them the worshipper praises and flatters the god, offers him the soma juice, and calmly asks for temporal blessings in return. Max Müller says, " The language of the simple prayers is more intelligible to us than anything we find in the literature of Greece or Rome, and there are here and there expressions of faith and devotion in which even a Christian can join without irreverence."

Who then are the gods upon whom he calls? First, the spirits of his dead ancestors, and therefore different for every family: next the aspects of nature personified with exquisite poetry, and so distinctly described that they might almost be painted. But we must remember that there must have been a long process of development, centuries before their beliefs reached even the stage in which we find them in the Rig Veda 1000 B. C. Max Müller has succeeded, in his lectures delivered in 1878, in bringing vividly before us the gradual awakenings which led up to even that degree of expression. The Aryans called a river the " runner" or "noisy," or " the mother which nourished the fields," or the " defender " as forming a boundary between two countries; we say "it rains," they said "the rainer rains," "the blower blows:" everything was active, and therefore must be a person. It was almost impossible to get rid of the idea of a person connected with everything active. It is generally supposed that gender was the cause of personification; on the contrary, it was the result. When they wished to say that a thing simply existed, then came a great difficulty to these pioneers of thought and its expression, which is language. " As the most general act of all human beings is to breathe, they said things breathe, when we say things are. The verb *as* means to breathe; and in Sanskrit those who breathe, who are, are called Asura, the oldest name for the living, breathing gods. The same verb *as* exists in Norse, where the gods are called Æsir: it is our English *is*. When the word to breathe was found inconvenient, as for instance if applied to a tree, they took the root *bhu*, to grow; and called the earth, the growing one; in English to be. When something vaster was wanted, the root *vas*, to dwell; English, I was: they applied to those things which could not breathe or grow. We say the sun is there; they said the sun breathes: we say the moon exists or is; they said the moon grows: we say the earth exists; they said the earth dwells." These were called *deva*, or bright; gradually, during a thousand years, one quality shared by many objects came to be used as a general term for the gods: the *devas*, the bright ones. Almost every object which is semi-tangible is included amongst them. Mountains and rivers; the sun, dawn, these can be seen, though not actually touched. The next step embraced in the devas only those which could be heard, not touched, nor seen, —

the thunder, the wind, the storm. Then they called the sun like light, next the bringer of light; the sky, bending over and protecting the earth like a father, next a father. Now these are wholly intangible. They are asked to listen ; to grant favors ; to protect men, and this point must have been reached before the Aryans separated, since we find the name Heaven-Father in every Aryan language.

Fortunately, we are able to go more into details, and see how the gods of other mythologies took shape, by examining closely the Sanskrit devas. There is some doubt about the number of them, but they are usually said to be twelve. If there are fewer than in the other mythologies, it is because ideas are in an elementary condition ; and the characteristics of the gods are not so often interchanged, as in the more crystallized state of Greek and Teutonic mythology. They are sometimes interchanged, and each god is at times represented as supreme and absolute over all the others. There are no settled families. The father sometimes becomes the son ; the brother becomes the husband ; she who is the wife in one hymn becomes the mother in another. But this very indistinctness and difference show us how naturally and gradually all Aryan mythology grew up. It was but the utterance of childish minds about the world around them, feeling their way towards clearness. This makes the incalculable value of the Rig Veda. Müller says : " While Hesiod gives us a past theogony, we see in the Veda the theogony itself; the very birth and growth of the gods, that is of the word for gods; and in its later hymns the subsequent development of these divine conceptions." In its unsettled and growing myths we have the foundation of the gay and brilliant mythology of the Greeks, as well as the dark and sombre mythology of the Teutons. It contains those elements which have been expanded into such innumerable forms, and which were never understood until they were illuminated by this oldest book of the world. Max Müller says, " It is the oldest, because it contains the earliest phases of thought and feeling."

It is hard to define and limit the work of each god, and his personal character. Dyaus is the most ancient name for the supreme god. It is derived from a root which means to shine, or bright; and becomes Daevas, in Zend; Theos, in Greek; Deus, in Latin; Divus, in Italian; Dieu, in French; Devil, in English. It meant at first the bright sky, the heaven above us. Among the Hindus, Dyaus, the heaven, married Prithivi, the earth, and they became the father and mother of the other Hindu gods. But the sky, originally the bright, the light-giver, was replaced by various gods who represented the different actions of the sky, such as the rain, the storm; and the power of Dyaus is almost given up to his son, Indra, the rain-bringer. Because the Indian land is parched up by the scorching sun, and depends upon the rain for its fertility, the rain is more grateful there than elsewhere. It pours down in resistless torrents, so Indra is a strong impetuous warrior, drunk with soma juice. He drives a chariot whose rolling wheels are heard far off; that is the thunder. It is drawn by pawing and champing steeds, the clouds : he bears a resistless lance ; that is the lightning. The lightning pierced the dark storm-clouds and set free the rain, and thus put an end to the drought. There is another explanation of the dark storm-clouds piled up into hollow cavernous forms. The Aryans called the sky a plain; the bright clouds which wandered over it they called cows, guarded by a lovely maiden, Sarama, the dawn; and the dark clouds they called a snake shut up in a cave. He was said to have stolen the cows and the maiden, and to have brought them into his hollow cave. So Indra takes on another character. As the sky shines out bright and serene, when a storm has passed away, Indra next becomes the god of the clear, cloudless sky. In this he usurped the character of Dyaus. So the Hindus said that Indra had killed the snake who had stolen treasures and a maiden. I describe this second personification of dark clouds because Indra in this becomes the original of every hero who delivers a distressed damsel by fighting with a monster; whether he is Perseus in Greek; or St. George in the Middle Ages. We shall meet him many a time. As the bright clear sky, Indra has golden locks and a beard which flashes like gold as he hastens over the heaven. His arrows have a hundred points, and are winged with a thousand feathers. All this sounds so very like the Greek mythology which we learned in our childhood, that it is hard to realize that it grew up in India five thousand years ago.

HYMNS TO INDRA.

" He who as soon as born is the first of the deities, who has done honor to the gods by his deeds; he at whose might heaven and earth are alarmed, and who is known by the greatness of his strength : he, men, is Indra.

" He who fixed firm the moving earth, who spread the spacious firmament; he is Indra.

" He who, having destroyed Vritra, set free the seven rivers ; who recovered the cows ; who generated fire in the clouds ; who is invincible in battle : he, men, is Indra.

" He to whom heaven and earth bow down ; he at whose might the mountains are appalled ; he who is drinker of the soma juice ; the firm of frame ; the adamant-armed ; the wielder of the thunderbolt : he, men, is Indra. May we envelop thee with acceptable praises."

" Showerer of benefits, destroyer of cities, propitiated by our new songs, reward us with gratifying blessings."

" Quaff the soma juice, satiate thy appetite, and then fix thy mind on the wealth that is to be given to us."

" Slayer of Vritra, ascend thy chariot, for thy horses have been yoked by prayer. May the sound of the stone that bruises the soma attract thy mind towards us."

Indra is accompanied by the Maruts, the storm winds. This is the same root as the Greek Ares, and the Latin Mars ; and the Teutonic Thor Miolnir, the god of war in each mythology. These Maruts overturn trees and destroy forests ; they roar like lions ; they shake the mountains ; they are swift as thought ; they are brothers of whom no one is the elder, no one the younger : this is a perfect picture of the wind ; and in this character of the Maruts we see blind strength and fury without judgment.

HYMN TO THE MARUTS.

" 1. For the manly host, the majestic, the wise, for the Maruts, bring thou, O poet, a pure offering. Like a workman, wise in his mind and handy, I join together words which are useful at sacrifices.

" 2. They are born, the tall bulls of Dyaus, the boys of Rudra, the divine, the blameless, pure and bright like suns, scattering raindrops of awful shape like giants.

"3. The youthful Maruts, they who never grow old, the slayers of the demon, have grown irresistible like mountains. They shake with their strength all beings, even the strongest on earth and in heaven.

"4. They deck themselves with glittering ornaments for show; on their chests they fix gold [chains] for beauty ; the spears on their shoulders pound to pieces ; they were born together by themselves, the men of Dyaus.

" 5. They who confer power, the rovers, the devourers of foes, they make winds and lightnings by their powers. The shakers milk the seventy udders [clouds], roaming around they fill the earth with milk [rain].

"7. Mighty are you, powerful, of wonderful splendor, firmly rooted like mountains ; yet lightly gliding along ; you chew up forests, like elephants, when you have assumed vigor among the red flames.

"8. Like lions they roar. The far-sighted Maruts, they are handsome like gazelles, the all-knowing. By night, with their spotted deer [that is rain clouds] and with their spears [lightnings] they rouse the companions together, they whose ire through strength is like the ire of serpents.

"9. You who march in companies, the friends of man, heroes, whose ire, etc., salute heaven and earth. On the seats of your chariots, O Maruts, the lightning stands, visible like light."

"12. We invoke with prayer the offspring of Rudra, the brisk, the bright, the worshipful, the active. Cling for happiness' sake to the strong host of the Maruts ; the chasers of the sky, the vigorous, the impetuous.

"13. The mortal whom ye, Maruts, protected with your protection, he indeed surpasses people in strength. He carries off food with his horses, treasures with his men ; he acquires honorable strength and he prospers.

"14. Give, O Maruts, to the worshippers strength, glorious, invincible in battle, wealth-conferring, praiseworthy, known to all men. Let us foster our kith and kin during a hundred winters.

"15. Will you then, O Maruts, grant unto us wealth, durable, rich in men, defying all onslaughts? wealth a hundred and a thousand fold, always increasing? May he [you] who is [are] rich in prayers [that is the company of the Maruts] come early and soon!"

But the wind has a gentler side to its character as it sinks down into a faint breeze. So the Maruts in the Veda "assume again the form of new-born babes." And this is exactly the story told in Greek of Hermes, as we shall see.

The soft music which the faint breeze makes becomes the reed pipe of Pan; the music of the Sirens; the lyre of Orpheus, which makes the beasts and trees dance; the harp of Arion, which charmed the fishes; the marvellous pipe of the pied piper of Hamelin, in the Middle Ages. The wind as a harper is one of the primary myths, organized before the separation of the Aryans, and found also in two Turanian nations, — the Finns of Northern Europe and the Indians of Central America. There is another office which the wind performs. It wreaks its fury, uproots the trees, penetrates into the most hidden corners; then, with a low whistling sound like mocking laughter, it passes on its way. This also is very plainly told in the Greek myth of Hermes, and the peering thief is visible as Peeping Tom of Coventry, who can see through a cranny.

The sun becomes in Sanskrit several persons as performing different acts, — Mitra, Vishnu. The holiest verse in the Vedas is addressed to it. "Earth, Sky, Heaven! Let us meditate on the most excellent light and power of that generous, sportive, and resplendent sun. May he guide our intellects!" It does not fill so large a place in the Sanskrit as in the other mythologies. As Vishnu, it receives its light from another power. It is called the wide-stepping, and traverses the heavens in three strides. This must be the rising, culminating, and setting of the sun. Vishnu comes forward in the later Brahmanical mythology, and there has ten incarnations which are called Avatars.

Every mythology has its drink of the gods, but in Sanskrit only does it become a person. You will notice that all the hymns offer the soma; it is the moon plant, and its juice becomes a fermented liquor. The Hindu fancied that the intoxication produced by it was a higher state of existence than his ordinary life. He felt endowed with new powers while under its influence. It seemed to him a gift worthy of the gods, and when he fancied that they were angry, he tried to appease them by pouring out libations of the precious juice. Here is one of the most beautiful hymns in the Rig Veda, which is addressed to Soma : —

"Where there is eternal light, in the world where the sun is placed, in that immortal, imperishable world, place me, O Soma.

"Where King Vaivasvata reigns, where the secret place of heaven is, where these mighty waters are : there make me immortal.

"Where life is free, in the third heaven of heavens, where the worlds are radiant : there make me immortal.

"Where wishes and desires are, where the place of the bright sun is, where there is freedom and delight : there make me immortal!

"Where there is happiness and delight, where joy and pleasure reside, where the desires of our desire are attained : there make me immortal!"

Agni is another god who is distinctively Hindu ; he is the fire ; from the root we have the Latin ignis, the English ignite; but the word does not appear in the other Aryan families as the name of a deity. There is no folk-lore connected with him, and his person does not reappear as the other Hindu deities constantly do. The Hindus were struck by its sudden appearing and disappearing ; its agile movements, and called it " the quick ; " or by its crackling noise, they said : " neighing like a horse that is greedy for food, it steps out from its strong prison." This is wonderfully descriptive. The first and last hymns of the Rig Veda are addressed to Agni because he was their favorite god. They considered him the messenger between them and heaven, who carried up their offerings to Dyaus-Pitar. If the flame rose bright and clear, they thought their offerings were accepted ; if it died down in smoke, that they were refused. They sacrificed clarified butter to him, thinking it to be his favorite food. Of course, any fire will burn brighter if clarified butter be poured upon it. Agni was the lord and protector of every household. No family could be established until the new-made husband had erected an altar, and kindled upon it the sacred fire, which was ever after kept perpetually burning. If by any misfortune it was extinguished, it could only be lighted again by rubbing together two sticks of wood, by friction ; or by a burning-glass brought down from the sun ; and only the husband or wife could ever touch it. Everything most sacred was associated with the household fire, which was thus the bond of union of the family. All this was exactly repeated, among the Romans, in the worship of Vesta.

And now we come to the loveliest and most widely spread of all the Vedic deities, Ushas, the dawn, the same root as our word usher. She was a pure and white-robed being, from whose presence every dark thing fled away, night and ghosts, and wild beasts and robbers. In the dawn of India, there is a peculiar whiteness in the atmosphere, a delicious coolness, a serene stillness, which form a refreshing prelude to the heats of the day, and a contrast to the gloom of the night. It is no wonder that the dawn seemed a lovely thing to them, as she brought back their beloved sun. You will never guess who is the favorite animal of the Veda. It is the ass, because it is the first to awaken and announce the coming of the lovely Ushas. She was accompanied by the Aswins, twin horses; these are morning and evening, since the darkness comes at evening as well as at morning, and these are the originals of the twin brothers whom we meet in every literature like Castor and Pollux. Ushas never grows old, but she makes others old. She reappears as Eös in Greek, as Aurora in Latin, always the same radiant being.

HYMN TO USHAS.

"Ushas, nourishing all, comes daily like a matron, conducting all transient creatures to decay.

"The divine and ancient Ushas born again and bright with unchanging hues, wastes away the life of a mortal, like the wife of a hunter cutting up the birds.

"How long is it that the Dawns have risen ? How long will they rise ?

"Those mortals who beheld the pristine Ushas dawning have passed away ; to us she now is visible, and they approach who will behold her in after times."

ANOTHER.

" She shines upon us like a young wife, rousing every living being to go to his work.

" She rose up, spreading far and wide, and moving towards every one. She grew in brightness, wearing her brilliant garment. The mother of the cows [the clouds], the leader of the days, she shone gold-colored, lovely to behold.

" She, the fortunate, who brings the eye of the god, who leads the white and lovely steed of the sun, the dawn was seen revealed by her rays : with brilliant treasures she follows every one.

" Shine for us with thy best rays, thou bright Dawn, thou who lengthenest our life, thou, the love of all, who givest us food, who givest us wealth in cows, horses, and chariots.

" Thou daughter of the sky, thou high-born, give us riches, high and wide."

" Thou, who art a blessing when thou art near, drive far away the unfriendly, make the pastures wide, give us safety. Remove the haters, bring treasures ; raise up wealth to the worshipper, thou mighty Dawn."

ANOTHER TO INDRA AND USHAS.

" This strong and manly deed also thou hast performed, O Indra, that thou struckest the daughter of Dyaus, a woman difficult to vanquish.

" Yes, even the daughter of Dyaus, the magnified, the Dawn, thou, O Indra, a great hero, hast ground to pieces.

" The Dawn rushed off from her crushed car, fearing that Indra, the bull, might strike her.

" This, her car, lay there, well ground to pieces. She went far away."

This is the germ of the story of Daphne and of Europa. The dawn is also called Dahana, and she is

Sarama, who guarded the cows, carried off by a monster (the dark clouds), and rescued by Indra.

In Sanskrit she has another name, Ahana, and reappears in Greek as Athene : in the Veda it says that Ahana sprang full-born from the forehead of Dyaus; in Greek that Athene sprang full-born from the forehead of Zeus. The meaning is plain. The dawn is the child of the sky ; as Athene, she possesses the penetrating power of the light, the calm wisdom which pierces through every-thing, as Athene's eyes pierce through every disguise. She has another and unexpected name, — Ahana, the dawn,is also Aphrodite, who springs from the water ; that is the morning often appears at the edge of the ocean where it seems to join the sky, and Aphrodite brings with her the dazzling loveliness of the early morning, and of the sea-foam. There are many other applications, but we have not time for them all. Urvasi is another name, as such she is a nymph married to a mortal hus-band whom she can never see. If she looks upon him, she will vanish. Of course the dawn can never see the sun : one must disappear before the other. So here, in Sanskrit, is the origin of all the stories of beings who cannot gaze upon each other, although united in the closest love. It is Eros and Psyche in Greek ; Cupid and Psyche, in Latin ; Melusina and Count Raymond, of Toulouse, in the Middle Ages ; Beauty and the Beast, in the nursery tale ; and a thousand more. This dawn myth is another of the primary Aryan myths, and one of the most fertile.

The work of all these gods is purely physical ; but it would be unjust to say that these are their only gods. Max Müller says, " Heaven-Father was a better word

than fire or storm-wind ; but the Hindu soon perceived
that this was too human a name to give to that Infinite
whose presence he felt everywhere." That part of the
sky behind the dawn, from which she came every morning, from which light came back to the world, was
called Aditi, the boundless, the beyond. She was one
of their earliest deities ; so this idea of something infinite, behind and beyond the other deities, was an early
conception. "The thought is so abstract that we have
fancied it purely modern. There was a visible revelation of the infinite in that golden sea of light behind the
dawn, something which eluded our grasp while the dawn
itself came and went." As light came from the east,
it was looked upon as the home of the bright gods ;
and then came the thought that the dead had joined
these bright gods in their birthplace, the East. Aditi,
the boundless, is connected with the thought of immortality ; for one poet sang : "Who will give us back
to the great Aditi, that I may see father and mother?"
This is one of the first intimations of immortality. In
this boundless infinite beyond, the dead must be living
with Aditi.

FUNERAL HYMN.

"Approach thou now the lap of Earth, thy mother,
The wide-extending Earth, the ever kindly :
A maiden soft as wool to him who comes with gifts,
She shall protect thee from destruction's bosom.
Open thyself, O Earth, and press not heavily ;
Be easy of access and of approach to him,
As a mother with her robe her child
So do thou cover him, O Earth."

ANOTHER.

"Open thy arms, O Earth, receive the dead
With gentle pressure and with loving welcome ;
Embrace him tenderly, e'en as a mother
Folds her soft vestment round the child she loves.
Soul of the dead, depart : take thou the path —
The ancient path — by which our ancestors
Have gone before thee.   Thou shalt look upon
The two kings, mighty Varuna and Yama,
Delighting in oblations.   Thou shalt meet
The fathers, and receive the recompense
Of all thy stored-up offerings, above.
Leave thou thy sin and imperfection here ;
Return unto thy home once more ; assume
A glorious form.   By an auspicious path
Hasten to pass the four-eyed brindled dogs,
Advance to meet the fathers who, with hearts
Kindly disposed towards thee, dwell in bliss
With Yama ; and do thou, O Mighty God,
Intrust him to thy guards to bring him to thee.
And grant him health and happiness eternal."

Yama was the judge of the dead.   He had a dog
with four eyes and wide nostrils, whom he sent to earth
to collect those about to die, something like the Greek
dog, Kerberos, a primary myth.   This idea of a judge
implies a distinction between right and wrong, the good
and the bad.   Here is the manner in which it arose.

By the return of day and night, the weekly changes
of the moon, the successions of the seasons, gradually
grew up a sense of something fixed and settled ; of a
law pervading all nature, and as soon as they had formed
the thought, they put it into a word, Rita.   It expressed at first the settled movement of the sun, the

path of the sun, which was to them the path of Rita. And so they tried to grasp this unknown power which formed the order of nature, by calling him Rita. Rita was the power that settled the path of the sun. The sun moved in the path of Rita. The abode of Rita was in the east, and the path of Rita was every day the same ; the moon and the stars also travelled in the path of Rita ; finally every good thing travelled in the path of Rita. Now, there is no translation of this, except the straight path, the right path ; and when it was once understood that the sun, the moon, the dawn overcame the darkness by following the path of Rita, the path of right, the worshippers took their next step, and prayed that they too might follow on the path of Rita, the right path, and thus overcome sin, which was the same to them as darkness, because evil-doers never cross the path of Rita, it is said. With this came up, of course, the idea of right and wrong ; of a law to be obeyed, and a wrong-doing to be punished.

This conception of Rita, of right and wrong, belongs to the Hindus and the Persians ; it is not a conception of the undivided Aryans, so we do not find it among the Greeks and Latins. This was never before so clearly explained ; it is contained in Max Müller's Lectures, published in 1878.

Mr. Cox says : " There is in the noblest minds a certain consciousness of sin, even without breaking any positive law, and this sense of sin weighed heavy on the mind of the thoughtful Hindu." At such times he addressed himself to Varuna, the All-Surrounder, that is the sky as brooding over and covering and surrounding the earth. These hymns to Varuna are most beautiful and deeply religious.

HYMN TO VARUNA.

"Let me not yet, O Varuna, enter into the house of clay : have mercy, almighty, have mercy.

"If I go along trembling like a cloud driven by the wind : have mercy, almighty, have mercy !

"Through want of strength, thou strong and bright god, have I gone to the wrong shore : have mercy, almighty, have mercy !

"Thirst came upon the worshipper though he stood in the midst of the waters : have mercy, almighty, have mercy !

"Whenever we men, O Varuna, commit an offence before the heavenly host, whenever we break the law through thoughtlessness : have mercy, almighty, have mercy ! "

ANOTHER.

"However we break thy laws from day to day, men as we are, O god, Varuna.

"Do not deliver us unto death, nor to the blow of the furious, nor to the wrath of the spiteful. Absolve us from the sins of our fathers, and from those which we have committed with our own bodies.

"Release the poet, O king, like a thief who has feasted on stolen cattle ; release him like a calf from the rope. It was not our own doing, O Varuna, it was necessity, an intoxicating draught, passion, dice, thoughtlessness ! "

Varuna's characteristics in the Rig Veda are perpetually suggesting the idea of a Divine Being, who made and upholds all things. Another hymn says : —

"Varuna dwells in all worlds as sovereign ; indeed the three worlds are embraced by him. The wind which resounds through the firmament is his breath. He has placed the sun in the heavens and opened a boundless path for it to traverse.

He has hollowed out the channels of the rivers. It is by his wise contrivance that, though all the rivers pour out their waters into the sea, the sea is never filled. By his ordinance the moon shines in the sky, and the stars which are visible by night disappear on the approach of daylight. Neither the birds flying in the air, nor the rivers in their sleepless flow, can attain a knowledge of his power or his wrath. His spies behold both worlds. He himself has a thousand eyes. He perceives all the hidden things that have been or shall be done."

In such hymns Varuna is plainly the supreme god, as the others had been in their turn.

Gradually the Hindu seems to have risen to a higher conception, and all these gods seemed to him but different names for one great being. One hymn says, " Wise poets make the beautiful-winged one manifold by words; though he is but one." Another says, "Thou, Agni, art Indra, bountiful to the excellent; thou art Vishnu, the wide-stepping; son of strength, in thee reside all the gods."

That mysterious principle of life, which is sought to-day in protoplasm, but which eludes our keenest search, our latest knowledge, becomes to the thoughtful Hindu one god, high over everything; but manifesting himself in many different ways and mingling in the affairs of men. The Rig Veda contains this idea. M. Langlois says, " The perpetual struggle of nature, the contrast of heat and cold, light and darkness, seemed to him the movement of some awful mysterious Being. This life of nature, independent of individuals, found in the vegetable and animal world, changing its form, dividing itself, spreading everywhere; found also in the spiritual world, where it creates thought and religious feeling: all this

3

animation of moving mind and matter the Aryans considered to be a person.   He is called Asoura Medhas,
the wise living one."   Afterwards he was called Viswakarman, the maker of all things ; then he grew to be
Pragapati, the one lord of all living things.   Thus they
expressed their growing thoughts, struggling ever to a
higher conception.

HYMN TO ONE GOD.

" In the beginning there arose the source of golden light.
He was the only born lord of all that is.   He established the
earth and the sky.   Who is the God to whom we shall offer
our sacrifice ?

" He who gives life, He who gives strength ; whose blessing
all the bright gods desire ; whose shadow is immortality ;
whose shadow is death : who is the God to whom we shall
offer sacrifice ?

" He who through his power is the only King of the breathing and awakening world ; He who governs all, man and
beast : who is the God to whom we shall offer our sacrifice ?

" He whose power these snowy mountains, whose power the
sea proclaims, with the distant river ; He whose these regions
are, as it were, his two arms : who is the God to whom we shall
offer our sacrifice ?

" He through whom the sky is bright and the earth firm ;
He through whom the heaven was established, nay, the highest
heaven ; He who measured out the light in the air : who is
the God to whom we shall offer our sacrifice?

" He to whom heaven and earth, standing firm by his will,
look up, trembling inwardly ; He over whom the rising sun
shines forth : who is the God to whom we shall offer our
sacrifice ?

" Wherever the mighty water cloud went, where they placed
the seed and lit the fire, thence arose He who is the only life

of the bright gods : who is the God to whom we shall offer our sacrifice ?

" He who by his might looked even over the water clouds, the clouds which gave strength and lit the sacrifice, He *who is God above all gods:* who is the God to whom we shall offer our sacrifice ?

" May he not destroy us : He, the creator of the earth ; or He, the righteous, who created the heavens ; He who also created the bright and mighty waters : who is the God to whom we shall offer our sacrifice?"

At times the Hindu rose to the height of loving this being without hope of reward.

" Thou, even Thou, art mother ; Thou my father ; Thou my kinsman ; Thou my friend ; Thou art knowledge ; Thou art riches ; Thou art my all, O God of Gods, Thou art my protector in all places. Then what fear or grief can there be to me ? "

And here closes what has a universal interest for all humanity. The next period is the Hindus' alone.

We wonder, as we read, who wrote these poetical powerful hymns. They were at first composed by each head of a family ; this is why they are so numerous, and seem a little monotonous. He uttered his hymn, he burst into song, while he laid his sacrifice on the sacred fire, and poured out his oblation on the sacred grass. How rich the early Aryan nature must have been ! how full of imagination and tenderness, to have produced a nation of poets ! The religious bard or singer seems to belong to every race and every age. In the second stage of civilization among the Hindus, rose a class of relig- ious bards called Rishis, who wrote the hymns ; and a class of priests called Brahmans, who performed the sacrifices. The sacrifice of a horse, called an Aswe-medha, is mentioned in the very latest hymns of the Rig Veda. It was the first step towards an organized priesthood.

The Rig Veda was not translated at all until 1833. Then a few hymns were published in a pamphlet by Rosen, a German. Complete translations were made by Langlois in French; and by Wilson in English, from 1848 to 1857. But translators are still at work upon it. At first the Brahmans would not teach the Sanskrit in which the Vedas were written; would scarcely allow foreigners to look at the books even. All the enormous influence of the East India Company was brought to bear upon them for years, and much money spent for books and teachers. Mr. Wilson devoted years of study to his translation of the Rig Veda. Finally, with a modest consciousness of good work well done, with an honorable pride, he walked into the office of a London publisher and informed him that he had a treasure to offer, the Rig Veda. The publisher looked blankly at him, " And pray, sir," said he, " what is the Rig Veda?" I hope that we are now better informed than he.

CHAPTER II.

BRAHMANISM AND THE MAHA BHARATA.

THERE are in Sanskrit literature four distinctly marked periods. First, the Vedic, which we have examined, — a joyous age of simple prayers and kindly gods and family independence. Second, the Brahmanical period; therefore we come now into a new atmosphere of thought. We leave behind us the gods which belong to all the Aryan race, and go on to speak of those which are distinctively Hindu. Their new gods represent one phase of the Aryan nature, its mysticism. Another phase, its energy, is displayed in the epic poem of the Maha Bharata. So our subject is the rise of Brahmanism, and the Maha Bharata.

In our last chapter we examined the Rig Veda, which is called sometimes a *sanhita*. The word means a collection, and we found the Rig Veda to be one general collection of hymns and prayers. In it we saw worshipped the sun, the sky, the dawn; finally, one god, the lord of·all these, a mysterious self-existent person, called sometimes Asoura-Medhas, the wise being; sometimes Viswakarman, the maker of all things. But the new religion is a denial of all these. One of the poets said these gods are only names; still he maintained that there was a real god, one alone; but, instead of making him a masculine name, they now made him a neuter name. They considered neuter names to be higher than either masculine or feminine. They wanted to get as far away from human nature as they could to express this divine being. They gave him two neuter names, — Atman, which belongs to philosophy, and to which I shall allude in the Sanskrit metaphysics ; and Brahman, which belongs to religion and literature. They are best translated by what we call the soul of the world ; what they called the breath of the world. It means the supreme self-existent spirit in repose. Brahman is too vast to be understood by. one single mind, or to be confined to one spot. He pervades everything : he has no form and no characteristics : he is not a person at all. But when he moves from this passive condition and begins to act, then the Hindus gave him other names. First, he wished to create nature and man ; then he took the name of Brahmā, nominative masculine, the creator. Next he wished to sustain and support all this creation, so he took the masculine name of Vishnu, the preserver. This is only enlarging the Vishnu, whom we found in the Rig Veda as a name for the sun. Vishnu had ten incarnations when he descended to live among men, which are called Avatars. Monier Williams says, " Vishnu is the most human and humane god of the Hindu pantheon, — a kind of protest in favor of a personal deity, as opposed to the impersonal pantheism of Brahman."

Next, Brahman wished to punish all this creation, so he took the character of Siva, the destroyer. This is only an enlargement of Rudra in the Rig Veda, the god of storm and tempest, chief of the Maruts. All these are far above the old Vedic deities. Indra alone retains any prominence. Varuna now becomes the god of the waters; and is the same as Nereus in Greek, Neptune in Latin. Each of these gods has a heaven of his own, but Brahman has no local habitation.

One writer says, "From the restlessness of false religions, the gods, being subjective, change with the minds of the people who created them. There are endless avatars in Brahmanical mythology, reproducing the dreary monstrosities of the Hindu mind." They showed their imagination in a curious freak. To denote power they increased the bodies of their gods: Brahmā the creator, has four faces: Siva, the destroyer, has five heads: Indra, the clear sky, has one thousand eyes: all the new gods and goddesses have four arms.

Among several of the Aryan nations are traditions of early ages of goodness and happiness, then a gradual deterioration, like the four ages of Hesiod in Greek. The Hindus had also vast periods of time, which they called Yugas. They agree better with modern science than the Greek periods, for a Yuga was 4,320,000 mortal years: no shorter period would have filled the vast imagination of the Hindu. One thousand of these Yugas constituted one day of Brahmā; then the creator will sleep and all nature — including the gods, Brahmā, Vishnu, and Siva — will become dissolved; melt away into Brahman, simple being.

As a natural result, the Brahmans taught the doctrine of metempsychosis. Mr. Thompson says, "It is the most novel and original idea ever started in any age or country; undoubtedly, too, its place of invention is India; Egypt took it from there; Greece took it from Egypt; Pythagoras took it in person. It implies the eternity of the soul." It teaches that the Supreme Spirit, Brahman, formed everything by changing himself into matter. He divided himself into innumerable existences; into gods, heroes, human beings, animals. plants, even into stones. All these are not only emanations from Brahman, they are actually a part of him, smaller or larger pieces of him. That small piece of Brahman, forming a man, had a body which died; then the soul passed into another body. If a man's deeds had been sinful, he went into a lower body, even as low as a stone; if good, he was born again into a higher body; but he must expiate the sins done in a former body. The doctrine somewhat diminished the sense of personal responsibility; for great talents and goodness, or great sins and wickednesses, were both considered to be the result of powers and habits belonging to some previous existences; yet there was not supposed to be any recollection of these existences in the mind. "Through speaking ill of his preceptor a man will be born again an ass; if he reviles his preceptor, a dog; if he envies him, an insect." Another said, "If a man steals grain, he shall be born again a mouse; if milk, a crow; if he steals horses, he shall be afflicted with lameness in a future existence; if he steals cloth, with leprosy." What a constant terror to evil-doers this thought would be!

The doctrine was particularly unpleasant to the Hindus, for motion in their hot climate is often intolerable; but it will account for the great kindness which they show to animals. The soul goes on through a series of transmigrations, — the various hells but purgatories, the various heavens but temporary resting-places, — till it reaches the height of its capacities, its final condition, absorption into Brahman. The Veda says, "As the web issues from the spider, as little sparks proceed from fire, so from the one soul proceed all breathing animals, all worlds, all the gods, and all beings." Next it says that all these exist separately for a time, but at length all are absorbed into their source, the Supreme Spirit. "As from a blazing fire consubstantial sparks proceed in a thousand ways, so from the Imperishable Spirit various living souls are produced; and they return to him too." So all personal life, all individuality, is lost, as seen from the following text: "As flowing rivers are resolved into the sea, losing their names and forms, so the wise man, freed from name and form, passes into the Divine Spirit, which is greater than the great. He who honors that Supreme Spirit becomes spirit." Such was their ideal. M. Barbier describes this mysticism. "The ideal life is to lose yourself in the divine essence, to detach yourself from the trifling interests of humanity, to feel a contempt for all religious and moral laws, and the nothingness of all creation in comparison with the divine love. Little by little, by prayers and meditations, absolute renunciation of the will, and rigorous mortification of the body, to rise above this earthly life; even above the heavenly life; to annihilate yourself in the great whole until the believer cries out, 'I am in God,' next, 'I am God.'" One text says "Thou art I; I am thou: of what kind is the difference? Like gold and the bracelet, like water and a wave."

This is not at all the spiritual communion which Christianity teaches; it is absolute loss of all identity. This was the goal to which they pressed forward, through penance and austerities and transmigrations.

And this Brahman in which they wished to lose themselves is not a person at all, like the gods of the Rig Veda. He is the principle of life, whether you give him the subjective name Atman; the objective, Brahman. Mr. Thompson says, "Brahman has no cause, no origin, is not produced by anything; but he is eternal, universal, single, independent, free from any characteristics, sovereign." It is almost impossible for the human mind to grasp this idea: but the Indian intellect reached it without influence from any other nation. What we call Pantheism sometimes, and sometimes Nature, comes nearest to conveying the thought to us. But this doctrine of identification with the supreme principle of the world is not found in the Rig Veda. No metempsychosis comes in there, no asceticism as steps to that result. The Rig Veda distinctly teaches that the soul has a personal, individual existence after death, as well as that it is eternal.

Under this new religion, gradually and naturally, society separated itself into classes; but these classes, instead of being pliable like society elsewhere, hardened into an iron framework, which has remained unchanged for centuries. In the Veda, where caste is indicated, it is quite different from what it afterwards became.

The word Brahman applied to a human being meant, first, one who offered a prayer to the Supreme Being, Brahman. Next, these prayer-offerers became the religious teachers of all others: every one was obliged to learn the Veda by heart; but they claimed that they alone had the right to teach it. Then they took the last step and announced that they alone could offer sacrifices: a long period must have elapsed since the father of the

family offered his own simple prayer, and performed his
own sacrifice. A form for worship and sacrifice grew
up, and this brought about the other three Vedas.
They are far less interesting and valuable than the Rig
Veda, and, whenever we say " the Veda," we mean the
Rig Veda. The others were formed when the Aryan
invaders had penetrated far into the land; the Sama
and Yadjour Vedas when they had reached the south-
eastern slope of the Himalaya Mountains; the Atharva
Veda upon the very banks of the Ganges.   .

The three later Vedas are liturgies for worship and
rules for performing the sacrifices. They give rules for
the great public ceremonials, where three sacred fires
burned upon three sacred hearths, for the worship of the
family, and the private devotion of the individual. Not
merely the custom itself, but every motion and every into-
nation of voice was prescribed by rule ; and these motions
and accents were as divinely inspired as any other part
of the Vedas. For the Brahmans claimed that the four
Vedas were directly revealed to the religious bards (the
Rishis), that they issued like breath from the Divine
Being. They were divine knowledge received through
the ear: not merely the thoughts but the actual words
were revealed. Therefore the change of a letter or an
accent was a sin ; and this revelation made to a class of
holy men was transmitted by repetition in the exact form
in which it had been received. It is difficult to determine
at what time the Brahmans set up the claim that the Veda
was divinely revealed, and therefore infallible. As all the
Hindus (except the Sudras) were obliged to learn the
Veda, it is plain that the Brahmans had employment
enough. They soon grew rich, for they received payment

for teaching the Veda, for offering prayers and sacrifices : one kind of sacrifice required the services of sixteen different classes of Brahmans. "These Brahmans were men who were intellectually superior, and they took advantage of the strong sense of religion, which was natural to the Hindu Aryan, to make themselves powerful." They claimed that they were born from the mouth of Brahma, and, therefore, formed the first caste.

As the shepherd tribes rested from their wanderings and settled upon the land, they became agriculturists. They needed some one to protect them from their enemies : there are always men who would rather fight than till the ground, — so the second caste grew up, the Kshatriyas or warriors. After a while they became kings over the peaceful farmers and merchants, and were called rajas. In fact the rajas were always taken from the Kshatriya or warrior caste. They always had a Brahman priest, however, for their adviser, like the kings of the Middle Ages in Europe.

Then the quiet farmers and merchants formed themselves into a third caste called Vaisyas. The root *vis* enters into this word : it means to enter into, sit down upon, like the Latin *vicus*, a village, and the English termination *wick* of the name of a town. It has a secondary meaning in *vis*, man of the people, *vis pater*, the father of the people. Sometimes, though very seldom, some Vaisya would gain great wealth : then he would hire Brahmans to perform his prayers and sacrifices, and Kshatriyas to become his body-guard. These three castes were all noble, all obliged to learn the Veda by heart. Each boy had a sacred cord tied around his waist, and was then called " twice born : " this corresponds to our rite of baptism. The Brahman boy was invested with the sacred thread at eight years of age ; the Kshatriya, at eleven ; the Vaisya, at twelve.

The Sudras, the fourth caste, did menial work. They were servants but not slaves, and their condition was far superior to the Helots of the Greeks, or the serfs of the Middle Ages, for they were not attached to the soil. They were not allowed to learn the Vedas, and this drew a sharp line between them and the three " twice-born " castes.

At the beginning of this Brahmanical period, took place the events which form the subject of the epic poems, although the poems themselves were not written down until after. They are two,— the Maha Bharata,and the Ramayana. They are quite old enough to be valuable, and they show a civilization far beyond the primitive simplicity of the Rig Veda. We find a degree of civilization which will be surprising to us : palaces and chariots and jewels ; fruits and flowers ; domestic love and womanly freedom, in an age and country which we are fond of calling heathen. Of course the pictures of life and manners which they give must be faithful, since the Aryans who entered India were utterly separated from other Aryan nations. We cannot too often recall to mind that all the writings of Sanskrit literature are utterly uninfluenced by contact with other minds, and this makes them as wonderful as they are exquisite : they are the spontaneous expression of the mind of man at its very first awakening, and we may well be amazed to find them so interesting in thought, so charming in form. Many scholars, among them Dean Milman, consider them more beautiful than those of any other nation.

It is impossible to know when the Maha Bharata was

written : the critics conflict so much. Monier Williams thinks it later than the Ramayana. Wheeler places it much earlier : one critic fixes it at 1500 b. c. ; another at 200 b. c. But this may be reconciled by assuming that the Maha Bharata was rewritten at a later date than it originated. We can but judge from the internal evidence of the book itself, the only guide in most Hindu chronology ; and the manners portrayed in the Maha Bharata are much earlier than those of the Ramayana, especially the freedom of the women. The Rig Veda may be called patriarchal : it has first the family, then the tribe, then an indication of the feudal lord. But the Maha Bharata is completely feudal. Its raja was a feudal lord, but little more powerful than his vassals. The priests were advisers and friends, not tyrants, and the tone of the poem is very brave and warlike. Throughout it we are constantly amazed at meeting customs which we supposed peculiar to the Middle Ages of Europe ; but which must have been common to the early civilization of every Aryan family, if they are found in its earliest literature. The Swayembara was an institution which greatly resembled the tournaments of the Middle Ages. The different young noblemen displayed their prowess before the raja, and the ladies of the royal family, who then chose one of them for her husband. The position of woman was, therefore, quite different from what it afterward became in India. The driving of chariots was a favorite amusement and accomplishment with the ancient Kshatriyas just as with the ancient Greeks. If the raja did not himself drive, his charioteer was his confidential friend and adviser. In the lassitude brought on by a hot climate, gambling was then, as now, a passion ; rajas played together for days until one had lost everything he possessed, and was driven out as an exile. The great sacrifice called an Aswemedha was a high solemnity. The animal sacrificed was a horse, and we find the same animal selected by the Teutonic families : a horse was sacrificed to Odin, the god of the Norsemen ; but we seldom read of a horse sacrifice among the Greeks and Romans.

Wheeler, in his history of India, says that " the Maha Bharata is the most voluminous, and, perhaps, the most valuable epic which has hitherto been preserved in any written language." And this is great praise from him, as he is not at all enthusiastic. There is no complete translation in existence, as fifteen octavo volumes would be required. For the Maha Bharata is seven times as long as both poems of Homer combined, and twenty times as long as the Nibelungen Lied. " In India everything is on a colossal scale. Not only are the mountains higher, and the rivers longer, but the poems also are more voluminous." M. Fauche left at his death an unfinished translation in French in ten volumes, but it is so diffuse that it is tedious.

The Maha Bharata is regarded with the most awful reverence by the Hindus : to read it, or even to listen to it, will prevent a Hindu from committing any sin for that day ; will ensure prosperity in this world and eternal happiness hereafter. The changes and additions made to it by the Brahmans have greatly injured its simplicity and freshness ; but these can be detected, and it will ever remain most noble and interesting in spite of them. Extravagant stories are told : billions and trillions of men are said to have been engaged in the battles ; showers of blood to have fallen

from the skies; but all these may be traced to the wish
which the Brahman singer felt to glorify the Kshatriya
ancestors of the raja to whom he sang. For the Maha
Bharata was originally a collection of ballads sung to some
raja. It is naturally greatly wanting in unity: it is a vast
collection of Hindu mythology, legends, and philosophy,
rather than a poem with one subject. But it is our only
source for the history of the period; for the Hindu, it
will be remembered, never wrote history. Its events took
place when the Aryan invaders had penetrated as far as
the city which we call Delhi. The main action of the
poem, however, is the quarrel between the Kauravas and
the Pandavas, who were first cousins, and descendants
of Bharata, a great Indian hero. The word Maha
always means great, so Maha Bharata means the
great war of Bharata. Mr. Wheeler says, "This war
was not a contest with a foreign invader nor a domestic tyrant, not a crusade of religion. It was simply
a struggle between kinsmen for land and throne."
Mr. Wheeler, therefore, rejects all symbolism, and treats
it simply as history. But symbolism is as true an
expression of our faculties as history, and cannot so
coolly be thrust aside. According to modern interpretation, a deeper meaning underlies this contest; it becomes
that same struggle between light and darkness which we
saw in the Rig Veda, and which is in reality that ever-
recurring strife between good and evil which we find in
every Aryan family, and whose origin I shall refer to
again. The heroes of the Maha Bharata are plainly the
same as the gods of the Rig Veda, and can clearly be
traced to that. In the Maha Bharata, then, the Pandavas are good and beautiful and strong. Their chiefs

are five brethren, each of whom has a distinct individuality. Bhima, a giant like the Greek Herakles, is one
of them : he carries a club or mace for weapon. The
most interesting hero in our eyes is Arjuna. His name
means " dazzling radiance," and he possesses the qualities
of Indra : the god has come down to be the hero of an
epic : his weapon is the unerring bow and arrow, he is
therefore a solar myth. But the favorite hero in the
Hindu's eyes is the Raja Yudishthira, who never manifests the slightest feeling, but shows a cold, passionless
stoicism.

The Kauravas are wicked and weak ; but as Hector
was noble among the wicked Trojans, so is Karna beautiful and brave among the wicked Kauravas. He is also
a form of the solar myth : his mother was a mortal maiden ;
his father was the shining sun. When he was born, he
wore golden ear-rings, and a golden coat of mail enveloped him like a shell. In the German mythology, one
hero is called the " horny Siegfried " because he wore a
coat of mail like horn. When Karna was born he was
put into a basket and floated far away. This same circumstance is told of Perseus in Greek and Scif in Anglo-
Saxon, and other Aryan heroes. He was picked up by
a wagon-driver ; brought up and educated by him. His
coat of mail grew with his growth : he could take it off
and on at pleasure, and was invincible when he wore it.
On a certain day a Swayamvara was held, and it was
announced that whoever should bend a certain enormous
bow and shoot the arrow into the mark, should gain the
hand of a lovely princess, Draupadi, the lotus-eyed. All
the rajas had tried and failed ; then Karna comes forward
and bends the bow, and the lotus-eyed princess calls out,

4

"I will not wed the base-born son of a wagon-driver," so poor Karna is obliged to give up the bow. Then Arjuna comes forward, bends the bow, and shoots the arrow, and hits the mark, and gains the princess. The practice of polyandry prevails, and she becomes the wife to the five brethren. Then the cousins gamble together, and the raja of the Pandavas gambles away his right to the kingdom and his wife. So all the Pandavas are exiled into the jungle, but the wife is given back to them: this exile into the jungle is a favorite punishment among the Hindus. When they became weary in their wanderings, the giant Bhima would carry his fatigued brethren and their afflicted wife upon his shoulders, or under his arms, and walk on as before. Finally, the difficulty is settled by a grand battle of eighteen days. But the interest lies in the single combats, and these sound like the stories of the Middle Ages. Here, in this first heroic poetry of the Aryan mind, is the type which recurred at different ages in each Aryan race. Karna and Arjuna are to settle the question by single combat; but the evening before, Karna's true mother comes to him and reveals his birth to him: he is really the half-brother of Arjuna, and begs him to join the side of the Pandavas. But he refuses to desert his friends. They fight, and the victory is uncertain, when Karna is slain from behind, like so many other warriors in Aryan poetry, — Achilleus, in Greek; Siegfried, in German.

Then all the widows come to the battle-field to mourn. How much freedom the women had in these first ages, to come to so public a place! They dishevel their long black hair and sit by the corpses. The mother of the raja said, "The wise and the learned always used to sit around this son of mine, and nearly all the rajas of the earth took their stations near him, and prided themselves on it as a promotion; but this night the jackals alone have been his courtiers." Then the widow of the raja placed her husband's head upon her lap, and the mother said, "This woman whom neither sun nor moon was once worthy to look upon, see how she now sits here bareheaded." The bodies are gathered into great heaps and burned, but each raja had a funeral-pile of his own. Among the Aryan nations, burning and burying were each used for the dead, — burning by the wandering tribes; burying. by those who settled on the land. But burning was never adopted by the masses ; only used for great chieftains. In the Iliad, Hector's body was burned ; among the Teutons it is constantly mentioned, as we shall find later on.

• Another most touching passage is the description of the dead arising at night from the waters of the Ganges to revisit their friends. ·Mr. Wheeler thinks this one of the " grandest pictures ever presented to the human eye." It certainly shows that " touch of nature " which " makes the whole world kin." The longing of the human heart to see its dead again must be universal, if it were felt so long ago, so far away, so independently of foreign influence. Does it not show how natural and spontaneous it is to believe in immortality ; to feel that those who are dead to us are living in another life? The action of the widows has a Hindu tone, but the rest is of all times and all nations.

"After this, while all were talking together of the husbands, and the sons, and the kinsfolk whom they had lost in the great

wars of the Maha Bharata, the Sage Vyasa appeared among
them and said, ' I will this day heal all your griefs. Go you all
to the river Ganges and bathe therein, and there each one of
you shall behold the kinsman for whom you have been sorrowing.' So they all went down to the river, and chose a bathing
place for themselves and families, and Vyasa said to them, —
' You shall see this night whom you desire.' And the day
passed away so slowly that it seemed like a whole year to them,
and at last the sun went down, and they all bathed in the river
by command of Vyasa, and said their prayers and went and
stood near him ; and Yudishthira and his brethren were on
the side of Vyasa. and everybody else stood where places could
be found. Vyasa then went into the water and prayed and
bathed, and he then came out and stood by Yudishthira, and
called out the names of each of the persons who had been slain,
one by one. At that moment the river began to foam and boil,
and a great noise was heard rising out of the water, as though
all the slain men were once again alive, and as though they,
and their elephants, and their horses, were bursting into loud
cries, and all the drums and trumpets and other instruments
of music of both armies were striking up together. The whole
assembly was astonished at this mighty tempest, and some
were smitten with a terrible fear when suddenly they saw
Bishma and Droma in full armor seated in their chariots, and
ascending out of the water with all their armies arrayed as they
were on the first day of the Maha Bharata. Next came forth
Abhimanya, the heroic son of Arjuna, and the five sons of
Draupadi, and the son of Bhima with his army. After him
came Kuna and Duryodhama and Sankivar, and the other sons
of Droma, all in full parade, seated upon their chariots, together
with many other warriors and rajas who had been slain. All
appeared in great glory and splendor, and more beautiful than
they were when all alive, and all came with their own horses
and chariots, and runners and arms. And every one was in perfect friendship with each other, for enmity had departed from
amongst them. And each one was preceded by his bards and

eulogists, who sang his praises, and very many singing men and dancing girls appeared with them, singing and dancing. Now, when those warriors had come out of the river their widows and orphans and kinsfolk were overjoyed, and not a trace of grief remained amongst them, and widows went to their husbands, and daughters to their fathers, and mothers to their sons, and sisters to their brothers, and all the fifteen years of sorrow which had passed away since the war of the Maha Bharata were forgotten in the ecstasy of seeing each other again. Thus the night passed away in the fulness of joy; but when the morning had dawned all the dead mounted their chariots and horses, and disappeared ; and those who had gathered to behold them prepared to depart, and Vyasa the Sage said that the widows who wished to rejoin their dead husbands might do so, and all the widows went and bathed in the Ganges, and came out of the water again and kissed every one the feet of Yudishthira and his wife Gandhavi, and went and drowned themselves in the river, and through the prayers of Vyasa they all went to the places they wished and obtained their several desires."

The Hindus justify from the Vedas the Sati, or custom of burning widows upon the funeral pile of their husbands. But the Sati is not found in the Rig Veda : on the contrary, it is forbidden there.

Mr. Alger, in his work on " Oriental Poetry," calls the close of the Maha Bharata " the culminating point of the poetry of the world." He says, " 'To the touched hearts and impressed imaginations of the reader, Hastinapur becomes a nobler name than Troy."

The Pandavas conquer ; Yudishthira gains the throne, but he is still unsatisfied. He feels that all who wish for true happiness and rest of mind must abandon worldly things, and seek for union with the Infinite. We fancy this to be a modern doctrine : it is as old as

the soul of every Aryan. It has been said that this was
added by the feeling of a later age than that which expressed itself in single combats and Swayamvaras; and
yet this idea was more or less present to the Hindu in
every stage of development. It was prompted by that
spiritual element which is so much stronger in the Sanskrit literature than in the literatures of Greece or Rome.
Yudishthira tells his four brethren and their one wife, of
his restless yearnings, of his intention to renounce that
throne which had cost such blood and treasure, and go
forth to seek the heaven of Indra. So he takes off his
royal robes, and the six clothe themselves in the garb of
pilgrims, and wander forth together, accompanied by a
faithful dog. All gradually drop down by the way, except the cold, stoical Yudishthira; he reaches at length
the heaven of Indra. But Indra will not admit the dog:
Yudishthira refuses to abandon a faithful friend, and
Indra consents. Then Yudishthira inquires for his four
brethren and the tender princess Draupadi, the faithful
wife. Indra informs him that they are in hell. So he
refuses to stay in heaven without them, goes down to hell
and hears the voices of his brethren in dreadful torment.
The hell is even worse than Dante's: there is a darkness which can be felt, the wicked are burning in flames
of fire. It is a dense wood whose leaves are sharp
swords; the ground is paved with razors; the path
strewn with mutilated corpses. The brethren implore
Yudishthira not to leave them, and he promises to stay
and share their torments. Then Indra tells him that
these were all maya or illusions to try his character:
the four brethren, and Draupadi, the lotus-eyed, are
really in the heaven of Indra, where they live happily
ever after.

In the poem there are innumerable episodes. One of them relates the adventures of the playful Krishna, who was married to sixteen thousand damsels, each of whom thought herself his only wife. This really means that Krishna is the sun, reflected in sixteen thousand dew-drops. Another episode is met again in Keltic folk-lore: it tells of a city with all its inhabitants submerged, drowned for its wickedness. Here is another little touch which suggests the Middle Ages. Each hero carries a conch-shell for a trumpet, which has a name, as if personified. We are accustomed to the naming of swords, but this is still more hero-like. Arjuna blew his shell, called Deva-datta, "the god-given;" the words sound like Latin: Yudishthira blew his, called " eternal victory."

There is another episode of the Maha Bharata, which may be quoted for its beauty simply, but also for the close resemblance it bears to the story of Alkestis in Greek literature. Like her, the heroine is willing to die for her husband; and these two nations unconsciously worked out the same idea. Its root, therefore, must have been the same; we shall learn the meaning when we take up the Greek form of the thought. Savitri, the beautiful daughter of a king, loved Satyavan, the son of a hermit, but was warned by a seer to overcome her attachment, as he had only one year to live. " Whether his years be few or many, be he gifted with all grace or graceless, him my heart hath chosen, and it chooseth not again," she replied; and they were married. The bride strove to forget the ominous prophecy; but as the last day of the year approached, her anxiety became irrepressible. She exhausted herself in prayers and

penances, but dared not reveal the fatal secret to her
husband. At last the dreaded day arrived, and Satyavan set out to cut wood in the forest. His wife asked
leave to accompany him, and walked behind with a
heavy heart. He soon made the wood resound with his
hatchet, when suddenly a thrill of agony shot through
his temples, and feeling himself falling he called out to
his wife to support him.

" Then she received her fainting husband in her arms and sat
    herself
On the cold ground, and gently laid his drooping head upon
    her lap.
                    All in an instant she beheld an awful shape
Standing before her, dressed in blood-red garments, with a
    glittering crown
Upon his head ; his form, though glowing like the sun, was
    yet obscure,
And eyes he had like flames, a noose depended from his hand ;
    and he
Was terrible to look upon, as by her husband's side he stood
And gazed upon him with a fiery glance. Shuddering, she
    started up
And laid her dying Satyavan upon the ground, and, with her
    hands
Joined reverently, she thus with beating heart addressed the
    shape,
' Surely thou art a god; such form as thine must more than
    mortal be !
Tell me, thou god-like being, who thou art, and wherefore thou
    art here ?' "

The figure replied that he was Yama, king of the dead ;
that her husband's time was come, and that he must
bind and take his spirit.

" Then from her husband's body forced he out, and firmly with
    his cord
Bound and detained the spirit, clothed in form no larger than a
    thumb.
Forthwith the body, reft of vital being and deprived of breath,
Lost all its grace and beauty, and became ghastly and motion-
    less."

After binding the spirit, Yama proceeds with it towards the place of which he is guardian ; the faithful wife follows him closely. Yama bids her go home
and prepare the funeral rites, but she persists in following, until Yama, pleased with her devotion, grants her
any boon she pleases, except her husband's life. She
chooses that her husband's father, who is now blind, may
recover his sight. Yama consents, and bids her now return home. Still she persists in following. Two other
boons are granted in the same way, and still Savitri
follows closely on the heels of the king of death. At
last, overcome by her constancy, Yama grants her a boon
without exception. The delighted Savitri exclaims, —

" Nought, mighty king, this time hast thou excepted : let my
    husband live ;
Without him I desire not happiness, nor even heaven itself ;
Without him I must die. ' So be it ! faithful wife,' replied
    the king ;
Thus I release him, and with that he loosed the cord that
    bound his soul."

But the most beautiful, as well as celebrated of the
episodes, is the story of Nala and Damayanti. It has
been translated into many modern languages. I will give
you Wheeler's prose translation. It is told in the most

naïve and delicious manner. Damayanti talks to the mountains and trees as if they were living beings.

There is one point in which the Indian epics are different from those of every other nation. The gods themselves take upon them a human form and take part in the action. But I think this is an interpolation of the Brahmans, for it is contrary to the natural processes of the human mind. Whereas, it is quite natural to lend to the hero the characteristics of a god; more fitting to raise a mortal than to degrade a deity.

One trait which reveals the gods is found in other poems. The Greek and Latin gods never wink. In the Iliad Helen recognizes Aphrodite by her "marble eyes." They mean the full, fixed eyes of the Hindu deities, which puzzled commentators, until they were found in Sanskrit literature.

THE STORY OF NALA AND DAMAYANTI.

In ancient times there lived in Nishadha a certain raja named Nala; and he was handsome, brave, majestic, and splendid, gifted with the choicest virtues, renowned for his skill in archery and in taming horses, of unblemished truth, admired by noble women, but loving dice exceedingly; and he was also deeply read in the Vedas, and had brought every sense and passion under control. Farther south, in the city Vidarbha, reigned Raja Bhíma, terrible in strength, whose blooming and slender-waisted daughter, Damayanti, was famous among all the rajas for her radiant charms and exceeding grace. And Nala, the tiger among rajas, had so often heard of the exquisite loveliness of Damayanti, the pearl of maidens, that he was enamored without having seen her ; and the soul-disturbing Damayanti had, in like manner, so often been told of the god-like comeliness and virtues of the hero Nala, that she secretly desired to become his bride.

Now, on a certain day Raja Nala wandered to a grove and pondered on his deep love for Damayantí, when a flock of swans with golden plumage flew into the grove, and he caught one of the bright birds. And the bird cried out, " Slay me not, O gentle raja, and I will so praise thee in the presence of Damayantí that she shall think of no other man but thee." So Nala set it free ; and the bird of golden wing flew away with all its companions to the city Vidarbha, and entered the garden of Raja Bhíma. And the beautiful Damayantí was sporting with her maidens in the garden, when they all beheld a flock of swans who dropped their golden plumes; and the slender-waisted chased the bright birds about the garden, when suddenly a swan turned round to Damayantí and said in the language of men, " O Damayantí, thou art the loveliest of maidens, and Nala is the handsomest of heroes ; if the peerless wed the peerless, how happy will be the union ! " Then the royal maiden softly said to the bird, " Speak the same words to Nala." And the bird fluttered its golden wings, and flew away to Nishada, and told all to Nala.

Meanwhile the beautiful maiden grew pale and dejected in her father's court at Vidarbha. She could not sleep, she often wept, she found no joy in banquets or in conversation, and she gazed upon the sky at night-time with a look of wild distraction; for her heart was wholly possessed with a deep love for Nala. So the maidens told her royal father that Damayantí was fading away into a deep melancholy. And the Raja of Vidarbha said, " My daughter is full-grown, and must be given away in marriage." And he sent Brahmans round the world to proclaim a Swayamvara; and all the rajas of the earth who had heard of the divine loveliness of Damayantí flocked to the court of Bhíma, with all the pomp of chariots and horses, and elephants, and armies. And Bhíma welcomed them all with due courtesy, and entertained them well.

Now, at this time the holy sage Nárada ascended on high to the heaven of Indra. And Indra gave him honorable welcome, and said, " Where, O sage, are all the rajas, that they come not to my abode?" And Nárada replied, "O cloud-compeller, all the rajas and their mighty sons have gone to the Swayamvara of Damayantí; for she, the loveliest of maidens, is about to choose a husband for herself." Then the gods were stricken as they heard of the transcendent beauty of Damayantí, and they exclaimed, "We, too, will go to her Swayamvara!" And Indra, lord of Swarga, and Agni, god of fire, and Varuna, who rules the seas, and Yama, who judges the dead, called for their celestial chariots, and drove through the air to the city of Vidarbha; and, as they approached the earth, they beheld the hero Nala, as radiant as the sun and as comely as the god of love; and they stayed their chariots in the blue air, and said to the heroic one, "O Nala, we pray you to do our bidding." And Nala stood with folded hands, and said, "Whatsoever you command, that will I do." So Indra, sovereign of the gods, said to Nala, "Go now and tell the fair daughter of Bhíma that the four immortal gods have come from heaven to woo her, and that she must choose from amongst them whom she will." But Nala replied, "Oh! spare me this; for I, too, am enamored with the damsel, and how can I woo her for another?" But all the gods spoke out with one accord, "Have you not pledged yourself to do whatsoever we command? Delay not, therefore, nor belie your word." Then Nala said, "The palace of Bhíma is strongly guarded, and I cannot enter the presence of the maiden." But Indra replied, "No man shall stop you; only go." Then Raja Nala entered the palace of Bhíma, and no man hindered him; and he reached the inner apartments, and beheld the beautiful damsel sitting amongst her maidens; and, when the damsels saw him, they sprang from their seats, and marvelled at his wondrous beauty. And Nala smiled sweetly upon Damayantí; and she, with lovely eyes, smiled sweetly in return, and said, "O hero, how came you hither? Have you escaped the guards my father has set around us?" Then Nala replied, "O loveliest of damsels, my name is Nala, and I am a messenger from the gods, and through their power I have passed the gates unseen by men. Now, the four gods desire to wed you, and pray you to choose one of their number to be their lord." And Damayantí bowed in reverence to the gods, and then smiled again upon Nala, and said, " O raja, the language of the golden-plumaged swan has kindled my soul, and I will choose no other but you; and, if you spurn my love, I will take poison, or plunge into the water or the fire." And Nala replied, "O beautiful maiden, how can you choose a mortal man in the presence of the bright gods? How can you refuse to be arrayed in heavenly raiment, and bright amaranthine flowers, and all the glory of the celestials? Where is the damsel who would not wed the radiant Agni, god of fire, whose mouths consume the world? or the bright Indra, sovereign of the gods, at whose dread sceptre all the assemblies of the earth are forced to do justice and work righteousness? or the majestic Varuna, lord of waters? or the mighty Yama, judge over all the dead?" But Damayantí trembled at the words of Nala, and her eyes were filled with tears, and she said, "I will pay due homage to all the gods; but you only will I choose to be my lord." And Nala went his way, and told to the expectant gods all that Damayantí had said.

2. THE SWAYAMVARA OF DAMAYANTI.

At length the day of happy omen, the great day of the Swayamvara, dawned upon the city of Vidarbha. And all the rajas, sick with love, passed through the glittering portals and the court of golden columns, and entered the Hall of State, like lions entering their mountain lairs. And all the rajas were adorned with fragrant garlands, and rich ear-rings of costly gems were hanging from their ears. And some had long arms, robust and vigorous as the ponderous battle-mace; while others were as soft and delicately rounded as a smooth serpent. With bright and flowing hair and arched eyebrows, their faces were as radiant as the stars; and they filled the Hall of State, as the serpents fill the under-world, or as tigers fill the caves in the mountains. But, when Damayantí entered the hall, every eye was fixed, and every soul entranced at her dazzling loveliness; and all the rajas gazed upon her beauty, and were stricken with deep and passionate desire. Then the name of every raja was proclaimed aloud, and Damayanti glanced around her at the glittering crowd of suitors, and she saw in her dismay that there were five Nalas in the hall, for each of the four bright gods had taken upon himself the form of Nala. And Damayantí trembled with fear, and after a while she folded her hands in reverence to the gods, and said in sad and humble tones, " Since I heard the language of the swan, I have chosen Nala for my lord, and have thought of no other husband. Therefore, O gods, I pray to you that you resume your own immortal forms, and reveal Nala to me, that I may choose him for my lord in the presence of all." And the gods heard the piteous prayer of Damayanti, and they wondered at her steadfast truth and fervent love; and straightway they revealed the tokens of their godhead. Then Damayantí saw the four bright gods, and knew that they were not mortal heroes; for their feet touched not the earth, and their eyes winked not, and no perspiration hung upon their brows, nor dust upon their raiment, and their garlands were as fresh as if the flowers were just gathered. And Damayantí also saw the true Nala; for he stood before her with shadow falling to the ground, and twinkling eyes, and drooping garland; and moisture was on his brow, and dust upon his raiment; and she knew he was Nala. Then she went in all maidenly modesty to Nala, and took the hem of his garment, and threw a wreath of radiant flowers round his neck, and thus chose him for her lord. And a sound of wild sorrow burst from all the rajas; but the gods and sages cried aloud, " Well done !" And Nala turned to the slender-waisted damsel and said, "Since, O maiden with the eye serene, you have chosen me for your husband in the presence of the gods, know that I will be your faithful consort, ever delighting in your words; and so long as my soul shall inhabit this body I solemnly vow to be thine, and thine alone."

Then the blest pair approached the gods with reverence, and the gods gave rare gifts to Nala. To him Indra gave the sight which sees the unseen in the sacrifice, and the power to go unhindered where he pleased; and Agni gave him the mastery over fire, and power over the three worlds; and Varuna gave him the mastery over water, and the power of obtaining fresh garlands at will; and Yama gave him a subtle taste for food, and eminence in every virtue.

Then Raja Bhíma in his joy and pride performed the marriage rites of his beautiful daughter and her chosen lord, and in due time Raja Nala carried away his bride to his own city. Thus the tiger among rajas obtained the pearl of maidens; and henceforth the bliss of Nala and Damayantí was equal to that of the giant-slayer Indra and his beautiful Sachí. Radiant and excellent as the sun, Nala ruled all the subjects of his raj with a just and equal sway. He performed an Aswemedha, with many rich gifts to holy men; and Damayantí bore him two children, — a handsome son named Indrasen, and a beautiful daughter named Indrasena.

3. THE GAMBLING MATCH BETWEEN NALA AND PUSHKARA.

Now, when the bright gods were returning from the Swayamvara to the heaven of Indra, they met the evil spirit Kali, accompanied by Duápara. And Indra said to Kali, " Whither art thou going, O Kali?" And Kali replied, " I am going to the Swayamvara of Damayantí ; for I have set my heart upon having her for my bride." And Indra laughed and said, " The bridal of Damayantí is ended, for in our presence she chose Raja Nala to be her lord." Then Kali was filled with rage, and, bowing with reverence to the gods, he said, " Since she has preferred a mortal man to the immortal gods, heavy shall be her doom." But the four gods replied, " It was with our consent that Damayantí chose her lord ; and what maiden would not incline to one so virtuous as Nala? And he who has read the Vedas, and constantly adores the gods with pure offerings, and is gentle to all living creatures, and true in word and deed, he is equal to the immortal gods." Then the gods ascended on high, but Kali said to Duápara, " I will not stay my wrath, but henceforth I will keep watch on Nala, and you shall abide in the dice ; and when the hour comes I will enter his soul and gain the mastery over him until I have cast him out of the raj and parted him from his sweet bride." And from that hour the two evil spirits, Kali and Duápara, dwelt in the palace of Nala.

Twelve years passed away, and none in all the world were so supremely blessed as the beautiful Damayantí and her husband Nala. But on a certain evening Nala failed in duty, for he prayed to the gods with feet unwashen ; and Kali seized the opportunity, and straightway entered into him and possessed his inmost soul. And Nala had a brother named Pushkara, and Kali said to Pushkara, "Go you and play at dice with Nala, and I will make him the winner of his raj." And Pushkara challenged Nala to a game at dice, and Nala and Pushkara sat down to play in the presence of Damayantí. And they played for gold and jewels and raiment, and for chariots and horses ; but Nala was worsted at every throw, for Duápara embodied the dice, and Kali had mastered him body and soul. Then the faithful friends of Nala prayed him to throw no longer ; but he was maddened with the love of play, and shut his ears to all they said. And all the chief men of the raj assembled at the gate of the palace to arrest the frenzy of the raja. And the charioteer entered the hall and said to Damayantí, " Lo, all the city are gathered together, for they fear lest some dire misfortune befall the raja." And Damayantí was stricken with deep sorrow, and she entreated the raja to listen to the voice of his people ; but he turned away from her beautiful and tearful eyes, and answered not a word ; and so the play went on, and the people returned to their houses, saying, " Surely this gambler cannot be the raja." And when Nala had lost all his treasures, the sorrowing Damayantí told her nurse to summon the council ; and the council assembled at the palace, and Damayantí announced their presence to Nala, but he heeded not her words ; and she was filled with shame, and left the hall and went to her own rooms.

Then Damayantí sent for the charioteer and spoke to him winningly, and said, "You know what trust my lord, the Raja, has ever placed in you. Go now and harness the steeds to the chariot, and take my children to my father's city and leave them in my father's house ; and then dwell there, or go wherever you will." And the charioteer went to the council and obtained their consent ; and he took the noble boy and the beautiful maiden to the city of Vidarbha, and he gave them in-to the charge of Raja Bhíma ; and then he went his way with great sadness of heart to the city of Ayodhyá and entered the service of Raja Rituparna.

Meanwhile, Nala had lost all his treasures, and his chariots and his horses ; and he staked his raj and the vestments which he wore, and he lost all to Pushkara. And Pushkara smiled and said, "O Nala, you have lost your all, excepting only your wife, Damayantí." At these words the heart of Nala was rent asunder, and he said not a word. And he took off all his robes and raiment and looked sadly upon Pushkara, and went out with but a single scanty covering, and Damayantí al-so had but a single covering, and she followed him slowly be-hind.

4. THE EXILE OF NALA AND DAMAYANTI.

Then Pushkara proclaimed throughout the city, "Whoever shall give food or shelter to Nala shall be put to death."

And for three days and three nights Nala lived on fruits and roots, and his sorrowing Rání followed behind him and did the same. Then Nala saw a flock of birds upon the ground and he said within himself, "This day we shall have food." And he threw his only garment upon the birds, but they flew into the air and carried the garment with them. And the birds

5

spoke in human language and mocked Nala in his misery, and said, "O foolish Nala, we are the dice, and we came hither to rob you of your covering, for whilst you had a single garment left our joy was small." Then Nala was in an agony, and he said to Damayanti, "Weep not for me, but go to the house of your father; yonder lies the road, and it passes through woods that have abundant fruits, and on the way are many hermitages of pious sages." But Damayanti burst into tears and replied, "O my lord, your words will break my heart: How can I leave you in this lonely wood, when you have been robbed of all? No, I will stay and soothe your weariness, for the wisest physicians say that a true wife is the best balsam in every time of sorrow. If I go to my kindred it must be with you, and we must both go together." But Nala had not the heart to take refuge in the house of his wife's father; and he said, "I will not seek refuge in your father's raj; once I went there in joy and pride, but now should I appear there I should only increase my shame."

So Nala and Damayanti journeyed on together, and they made one garment suffice them. And they came to a brook and Nala caught two fishes and laid them before his wife and went into the brook to bathe; and Damayanti in her hunger put her hand upon the fishes, but the touch of her fingers revived them like a draught of soma and they sprang back into the water. And when Nala returned he thought that Damayanti had eaten the fishes, but he said nothing, and so they still wandered on.

Now when both Raja and the Rání were wearied with their toil, and faint with thirst and hunger they reached a little hut, and there they lay and slept upon the bare ground. And Damayanti was oppressed with sleep, but Nala was distraught with sorrow. And Nala awoke and thought of the raj he had lost, and the friends who had deserted him, and of his weary wandering in the jungle; and he grew frantic, for the evil spirit of Kali was working within him; and he said within his heart, "If Damayanti remains with me she must bear certain sorrow, but if I leave her she may return to her father's house:

If I go, I know not which is better for me, — life or death ; but for her, no one will harm a wife so devoted and so beautiful." Then Nala pondered how he should divide the single garment between them ; and he saw a sword that lay in the cabin, and he severed the garment in two, and he clothed himself with the half of the garment. Then he fled into the jungle, but came back again and beheld his wife sleeping, and he wept bitterly and said, " My love, whom neither sun nor moon dared look upon, how will she awake ? How will she wander alone through the deep jungle haunted by serpents and wild beasts ? May the sun god and the god of wind protect her, though her virtue is her best guard." Then the mind of Nala was swayed to and fro, first by love and then by despair, until at last he left his wife alone in the hut, and rushed like one who is mad into the depths of the jungle.

5. NALA'S DESERTION OF DAMAYANTI.

Now when the slender-waisted Damayantí awoke from her deep slumber and found herself abandoned in the jungle, she shrieked aloud in grief and pain, and ran about the wood leaping in madness; and she sobbed very bitterly and said, " May that evil one who has caused this dreadful suffering to Nala be smitten by a curse more fatal still." Thus she went wailing through the forest, until suddenly there came a great serpent and seized her in his grasp and coiled around her ; and she cried out in great terror, and a huntsman heard her screams, and shot an arrow at the serpent's face, and released her from her peril. Then the huntsman brought her water and food, and refreshed her ; and at his bidding she told him all her story, but as he gazed upon her beautiful form, which was scantily covered by half a garment, a deep passion burned within him, and he whispered words of love. Then Damayantí was filled with wrath, and she cursed him in her bitterness of soul, and he fell down dead like a tree that has been stricken with lightning.

Then Damayantí wandered on in quest of Nala until she met a caravan of merchants, with elephants and camels and chariots and horses; and when the people saw her so beautiful and noble, and yet so pale and worn, they took compassion on her; and they told her they were going to the city of Chedi. And Damayantí went with the caravan, and when it was evening they came to a pleasant lake fragrant with lotus flowers, and they pitched their tents and encamped there. But at midnight there was a great cry, for a horde of wild elephants of the jungle rushed down upon the encampment, like mountain-tops rolling down to the valley; and they trampled upon the sleeping people, and crushed many with their heavy tread, and gored others with their fierce tusks. And the merchants shrieked aloud with terror, and some began to fly and others stood gasping, blind with sleep; whilst many struck each other down, or stumbled over the rough ground, or climbed the trees, or hid themselves in the holes in the earth. And, Damayantí awoke amidst the dreadful turmoil; and some said that she was a woman of evil omen and had worked all the mischief; and she was filled with shame and fear, and fled once again into the depths of the jungle.

After many days Damayantí entered the city of Chedi, and she was famished and distressed, and broken down with sorrow. And she was clad in only half a garment, and her long hair was hanging dishevelled over her shoulders, and her gaze was wild and distracted, and her face was emaciated from long fasting. And the people of the city thought that she was mad, and a crowd of boys followed her and mocked her. And, as she approached the gate of the palace, the mother of the raja beheld her from the terrace, and sent her waiting-woman to bring the wanderer in. Damayantí entered the palace and told how her husband was a raja, who had lost his all by dice, and how she had followed him into exile through the greatness of her love, but how he had left her in the jungle with only half a garment. And the eyes of Damayantí were filled with tears, and the gracious lady bade her take up her abode in the palace while the servants of the household went abroad in search of Nala. And Damayantí said to the mother of the raja, "O mother of heroes, I will dwell with you, but I will not eat the victuals left by others, nor wash the feet of others, nor converse with strange men." And the mother of the raja agreed, and called her daughter Sunadá, and bade her take Damayantí to be her friend. And Damayantí dwelt in the palace many days as friend and companion of the princess, Sunadá.

6. ADVENTURES OF NALA.

Now when Rajah Nala left Damayantí in the hut, he beheld a great fire in the forest, and he heard a voice crying, "Hasten, Nala, and come hither !" And Nala remembered that on his bridal day, the god Agni had given him power over fire; and he plunged into the bright flame and saw the raja of serpents coiled up in a ring. And the serpent said, "I deceived the sage of Naradá, and he has cursed me, that fire should surround me until you save me." And the serpent shrank to the size of a finger, and Nala lifted him up and carried him out of the fire. Then the serpent bit Nala, and immediately the form of Nala was changed into that of a deformed dwarf, so that no man could know him. And the serpent said to Nala, "My poison shall work on the evil spirit who has entered your soul, until he leaves you free. Take now the name of Váhuka and enter the service of Rituparna, Raja of Ayodhyá, and you shall teach him the art of taming horses, and he shall teach you all the secrets of the dice ; therefore, sorrow no more, O Nala ! for you shall see again your wife, your children, and your raj ; and when you would again resume your proper form, put on this change of raiment and think of me." So saying, the serpent gave a change of raiment to Nala, and vanished away from his sight.

Then Nala journeyed on to the city of Ayodhyá, and offered his services to Raja Rituparna, both as a tamer of horses, and as skilled in the art of cooking viands ; and the Raja engaged him, and bade him take heed that the horses were swift of foot ; and he gave him Várshneya and Jívala to be his adjutants. Now Várshneya had been charioteer to Nala, and had driven his children to the city of Vidarbha ; but Nala's form had been changed by the serpent, and Várshneya knew him not. And every evening Nala used to sing this single verse : —

"Where is she whom I left in the jungle, to suffer hunger, thirst
   and weariness ? "
"Does she think of me, her foolish lord, or does she sit in the
   presence of another ? "

And Jívala said to Nala, "Who is she, O Váhuka! for whom you are grieving?" And Nala answered, "A man there was bereft of sense, who had a faithful wife, but in his foolishness he forsook her in the wilderness ; and ever since that time the man wanders to and fro in despair, for, whether she lives or no, he cannot say."

7. DISCOVERY OF DAMAYANTI.

Meantime, Raja Bhíma of Vidarbha had sent holy Brahmans to every land in quest of his daughter, Damayantí, and her husband, Nala ; and the joyful Brahmans, hoping for rich re-wards, went through every city and every clime, but nowhere could they find a trace of those they sought. At length a certain Brahman, whose name was Sudeva, went to the pleasant city of Chedi, and there he saw the slender-waisted Damayantí, standing in the palace by the side of the princess Sunadá ; and her beauty was dim, and seemed like the sunlight struggling through a cloud, yet he failed not to see that she was the daughter of Raja Bhíma. And the Brahman spoke to her say-ing, "O daughter of Bhíma, your father has sent me to seek for you ; and both he and your mother and your brethren are all well ; and so too are your little ones, who are dwelling in your father's palace."

And Damayantí remembered Sudeva, and made inquiry

about all her friends. And the mother of the raja came in and
saw her talking to the Brahman ; and presently she took the
Brahman aside, and said, "Who is this lady to whom you have
spoken ? Who is her father, and who is her husband?"
Then the Brahman told all to the mother of the raja, and he
said, "I knew she was the daughter of Bhima, because of her
peerless beauty ; but from her birth a lovely beauty-mark was
to be seen between her eyebrows, and now it has passed away."
When the princess Sunadá heard these words of the Brahman,
she took water and washed away the traces of tears that were
between the eyes of Damayantí, and the beauty-mark was
present to the eyes of all. Then the mother of the raja exclaimed to Damayantí, "You are the daughter of my sister!
I know you by the mark, for I myself was present at your
birth. Lo, all I have is yours !" And Damayantí bowed to
her mother's sister, and prayed that she might be sent to her
two children at Vidarbha. And the palanquin was prepared,
and a guard was ordered, and Damayantí was carried to her
father's palace at Vidarbha. And when she saw her children
her heart was filled with joy, and she passed the night in sweet
slumber; but in the morning she went to her mother and softly
said, "O mother, if my life is dear to you, I pray you to
do all you can to bring back Nala." And her mother went to
Bhima and said, "Your daughter is mourning for her husband, Nala."

Then Raja Bhima sent the Brahmans once again to every
land in search of Nala ; and, before the Brahmans departed,
Damayantí sent for them, and entreated them to cry aloud
these words in every public place, "Whither didst thou go,
O gambler, who severed thy wife's garment, and left her in
the lonely forest, where she still sits sorrowing for thee ?" So,
the Brahmans went forth to all lands, and they searched everywhere, in crowded cities and in quiet villages, and in the hermitages of holy men, and everywhere they repeated aloud the
words of Damayantí, but no man took heed of the question
respecting Nala.

8. DISCOVERY OF NALA.

Now, after a while, a certain Brahman went to the great city of Ayodhyá, where reigned Raja Rituparna, and where Nala was dwelling in the guise of a charioteer and under the name of Váhuka. And the Brahman cried aloud the question of Damayantí in all the streets and ways and market-places in the city; but no man heeded him. So he took leave of the raja and prepared to depart, when Váhuka came to him, and groaned in anguish and wept bitterly, and said, " Even in the extremity of misery a noble woman is mistress of herself ; and, even when abandoned by her husband, she will not give her soul to anger." At these words the Brahman left the city of Ayodhyá with all speed, and hastened to the city of Vidarbha, and told Damayantí all that Váhuka had said; and the eyes of Damayantí overflowed with tears, for she thought that she had found Nala. Then Damayantí went to her mother, and said, "O mother! I must send a message to the city of Ayodhyá which my father Bhíma must not hear; and I will deliver it in your presence to Sudeva, that best of Brahmans, who found me in the city of Chedi ; and as he brought your daughter to her father's house, so may he swiftly bring my royal husband from the city of Ayodhyá." So she sent for Sudeva, and requested him, in the presence of her mother, to go to the city of Ayodhyá, and to seek out Raja Rituparna, and say to him as if by chance, " Damayantí, daughter of Raja Bhíma, is about to choose a second husband, and all the rajas and sons of rajas are hastening to Vidarbha. If you would be there, you must make good speed; for to-morrow is the appointed day, and at sunrise she makes her choice; for Raja Nala cannot be found, and no man knows whether he be alive or dead."

And Sudeva went to the city of Ayodhyá and performed the bidding of Damayantí; and, when Rituparna heard the tidings that Damayantí was about to choose another husband, his heart burned to be there, but the way was far. Rituparna

went to Váhuka, his charioteer, and spoke to him with winning words like one that asks a favor, and said, " On the morrow the daughter of Bhíma will choose a second husband; I,
too, would seek to win her, but the city of Vidarbha is afar
off. Say, then, if you have horses that can reach it in a single
day." Then the heart of Váhuka was smitten with anguish,
and he wondered that the holy Damayantí should be driven to
a deed so unholy, and he thought within himself that he would
see if the tidings were true. So he folded his hands in reverence to the raja, and said, " I promise in a single day to reach
the city of Vidarbha." And he went to the stables of the
raja, and pondered long over the horses ; and he chose four
that were very slender, but fleet and powerful for the road,
and they had broad nostrils and large jaws ; and he har-
nessed them to the chariot of the raja. But when Rituparna
saw the slenderness of the coursers, he cried out, " What steeds
be these ? Have they strength and wind for such a journey ? "
And Váhuka replied, " These horses will not fail to carry you
to Vidarbha, but, if you desire others, tell me which you will
have, and I will harness them." But the raja said, " You know
the horses best, and may harness what you will."

9. NALA'S DRIVE FROM AYODHYÁ TO VIDARBHA.

Now when the chariot was ready, Raja Rituparna took his
seat, and commanded Várshneya to ascend likewise, whilst
Váhuka drove. Then the fiery horses began to prance and
paw the air; but Váhuka gathered up the reins, and cried out
to the horses in a soothing voice, and they sprang into the air
as if they would unseat their driver, and then tore along the
ground as•swift as the wind. And the riders were wellnigh
blinded with speed ; but the raja marvelled and rejoiced
greatly at the driving of Váhuka; and Várshneya said within
himself, as he felt the rattling of the chariot and beheld the
driving of Váhuka, " Either this Váhuka must be the charioteer
of Indra, or else he is my old master, Raja Nala."

Thus the chariot flew along, like a bird in the air, through the deep forests, and over the rivers and mountains and broad lakes. And the raja dropped his mantle, and prayed Nala to halt a moment and pick it up; but Nala said, " The mantle is miles behind, and we cannot return to recover it." And they passed a certain tree, and the raja said to Nala, " Mark now my skill in numbers; for I know the secrets of dice and the rules of calculation. On these two branches hang fifty millions of leaves and two thousand and ninety-five berries." And Nala descended the chariot to count the leaves and berries, and, whilst the raja cried out that he could not wait, Nala persisted, and after a while Nala found that the numbering of the raja was true to a single leaf. And Nala said, " O raja, teach me this skill of yours, and you shall learn from me all the secrets that I know in horsemanship." And the raja did so; and, when Nala knew the secret of the dice, the evil spirit Kali went out of him, and Kali vomited the poison of the serpent that was burning within him. And Nala would have cursed Kali; but he fled away and entered a tree. Thus Nala was released from his sufferings; but still he took not his own form of Nala, but remained in that of Vâhuka the charioteer.

Now when it was near the setting of the sun, the chariot approached the city of Vidarbha, and the heart of Nala beat faster and faster; and, when they reached the city gates, the watchmen on the walls proclaimed the coming of Raja Rituparna; and the rushing of the horses and rolling of the chariot-wheels were like the thunder which heralds in the coming rain ; and the peacocks on the palace walls raised their necks and clamored, and the elephants in the stables roared tumultuously. And the heart of Damayanti thrilled with delight as she heard the old familiar sound of her husband's driving, and she said, " Unless Nala comes this day, I will no longer live, but will perish by the fire."

10. DAMAYANTI RECOVERS HER HUSBAND.

Then Damayanti ascended to the terrace on the roof of the palace, and looked down into the middle of the court; and she saw Raja Rituparna, and her old charioteer Várshneya, and the dwarfish and deformed Váhuka; and she beheld her father Raja Bhíma receive Rituparna with all courtesy, although amazed at the suddenness of his coming ; and she remembered Várshneya, and thought that he had learned to drive furiously, like Nala; for she knew not Váhuka, because of his altered form. But still her heart thrilled, and she pondered deeply; for she remembered what Váhuka had said to the Brahman. And she called her fair-haired handmaiden, Kesiní, and said to her, " Go, my little maid, and speak to that chariot-driver who is short of stature, and find out who he is; and do you repeat to him the message which was brought to me by the Brahman, and tell me what he says." So, whilst Damayanti watched from the terrace, the blameless little maiden went into the middle of the court to speak to Nala.

Meantime Nala had taken the chariot to the stall ; and, after he had tended to his horses, he mounted the chariot and sat there alone. And the fair-haired Kesiní went to him and said, " I salute you, O charioteer! and pray you to hear the message of my mistress Damayanti. She desires to know whence you came and wherefore you have come." Nala answered, " When my master, the raja, heard that Damayanti would wed again, and would choose another husband on the morrow, he bade me drive him hither with all speed; and, lo ! we have come this day all the way from the city of Ayodhyá." Then Kesiní said, "And who is that other charioteer who came with you ? " Nala answered, "That is the renowned Várshneya, who was once the charioteer of Nala; and, when his raja went into exile, he took service with Rituparna. And I, also, serve Rituparna; for I am his charioteer, and the chief of all his cooks." And Kesiní said, further, " Does Várshneya know aught of Nala?" Nala answered, "It was Vársh-neya who brought the children of Nala to this city, and then he went his way, and heard no more of his old master." And Kesiní said, still further, "The Brahman that lately went to the city of Ayodhyá was commanded by my mistress to cry aloud in every place, 'Whither didst thou go, O gambler! who severed thy wife's garment, and left her in the lonely forest, where she still sits sorrowing for thee?' Now, it was you who gave the Brahman his answer back; so I pray you to repeat that answer again, for my mistress desires to hear it." At these words of the blameless little maiden the heart of Nala was wrung with a deep sorrow, and his eyes overflowed with tears, and, with a voice half choking from weeping, he thus repeated his reply, "Even in the extremity of misery a noble woman is mistress of herself; and, even when abandoned by her husband, she will not give her soul to anger." And Nala wept afresh; and the maid went back to Damayantí, and told her all that Váhuka had said, and described to her the bitterness of his sorrow.

Then Damayantí was still heavy at heart, wondering whether the charioteer could possibly be Nala; and she said, "Go again, O Kesiní, and watch this man, and observe all that he does, and see that no fire or water be given to him; and whatsoever he does, be it human or divine, come back and tell to me." And Kesiní went out and watched Nala, and presently she returned and said, "O Damayantí, never before did I behold a man so god-like; for if he approaches a low portal he never bows his head, but the portal rises above him; and when he prepared to dress the victuals for his master, the vessels were filled with water directly he looked at them; and when he had washed the meat he held some blades of grass towards the set-ting sun, and they blazed with fire of their own accord." And Damayantí remembered the gifts which the gods had given to Nala on his marriage-day, and she said with a gentle voice, "Go again, Kesiní, and bring me some of the meat which the charioteer is cooking." So the little maiden went into the kit-

chen and brought some of the food to Damayantí, and Damayantí tasted it and cried aloud, " The charioteer is Nala ! " And
her heart was stirred with vehement emotion, and she directed
her maid to carry her two children to the charioteer. And
when Nala beheld his son and daughter, as beautiful as the
children of the gods; he wound his arms around them and
pressed them to his bosom, and burst into a flood of tears ; and
he said to Kesiní, " O blameless maiden, the children are so like
my own, that I have been compelled to weep."

When Damayantí heard from her handmaid of the deep
affection of the charioteer, she was seized with a deep longing
to behold Nala, and she sent Kesiní to her mother, saying, " We
have watched the charioteer most closely, and we suspect him
to be Nala, only that his form is changed. I pray you, therefore, either to permit him to be brought to you, or give me
leave to have him brought to me, with or without the knowledge of my father." So the mother of Damayantí told to
Bhíma all the secret counsel of his daughter, and the raja
permitted Damayantí to summon the charioteer.

Then Damayantí sent for Nala, and as she saw him she
trembled greatly, and her hair was dishevelled about her shoulders, and she was arrayed in a mantle of scarlet, and the eyes
of both Nala and Damayantí overflowed with tears. And Damayantí was almost overcome by her strong emotion, and she
said, " O Vahuka, did you ever know an upright and noble man
who abandoned his sleeping wife in a wood ? Who was he
who thus forsook a beloved and blameless wife but Raja Nala ?
He who was chosen by me, and for whom I rejected the gods ;
me, whose hand he had clasped in the presence of the immortal
gods ; me, to whom he had plighted his faith before the nuptial
fire : where is that promise now ? "

And Nala gazed upon his long-lost wife like one in a dream,
and he said, " I lost my raj by the dice, but the evil was
wrought by Kali; I forsook you in the jungle, but the guilty
deed was the work of Kali. Long time has Kali dwelt within
me, but now he is subdued and gone, and for thy sake I made

haste to come hither. But how may a high-born woman choose a second husband? Yet heralds are proclaiming throughout the world that the daughter of Bhíma will celebrate a second Swayamvara."

At these words Damayantí trembled and said, " Do not suspect me of such shameless guilt. The Brahman proclaimed a second Swayamvara only to find thee, and to bring thee here. I call on the all-seeing wind, the sun, the moon, who are the three gods who govern the three worlds, to attest the truth of what I say." Then the voice of the wind was heard in the air, " Nala, she has neither done nor thought evil, but for three long years hath treasured up her virtue in all its fulness. The second Swayamvara was a plot to discover thee. Thou hast met with the daughter of Bhíma, and the daughter of Bhíma has met thee. Take thy own wife to thy bosom!"

Even as the wind was speaking, the flowers fell in showers from heaven, and the gods sounded sweet music ; and every doubt of the blameless Damayantí passed away from the mind of Nala, and he threw off his disguise and put on the garments that the serpent had given him, and at once resumed his proper form as Raja Nala. And Damayantí shrieked aloud, and embraced her husband ; and Nala, radiant as of old, clasped her to his heart, and the children were brought in, and the night passed away in the fulness of joy.

11. NALA RECOVERS HIS RAJ.

And when the white-robed dawn was awakening a sleeping world, the sound of rejoicing ran through the city of Vidarbha. In every street the people exulted in the safe return of Raja Nala, and adorned the houses with banners and garlands, and hung chains of flowers from door to door, and strewed the roadways with leaves and blossoms. And all was gladness in the palace at Vidarbha, for Raja Bhíma was transported with joy when he beheld the long-lost husband of his beloved daughter ; and Raja Rituparna was filled with wonder and delight when

he knew that his fiercely driving charioteer was no other than
Raja Nala. Then they took counsel together how they might
compel the evil-minded Pushkara to restore the raj to his
elder brother. And Nala had learned the whole art of throwing dice from his old master, Raja Rituparna, and he saw how
Pushkara had won the raj, and resolved to win it back in like
manner. So when one month had passed away and Nala was
perfect in the game, he set off to Nishadha, with elephants and
horses and chariots, and challenged his brother Pushkara to
another throw, in which he would stake Damayantí against the
raj ; and the wicked Pushkara eagerly agreed and exulted in
the certainty of winning the wife of Nala. But the throw was
against Pushkara, and thus Nala won back his raj and all his
treasure ; but, when Pushkara humbled himself before him,
Nala forgave him all, and dismissed him with many gifts to his
own city. Then Nala returned to Vidarbha and brought away
his beautiful Damayantí ; and henceforth he reigned at Nishada, as Indra reigns in heaven, and performed every holy rite
in honor of the gods, with all the munificence of a royal
devotee.

CHAPTER III.

BUDDHISM AND THE RAMAYANA.

A S these studies are literary and not theological, it may be wondered that I allude to the two religions: it is because we could not understand the poems without them. The Maha Bharata, with its Swayamvaras and single combats and feudal tone, is transitional. The Brahmanical age soon became a gloomy sacerdotal period, where Brahman priests tyrannized over the Kshatriya rajas; and therefore we shall trace next the rise of Buddhism, and the epic poem, the Ramayana, which form the third period, called the Buddhist period.

The Brahmans based their authority upon the Vedas, which we spoke of in our last chapters, and also on the laws of Manu, their great lawgiver, which is the oldest code of laws after the three Vedas. They contain old material; but, in their present form, they are of much later date than the three Vedas. They were not revealed in their actual form like the laws in the three Vedas; the thought was sacred, but written down in human words, and handed down by *smriti*, tradition, instead of *sruti*, revelation, so that sometimes a letter or a word might be changed. The word Manu is the same as the Greek Minos, which also means lawgiver, and has the same root as our words " mind " and " man."

Therefore it is not probable that he was a real person. The code of Manu means probably the laws of a man, instead of the laws revealed by the gods in the three Vedas. ▪

These laws of Manu give rules for the religious observances, the civil customs, and the domestic life of priests and laymen. By their commands, the Hindu knows how to act towards his gods, his fellow-citizens, and his family. And those remarkable village communities, still existing in India, are governed by Manu's laws. Many of them seem to us trivial and subservient; I fear we shall not admire our Hindu brethren in them as much as we did in the Rig Veda and the Maha Bharata. A few noble ones are scattered throughout, like these : —

"The witness who speaks falsely shall be fast bound under water in the cords of Varuna ; and shall be wholly deprived of power to escape torment during one hundred transmigrations. Let mankind therefore give no false testimony. The soul is its own witness : offend not thy conscious soul, the supreme internal witness of men."

"The sinful have said in their heart, 'None sees us'; yes, the gods distinctly see them, and so does the spirit within their breasts."

These laws are quite different from our idea of a code ; there is no systematic arrangement in them. The real laws for government and civil customs, which ought to form the greatest part of any code, occupy part of three books. There are twelve books in all : of these, six are devoted to the duties of Brahmans ; two, to the duties of Kshatriyas, including rajas ; one book, to the other two castes. The state of society is pure, unmixed

6

Brahmanism. The world evidently was created for the Brahmans. They are the great central body around which everything revolves. They are bound together by most stringent rules, and the other three castes were powerless to resist them, because they were forbidden to combine, by equally severe laws. These are rules : —

"A Brahman, whether learned or unlearned, is a mighty divinity; just as fire is a mighty divinity, whether consecrated or unconsecrated."

"From priority of birth, from superiority of origin (in being born from the mouth of the Creator), from possession of the right of teaching the Rig Veda, from being the first to receive the sacred thread, the Brahman is lord of all the classes."

"A raja must never kill a Brahman, though he be found guilty of all possible crimes; let him be expelled from the kingdom unharmed in body, and intact in property. There is no greater injustice on earth than killing a Brahman. The raja, therefore, must not harbor a thought about putting him to death."

"The superiority of the Brahman is by birth and divine right; it is as much a law of nature and divine appointment as the differences between elephants, lions, and horses."

"Although the kings rule by divine right, they are expected to be fathers to their people. Determination not to retreat in battle, protection of the people, and obedience to Brahmans, are the best duties of kings, and secure their felicity in heaven."

We learn that coined money was not common, from the laws about interest, which was allowed for borrowed goods, but was always paid in kind, if fruit, grain, or wool. The laws about property are very patriarchal, and suggest the early tribal government of the Aryan race: they did not allow the owner to make any will:

there is no such word as "will," or "testament," in the Sanskrit language. In any patriarchal state of society all property was held in common, the head of the family being the head partner. The family was a corporation, and the property could not be divided until the father and mother were both dead: if the father died first, the eldest son managed the family until the mother died. Women had no legal title to the property; if unmarried, a share was generally given to them. Married women had no property except gifts which had been made them: for instance, —

"Whatever was given over the marriage fire, whatever she received while being led in procession from her father's to her husband's house, whatever was a gift from her husband as a token of affection, or a similar gift from her mother, her brother, or her father, — these were her own peculiar property."

If a man had no son, his daughters inherited, but this almost never occurred. The other laws about women would sound very strangely to the advocates of woman's suffrage. These are literal quotations : —

147. "By a girl, or a young woman, or by a woman advanced in years, nothing must be done, even in her own dwelling-place, according to her mere pleasure."

148. "In childhood a female must be dependent upon her father; in youth, on her husband; her lord being dead, on her sons; if she have no sons, on the near kinsmen of her husband; if he have left no kinsman, on those of her father; if she have no kinsmen, on the sovereign. A woman must never seek independence."

150. "She must always live with a cheerful temper, with good management in the affairs of the house, with great care of the household furniture, and with a frugal hand in all her expenses."

154. "Though a husband should be unobservant of approved usages, or devoid of good qualities, he must constantly be revered as a god by a virtuous wife."

155. "No sacrifice is allowed to women apart from their husbands, no religious rite, no fasting; as far only as a wife honors her husband, so far is she exalted in heaven."

156. "Women have no business with the text of the Veda."

157. "A husband must never eat with his wife, nor look at her while she is eating."

158. "The names of women should be agreeable, soft, clear, captivating the fancy, auspicious, ending in long vowels, resembling words of benediction."

When Gandhari, a princess, heard that her future husband was born blind, she from that moment showed her respect for him by binding her own eyes with a handkerchief and always remaining blindfold in his presence. She had evidently learned the spirit of Manu. There are other laws which seem very suitable to the climate of India: against cutting down green trees for fuel; against selling a garden, or a tank of water. But the laws against selling a wife, a child, or a cow are less consonant to our ideas.

But the rules for daily life are the most curious of all. There was a fixed form for Brahmans, another for rajas, but the whole life of every twice-born man was marked out. Before his birth even, his parents had to perform certain sacrifices, without which the child could not become a member of society, or, what was the same thing with the Brahmans, a member of the church: after his birth certain food must be given to him in a certain way. From seven to eleven years of age his student-life began. He was sent away from home, and given to a master to be educated; and his education consisted in learning the Vedas by heart. Some students remained twelve years, which was the shortest period allowed; others, forty-eight years; others, all their lives. From nineteen to twenty-two came the second stage, — that of married life. His wife must be from eight to twelve years of age, chosen by certain rules. Then a new house must be erected, and the sacred fire kindled according to a prescribed form. Then his daily life began: their theory of life was, that man is born a debtor, and he must repay this debt by five sacraments, performed every day.

First. Homage to his dead ancestors, by offering them cakes of rice and meal mingled with water. There was, in addition, a funeral offering to deceased ancestors, monthly, on the new moon, and annually, on the anniversary of their deaths, as far back as great-grandfather. The family was a corporation, consisting of father, grandfather, and great-grandfather, among the dead; son and grandson, among the living; and the oblation from the living to the dead was the bond of union. No one could go to heaven unless he had a son: the dead spirit could not rest till its funeral rites had been performed by a son.

Second. To all beings, by throwing rice grains on the house-tops, or outside the door, for animals to devour.

Third. To the bards who received the revelation of the Vedas, this was done by repeating the Vedas. The twice-born man was to go in an easterly or northerly direction, wearing the sacred thread over his shoulders. Having rinsed his mouth, he was to sit down on sacred Kusa grass whose points were directed towards the east; then, to draw in his breath three times, to say the sacred syllable Aum (Om), which is the condensed essence of the four Vedas; then, the three mystical words, earth, air, heaven; then, the holiest verse of the Veda, " Let us meditate on the most excellent light and power of that generous. sportive, and resplendent Sun; may He guide our intellect"; then, as many more verses from the Vedas as he chose, in a low tone, or even inaudibly. This was the most meritorious of all religious acts, and made him fit for final beatitude and absorption into Brahman, whether he performed other acts or not.

Fourth. Homage to men by hospitality. Here is a very pleasing encouragement to this duty : —

" Grass and earth to sit upon, water to wash the feet, and affectionate speech, are at no time wanting in the mansions of the good, although indigent. . . . No guest must be dismissed in the evening by a householder: he is sent by the retiring sun, and, whether he come in fit season or unseasonably, he must not sojourn in the house without entertainment."

Fifth. Homage to the gods, by an offering thrown on the sacred fire. I describe these five sacraments so minutely that one may have some slight idea of the net-work of forms which enveloped every moment of the Hindu's day and night. The laws of Manu and the Vedas say, " The man who does not perform these five sacraments every, day lives not, although he may breathe." As time went on, a Guru, or family priest, was established in every household. But he was far more than a teacher, — far more, even, than a mediator between the gods and man : he was the present god, the actual, visible incarnation of Brahman. The re-

ligion of the Hindus, therefore, came gradually to con-
sist in performing all the ceremonies, obeying all the
rules, maintaining caste, and, finally, in doing penances to propitiate the anger of the new gods; for to
break any of these forms was a fearful sin. The joyous feasts of the Kshatriya rajas, where bards sang the
glories of their ancestors, were turned into gloomy
sacrifices and penances to appease the wrath of Siva.
Severe penances inflicted by the persons themselves
were more honorable than legal penalties inflicted by a
judge. Here is one penance: —

"He who says 'Hush!' or 'Pish!' to a Brahman, or 'thou'
to a superior, must immediately bathe, eat nothing for the rest
of the day, and appease him by clasping his feet with respectful salutation. . . . He who has committed a crime for the first
degree shall be absolved if he attend a herd of cattle for one
year, mortifying his organs, and continually repeating the texts,
living entirely upon food given by charity."

So the slightest neglect of these duties brought loss of
caste in this world, and eternal punishment in the next.
Meditations were considered especially holy; and the
Hindu sat under a tree for years meditating upon
Brahman. One man meditated so long that ants threw
up a mound as high as his waist without being disturbed, and birds built their nests in his clotted hair.
One traveller saw a man standing motionless and meditating with his face towards the sun. After sixteen
years he revisited the spot, and found the same man in
the same place: he had been there ever since. To
appease the new gods, they also practised the most
dreadful austerities. During the three hottest months,

April, May, and June, one man sat between four blazing fires, with a burning sun above his head. He stood on one leg, gazing at the sun; then he stood on his head for three hours, with his feet in the air. Out of many laws and penances, the few I have given will bring the daily life of the Hindu before you, and easily account for the necessity of some change. Human nature could bear no more. There was one relief afforded by Brahmanism; but it was applicable only to one class of people, necessarily very few in number. When the householder among the Hindus had reared up a son and a grandson, to perform the funeral sacraments, he reached the third stage of that life which every twice-born man wished to lead. He had then done all that this world required of him, and was at liberty to begin the fourth stage. He said farewell to his family, he gave away all his share in the family property, and he retired to the forest. He became what we call a hermit. He meditated upon life and death; instead of performing a peculiar sacrifice to free himself from transmigration and second birth, he went through it mentally, and obtained the same result. Then he took another step, and sought to concentrate his thoughts on Brahman, to bring himself into absolute communion with the eternal soul of the world. As soon as he had reached this point, he could no longer remain separated from his parent existence. In order that he might the sooner be absorbed into Brahman, he killed himself. Now, this fourth stage, this forest life, was not exile: it was, on the contrary, the highest privilege of a twice-born man. It could only be allowed after he had passed through the other stages, —

had been a student, a father, and a grandfather. Therefore this high glory was not attainable by all. One would fancy that the past steps would be discarded, and this desirable condition become the prerogative of all; but the great peculiarity of Brahmanism is that it preserved every religious thought which had been handed down; it never outgrew anything and put it away. There are still families where the son learns the Vedas, the father performs the daily sacrifices, the grandfather becomes a hermit, gives up all sacrifices, and seeks absorption into Brahman. But, for the ordinary man, the innumerable penances and sacrifices, the system of caste, and the dread of transmigration, weighed heavier and heavier upon the priest-ridden people; and at length a religious reformer arose.

The rise of Buddhism was simply one of those reactions which will occur when opinions have been pushed too far. It brings us to the third, or Buddhist, period of the literature. Max Müller says that the Sanskrit literature before this period is what is really historically important, — of use in tracing the development of the human mind and the rise and growth of ideas; and adds, " What would Plato and Aristotle have said if they had been told that in their time existed in that India which Alexander had just discovered, an ancient literature far richer than anything they possessed in Greece ?" There were ten thousand separate manuscripts in Sanskrit before Alexander conquered India. Now at length we get a date. Sakya Muni was born 623 b. c., died 543 b. c.; the era commenced about 500 b. c. Gautama was the tribe of his clan, he belonged to the warrior caste, and therefore, in the eyes of the

Brahmans, was utterly disqualified from ever becoming a religious teacher. He was more: he was a prince, the son of a raja. He became Buddha, or "the enlightened," and he founded Buddhism. It increased so much that it became the state religion of India, under the Constantine of India, Asoka, 245 B. C. It was carried far and wide by Buddhist missionaries, — to Thibet, to China, to Siberia, to Ceylon. The Turanian races proved peculiarly susceptible to its influence, and it numbers more than one third of the human race to-day. This account of its origin is taken from an Indian book : —

"One day when the prince drove through the eastern gate of the city, on his way to one of the parks, he met on the road a man broken and decrepit. 'Who is that man?' said the prince to his coachman. 'He is small and weak; his flesh and his blood are dried up; his muscles stick to his skin; his head is white; his teeth chatter; leaning on his stick he can hardly walk, stumbling at every step. Is there something peculiar in his family, or is his the lot of all created beings?' — 'Sir,' said the coachman, 'that man is sinking under old age. This is the appointed end of all creatures.' — 'Alas!' said the prince, 'are creatures so ignorant, so weak and foolish, as to be proud of the youth by which they are intoxicated? Coachman, turn my chariot quickly. What have I, the future prey of old age, to do with pleasure?' Another time the prince drove through the western gate, to a pleasure garden, when he perceived on the road a man suffering from illness, parched with fever. Having questioned his coachman and received the answer he expected, the prince cried, 'Alas! health is the sport of a dream. Who having seen this frightful spectacle could think of pleasure?' A third time he was driving to a pleasure garden, when he saw a dead body lying on a bier, covered with a cloth. The friends stood around weeping. The prince cried out, 'Woe to this life, where a man remains so short a time! If there were no old age, no disease, no death! Let us turn back. I must seek how to accomplish deliverance.' Again, he drove through the northern gate, to a pleasure-ground. He met a devotee, a mendicant. He had renounced all pleasures, all desires, and led a life of austerity. He sought to conquer himself. 'That is well,' said the prince. 'The life of a devotee will be my refuge: it will lead to real life, to happiness, to immortality.' He turned his chariot, and went back to the city."

There is something morbid and unhealthy in this. So after a day of revelry and mirth Prince Sakya Muni left his father's palace at night without saying farewell to his sleeping wife, and went out into the world to relieve its miseries, and to seek deliverance from them. He put on the yellow dress of a beggar, and begged his food from door to door. He began by doing charitable works: he taught the ignorant Sudras; he fed the poor; he nursed the sick. Since old age, sickness, and the loss of friends made life only a misfortune, Gautama felt that the good man would pass his own life in trying to alleviate the miseries of others. Then he meditated, sitting under a tree; after seven years he became enlightened; then he taught his doctrine. He denied that the Vedas were revealed, and were therefore infallible authority. His followers said that the Brahmans established all the ceremonies, as a means of livelihood. This was one of the great points of difference between Brahmanism and Buddhism. Buddha denounced caste, and divided mankind into two classes: laymen, those who are still attached to the world; and ascetics, those who wish to be delivered from it by mortifying themselves and performing works of charity. He admitted Sudras to be ascetics as well as twice-born men. Now, these ascetics are not very unlike the hermits of the fourth stage among the Brahmans; the difference being that Buddha admitted all men of any caste to this stage at once. He gave them individual freedom without going through the preliminary stages which the Brahmans insisted upon. He denied that sacrifices would take away sins, and taught that men should be pure, gentle, patient, and courageous; that they should do good deeds and show sympathy to every living thing, especially to animals; that is, he taught a lovely life, and he led such a life himself. He gave five commandments to laymen, — thou shalt not kill, steal, commit adultery, become intoxicated, lie; thus he gave them a pure and simple religion.

All this sounds very much as a matter of course to us brought up under Christianity. We must throw ourselves into the life and thought which existed around the Buddha before we can comprehend what an immense advance he made upon Brahmanism. For the ascetics Buddhism cannot receive such unqualified praise. It was stern and inexorable for them; it stripped life of every illusion. The ascetic renounced five things, — wife, children, property, life, and self. Instead of crushing out the passions by austerities, Buddha said that all the objects for which men strive — wealth, pleasure, power, human affection — are but Maya (vain illusions); that we should hush our mind into dreamy contemplative repose, and cease to desire anything. " Not nakedness, nor platted hair," he said,

"nor dirt, nor fasting, nor lying on the earth, not rubbing
with dust, nor sitting motionless, can purify a mortal
who has not overcome desires." This dull indifference
would lessen the sufferings caused by the "endless vor-
tex of transmigration." But Buddha taught the doctrine
of transmigration distinctly; that the wicked passed
through one hundred and thirty-six different hells, the
good through as many heavens, temporary purgatories,
before reaching the final result. After successive births
in this world and others, death would become the greatest of blessings, and the good man would be rewarded
by what? — by utter disappearance, Nirvana; and the
better he was, the sooner he would pass through the
necessary transmigrations and reach this result.

There has been endless discussion about the meaning
of Nirvana. The latest authorities say that it is not
exactly annihilation, though practically it amounts to
the same thing. " It may rather be figured under the
form of the morning mist disappearing in space, — not
destroyed, yet not cognizable by any human sense, or
to be described by any form of words." It has been
the fashion of late years to glorify Buddhism; it may
have been a lovely life, but it is a dreary creed.
Mr. Wheeler says: "Brahmanism answers to the natural instincts of the human heart, that good deeds will
be rewarded, and bad ones punished, in a future life.
But Buddhism is essentially an aristocratic creed,
suitable only to the philosophic yearning of a rich and
noble class, in whom self-indulgence in every pleasure
had produced a surfeit. They were driven by sheer
satiety to a life of abstinence and contemplation, which
tended to a dreamy existence of eternal repose and

undisturbed slumber, where all individuality was lost in the ocean of Nirvana." The different authorities agree that Buddhism is practically atheism. It can hardly be called a religion at all, for Buddha recognized no supreme god. The only god was what man himself could become. Of course there was no need of sacrifice to propitiate an angry god. There was no need of prayer either, for there was no god to pray to. Strictly speaking, a Buddhist never prayed, — he only meditated. There was no need of a priest, for there was nothing for him to do. Indeed, the ascetics are much more like our idea of monks, than of priests.

Buddhism spread with incredible rapidity. Convents and monasteries sprang up all over India, filled with monks and nuns, seeking deliverance by meditation. Whenever a scorching wind blew over the plains, a disgust of life seemed to seize upon all mankind, and the lazy dreaming of a Buddhist convent or monastery seemed to offer the speediest relief from the misery of existence; which may account for their number. At first there was no ceremonial; but since human nature is prone to worship something, they afterward worshipped Sakya Muni Gautama, the Buddha. His tooth is still preserved in a temple of Ceylon, which is, therefore, the most sacred spot of the world to all Buddhists. It was shown to the Prince of Wales during his visit to India, but is seldom seen by profane eyes. There were temples built also; in each of them was a statue of the Buddha, and these rock-hewn temples, whose ruins exist in India, are the admiration of architects, as well as of uneducated travellers. Instead of raising a lofty building upon a plain, as we do, the Buddhists selected some high rock or mountain. They levelled a space in front of it; they excavated the inside and formed one lofty room. They carved the face of the rock into a beautiful façade, with doors and one immense window, through which the light streamed into the interior, which they had hollowed out. The effect is most curious and beautiful. Grass and trees grow above the temple front, as if some lovely building had been pushed bodily inside a mountain and only its front could be seen. One may wonder that they are in ruins, for they would have resisted the mere attacks of time; but finally war arose in India, — a religious war between the Brahmans and the Buddhists. The monasteries and temples were burned: the Buddhists utterly driven out of India, to Ceylon and Burmah. They have never been allowed to return to the land where their religion originated. The power of organization and caste proved too strong to be permanently overcome: Buddhism too lost its energy and simplicity; and then arose the fourth period of Sanskrit literature, — the Brahmanical revival. It is put at different dates, from A. D. 300 to A. D. 800, and it is still in force in India.

In these dark and troublous times of religious warfare arose a poet named Valmiki. He is supposed to have lived at the close of the Buddhist period, or the beginning of the Brahmanical revival; and he rewrote the other epic poem of India, the Ramayana. There are two other Ramayanas, but this is considered much the best. He gives an account of the youth of the hero Rama, and his contest with the giants and demons of the island of Sanka, to recover his wife Sita, whom they had stolen. Valmiki must have derived his original plot

from an old Vedic tradition of a hero Rama, who drove
out the inhabitants of the Dekhan, or Southern India.
This must have been a contest between the Aryan invaders and the Turanian aborigines. But Valmiki takes
a wider sweep; he had a lofty religious purpose. "He
wished to afford consolation to the soul," Mr. Wheeler
says, "when the world seemed to be going wrong, and
the divine government doubtful." In his poem Rama is
an incarnation of the god Vishnu; Sita, of Vishnu's wife,
the goddess Lakshmi: and he is sent into the world to
deliver the Brahmans from the persecutions of the
Buddhists. The plot is simple, and the poem is unlike
the Maha Bharata; first, because it has only one hero
and heroine; and, second, because it is written by a
person whose name we know. It would form about six
volumes octavo: the three periods, Vedic, Brahmanical,
and Buddhist, are strangely mixed up in it. I think
there can be no question that it is later than the Maha
Bharata; for a vast interval of thought separates the
patriarchal and feudal manners of the Maha Bharata
and the monarchical tone of the Ramayana, where
despotism is checked only by the power of the priests.
The Ramayana is more than religious; it is sacerdotal:
this is the only fault of the poem: beautiful as it is, it
is marred by the fault of the Hindu character, its sub-
serviency to priestly tyranny. Everywhere we find in
it this hierarchy of priests, mediators between the gods
and men, forbidding any sacrifice to be offered except
by themselves, interfering in the family life; and thus
exercising powers which were never allowed them in the
Maha Bharata. Monier Williams says: "There are
few poems in the world's literature more charming than

the Ramayana. Its moral tone is far above that of the Iliad. It teaches the hopelessness of victory without purity of soul, and abnegation of self." In one thing all the critics of Sanskrit epics agree, unbounded admiration.

To a modern mind it is also a most amusing book. It is so new, so different from other books, that it is delightful to a reader seeking a new sensation. The civilization is so unlike our own, that we seem to be living in another world, and can hardly realize that such customs ever existed. It is as marvellous as a fairy tale, as *naïve* as a child's prattle: the pictures of scenery are lovely, and yet it has a human element. The descriptions of childhood are especially charming; the domestic life of Rama and Sita, most tender and perfect; and the characters, noble and lovely. The friendly monkey, Hanuman, is a model of every virtue. There is no female character in all Greek literature so modest and loving, yet so firm and brave, as Sita, who is gentle, yet high-spirited. The translation in poetry by Griffith is very unsatisfactory and disagreeable; he has introduced so many episodes, and taken away the *naïveté* of the story. I shall use Wheeler's prose translation, which has the merit of being simple and unpretending. To the Hindu, the Ramayana becomes a deeply religious poem. It is regarded with the most awful reverence, equally with the Maha Bharata, although both belong to Smriti, tradition. It closes with the promise that whoever reads or listens to the Ramayana will be freed from all sin. The mere utterance of the name of Rama (because he is an incarnation of Vishnu) is equal in religious merit to giving one hundred ornamented cows to a Brahman, or to performing an Aswemedha. So, in the cool of the evening, when the labors of the day are over, some Brahman priest appears in an Indian village, and all crowd around him with respectful attention, while he reads from palm-leaves the story of Rama.

The Aryan invaders had now reached the very centre of the country, and established themselves with power and splendor. The story opens with a description of the famous city of Ayodhya, the modern Oude, — to-day a heap of ruins, but formerly the most magnificent city in Hindostan. It gives us the Hindu ideal, and paints —

"temples richly decorated; stately palaces, with domes like tops of mountains ; surrounded by pleasant gardens, full of birds and flowers, and shady groves of trees loaded with deli_cious fruits. And the tanks in the city were magnificent beyond description, and covered with the white lotus. The city was perfumed with flowers and incense, and decked out with gorgeous banners ; and it was ever filled with the sweet sounds of music, the sharp twanging of bows, and the holy chanting of Vedic hymns. The city was encompassed round about with very lofty walls, which were set in with variously colored jewels ; and all around the walls was a moat filled with water, deep and impassable. No one was poor, or wore tarnished ornaments ; no one was without fine raiment and perfumes, or was unclean, or fed upon unclean things, or neglected the sacraments, or gave less than a thousand rupees to the Brahmans. No man was without learning, or practised a calling that did not belong to his family or caste, or dwelt in a mean habitation, or was without children and kinsmen. Inspecting the world by his spies, as the sun inspects it by his rays, the Maharaja found no person of hostile mind ; and he shone resplendent, and illuminated the whole earth."

Now this civilization, and also that described in the demon's home at Lanka, are far higher than anything found at Troy or Sparta or Ithaca. Only the allusion to spies shows that it was a despotism. There were no spies over the haughty vassals in the Maha Bharata. In this blissful spot Rama is born by a miraculous birth; his father being a god, his mother the Ranee, or queen. I will quote part of the lovely description of his childhood, peculiarly Hindu, as showing their great fondness for children. It gives a pleasanter idea than we had before of their domestic life; though one can hardly imagine Beaconsfield or Gladstone summoned from the cares of empire to hush the cries of a little prince.

" And Rama was a very lovely babe; and as he slept in a white cot he appeared like a blue lotus floating upon the waters of the Ganges. [His complexion was dark, evidently.] When Rama was sufficiently grown to run about, he was the delight of his mother and the Maharaja. So it happened one evening the full moon arose in all its splendor, and Rama felt a very strong desire to have the beautiful moon to play with for a toy. And he put out both little hands towards the moon, in order to obtain it; but his mother could not understand what he wanted, and thereupon he tried to beat her. And she asked him many times what he wished to have, and he continued to point to the moon; so that at last she came to understand what it was that he wanted, and she said to him, ' Do not desire, O my child, to possess the moon; because it is a thousand miles off, and it is not a plaything for children, and no child ever got it. If you wish, I will bring you some jewels that are brighter than the moon, and you can play with them.' So saying, she brought some beautiful jewels, and placed them before the little boy; but Rama threw them away in anger, and began to cry, until his eyes were red and swollen with weeping. Now, by this time a number of women were gathered around him, but no one could console him. One said, 'Perhaps he is hungry'; but he refused to take any food. Another said, 'Perchance he is sleepy'; and she took him on her lap, and sung him the lullaby; but she could not quiet him, and he still continued to cry. Then one of the women said, 'The goddess Susti has become unpropitious, and must be propitiated with offerings of curds, plantains, and fried paddy.' Another said, 'A ghost is troubling him; so send for a man who can repeat a verse and drive the ghost out.' But all these were of no effect, and Rama was still as unpacified as before. So the Rance sent for the Maharaja; and, when the Maharaja heard that Rama was ill, he came to him immediately, and tried his utmost to console the child; but he could do no more than those who had tried before him, and Rama continued to cry, and would not be comforted. Then the Maharaja sent for his chief councillor of state, and told him all that had happened; and when he heard that Rama was crying for the moon, he desired those about him to bring him a mirror. So a mirror was brought, and placed in the hands of Rama; and when Rama saw the image of the moon in the mirror, he was fully satisfied, and left off weeping, and was soon as merry as before, and the whole family were at ease."

When grown up, after various adventures, Rama hears that whoever can bend an enormous bow, and shoot its arrow, shall win the lovely princess Sita for a bride. The age of Swayamvaras has passed away; but Sita willingly accepts Rama, who bends the bow, after numerous other suitors have failed; and they are married. After a while they are banished into the jungle for fourteen years, — a favorite form of punishment in India. Rama is unwilling that Sita should accompany him; but she finally prevails upon him, in a speech which follows : —

" ' O beloved one, I must depart to the great forest ; and do you remain here, obedient to the command of Raja Bharata, and never praise me in the presence of Bharata, for a raja cannot bear to hear the praises of any one beside himself.'

" Sita, angry but yet humble, replied as follows : ' O Rama, what words are these ? A wife must share the fortunes of her husband ; and if you this day depart to the forest, I must precede you and smooth the thorns. Wherever the husband may be, the wife must dwell in the shadow of his foot. I shall live in the jungle with as much ease as in my father's house, and shall enjoy happiness with you in the honey-scented wood ; I have no fear, and I long to roam in the forest with you, and view the lakes and rivers, and the flowers and water-birds. I will be no burden to you, but if you leave me I will die.'

" Then Rama, wishing to turn the mind of his wife from going with him into the forest, spoke to her as follows : ' O Sita, the forest is not always pleasant, but I know it is always dangerous. You are very delicate and the beloved daughter of a raja ; you have never been in the sun out of your own room ; how then can you brave the dangers of the wilderness ? You are surrounded and attended every day by your maids ; how then can you go out into the jungle without a servant near you ? Your feet are as delicate as the petals of the lily, and the pebbles and briers will affect you grievously : you are like butter which will be melted away by the sun at mid-day. You will have to cross many rivers, in which there are serpents, and crocodiles, and sharks. The roaring of the lions and the thundering of the cataracts are fearful to hear. The roads are infested with wild elephants and filled with thorns ; and the jungle is covered with rank weeds, in which venomous snakes lie concealed, so deadly that their breath alone will kill a man. Sometimes you will have to subsist upon grass-seed ; sometimes upon bitter roots and fruits ; and sometimes you will not even find these things, and will have to fast for many days. At times you will be athirst, and there will be no water. For garments, you will have to wear the bark of trees, or the skin of an antelope ; and at night you will have to sleep upon grass, or upon the bare earth. Reptiles, mosquitoes, flies, scorpions, and fierce birds will bite and sting you, and afflict you in your sleep. Fearful Rákshasas infest the wilderness, and will eat up a whole man at a single meal. Your beautiful locks of hair will become a tangled mass, and will lose their color from want of oil. Besides all this suffering, you will be without friends ; and how can this be endured by a woman ? It is my knowledge of all that you will have to suffer that prevents my taking you with me. Exposure to the heat, cold, and wind render the frame lean and emaciated. What enjoyment then can you experience in the forest, whilst I shall be filled with distress at the sight of your afflictions ? You are dearer to me than my own life, and I cannot consent to your suffering pain on my account ; so take my advice and remain at my house. Though I may be travelling in distant parts, yet still you shall always be present in my thoughts ; and though separated in our eyes, we shall never be separated in our hearts. Moreover, separation often increases affection, and he 'alone can perfectly enjoy the felicity of connubial love who knows what it is to have been separated from his wife. So bear all these things in your mind, and relinquish your plan of accompanying me, and do you determine to remain here.'

"Hearing the words of Rama, Sita was greatly distressed, and her eyes were filled with tears, and she replied in a low tone thus : ' O Rama, I am fully aware of all the evil things that have been described by you, but in your presence all that is evil will be turned to good ; the fierce animals of the jungle, the elephants, the lions, the tigers, and all the beasts of prey, will fly when they behold you ; the grass and the seeds, the roots and the fruits, will in your presence be more delightful than amrita ; and if I should fail to procure these things for food, I can never be deprived of the amrita of your words. As for garments of bark and antelope's skin, I am not sorry to wear them, for the goddess Párvatí wore them for the sake of her husband Siva. Sleeping with you upon a bed of grass will give me more delight than sleeping by myself upon a bed of the softest down; without you my life is not worth preserving, but with you not even Indra can terrify me. O my lord, by following my husband through affection, I shall be faultless, for the husband is the chief deity of the wife. It is written in the Vedas that the woman who always attends upon her husband, and follows him like a shadow in this life, will in like manner follow him in the world of spirits, it becomes you, therefore, O Rama, to take me with you, that I may share in your pleasures and in your pains, for the desert with all its evils is far better in my sight than all the pleasures of this palace without you.' "

They wander about in the jungle for ten years, and describe the beautiful scenery in a most vivid manner. They visit the dwellings of the most celebrated hermits ; a female hermit, named Anasuya, talks to Sita, who tells her of her birth, and says, —

" My preceptor taught me ever to reverence my mother earth, and to strive to be as pure and true and brave as she, and he called me Sita, because I sprung out of a furrow of the ground." Anasuya says, " Thou hast indeed the courage of the brave earth-mother, for thou hast not feared to face the scorching heat, and the biting winds, and the angry storm ; and thou art as noble, too, Sita, for thou hast lavished thy beauty on the sorrowful, and hast sought to make even the path of exile sweet to thy beloved."

Now these hermits are Brahmans, and saints into the bargain. These holy beings are disturbed in their worship by Ravana, a giant, and the Rakshasas, demons who accompany him. But these are no ordinary demons ; they are worse, — Buddhists in disguise. The saints beg Rama to assist them against the demons ; but he refuses at first, because he is not a Brahman, only a Kshatriya. Finally, Ravana fills up the measure of his crimes, and carries away the faithful Sita. She is not, like the Grecian Helen, a willing victim; she is borne struggling through the air, to the demon's home at Lanka.

"Adorned with golden ornaments, and arrayed in yellow silk, Sita appeared in the air like a flash of lightning. She, bright as the most burnished gold, appeared, while held by the black raja of the Rakshasas, like a thread of gold round the loins of an elephant. Ravana wishes to make her his wife, and says, 'Cast aside your foolish hopes of rescue, and consent to become my chief Rani.' She replies in anger: 'The day is not far off, O wicked Ravana! when your golden Lanka will be a heap of ashes, and your numberless army fall under the arrows of Rama. As for your bravery, you need say nothing. I know its worth from the stealth with which you carried me away. There is as much difference between you and Rama as there is between a mouse and a lion; a hedgehog and an elephant; a mosquito and a hawk; a glow-worm and the noonday sun; a grain of sand and a precious stone; a star and the full moon; a burnt brick and a mountain; the river Carannasa and the Ganges. Boast as long as you do not meet Rama; but the moment he is here, consider yourself and your whole family as dead persons.'"

Rama rouses himself. He forms an alliance with the bears and monkeys of the Dekhan, or Southern India. This introduction of the bears and monkeys gives a delightfully Hindu tone to the story. They continually compare their heroes to animals. You remember that Nala was the "tiger among rajas," and the highest beauty attributed to a Hindu heroine is that she has "the rolling gait of an elephant." The monkeys were supposed to be descended from the gods, and to be

saints and Brahmans, stronger and better than men;
they have supernatural powers and talk in human speech.
The animals of Æsop are borrowed consciously, — we
shall see how in another chapter; but these animals who
speak appear among the Norse, and the German families of the Teutonic branch: Reynard, the fox, Bruin,
the bear, are brothers of the good monkey, Hanuman in
the Ramayana; but they are not borrowed nor stolen.
They arose spontaneously from the Aryan feeling. Now
the monkeys of Southern India really are wonderfully
intelligent and strong. They swing themselves over
immense distances by their long arms, and seem superior
to human beings: so it is not strange that the Hindus
deified them. These good monkeys prove to be most
friendly. Hanuman takes a flying leap of sixty miles,
from the main-land to Lanka; and he and the other
monkeys build a bridge of stone, sixty miles long,
across the deep ocean. Actually the Buddhists had
been driven to Ceylon; so it became the demon's home:
a chain of rocks extends now from the main-land to the
island of Ceylon; so that every vessel to or from the
Ganges must circumnavigate that island. The Hindus
firmly believe it to be Rama's bridge: the stones which
crop out through Southern India are said to have been
dropped by the monkey builders. On this bridge the
army crosses to Lanka, and Rama engages in single combat with the giant, Ravana. He is like the Hydra, or
hundred-headed serpent, whom Herakles kills in Greek
mythology; for Ravana has ten heads, and one grows
again as fast as Rama cuts it off. Finally Rama is
roused to the last degree; he shoots the terrible arrow
of Brahma, the Creator, and not till then does the mon-

ster fall dead. Gods and demons are watching the contest from the sky, and flowers fall down in showers on the victorious hero. This lovely idea constantly recurs through all the Hindu literature. There are no wanton cruelties on the battle-field. The victors refuse to give Ravana a funeral pile; but the generous Rama said, " I am much grieved to hear these words from you; Ravana is now dead, and he is therefore no longer your enemy, but your elder brother, and it is proper for you to perform his funeral rites." And he gives the giant a splendid funeral pile; his body is consumed by fire, which is quite different from the treatment of Hector's dead body by Achilles.

Then Rama allows Sita to come into his presence on foot, in the sight of the whole army. This shows that on grand occasions women were seen in public, even at this late period: it was not until after the Mohammedan conquest, A. D. 1000, that they were so entirely enslaved. Joy and grief and anger divide Rama's heart: Sita was carried away against all her own struggles and efforts, it was true; but as she spent so long time in the palace of Ravana, Rama is not willing to receive her as his wife until she has proved her innocence by going through the ordeal of fire. This seems like a princess of the Middle Ages, but it must be a custom of all the Aryan families, if we find it here.

" 'Agni, God of purity!' prayed Sita among the flames, 'if I am true, and clean, and bright of soul as thou, then prove my innocence to Rama and all this host.' Agni brings her out of the fire unhurt. [The Vedic Agni reappears here.] Then Rama wept, and said, 'It was needful there should be no speck on thy soul's whiteness, for thine own sake first, then

for the sake of all these here ; that they might learn that loveliness of outward form cannot make vice more tolerable ; and
that where there is not utter reverence, there is no true
love.' "

Then all return in triumph to Ayodhya. But the
Brahmans are still unsatisfied. They banish Sita into
the jungle for fourteen years. She bears this trial with
the perfect meekness of a typical Hindu wife, and after
this is allowed to live happily ever after. Stripped of
that religious meaning which makes it sacred to the
Hindu, it has yet a religious meaning to us. For the
Ramayana is but one more form. one other aspect, of
that contest between good and evil which has gone on
in every country to which the Aryans carried the ideas
they had imbibed in their common home. Even the
sceptical Monier Williams acknowledges the Ramayana
to be a contest between good and evil. We shall meet
this strife in every Aryan literature which we shall take
up in turn. It will take on the different local coloring,
but it will be at heart the same, varying with the varying climate. For Rama is a very simple form of the
solar myth, more easily traced than Arjuna and Karna.
His birth is supernatural ; he wins his bride by bending
a bow ; he suffers for the good of others ; he fights with
the powers of evil and darkness ; he wins by a magical
weapon, which he alone can use. His bride is Sita, a
nymph of celestial birth ; the name means "a furrow " :
she is therefore the earth married to the sun. In the
bright clime of India the conflict of nature is brief ;
so the sun, victorious over the darkness, returns in joyful triumph to its early home.

CHAPTER IV.

SANSKRIT PHILOSOPHY, FABLE, AND DRAMA.

WE have spoken of the Hindu religions and forms of worship, — their austerities, sacrifices, and meditations. There was never a nation so priest-ridden as the Hindus: yet they indulged in the most unrestrained freedom of thought. India is, above all others, the country of theology and metaphysics ; and nowhere else have these taken such a hold upon a nation. Mr. Dasent says : —

" In this passive, abstract, unprogressive state they have remained, stiffened into castes, and tongue-tied and hand-tied by absurd ceremonies. Heard of by Herodotus in dim legends ; seen by Alexander ; trafficked with by imperial Rome and the later Empire ; becoming fabulous in the Middle Ages ; rediscovered by the Portuguese ; alternately peaceful subjects and desperate rebels to England ; — they have been still the same immovable and unprogressive philosophers, though akin to Europe all the time."

Their history is intellectual, not political, — a history of opinions, not of actions. Greece might fade away ; Rome might arise and shake the world ; Christianity, with gentle but irresistible power, might penetrate into every other country ; but India dreamed on. Not until it was first conquered by the Mohammedans, A. D. 1000, was India influenced by the rest of the world ; and even that war was a religious war. Yet a peculiar and beautiful architecture grew up there, as well as literature ; so there must have been a varied life of the mind : this very isolation and independence give an interest and value to what they did. Left to itself, the imagination took an undue share of the mind. And there was never a time when the Hindu did not speculate. Even in the Rig Veda we find one of the original hymns (that one to which I alluded in the first chapter) full of ideas which would seem to imply a long previous period of metaphysical speculation. After all, is it not natural that man should speculate? — should wonder from whence he came and whither he is going? This hymn has the conception of a state when nothing existed except the Supreme Spirit. Max Müller says, " Many of its thoughts would seem to come from mystic philosophers, rather than simple shepherds ; but there they are, in this oldest book of the world." I should prefer a prose translation, but have not been able to find it. The poem is certainly one of the grandest in all literature. The word rendered " love " by this translator is not at all what we mean by the same word. This Kama is the same thing as Eros in Greek or Wuotan in German. Kama, like Eros, afterwards became the god of love ; but originally, and here in this connection it means the wish or desire of the mind to perform some action before the will has resolved to do it. This is rather metaphysical, but I think there is no clearer way of stating it ; for, of course, the wish to do anything precedes the will or resolution to do it. In Greek as well as Hindu mythology, Kama and Eros are among the oldest deities, and are self-existent.

" Nor aught nor naught existed : yon bright sky
Was not, nor heaven's broad roof outstretched above.
What covered all ? what sheltered ? what concealed ?
Was it the water's fathomless abyss ?
There was not death ; hence was there naught immortal.
There was no confine betwixt day and night.
The only One breathed breathless in itself ;
Other than it, there nothing since has been.
Darkness there was, and all at first was veiled
In gloom profound, an ocean without light.
The germ that still lay covered in the husk
Burst forth, one nature from the fervent heat.
Then first came Love upon it, the new spring
Of mind, — yea, poets in their hearts discerned,
Pondering, this bond between created things
And uncreated.   Comes this spark from earth
Piercing and all-pervading, or from heaven ?
Then seeds were sown, and mighty power arose,
Nature below, and Power and Will above :
Who knows the secret ?   Who proclaimed it here
Whence, whence this manifold creation sprang ?
The gods themselves came later into being.
Who knows from whence this great creation sprang ?
He from whom all this great creation came,
Whether his will created or was mute,
The Most High Seer that is in highest heaven
He knows it, — or perchance e'en He knows not."

This last expression of doubt seems sad and startling,
after the poet had so firmly asserted his belief in one
overseer and creator.   Sanskrit literature has an immense number of books upon metaphysics.   There are
six systems of philosophy ; the very thought of these is
appalling.   Victor Cousin says, " The history of metaphysics in India is an epitome of its history every-

where." It is curious to know that the same problems which agitate speculative minds to-day agitated the dreaming Hindu three thousand years ago. The metaphysical books which grew up in Sanskrit without the slightest contact with other minds go over the same ground with the mental philosophy of Greece 600 B.C., or of Germany to-day. The books sound as if they had been written yesterday, and no more is known on the subject of metaphysics than the Hindus knew. Max Müller says: "We find in many cases a treatment of philosophical problems which will rouse surprise and admiration, — the whole development of philosophic thought in a nut-shell." Mr. Thompson says: "There are few countries where philosophy has developed itself clearly, independently, and spontaneously. Greece and India may be considered as the only two such: the great systems of China, Persia, and Egypt are a species of religious mysticism."

The rise of philosophy in India was much like the rise of the new Brahmanical religion, and, if you have followed that, you will understand this. The Aryans in India always speculated; but there was a long period before their speculations crystallized into a definite system, — a long time before the brave warriors who invaded and conquered this fertile land became a nation of priest-ridden dreamers.

They gradually succumbed to the enervating climate, which brought on inertia and sloth. The first system of metaphysics was written by Kapila about 700 B. C. It was adopted by a few thoughtful men of the twice-born castes, whose speculations were winked at by the religious teachers. They were allowed to speculate as much as they pleased, to believe what they chose, if they would faithfully observe those rules and forms of worship which are described, maintain caste, the ascendency of the Brahmans, and their exclusive right to be teachers of religion and philosophy. "All the founders of philosophy were Brahmans themselves, and probably school-teachers," Mr. Thompson says. The important period in metaphysics is therefore the period before the rise of Buddhism. Just as in the poetry, there are four periods of metaphysics : — First, the Vedic, with the hymn just quoted, not interpolated. Second, the Brahmanical, — that of Kapila. Probably the Hindus would have been contented to dream on forever, meditating under a tree, if the Brahmans had been more prudent. But their yoke grew to be intolerable, and the Buddha arose, and founded a philosophy as well as a religion. It was a tremendous social revolution also, for it opened metaphysics to the whole people, as it had religion : everybody speculated, instead of a small knot of cultivated men. Buddhism increased so fast and so far that the Brahmans in despair felt that something must be done. So they very wisely ceased to oppose the Buddhist philosophy. They merely remarked that all these doctrines upon which the Buddhist philosophers prided themselves could be found in the Vedas, hinted at, if not clearly expressed. Then they proceeded to interpolate into the Vedas and the epic poems the doctrines which they wished to find there. This brought about the fourth period of philosophy, — the Brahmanical revival. In it the Brahmanical metaphysics of Kapila took a broader ground and a peculiar mysticism. It is impossible to define what they did think, as a mystical meaning was given to every difficulty. They claimed that the foundation of all philosophy was found in an original part of the Vedas, called the Upanishad, or mystical doctrine. These are vague, mystical speculations about the origin of the world and of man, and the character of the Supreme Being., They mean literally "sessions," — that is, assemblies of pupils around a master. "They do not contain a completed system of philosophy. They are, in the true sense of the word, guesses at truth," Max Müller says. The first Brahmans always included them in their sacred code. They belong to Sruti, that is, revelation: for the philosophy of the ancient Rishis was as sacred to them as their hymn of praise. As everything in the Upanishads is sacred truth, all the opposing systems of metaphysics justify themselves from these. Brahmanism and Buddhism divide the six systems of metaphysics between them. And I will simply mention those features which distinguish the Hindu from the other metaphysics of the world.

I described fully, in the second chapter, that the Supreme Spirit, after receiving various names, was finally called Brahman when in a state of repose; that he divided himself into innumerable pieces, — into gods, heroes, human beings, animals, plants, — even into stones. Finally, all these emanations from Brahman were absorbed back into him.

"There is one only Being who exists :
Unmoved, yet moving swifter than the mind :
Who far outstrips the senses, though as gods
They strive to reach him : who, himself at rest,
Transcends the fleetest flight of other beings :

8

> Who, like the air, supports all vital action.
> He moves, yet moves not ; he is far, yet near ;
> He is within this universe and yet
> Outside this universe : who e'er beholds
> All living creatures as in him, and him,
> The Universal Spirit, as in all,
> Henceforth regards no creature with contempt."

Now exactly the same idea comes into the Brahmanical philosophy : only now the Supreme Spirit in a passive state is called Atman. Max Müller says, "The conception of Atman was too transparent for poetry, and therefore was handed down to philosophy, which afterwards polished and turned and watched it as the medium through which all is seen, and in which all is reflected." It is the same word as the Latin *animus*, and it means breath or air. It is the idea of the principle of life pervading everything, like the air, accompanying all beings wherever they go : of something incessantly round us, like the atmosphere. We shall meet this again in the Teutonic mythology : Tennyson has the same thought when he says, —

" Closer is he than breathing, nearer than hands or than feet."

But Atman lost its meaning of breath very soon, and took a still more abstract meaning. It became the self, like our reflective pronoun, I, myself; he, himself. The self is he who uses the mind and the senses, but is distinct from them ; for instance, the eyes are but instruments to see with, used by some one who is the seer, the self. So Atman was called the self of the universe, who existed before all created things, and each individual was a piece of Atman. His highest aim, therefore, was to recognize consciously the Atman within himself, put himself into harmony and identity with it, and be absorbed into it. The Upanishads taught, " Know thyself," that is, know thy own Atman, and recognize that it is a piece of the great Atman, that eternal self which underlies all the universe. " The Atman within thee is the true Brahman, from whom thou wert estranged by birth and death, who receives thee back again as soon as thou returnest to it." This was the final solution of the search after the Infinite. Atman became the subjective soul of the universe, — utterly without form, not a person at all, — even more impossible to seize than Brahman, the objective soul.

But the Buddhist metaphysics do not recognize any supreme spirit at all : disappearance was the end of each person, melting away like mist. " There is not much to choose between this and being absorbed like a drop of water." The philosophy of the Brahmans and the Buddhists reached the same conclusions as their religion : with the Brahmans pantheism, with the Buddhists atheism ; but we must not forget that the Buddhist religion taught men to lead lovely lives in spite of its dreadful doctrines. But both of these systems are mere schemes for getting rid of the evils of life by the extinction of all personal existence, all individuality. Buddhism is especially distinguished by its doctrine of Maya, or illusion. This teaches that the world does not exist ; it only seems to us to exist, through the medium of our own senses. If we had no eyes, there would be no light ; if we had no ears, there would be no sound ; if we had no senses, there would be no ideas formed in our mind. The doctrine has since been taught by Spinoza and Berkeley (the ideal theory) ; but Buddha went farther, and said, if there is no reality in all the creation, of course there is no creator : and thus he ignored spirit altogether. Buddha pronounced all metaphysical discussion vain and useless. In one of the Upanishads the soul is compared to a rider in a chariot ; the body is the chariot ; the intellect is the charioteer ; the passions are the horses ; the mind is the reins ; the objects of sense are the roads. The unwise man neglects to apply the reins ; in consequence of which, the passions, like unrestrained vicious horses, rush about hither and thither, carrying the charioteer wherever they please. We ought particularly to notice and remember this passage, because the same idea is found in the most celebrated passage of Plato : but this is from the very earliest metaphysical writings in the world. We do not know who wrote the Upanishads, but we do know the names of the six writers of the later metaphysical books. I will spare the reader a catalogue of names.

The metaphysical book best known outside of India is the " Bhagavat Gita," or Song of the Divine One. The god Vishnu became incarnate as Krishna, the charioteer of the hero Arjuna. Krishna has another name, Bhagavat, and while the two armies were drawn up in battle array he delivered this long discourse, at a very inopportune time. It was named from him " the divine " ; in this fourth period, the Brahmanical revival, it was written, and interpolated into the Maha Bharata. The author was a poet as well as a philosopher, and he sought to combine all the systems together, and put them under the patronage of the Brahmans, himself being a Brahman. It was the same spirit which induced Valmiki the poet to rewrite the Ramayana. Mr. Thompson says, " To unite the skilful and elegant poet with the clear and systematic philosopher, and these two with the shrewd and successful reformer, is an undertaking of no small merit, and this was achieved by the author of the Bhagavat Gita."

It is almost incomprehensible : it attempts to describe the supreme being Atman or Brahman, but I have been able to find only one passage which interests the general reader. Arjuna, the hero. hesitates to begin the battle, and win the throne through the blood of his kindred. But Krishna tells him that he must fulfil the duties of his caste, however unpleasant, and throw aside all considerations of affection. He consoles him, however, by these thoughts : —

" The wise grieve not for the departed, nor for those who yet
   survive.
Ne'er was a time when I was not, nor thou, nor yonder chiefs
   and ne'er
Shall be a time when all of us shall be not : as the embodied
   soul
In this corporeal frame moves swiftly on through boyhood,
   youth, and age.
So will it pass through other forms hereafter : — be not grieved
   thereat.
Know this, — the Being that spread the universe
Is indestructible. Who can destroy the Indestructible ?
These bodies that enclose the everlasting, inscrutable,
Immortal soul have an end : but the soul
Kills not, and is not killed ; it is not born, nor doth it ever
   die."

So Arjuna cheerfully kills all his kindred, knowing they will pass through transmigrations and be born again. To put the duties of caste above all others is the main object of the Bhagavat Gita ; it has had great influence in preserving the caste system in India, notwithstanding all the efforts of the Mohammedan and English conquerors. It belongs to the very close of metaphysics, and is eclectic, seeking to combine all the preceding systems. It is greatly admired by the Hindus ; — partly on that account, partly because they did not know what else to translate, it was chosen as the first direct translation from Sanskrit into English. It was published in 1785, and dedicated to Warren Hastings.

The Hindus to-day care nothing for the Vedas, except the Upanishads ; but there is an immense Brahmanical literature ; it is the foundation for their religion and theology, but does not come within our book, which is literary, and not theological. It has books of laws for the priests and people, and legends about the new gods, called Puranas. These Puranas are much studied at the present time. It grew up in the fourth period, the Brahmanical revival, and most of it was written about 300 A. D. India has but one literature accepted by all, the Sanskrit. The different modern dialects have no literature at all ; and the latest Sanskrit books are two plays, one written in 720, the other in 1100 A. D.

There is in Sanskrit an admirable and original scientific literature. It will be remembered that the system of counting by tens (the decimal system) was used among the undivided Aryans : how long ago we cannot tell. The figures which every modern nation uses come from the Hindus, and so does the game of chess. There are many books upon arithmetic and algebra. Here is a pretty question : —

"Eight rubies, ten emeralds, and a hundred pearls, which are in thy ear-ring, my beloved, were purchased by me, for thee, at an equal amount ; and the sum of the rates of the three sorts of gems was three less than half a hundred ; tell me the rate, auspicious woman ? "

One of their astronomers maintained that the earth moved on its own axis, which produced the alternations of day and night. Is it not amazing that he should have thus anticipated the Copernican system? The idea was not followed out by his countrymen, although there are books about astronomy which are very valuable. There are also books upon medicine and music, these three sciences being always the first to arise in every nation. The shepherds watch the stars and observe the influence of the moon upon the tides, so astronomy takes form There are always sickness and death, and it is the first instinctive effort of human nature to avoid them, among the tribes of our ancestors, as much as in our own complex civilization : so medicine naturally grows into a science very early. And as to music, we have already seen that a hymn to a god is the very first utterance of humanity. The shepherd priest bursts into a song, so his prayer is accompanied with music, at first simple, but soon reduced to rules. As to arithmetic, it is plain that no sort of commerce, no interchange of the simplest commodities, is possible without counting, and we can understand the rise of arithmetic. The early existence of algebra is difficult to explain, but at any rate they are all in Sanskrit literature, and, what is

very foreign to our ideas, these scientific and metaphysical books, like the Vedas and the Code of Manu,
are written in poetry, in astokas, stanzas of two lines;
and consequently there are books upon versification and
rhetoric. But there are none upon the fine arts, or the
mechanical arts.

Grammar, on the contrary, is the very last science to
arise. In the decay of original thought, many fall to
discussing outside form, and Sanskrit literature is no exception to this rule. There are hundreds of works upon
grammar: they are mostly commentaries upon Panini's
grammar, which is of portentous size, and contains
four thousand condensed rules. Alas for the schoolboys in that country! It is considered the most original product of all the Hindu has written. He regards
grammar as something to be loved and studied for its
own sake. Max Müller says, "There are only two
nations in the history of the world which have conceived independently the two sciences of Logic and
Grammar. Our grammatical terms come to us from
Greece, through Alexandria and Rome. In India its
history is parallel, yet independent." These books are
less interesting than the poetical literature, but they
show us that the scientific as well as the metaphysical
type of mind arose in India; although, as everywhere
else, at a later period than the poetical type.

In Sanskrit are many stories, which are chiefly interesting as being the foundation of some of the stories
of the Arabian Nights. That earliest of travellers,
Sindbad the Sailor, started on his journeys in India;
he has gone long and far since then, and was first
translated into Persian. But the stories seem slight

sketches compared with the completed glories of the Arabian Nights. The nursery tales are amazing as well as charming. The good heroines are most lovely and gentle ; the bad ones very shrewd and clever ; and in spite of the subordinate position which women are supposed to occupy in India, in these stories they express their minds with great freedom to the haughtiest rajas, and bring about the success of the plot by their own wit and energy. We find in India the cruel step-mother, the haughty elder sister, the gentle maiden whose mouth drops pearls and diamonds, the sleeping beauty killed by a Raksha's claw, the beautiful golden dress glittering like the sun, and the stupid ogre, called a Raksha here. There are two things that especially suggest other Aryan stories. The life of one princess is bound up in a gold necklace : it is stolen, and she dies ; it is brought back, and she comes to life. Another is of a raja who dies ; a beautiful marble statue of him is put in a little chapel, and every night he comes to life for a few hours. He might be a lunar myth. The lovely German story of Faithful John is almost word for word like the Sanskrit story of Rama and Lux and man. In fact, in reading the folk-lore, you find yourself in a familiar atmosphere, and you accept the theory which tells us that these stories are the original inheritance of every Aryan family, and a strong proof of relationship between them. I copy this one because it is the shortest.

HOW THE SUN, THE MOON, AND THE WIND WENT OUT TO DINNER.

One day, the Sun, the Moon, and the Wind went out to dine with their uncle and aunt, the Thunder and Lightning. Their mother (one of the most distant stars you see far up in the sky) waited alone for her children's return.

Now both the Sun and the Wind were greedy and selfish. They enjoyed the great feast that had been prepared for them, without a thought of saving any of it to take home to their mother; but the gentle Moon did not forget her. Of every dainty dish that was brought around, she placed a small portion under one of her beautiful long finger nails, that the star might have a share in the treat.

On their return, the mother, who had kept watch for them all night long with her little bright eye, said, "Well, children, what have you brought home for me?" Then the Sun (who was the oldest) said, "I have brought nothing home for you. I went out to enjoy myself with my friends, not to fetch a dinner for my mother." And the Wind said, "Neither have I brought anything home for you, mother. You could hardly expect me to bring a collection of good things for you when I merely went out for my own pleasure." But the Moon said, "Mother, fetch a plate; see what I have brought you." And, shaking her hands, she showered down such a choice dinner as never was seen before.

Then the Star turned to the Sun, and spoke thus: "Because you went out to amuse yourself with your friends, and feasted and enjoyed yourself without any thought of your mother at home, you shall be cursed. Henceforth your rays shall be ever hot and scorching, and shall burn all that they touch, and men shall hate you, and cover their heads when you appear."

(And this is why the Sun is so hot to this day.)

Then she turned to the Wind, and said : "You also, who forgot your mother in the midst of your selfish pleasures, hear your doom. You shall always blow in the hot dry weather, and shall parch and shrivel all living things, and men shall detest and avoid you from this very time."

(And that is why the Wind in the hot weather is still so disagreeable.)

But to the Moon she said : "Daughter, because you remembered your mother, and kept for her a share in your own enjoyment, from henceforth you shall be ever cool, and calm, and bright : no noxious glare shall accompany your pure rays, and men shall always call you blessed."

(And that is why the Moon's light is so soft and cool and beautiful even to this day.)

I will not apologize for reading this child's story, because in it you see so clearly how the objects in nature were personified. The long finger-nails are considered a great beauty in India.

It is in vain to hope to escape the moralist : he expands into large proportions in India. We used to suppose that Æsop the Greek invented these pretty stories, where animals speak, with a moral at the end which we carefully skipped. But a study of Sanskrit literature shows that they originated in India long before, without intercourse with any other people, — a growth indigenous to the soil. There are two collections, the Panchatantra and the Hitopadesa : the latter was taken as the second translation from the Sanskrit. in 1787. The morals and the stories of the Hitopadesa are so interwoven that you must swallow them both in spite of yourself : the fables are strung together, one within another, so that a new one is begun before the first one is finished. The fondness for animals which the Hindus showed arose before their belief in transmigration : but it doubled after this belief was established. 'How could one be cruel to an ape, or a jackal, or an elephant? he might be your dead uncle or first-cousin. Those introduced in the fables are chiefly those which surrounded the Hindu, — fishes and insects rarely come into the fables. Mr. Thompson says, "The characters given to each — the good-natured gullibility of the elephant, the bumptious stupidity of the ass, the insidious flattery of the jackal, the calm philosophy of the tortoise, and the folly of the ape — are proofs of the early attempt to affirm that they possessed souls." They were each true to their beast nature, at first. The attempt to turn them into men disguised, and make them moralize, is a secondary development.

"The fool who gives way to his anger, before knowing the truth, experiences regret, like the Brahman who killed his ichneumon. There was at Ayodhya a Brahman named Mathara. His wife one day went out to bathe, leaving him to take care of the baby. In the mean time the king sent for the Brahman to perform a sacrament for the dead, called a Parvana Sraddha. As soon as he had received this invitation, the Brahman, who was poor, said to himself, 'If I do not go there very quickly another will know it, and will receive the present for performing the Sraddha. When it is a question of receiving, of giving and performing a sacrifice, if one does not hurry, time will carry away all the benefit of the work. But there is nobody here to take care of the child. What am I going to do then? Well, I will confide the care of my son to this ichneumon, which I have supported for a long time, and which I love as if it were my child; then I will go.' The Brahman did as he said, and went to the sacrifice. The ichneumon saw a black snake which was coming towards the child, and killed it; when it saw the Brahman returning, it ran to meet him, with its jaws and paws all bloody, and rolled at his feet. The Brahman, seeing it in such a state, believed that it had devoured his child, and he killed it. He immediately approached to look, and saw the child safe and well, and the snake dead. He recognized then that the ichneumon had saved his son, and, seeing what it had done, he regretted his being carried away with anger, and fell into a deep melancholy."

The Welsh story of the dog Gellert comes to mind. The Hindus themselves claim that they invented teaching by fables ; and it is quite true that these fables were a secondary development of the beast epic, and were copied by the Persians very long ago. During the Greek and Persian wars they were carried into Greece ; there transformed again by Æsop. Does not this make history very living and real? Max Müller says, " The fables of the Hitopadesa and Panchatantra are excellent specimens of what story-telling ought to be."

This moralizing and philosophizing tone is found throughout Sanskrit literature : in the two epics, in the present rewritten form, are countless moral reflections and precepts ; in the poems and stories of this fourth period, the hero constantly turns aside from the plot to offer a few didactic thoughts. There are many poems, but they show the effect of a later and an artificial age ; they have nothing of the freshness and naturalness of the Rig Veda, nor of its universal value and interest ; they have not expressed the whole origin of literature like that ; but, nevertheless, it is most interesting to find these different branches of literature invented spontaneously ; and all show great skill in managing the difficulties of Sanskrit metre and grammar. One of them, the " Cloud Messenger," by Kalidasa, has a most poetical plot, and lovely descriptions of nature : a Yaksha is exiled from his wife, and sends her a message by the clouds floating over him : it is considered a most pure and perfect work of art. The Hindus of this fourth period wrote the following : —

"Now for a little while a child, and now
An amorous youth ; then for a season turned

Into the wealthy householder; then stripped
Of all his riches, with decrepit limbs
And wrinkled frame, man creeps towards to the end
Of life's erratic course; and like an actor
Passes behind Death's curtain out of view."

Of course one will at once think of Shakespeare's
" seven ages."

But when we read the drama, Sanskrit literature rises
to the level of every other literature ; and I do not hesitate to say that the Sanskrit plays equal all others,
except those of Shakespeare. This is high praise ; but
I have great authorities to support me. Mr. Fergusson
compares the exuberant Indian architecture to the rich
irregularity of Gothic architecture in Europe ; certainly,
the Sanskrit drama may be compared to the romantic
drama of Europe. Strange to say, in the twelfth century is a play where all the characters are vices and
virtues personified, just like the morality plays in the
Middle Ages ; which seems very surprising. This contest between the classic and romantic drama has engaged so much attention of late years, that the friends
of the romantic drama are delighted to find such perfect
examples of it, arising spontaneously, in this literature,
hitherto unknown : it is most curious that this drama,
uninfluenced by other human beings, should have taken
such a different form from the Greek drama. There
will be found in the Sanskrit plays strong feeling for
nature and lovely descriptions of scenery ; characters
noble and yet natural, tragic and comic, taken from
high and low life, in the same play, intermingled as in
real life. There will be witty dialogues, dramatic situations, and an amusing plot. None of them are unmixed

tragedies or comedies: a little suffering is given to touch the feelings; then a happy ending comes. The plays are divided into acts; they all have a prologue. The ordinary conversation is in prose; but reflections, and descriptions of scenery, and bursts of feeling, are in . lovely poetry. There is always a buffoon, who is some-times witty, always lively: he is a Brahman, a humble friend, not a servant; and makes an agreeable contrast to' the melancholy hero. Unmarried women of good family are introduced upon the stage; married women are allowed to go anywhere, and do as they please : all these characteristics belong to the romantic drama in every age and country. In India there are two peculiar-ities. First, unmarried women are not allowed to re-ply to their lover, although they may listen to him : they are always accompanied by a female confidant, to whom they speak, and she answers for them. Second, — and this is the great peculiarity of the Sanskrit plays, — the different characters speak different dialects in the same play : the higher male characters use Sanskrit; the lower male, and the female characters, Prakrit. There are but few plays in Sanskrit; not more than sixty have been discovered. One play is very long; it was seldom performed more than once, and was written to do honor to some high state ceremony. The earliest and best of them were written by Kalidasa. He wrote only three plays, and lived about 200 b. c., — perhaps 100 b. c. He was a contemporary of the poet who wrote the Bhagavat Gita, and also of Valmiki, who wrote the Ramayana; and thus belongs to the fourth period, — the Brahmanical revival. One of his plays is the Vikramorvasi, — the dawn myth put into a dramatic form. The nymph Urvasi is turned into a vine as soon as she beholds her lover; and she is the original of Psyche in Greek literature, of Melusina in the Middle Ages, of Beauty in the nursery tale of Beauty and the Beast, of all the beings who cannot gaze upon each other, though full of the tenderest affection or united in the closest ties; for the lover is the sun: Urvasi is but another name for the dawn, which of course never can see the sun. The vine, in one version of the play, bleeds and speaks when broken: it appears in this form in the Greek mythology and the ballads of the Middle Ages: from them it went into the poems of Tasso and Spenser; but it arose in the Sanskrit literature. For all nature was peopled with living forms, small as well as great: each mountain and brook was supposed to be a distinct individual. Perhaps the personifications are not as numerous as in the Greek and Teutonic mythologies, but they are present.

Kalidasa's best play is the charming Sakoontala, — the most artless, fresh, and poetical of books. Yet the characters are distinctly drawn and clearly defined, even the subordinate ones: the two constables who arrest the fisherman are as individual as the grave-diggers in Hamlet. The characters are noble, the situations dramatic; and one might fancy that the play was written in our own century, instead of almost two thousand years ago. This story of the ring is found in Greek literature, — the ring of Polycrates; also, in modern German. It must have been one of the stories of the undivided Aryans: the Germans must have copied it; but Herodotus could not. The events of the play took place in the Vedic period, and were copied from an episode of the Maha Bharata. We see this from the manners, especially the freedom of the women. It is probable that the present condition of the Hindu women was copied from the Mohammedan conquerors. Sakoontala was the third direct translation from the Sanskrit by Sir William Jones, in 1789. It spread over Europe in a very short time: Goethe read it, and wrote: —

" Wouldst thou the blossoms of spring? the autumn's fruits?
Wouldst thou what charms and thrills? Wouldst thou what
    satisfies and feeds?
Wouldst thou the heaven, the earth, in one sole word com-
    press?
I name Sakoontala, and so have said it all."

SAKOONTALA; OR, THE LOST RING.

ACT I.

Scene. — *A Forest.*

Enter King Dushyanta, *armed with a bow and arrow, in a chariot, chasing an antelope, attended by his charioteer.*

King *(looking about him).*

Charioteer, even without being told, I should have known that these were the precincts of a grove consecrated to peniten- tial rites. (*Alighting.*) Groves devoted to penance must be entered in humble attire. Take these ornaments. (*Delivers his bow and ornaments to the charioteer.*) What means this throbbing of my arm? Hark! I hear voices to the right of yonder grove of trees. I will walk in that direction. Ah! here are the maidens of the hermitage coming this way to water the shrubs, carrying watering-pots proportioned to their strength. I will conceal myself in the shade, and watch them.

9

Enter SAKOONTALA, *with two female companions, who converse, and water the shrubs.*

SAKOONTALA.

Ah! a bee, disturbed by the sprinkling of the water, has left the young jasmine, and is trying to settle on my face. Help, my dear friends! deliver me from the attack of this troublesome insect.

PRIYAMVADA *and* ANASUYA.

How can we deliver you? Call Dushyanta to your aid. These sacred groves are under the King's special protection.

KING (*advancing hastily*).

When mighty Puru's offering sways the earth,
And o'er the wayward holds his threatening rod,
Who dares molest the gentle maids that keep
Their holy vigils here in Kanwa's grove?

[*They converse.*

Nay, think not I am King Dushyanta. I am only the king's officer.

[*They converse.*

PRIYAMAVDA *and* ANASUYA.

Noble sir, permit us to return to the cottage.

[*All rise.*

SAKOONTALA.

A pointed blade of Kusa grass has pricked my foot, and my bark mantle is caught in the branch of a Kuruvaka bush. Be so good as to wait for me till I have disentangled it.

[*Exit with her two companions, after making pretexts for delay that she may steal glances at the* KING.

KING.

I have no longer any desire to return to the city. Sakoontala has taken such possession of my thoughts that I cannot turn myself in any other direction.

My limbs drawn onward, leave my heart behind,
Like silken pennon borne against the wind.

ACT III.

SCENE. — *The Sacred Grove.*

Enter KING DUSHYANTA, *with the air of one in love.* *Talks to him-self.* *Walks about.*

Ah! yonder I see the beloved of my heart reclining on a rock strewn with flowers, and attended by her two friends. Concealed behind the leaves, I will listen to their conversation.

SAKOONTALA *and her two attendants discovered.*

PRIYAMVADA.

I have observed that Sakoontala has been indisposed ever since her interview with King Dushyanta. She looks seriously ill. Dear Sakoontala! we know very little about love matters ; but, for all that, I cannot help suspecting your present state to be something similar to that of the lovers we have read about in romances. Tell us frankly what is the cause of your disorder.

[*They converse.*

SAKOONTALA.

Know then, dear friends, that from the first moment the illustrious prince who is the guardian of our sacred grove presented himself to my sight —

[*Stops short, and appears confused.*

PRIYAMVADA *and* ANASUYA.

Say on, dear Sakoontala, say on.

SAKOONTALA.

Ever since that happy moment my heart's affections have been fixed upon him, and my energies of mind and body have deserted me, as you see.

[*They converse.*

PRIYAMVADA.

I look upon the affair as already settled. Did you not observe how the king betrayed his liking by the tender manner in which he gazed upon her, and how thin he has become in the last few days, as if he had been lying awake thinking of her? An idea strikes me. Let Sakoontala write a love-letter. I will conceal it in a flower, and drop it in the king's path.

[*They converse.*

SAKOONTALA.

Dear girls, I have thought of a verse, but I have no writing materials at hand.

PRIYAMVADA.

Write the letters with your nail on this lotus leaf, which is smooth as a parrot's breast.

SAKOONTALA (*after writing*).

Listen, dear friends, and tell me whether the ideas are appropriately expressed : —

I know not the secret thy bosom reveals;
    Thy form is not near me to gladden my sight ;
But sad is the tale that my fever reveals
    Of the love that consumes me by day and by night.

KING (*advancing hastily towards her*).

Nay, Love does but warm thee, fair maiden, thy frame
    Only droops like the bud in the glare of the noon ;
But me he consumes with a pitiless flame,
    As the beams of the day-star destroy the pale moon.

PRIYAMVADA *and* ANASUYA.

Welcome, the desire of our hearts, that so speedily presents itself! Deign, gentle sir, to seat yourself on the rock on which our friend is reposing.

[*The* KING *sits down.* SAKOONTALA *is confused. All converse. Then* PRIYAMVADA *and* ANASUYA *move away. The* KING *and* SAKOONTALA *converse.*

ACT IV.

SCENE. — *The Garden of the Hermitage.*

Enter ANASUYA *and* PRIYAMVADA, *gathering flowers.*

ANASUYA.

Although, dear Priyamvada, it rejoices my heart that Sakoontala has been united to a husband every way worthy of her, nevertheless I cannot help feeling somewhat uneasy in my mind. You know that the pious king was gratefully dismissed by the hermits, on the termination of their sacrificial rites. He has now returned to the capital, leaving Sakoontala under our care, and it may be doubted whether in the society of his royal consorts he will not forget all that has taken place in this hermitage of ours.

PUPIL *(entering joyfully)*.

Quick! quick! come and assist in the joyful preparations for Sakoontala's departure to her husband's palace. This very day, her father proposes sending her to the king's palace, under charge of trusty hermits.

PRIYAMVADA.

See, there sits Sakoontala. Let us join them: the holy women of the hermitage are congratulating her and invoking blessings on her head, while they present her with wedding gifts and offerings of consecrated rice.

[*They approach and converse.*

SAKOONTALA.

Come, my two loved companions, embrace me both of you.

PRIYAMVADA *and* ANASUYA.

Dear Sakoontala, remember, if the king should by any chance be slow in recognizing you, you have only to show him this ring, on which his own name is engraved.

[*They converse. Exit* SAKOONTALA *with her escort.*

ACT V.

SCENE. — *A room in the Palace.* THE KING (*seated*).

CHAMBERLAIN.

Victory to the king! So please your Majesty, some hermits have arrived here bringing certain women with them: they have a message from the sage, Kanwa, and desire an audience.

[*They converse.*

Enter the HERMITS *leading* SAKOONTALA *attended by a matron,* GAU-TAMI; *and in advance of them the* CHAMBERLAIN *and the* DOMES-TIC PRIEST.

SAKOONTALA (*aside*).

What means this throbbing of my right eyelid? Heaven avert the evil omen!

HERMITS.

Victory to the king! (*They converse.*) The venerable Kanwa bids us say he feels happy in giving his sanction to the marriage which your Majesty contracted with this lady, and bids thee receive her into thy palace.

KING.

What strange proposal is this?

HERMIT.

Dost thou hesitate?

KING.

Do you mean to assert that I ever married this lady?

GAUTAMI (*to* SAKOONTALA).

Be not ashamed, my daughter. Let me remove thy veil: thy husband will then recognize thee.

KING (*wrapped in thought and gazing at* SAKOONTALA).

Holy men, I have resolved the matter in my mind, but the more I think of it, the more I am unable to recollect that I ever contracted an alliance with this lady.

[*All converse.*

SAKOONTALA.

If, then, thou really believest me to be the wife of another, and thy present conduct proceeds from some cloud that obscures thy recollection, I will easily convince thee by this token.

KING.

An excellent idea!

SAKOONTALA (*feeling for the ring*).

Alas! alas! woe is me! There is no ring on my finger!

[*Looks with anguish at* GAUTAMI.

GAUTAMI.

The ring must have slipped off when thou wast in the act of offering homage to the holy water of Sachi's sacred pool.

KING (*smiling*).

People may well talk of the readiness of woman's invention! Here's an instance of it!

[*All converse.*

GAUTAMI.

Speak not thus, illustrious prince : this lady was brought up in a hermitage, and never learned deceit.

KING.

Holy matron, e'en in untutored brutes, the female sex
  Is marked by inborn subtlety, — much more
  In beings gifted with intelligence.

SAKOONTALA (*angrily*).

Dishonorable man, thou judgest others by thine own evil heart, thou at least art unrivalled in perfidy, and standest alone, — a base deceiver, in the garb of virtue and religion, — like a deep pit whose yawning mouth is concealed by smiling flowers.

[*The* HERMITS *depart and will not take* SAKOONTALA *home with them; the* KING *will not receive her, so the* DOMESTIC PRIEST *leads her away with him. Then a voice behind the scenes cries, "A miracle!"*

PRIEST (*entering with astonishment*).

Great prince, a stupendous prodigy has occurred. Sakoon-

tala, as soon as the hermits had departed, was bewailing her
cruel fate, when a shining apparition in female shape descended
from the skies and bore her up to heaven.

ACT VI.

SCENE. — *A Street.*

Enter the SUPERINTENDENT *of police; with him two* CONSTABLES
dragging a poor FISHERMAN, *who has his hands tied behind his back.*

Both the CONSTABLES (*striking the prisoner*).

Take that, for a rascally thief as you are, and now tell us,
sirrah, where you found this ring, — ay, the king's own signet-
ring. See, here is the royal name engraved in the setting of
the jewel.

FISHERMAN (*with a gesture of alarm*).

Mercy! kind sirs, mercy! I did not steal it, indeed I did
not.

[*They talk.*

SUPERINTENDENT.

Let the fellow tell his own story from the beginning.

FISHERMAN (*makes a long story*).

One day when I was cutting open a large carp I had just
hooked, the sparkle of a jewel caught my eye, and what should
I find in that fish's maw but that ring.

[*Continues to talk.*

SUPERINTENDENT.

Well the fellow emits such a fishy odor, there is little doubt
of his being a fisherman. Come, we'll take him before the
king's household. On with you, you cut-purse!

[*All move on. Exit* SUPERINTENDENT.

FIRST CONSTABLE (*after an interval*).

The Superintendent is a long time away. My fingers itch to
strike the first blow at this victim here: we must kill him with

all the honors, you know. I long to begin binding the flowers around his head.

[Pretending to strike the FISHERMAN.

SECOND CONSTABLE.

Here's our Superintendent at last : see, he is coming towards us with a paper in his hand. We shall soon know the king's command ; so prepare, my fine fellow, either to become food for vultures, or to make acquaintance with some hungry cur.

SUPERINTENDENT (*entering*).

Ho there! set the fisherman at liberty : his story is all correct about the ring. (CONSTABLES *talk.*) Here, my good man, the king desired me to present you with this purse : it contains a sum of money equal to the value of the ring.

FISHERMAN (*taking it and bowing*).

His Majesty does me too great honor.

FIRST CONSTABLE.

You may well say so : he might as well have taken you from the gallows to seat you on his state elephant.

SECOND CONSTABLE.

Master, the king must value the ring very highly, or he never would have sent such a sum of money to this ragamuffin.

[*Looks enviously at the* FISHERMAN.

SUPERINTENDENT.

I don't think he values it as a costly jewel, so much as a memorial of some person he tenderly loves : the moment it was shown him, he became much agitated, though in general he conceals his feelings.

FISHERMAN.

Here's half the money for you, my masters. It will serve to purchase the flowers you spoke of, if not to buy me your good-will.

FIRST CONSTABLE.

Well now, that 's just as it should be.

SUPERINTENDENT.

My good fisherman, you are an excellent fellow, and I begin to feel quite a regard for you : let us seal our first friendship over a glass of good liquor.

ALL.

By all means.   [*Exeunt.*

ACT VII.

SCENE. — *Another Sacred Grove.*

CHARIOTEER.

Great prince, we are now in the sacred grove of the holy Kasyapa : if your Majesty will rest under the shade of this Asoka tree, I will announce your arrival.

KING (*feeling his arm throb*).

Wherefore this causeless throbbing, O mine arm ?
All hope has fled forever. — Mock me not
With presages of good, when happiness
Is lost and naught but misery remains.

Enter a CHILD *attended by two women, and playing with a lion's whelp.*

CHILD.

Open your mouth, my young lion, I want to count your teeth.

KING.

Strange, my heart inclines toward the boy with almost as much affection as if he were my own child.

ATTENDANT.

The lioness will certainly attack you, if you do not release her whelps.

CHILD (*laughing*).

O, much I fear her to be sure ! let her come.

[*Both converse. The* CHILD *pouts his under lip in defiance.*

KING.

I feel an unaccountable affection for this wayward child.
How blest the virtuous parents, whose attire,
Is soiled with dust, by raising from the ground
The child that asks a refuge in their arms!
And happy are they while, with lisping prattle,
In accents sweetly inarticulate,
He charms their ears, and with his artless smiles
Gladdens their hearts, revealing to their gaze
His tiny teeth just budding into view.

[*All converse.*

ATTENDANT (*entering with a china bird*).

See, what a beautiful Sakoonta [bird]!

CHILD.

My mother! Where? Let me go to her!

ATTENDANT.

He mistook the word Sakoonta for Sakoontala. The boy
dotes upon his mother, and she is ever uppermost in his
thoughts.

KING (*aside*).

That is his mother's name, Sakoontala, but the name is common among women.

ATTENDANT (*in great distress*).

Alas! I do not see the amulet on his wrist.

KING.

Don't distress yourself. Here it is: it fell off while he was
struggling with the lion.

[*Stoops to pick it up.*

Both Attendants.

Hold, touch it not for your life! How marvellous! he has actually taken it up without the slightest hesitation.

[*Both gaze in astonishment.*

King.

Why did you try to prevent my touching it?

Attendant.

This amulet was given to the boy. Its peculiar virtue is that when it falls on the ground no one except the father or mother of the child can pick it up unhurt: if another person touches it, it instantly becomes a serpent and bites them.

King (*with rapture*).

Joy, joy! are then my dearest hopes to be fulfilled?

Enter Sakoontala *in widow's apparel, her long hair twisted into a single braid.*

Sakoontala (*gazing at the* King, *who is pale with remorse*).

Surely this is not like my husband, yet who can it be that dares pollute by the pressure of his hand my child, whose amulet ought to protect him from a stranger's touch?

King.

My best beloved, I have indeed treated thee most cruelly, but am now once more thy fond and affectionate lover: Refuse not to acknowledge me as thy husband.

[*Both converse aside, the* Child *speaking.*

Sakoontala.

Rise, my own husband, rise! thou wast not to blame. My own evil deeds committed in a former state of being brought down this judgment upon me. How else could my husband, who is of compassionate disposition, have acted so unfeelingly?

[*All go to the presence of the sage* Kasyapa, *and converse.*

KASYAPA.

My son, cease to think yourself in fault : the delusion that possessed thy mind was not brought about by any act. of thine. By my divine power of meditation I ascertained that thy repudiation of thy poor, faithful wife had been caused entirely by the curse of the angry sage Durvasas, not by thine own fault, and that the spell would terminate at the discovery of the ring.

KING (*drawing a deep breath*).

O, what a weight is taken off my mind now that my character is cleared of reproach !

SAKOONTALA.

Joy ! joy ! my revered husband did not then reject me without good reason, although I have no recollection of the curse pronounced upon me : but probably I unconsciously brought it on myself, when I was so distracted at being separated from my husband so soon after our marriage.

CHAPTER V.

PERSIAN LITERATURE, — ARYAN AND SEMITIC.

IT is correct to write next about the Persians, the second branch of that brilliant Aryan race whose first appearing we have followed in India. We must utterly dismiss from our minds the Persian of to-day, effeminate, treacherous, a Mohammedan in his religion, a sensualist in his life, and go back to a period 2234 B. C., when there was Aryan government in Persia. We find a repetition of what occurred in India. An Aryan race, of brave, warlike shepherd tribes had come in, conquered the native Turanian tribes, settled in the land, absorbed the native dialect to make a new idiom, which is called *Zend*. It was an important witness in forming the new science of comparative philology, as all its words were like the Sanskrit, some of them identical with it.

Their sacred book is called the *Avesta*. It was translated into French in 1771, and excited much comment. For a long time it was sneered at as a forgery. Even the great Sir William Jones threw the weight of his scholarship against it, showing that the wisest men may sometimes make mistakes. This was before the period of the Sanskrit translations. Not until it proved to be such a valuable ally in explaining the words as well as the thoughts of Sanskrit literature, was it accepted as genuine. This sacred book, the Avesta, is another illustration of the first two periods of mental growth. It is written in poetry: its oldest portion is a collection of hymns; but the Avesta contains in one volume what expanded into four in India. First come the hymns, next the prayers, next the laws; and these three sacred books formed a liturgy which was used by the priests alone, when the people were not present. Each priest was obliged to repeat the three sacred books once every twenty-four hours, in order to purify himself; and he would recite them for others, if paid for doing so.

These were all written in Zend, and it is not too much to think that the hymns, which are much the oldest, may go back to the first Aryan date we have in Persia, 2234 B. C. The language is older than that used on the cuneiform inscriptions on the oldest monuments: it differs essentially from that used by Cyrus, 559 B. C., or that of the first great struggle between the Persians and Greeks, 490 B. C.; if not later than these, it must be earlier than the cuneiform inscriptions.

The fourth part of the Avesta consists of prayers, and confessions of sin: it formed a liturgy for the people. A very little of it is written in the Parsee language, and must be very much later than the rest. But the books have been so carefully collected and preserved that there is no doubt that they are genuine; and they sound as if they were.

It is almost impossible to understand the Avesta. The translator himself often gives up in despair. The hymns, priests' prayers, and laws are very obscure, and loaded down with repetitions; they are utterly unlike the simple reality of the Vedas. They are addressed first to Ahura Mazda; next to seven spirits, who appear to personify the powers of nature, but treated so dif-ferently from the Vedic manner that it is impossible to tell who is meant. The reader will at once recognize Ahura Mazda. He is often shortened into Ormazd, but is plainly the Asoura Medhas, "the wise spirit" of the Rig Veda, the one God, the mysterious principle of life. *Ahura* means spiritual; *Mazda*, maker.

The climate of Persia, then called Iran, was far more severe then than now; the winters were so long, the cold so intense, the darkness so profound, that gloom and suffering filled the heart. But the summers were so warm and brought such blessed relief to man and beast and earth, that the Aryans of Iran felt there must be a good god who protected them, and brought back light and heat and summer. Accordingly, Ahura Mazda becomes that good god, that kind creator of life and growth. But they considered him far above the other friendly gods, who sank down to mere servants to do his will. The kindly sun, the fertilizing rain, the pleas-ant light, were sent by this Supreme Being, his sub-jects, not his equals; they become the seven good spirits, called Genii. Since winter and cold and darkness re-turn, they are not really conquered by Ahura Mazda; therefore, they must be gods too, so they become Devas, or Devs, bad spirits. (The word Deva, however, as used originally in the Rig Veda, meant simply a spirit, and had nothing bad connected with it, although we derive our word devil from the same root.) Here, in this contest of nature, more severe in Iran than in India, arises our distinction between devil and angel. Over all these Divs ruled one supreme Div, called Ahriman, the spirit of darkness. He is constantly thwarting

Ahura Mazda; for instance, Ahura Mazda created a beautiful warm country; then Ahriman created Azhidahaka, the biting snake of winter. He has triple jaws, three heads, six eyes, a thousand strengths (that is, the strength of a thousand beings), and is slain by a mighty hero, Thraetaona. Does not this remind one of Indra killing Vritra, in the Rig Veda? He is the same; though the winter is to Persia what the drought was to India, the enemy most to be dreaded. But the Avesta teaches that finally Ahura Mazda will conquer Ahriman forever: then perpetual summer, peace, and prosperity will smile upon Iran. This same idea will be found in Scandinavian mythology.

These hymns, called Gathas, and these prayers, are said to have been written by different bards and priests. They have an antiquity greater than we can know, and they contain one thought which we found in the hymns of the Rig Veda, and do not find in the other Aryan languages. Max Müller, in his latest book, published in 1879, says : —

"Although we look in vain for anything corresponding to the word *rita* in the oldest Aryan languages, and cannot claim an antiquity for it exceeding the first separation of the Aryan races, the word and the thought existed before the Iranians, whose religion is known to us in the Avesta, became finally separated from the Indians. These two branches remained together a long time, and extended in a southeasterly direction, after they had separated from the others, who went in a northwesterly course. The word *rita* became *asha* in Zend ; and it is used to denote the right path, the universe following the law of *asha*. Think what it was to believe in a right order of the world ; all the difference between chaos and cosmos, between blind chance and an intelligent providence. It was an

10

intuition which underlaid the most ancient religion, older than the oldest Gatha of the Avesta, the oldest hymn of the Veda. It is far more important than the stories of Ushas, Agni, Indra, and the others."

The third part of the Avesta belongs to the next step of civilization. It is a code of religious laws, and it was written by a religious reformer named Zarathustra; we usually speak of him by the Greek form, Zoroaster. Some of the first laws order very severe penalties for killing dogs; and it was especially these which Sir William Jones ridiculed. But, on the contrary, these are the very things which prove the antiquity of the Avesta, because dogs would be especially valuable to a shepherd community, living near mountains, — such a country as the Persian Aryans actually did inhabit. These laws enforce the greatest purity of body; and also of mind, for here comes in the other and deeper side of this religion. The physical struggle of India becomes spiritualized in Iran. Zarathustra must have had deep spiritual insight; for he transferred this struggle from external nature to the heart of man. Asha was not the right path for the universe alone, but for each person: life became a contest between breaking these laws and obeying them, therefore. This involves two ideas: first, of a distinction between good and evil, which never was very prominent in India; second, of the power to choose between them. Zarathustra also taught that there were two spiritual worlds, to which all would return at their death. Finally, Ahura Mazda would conquer Ahriman, once and forever. Then would be a resurrection from the dead, when the good would be rewarded, the bad punished. He taught also another idea, which is so beautiful that I will give it to you iu the very words of the Avesta.

"Zarathustra said to Ahura Mazda, 'Where does the soul of the pure man go after his death?' Ahura Mazda said, 'When the lapse of the third night turns itself to light, the soul of the pure man goes forward: there comes to meet him the figure of a maiden; one beautiful, shining, with shining arms; one powerful, well grown, slender; one noble, with brilliant face; one of fifteen years, as fair in her growth as the fairest creatures.

"Then to her speaks the soul of the pure man asking, 'What maiden art thou whom I have seen here as the fairest maiden in body?'

"Then replies to him the maiden, 'I am, O youth, thy good thoughts, words, and deeds, thy good law; the law of thine own body.

"Thou art like me, O well-speaking, well-thinking, well-acting youth, devoted to the good law; thou art in greatness, goodness, beauty, such as I appear to thee.'"

So Zarathustra said that, besides the Genii, servants to do the will of Ahura Mazda, each individual had an attendant spirit called a Fravashi; not like our idea of a guardian angel, but the nature of the man himself, his own character, put into a spiritual body; and this Fravashi would be made pure and beautiful, or ugly and hideous, by the actions of the man himself. It would be this Fravashi which would arise for the resurrection and final judgment.

The religion of the Hindu Aryans was to dream; the religion of the Persian Aryans was to fight. It was while the Persians were brave, hardy, and poor, that they won their brilliant successes under Cyrus the Great, 559 B. C. Perhaps they owed their noble character to their noble religion; and it is curious to think what might have been, if they had not become corrupted by prosperity. If Marathon and Salamis had been gained by the Persians, the religion of Ahura Mazda, reformed by Zarathustra, might have overspread the heathen world. Even when conquered by Alexander, 334 b. c., the Persians retained their religion. Not until they were conquered by the Mohammedans, 641 a. d., did it lose its power. But the Persian nobles cherished a secret love for the religion of their ancestors, and kept it alive in the distant provinces. A few of them fled to India, where the small sect called Parsees exists to-day, and still observes the laws of Zarathustra. Some of the wealthiest men of Bombay are Parsees, and worship fire, as the symbol of the sun. Probably the caste system of India forced them into a caste of their own in self-defence. In the later times of Parseeism in Persia, Zarathustra's idea of a god was too abstruse and philosophical for the common people; and there were splendid temples built to the sun, whom they called Mithras. This is like Mitra, one of the names of the sun in the Rig Veda, it will be remembered. In these temples was an altar on which burned the sacred fire perpetually. I will quote the shortest and simplest hymn I can find in the Avesta. The others are incomprehensible: the sense is so overlaid with repetitions.

HYMN.

THE PRIEST SPEAKS.

"I invite and announce to the lords of the heavenly, the lords of the earthly, the lords of those who live in the water, the lords of those which live under heaven, the lords of the winged, the lords of the wide-stepping (that is, the cattle), the lords of the beasts with claws, the pure lords of the pure."

This means that he invites the spiritual presence of Ahura Mazda and the seven good Genii, and announces that he is about to perform the religious ceremonies. Then he drinks the Haoma juice, which is like the Vedic Soma, and eats the sacred bread. Then he says : —

"Good is the thought, good the speech, good the actions, of the pure Zarathustra. May the good spirits accept the hymns! Praise be to you pure song."

Here at last is the hymn : —

"1. Here praise I now Ahura-Mazda, who has created the cattle; who created purity, the water, and the good trees ;
"2. Who created the splendor of light, the earth, and all good.
"3. To Him belongs the kingdom, the might, and the power.
"4. We praise Him first among the adorable beings
"5. Which dwell together with the cattle."

This means the good spirits who protect the cattle, and would be much venerated by shepherds and farmers.

"6. Him praise we with Ahurian name Mazda.
"7. With our own bodies and life praise we Him.
"8. The Fravashis of the pure men and women we praise.
"9. The best purity we praise ;
"10. What is fairest, what pure, what immortal,
"11. What brilliant, all that is good.
"12. The good spirit we honor; the good kingdom we honor ;
"13. And the good rule, and the good law, and the good wisdom."

This one example is enough to show how much repetition there is : also, that ideas are worshipped, instead of the living, real people that crowd the Rig Veda. The word Asha is also applied to the right performance of the sacrifices. It means, then, correct in the pronunciation, or the form of sacrifice, without a mistake. The prayer Ashem means the right, proper prayer, the good prayer.

The form of prayer for the people is more interesting ; it is very much later. And, certainly, the prayers and confessions of sin are very beautiful. In the liturgies and the laws, Zarathustra is represented as conversing with Ahura Mazda. Here is a prayer : —

" 1. Zarathustra asked Ahura Mazda, 'Ahura Mazda, Heavenly, Holiest, Creator of the corporeal world, Pure One ! wherein alone is contained thy word, which expresses all good, all that springs from purity ? ' "

" 2. To him answered Ahura Mazda : ' The prayer Ashem, O Zarathustra.

" 3. 'Whoso utters the prayer Ashem with believing mind, from the memory, praises me, Ahura Mazda : he praises the water, he praises the earth, he praises the cow, he praises the trees, he praises all good things created by Mazda, which have a pure origin.'

" 4. Zarathustra asked Ahura Mazda, 'What is that prayer Ashem which in greatness, goodness, and beauty is worth all that is between heaven and earth, and this earth and those lights created by Mazda, which have a pure origin ? ' "

There are many more verses, — thirteen more ; but this is the last : —

" 15. To him answered Ahura Mazda : ' That prayer, O pure Zarathustra, when one renounces all evil thoughts, words, and deeds.' "

Here is the prayer : —

" 1. Purity is the best good.
" 2. Happiness, happiness is to him ;
" 3. Namely, to the best pure in purity."

Then come very long confessions of sin against those laws. The confession begins : —

" I praise the good thoughts, words, and deeds with thoughts, words, and deeds. I curse wicked thoughts, words, and deeds away from thoughts, words, and deeds. I lay hold on all good thoughts, words, and deeds. I renounce all evil thoughts, words, and deeds. I praise the best purity. I hunt away the Divs. I confess myself a follower of Zarathustra, an opponent of the Divs, devoted to the faith in Ormazd. I am wholly without doubt in the existence of the good Mazdayaçnian faith ; in the coming of the resurrection and the later body ; in the stepping over the bridge Chinvat ; in an invariable recompense of good deeds and their reward, and of bad deeds and their punishment, as well as in the continuance of Paradise, and the annihilation of Hell and Ahriman and the Divs ; that the god Ormazd will at last be victorious, and Ahriman will perish, together with the Divs and the offshoots of darkness."

Then there is a long list of sins, — pages of them. Repeating a sin without having previously repented of the first commission of it made the guilt greater than before.

And then the conclusion : —

" In what kind soever I have sinned, against whomsoever I have sinned, however I have sinned, I repent of it with thoughts, words, and deeds ! Pardon !"

This is the very depth of penitence.

From a literary point of view, the Avesta is far below

the Vedas; it has none of the lovely poetry which breathes through every line of the Rig Veda. Morally it surpasses the Rig Veda: those beautiful aspirations towards goodness which occasionally are poured out there become the settled principle of daily life in the Avesta. Historically it is very valuable to all believers in Christianity; for here is the source of the contest between good and evil which Christianity has so glorified. For the Avesta is the true development of the Rig Veda, rather than Brahmanism; and, in a history of thought, would come between the two.

The reader will remember that Indra and Vritra are purely physical in the Rig Veda; but in the Avesta, Azhidahaka, the biting snake of winter, is called in addition "the evil for the world, the wicked one, which Ahriman created for slaying the purity of the world," so under the later and spiritual interpretation of Zarathustra, the hero who slays him is all good fighting against all evil : and this idea came into Christianity in two ways. First, the Jews brought it back from their captivity in Babylon. Before that they had no idea of devils or bad spirits. M. Bréal says that " Satan, in Job, is meant for an angel, not a devil; he is an angel, that is, a messenger to do the bidding of the Most High. In 1st Chronicles xxi. 1, Satan appears as an evil spirit, and tempts David to number the people." (We must remember that the Books of Chronicles were not written down until long after the events described had taken place, — until the Jews had come back from their captivity in Babylon among the Persians.) M. Bréal says, " Through the Jews it came into Christianity, and is found very strongly expressed in the Book of Revelation." Mr. James Freeman Clarke says, "Such a picture as that by Guido of the conflict between Michael and Satan, such a poem as Goethe's Faust, or Milton's Paradise Lost, would never have appeared in Christendom but for the influence of Zoroaster's religion, first on Jewish, after that on Christian thought." There is another idea which the Jews brought back : Yama, the judge of the dead, in the Vedas, becomes Yima in the Avesta: instead of living in a spiritual world he lives here in a beautiful country, an earthly paradise. The souls of the good live there until the final judgment. I quote from the Avesta : "In the wide rule of Yima there was no cold, no heat, no old age, no death, no envy (the creation of the Divs). Father and son walked along together, fifteen years old in countenance, each of the two : the eatable food was inexhaustible : men and cattle were immortal : water and trees never dried up, all on account of the absence of the lie, until Yima, himself untrue, began to love lying speech : then when he, himself untrue, began to love lying speech, his majesty flew away from him visibly with the body of a bird." Here is the conception of the fall of a good spirit through haughtiness of mind : the reader will at once think of the fall of Satan. This belief in an earthly paradise constantly recurs in the literature of the Middle Ages : when we come to that, I shall refer to the second way in which these ideas reached Christianity.

There is one thing more which we probably owe to the Avesta and the Parsees. It will be remembered that the undivided Aryans used the moon to measure time : the words " moons " and " month " mean measures, and time was measured by months — that is, by moons — long before it was divided into weeks. The Parsees had a different Genius, or good god, for every day of the month, except the 1st, 8th, 15th, and 22d, which were sacred to Ahura Mazda. Although it is not yet fully proved that we get our division of time into weeks from the Aryans of Persia, I think it is a fair conclusion, and scholars say that it is probably so. If . I have dwelt so long upon the Avesta, it is because its historical value is so great; it is the inner meaning, the last resultant of the principles of the Rig Veda, and one would be incomplete without the other. We even could not understand literature itself without tracing its ideas back to their sources, — sources unknown and unsuspected one hundred years ago, despised and doubted when first made known; to have discovered them is a splendid triumph of the human mind; and to follow the footsteps of these great scholars is a lofty pleasure for us.

There is no literature in Zend except a religious one, a few books developing the principles laid down by Zarathustra. The Persian literature proper is comparatively modern. It was well known in Europe before the Avesta had been translated, or the two new sciences of comparative mythology and comparative philology formed. But Persia has a really great poem and a true poet. The great Sultan Mahmoud, who invaded and conquered India near A. D. 1000, felt that the glory of empire was not enough for him: he longed to be a patron of literature, so he ordered the poet Firdousi to collect and rewrite into an harmonious whole the legends and ballads relating to the history of Persia. Since the Mohammedan conquest of Persia, two hundred and fifty

years before, these legends had been kept alive by the
Persian nobles who had preserved in secret the faith of
their ancestors, the religion of Zarathustra ; but we owe
their present form to two Mohammedans, Mahmoud and
Firdousi. The poem is a true national epic, and is called
the Shah Nameh, or "Book of Kings." The Sultan
promised to pay him sixty thousand pieces of gold, one
thousand pieces as soon as each thousand couplets
should be completed ; but Firdousi preferred to receive
the whole amount at once, because he wished to build
stone ditches and drains to irrigate and improve his native city. After thirty-five years of toil the great poem
of sixty thousand couplets was completed ; but the prime
vizier of Mahmoud disliked Firdousi, and persuaded
the Sultan to send him sixty thousand pieces of silver.
Firdousi received them at the bath ; he was so indignant
that he on the spot divided the money into three parts,
gave one to each of the two slaves who had brought it,
the other to the attendant at the bath : then he wrote a
stinging satire upon Mahmoud and fled to his native
city, Tus. After some years Mahmoud repented, and
sent an elephant loaded with sixty thousand pieces of
gold to Tus : but at the gates they met the funeral procession of Firdousi. His daughter nobly refused the
gold, but his sister remembered the dream of Firdousi's youth : she took the gold and built the drains and
ditches in stone. So Firdousi became a benefactor to his
native city, but like others he suffered for an ungrateful
country, — like Dante, Tasso, Camoens. Ampère, the
French critic, calls him one of the great poets of the
world, and his story throws a mournful interest around
his poem. A magnificent French translation was begun

by the French government at ninety francs a volume, but the death of M. Mohl has left it unfinished : there is a poor translation in English, very much abridged, published in 1832.

We find collected in the Shah Nameh the national traditions for an estimated period of three thousand six hundred years. This is rather apocryphal, since he makes one king rule seven hundred years, and another one thousand. It describes the civilization founded by Djemschid, reformed by Zarathustra, and overthrown by Alexander. Alexander is called Sikander, and the Persians have certainly a right to claim him, as he adopted Persian manners. Of course it is not literal history, although it is carried down to the Mohammedan conquest in A. D. 641 ; it is rather a picture of the manners and the thought of the country and the time. There is a want of unity in it since so many kings and heroes are described ; it resembles in this respect the Maha Bharata, but it has nothing of that theocratic character, that government of the priests, which runs through the two Sanskrit epics. It is an heroic story of a brave and warlike people, pure in their lives and full of simple faith ; yet it has a religious meaning, and represents the contest between good and evil. Iran is the principle of light, and Turan of darkness ; Iran, which is Persia, being constantly at war with a country called Turan. From this comes our word Turanian, applied afterwards to all those native races which fought against all the other Aryan invaders. Each new hero who arises carries on the holy war, and is accompanied by good spirits called Peris and Genii. The Turanians are accompanied by Divs, both directly traceable to the Avesta, of course.

The heroes and heroines are so much alike that one becomes rather wearied with the repetition of the same adventures over and over again; but the poem is most interesting as a link in the history of the human mind, and as another proof of the brotherhood of the different Aryan families. These ballads must have grown up soon after the separation of the Iranians and Indians; they somewhat resemble the early feudal epic of their Hindu brethren, but not at all the later theocratic one. The literature of Greece had been well known in Persia by means of Zenobia and her prime minister, Longinus, seven hundred years before they were collected; yet the ballads seem utterly uninfluenced by Greek thought. Persia had been conquered by the Mohammedans two hundred and fifty years before their collection, yet there is no trace of the Arabian mind in them. The Crusades came one hundred years after they were collected, so that no influence could have been exerted by the Christians : they are an original growth, a product of the soil, and yet they are exactly like the chivalric romances which arose in Europe in the Middle Ages. The same brave and warlike heroes perform the most amazing feats of valor, and are attended by good and evil spirits : the same moon-faced heroines, with musky hair, and cypress-like forms, as much alike as a row of lay figures, fall in love at first sight. Yet the poem is most spirited, full of prodigies of valor performed by the different heroes, and the demons fly about with the most delightful profusion and energy.

It is easy to recognize in these heroes the ancient heroes and divinities of the Rig Veda and the Avesta, who have been made into men, and thus become the heroes of the epic poem. The greatest as well as the first king was Djemschid, distinguished for learning and wisdom. In his reign coats of mail were invented, swords and other armor; garments of silk were woven; desert lands were cultivated; vessels were put upon the rivers and seas; water and clay were formed into bricks to build him a splendid palace. In this palace he every year assembled Genii and Divs, men and beasts and birds. Over all these his empire extended. Nature herself was subject to him; for his government lasted seven hundred years. Nobody died, and nobody was ill. Then his heart was filled with pride. He said to his nobles, " Was there ever a king of such magnificence and power as I?" And the nobles replied, " Thou art the mightiest, the most victorious : there is no equal to thee." Then the just god beheld this foolish pride, and cast him down into utter misery. Does not this remind one of the story of Yima in the Avesta? Eugène Burnouf, the greatest Zend scholar in the world, says that Yima reappears in Djemschid.

The first great hero of the Shah Nameh is Feridun. A king named Zohak had committed dreadful crimes, assisted by a Div named Iblis. As his reward, Iblis requested permission to kiss the king's shoulder, which was granted. Then from the shoulder sprang two dreadful serpents. Iblis told him that these must be fed every day with the brains of two children. So the country gradually was becoming depopulated, as the object of Iblis was to destroy the human race. Then arose a youthful hero named Feridun. When yet a baby, he had been abandoned by his mother, and nursed by a cow. The reader will at once think of other

Aryan heroes who have been brought up by some friendly animal, — Romulus and Remus, or Œdipus. Feridun had been educated by a mountain hermit. He grew up beautiful and strong, and finally he killed the serpent-king Zohak, and delivered his country. Eugène Burnouf has discovered that Zohak is the same as Azhidahaka in the Avesta, — the biting snake; Feridun has been identified with Thraetaona, the hero of the Avesta. And thus another hero fights with a monster; that is, good fights with evil, for the contest has now become spiritualized. The poet Firdousi uses every opportunity to introduce religious and moral reflections; which are, however, both beautiful and appropriate. He says : —

> " Feridun
> First purified the world from sin and crime :
> Yet Feridun was not an angel; nor
> Composed of musk and ambergris. By justice
> And generosity he gained his fame.
> Do thou but exercise these princely virtues,
> And thou wilt be renowned as Feridun."

The second and greatest hero is Rustem. He is a compound of Herakles the Greek and Roland of the Middle Ages, as we shall see later. His infancy is protected by a marvellous bird, — the Simurgh. He is like the bird Garuda in Sanskrit, and develops into the roc of the Arabian Nights. When an infant only, he performs prodigies of valor, like Herakles; when a child, he kills an elephant. When grown up, the king and his army being shut up in the demon country by the king of Turan and his Divs, Rustem, all alone, performs seven labors, and frees the king. This is again like Herakles. But Rustem is as pious as he is brave. He prays to his god before every encounter, and gives thanks after every victory. He has a marvellous horse, whom he loves more than wife or child. These traits suggest Roland. He is in fact a perfect type of the mediæval hero, except in one thing, his indifference to women: he leaves his young wife, the daughter of a king, to look for his horse, which had strayed away, and never goes back to her, although he kindly sends once to inquire for her. Now, many of these traits identify him at once as a solar myth. If he is so much more pious than the Greek hero, it is that he expresses the simple faith of the noble Persian character. His marvellous strength when an infant is the power of the sun, resistless even at its rising; the seven labors which he performs for the good of others, the demons which he slays, are the dark clouds which obstruct his path. When in the middle of his life, Rustem feels that his labors for others have not been appreciated, and he sits apart, gloomy and sullen, in his tent, while the war goes on. This will at once suggest the wrath of Achilleus. It is the dark cloud again, obscuring the beneficent sun. The bride whom Rustem so coolly leaves is the same bride whom all the other solar heroes abandon, — the dawn. And at last, when Rustem dies, he is not killed in fair fight, but in ambush, — like Siegfried, slain from behind. There is one circumstance connected with the solar myth as represented by Rustem which only recurs once again in the other Aryan literatures. The great hero kills his unknown son, Sohrab. This comes into the old High German ballad of Hildebrand and Hadubrand; and this is simply a reversal of the usual form. Sohrab is also a solar myth, — the light of one day slain by another; for Rustem never grows old. The kings of the Shah Nameh pass away and die, and new ones arise; but Rustem is still the great champion. He may be said to have a thousand lives, like the light, which never dies. Matthew Arnold's exquisite translation is so well known that readers can at once refer to it for the episode of Sohrab and Rustem.

There is another hero in the Shah Nameh, named Isfendiyar, — also a solar myth, because he can be slain only by an arrow from one particular tree, the thorn; this is the same thorn which killed Siegfried in German, the mistletoe which killed Balder in Norse, the thorn which pricks the sleeping beauty. And of course Rustem, the summer, kills Isfendiyar, the dark winter. These four are the most famous heroes of the Shah Nameh; there are no women so sweet, yet so strong, as Damayanti and Sita, but a totally new type is introduced, Gurd-Afrid, an amazon who fights in armor like a man. This certainly proves the early independence of the Persian women; the later type of Persian woman is Mohammedan, not Aryan. Until this discovery it was considered that the Greek amazon, Atalanta, was the original; but the type belongs to all the Aryans, not to the Greeks alone.

The Persians of this late day still love and reverence the Shah Nameh. Many places are associated with its events. The ruins of Persepolis are called the throne of Djemschid. A traveller relates that, in 1830, he accompanied an embassy from Persepolis to Shiraz. One of the grooms began to recite verses from the Shah

Nameh, while they moved along. When he ceased, a nobleman of the embassy took up the passage where the servant left off. Rustem is still the national hero of Persia. Three hundred villages bear his name. Like Roland's with the Pyrenees, his name is associated with the province of Mazenderan. Stones in the desert are pointed out as the tracks that Rustem's camel left behind him. In the Persian wars, during the first centuries of this era, his exploits were still sung, like the exploits of Roland, sung at the battle of Hastings. There are hundreds of these ballads in Persia, which have been collected into Nameh, or books, but they do not equal the Shah Nameh. All belong to the Aryan period, pure and unmixed.

Of course, the Shah Nameh is not literal history ; so that you will not be amazed to find its heroes possessing the attributes of the solar myth. But it is curious that they should have also attached themselves to a real historical person. There is no doubt that Cyrus the Great lived, and conquered the Medes, and followed the religion of Zarathustra, and was a warlike Aryan, like all the early Persians ; but the stories told of him are too much like those of many another hero to be quite·true historically. We owe our account of Cyrus to Herodotus, the Greek. Before his birth it was predicted that he should destroy his grandfather ; so, as soon as he was born, Astyages ordered him to be exposed to death on a mountain-side. He was wrapped in golden and parti-colored robes, and left to die ; but the kind wife of a herdsman, filled with pity, nursed him and brought him up as her own child. Her name was Spaca, which means a dog, and it was always said

that Cyrus was nursed by an animal, like the heroes
Feridun and Romulus. When Cyrus grew up, he was
so strong and fair that the boys chose him to be king
in all their games. He acted like a king, — made laws,
and punished all offenders who disobeyed him. Then
one of the boys complained to his father. who was a
nobleman, and young Cyrus was brought before the
real king, Astyages. Then Astyages recognized him
to be the grandson whom he had exposed to die, and
sent him to his father, who was a Persian. When
Cyrus grew older, he raised an army of Persians, came
and conquered the Medes, and overthrew his grandfather, Astyages. Thus he fulfilled the prophecy that
he should destroy his own grandfather. The same
prophecy was made about Romulus and Perseus. It is
an historical fact that Cyrus did unite the Medes and
Persians, — those very Medes and Persians whom we
used to meet at our Sunday-school lessons; but it is
also true that the Aryan imagination of our Persian
brethren threw around him those circumstances which .
clearly indicate the solar myth, wherever found. The
sun often rises behind a mountain, wrapped in golden
and colored clouds, and the sun always destroys the
darkness, its father; for here comes in the strongest
proof of the mythical element attached to Cyrus, — the
name of the grandfather Astyages is the same word as
Azhidaka, the biting snake of the Avesta, and Cyrus
becomes another of the heroes of light fighting against
darkness and evil. It was not consciously composed,
of course, this story of Cyrus, but grew up spontaneously.

I came to the Shah Nameh utterly ignorant of what

it was, and was amazed as well as delighted, it was
so unlike my idea of Persian poetry. But when I
studied the modern poetry, I found what I had expected, — the luxuriance and indolence and Epicurean-
ism which we associate with the East, but which are not
found in the Sanskrit literature at all, nor in the ancient
literature of Persia. The modern Persian language is
an Aryan language, the child of Zend; but the thoughts
are Mohammedan and Semitic. You will remember
that there is no modern literature in Sanskrit. There
is a great deal in Persian. It has been the fashion in
France and Germany. Goethe wrote a whole volume
called the "West-Easterly Divan," which was a wonderful imitation of Hafiz.

Hafiz is the greatest of the modern Persians. He
lived in the fourteenth century, at Shiraz. He wrote
songs in praise of love and wine, the rose and the nightingale, the nightingale and the rose, until one gets very
weary of their monotony. The metre is very peculiar
and pleasing; it is called a Ghazel. They have a vague
mysticism running through them; and some devout
Mohammedans use them as a devotional book, and
claim that they have a spiritual meaning. The love
poems are said to describe the soul's love of God; but
I cannot think this Hafiz's own meaning. They are
interesting as an expression of one side of the national
character, although a very low side; for Hafiz was an
infidel and a sensualist. He belongs to the same class
as Anacreon in Greek, or Catullus in Latin. Hafiz
is so celebrated that we cannot ignore him in a sketch
of the national literature; but he will never have in
Europe the popularity he enjoys in the East. The

specimens I shall quote are very favorable to him. Out of a whole volume, they are the clearest I could find. The others seem confused and stupid; but certainly these are very pretty in their way. The rose is the national emblem of Persia, the bulbul (the nightingale) is the favorite bird, the cypress the favorite tree; and whenever one meets these three in a European poet, one may know that he has sat at the feet of Hafiz and Saadi.

"Without the loved one's cheek, the rose
　　　　　Can charm not.
The spring, unless the wine-cup flows,
　　　　　Can charm not.
The greenwood's border and the orchard's air,
Unless some tulip cheek be there,
　　　　　Can charm not.
The sugar-lipped, the fair of rosy frame,
Whom kisses nor embrace can claim,
　　　　　Can charm not.
The dancing cypress, the enrapturing flower,
If no nightingale gladden the bower,
　　　　　Can charm not.
The painter's picture, though with genius rife,
Without the picture that has life,
　　　　　Can charm not.
Wine, flower, and bower abound in charm, yet they,
Lack we the friend who makes us gay,
　　　　　Can charm not.
　　　Thy soul, O Hafiz!
　　　Is a coin that none prize;
　　　And it, though poured forth
　　　　　Largess-wise,
　　　　　　Can charm not."

> "'T is a deep charm which wakes the lover's flame;
> Not ruby lip nor musky locks its name.
> Beauty is not the eye, hair, cheek, or mole :
> A thousand subtile points the heart control."

Saadi is the other great writer of modern and Mohammedan Persia. He lived in the twelfth century of our era, one hundred and fifty years before Hafiz, and so was less corrupted by Mohammedan thought. He will have in Europe some portion of the popularity he enjoys among the Mohammedans. He travelled over Europe and Asia, and wrote many books. The best of them are the Gulistan, or "Rose Garden," and the Bostan, or "Fruit Garden." Their very names show the allegory of which the Semitic nations are so fond. They are composed of short stories in prose, with a moral in verse attached, which is supposed to be as valuable and beautiful as roses and fruits. In every sentence of the original, Persian and Arabic words are intermixed, as if we should make a sentence with English and Latin words; yet nevertheless he writes with charming ease: even through a prose translation the grace is felt, and the Gulistan would be accepted as the masterpiece of Mohammedan literature. It is witty and wise and shrewd. Saadi preaches and moralizes, and overflows with good sense. But he has no faith, no enthusiasm, no spirituality. This cool, calculating self-righteousness is exasperating to the last degree ; and one feels inclined to say that such a goodness, which comes only from prudent self-interest, is no goodness at all.

Here is one of the finest proverbs : —

> "O, square thyself for use : a stone that may
> Fit in the wall is not left in the way."

We give an extract from the Gulistan : —

" I was sitting in a boat, in company with some persons of distinction, when a vessel near us sunk, and two brothers fell into a whirlpool. One of the company promised a mariner one hundred dinars if he would save both the brothers. The mariner came and saved one, and the other perished. I said, ' Of a truth the other had no longer to live, and therefore he was taken out of the water last.' The mariner, laughing, replied, ' What you say is true; but I had also another motive in saving this one in preference to the other, because once, when I was tired in the desert, he mounted me on a camel, and from the other I received a whipping in my childhood.' I replied, ' Truly the great God is just; so that whosoever doeth good shall himself experience good, and he who com- mitteth evil shall suffer evil. As far as you can avoid it, dis- tress not the mind of any one; for in the path of life there are many thorns. Assist the exigencies of others, since you also stand in need of many things.' "

Here is the fatalism of the Mohammedans : —

" O thou who art in want of subsistence, be confident that thou shalt eat. And thou whom death hath required, flee not ; for thou canst not preserve thy life. With or without your exertion, Providence will bestow on you daily bread ; and if thou shouldst be in the jaws of the lion, or of the tiger, they could not devour you excepting on the day of your destiny."

The story of the perfumed clay is too old and fa- miliar to be quoted ; but it originated in Persia. " Je ne suis pas la rose ; mais j'ai vécu avec elle."

There are many poets belonging to this modern period in Persia, — said to be twenty-five thousand. I do not know who is left to form an audience. The period ex- tends from the eleventh century (the collection of the

Shah Namch) to our time. One of them, Omar Khay-
yam, the astronomer-poet, who died in A. D. 1123, was
translated a few years ago. He reads like Heine, full
of scepticism and irony. "This life is but an inn," he
cries; "let us eat and drink and be merry." Mr.
Emerson says, "The poet stands in strict relation to
his people; he has the overdose of their nationality."
It seems melancholy that the brave and believing Persians should be represented by the sensualism of Hafiz,
and the worldly wisdom of Saadi; but the Aryan element was not quite crushed out of Persia. Because
Persian poetry is the meeting of two distinct races, the
Aryan and the Semitic, two modes of thought, the Vedic and the Mohammedan, it has a universal interest, a
claim to consideration.

It burst forth first in mysticism, — that curious phase
of the Aryan race, which breaks out in every family,
modified by external surroundings, and is so prominent
in modern Persian poetry that it cannot be passed over.
The third great poet is Djellaleddin Roumi. His mystical poem, called the Mesnevi, is the third great poem
of Mohammedan literature. It is a fusion of the two
elements; but the mysticism which was barely perceptible in Hafiz preponderates in the Mesnevi. The doctrine is like the pantheism of Brahmanism, and it was
so fully explained in the second chapter that I need
not repeat the account. The individual is said to be a
piece of the Divine Being, and finally to be absorbed
into him. The believer cries out, "I am in God";
next, "I am God." There is a set of Mohammedan
mystics called Sufis, who admire and follow this poem.

We must return for a moment to the Shah Nameh.

It has an interest to us far more than these three poems, — far more than that of any mere literary monument of a past age. It is the source of many of our own ideas. The Persians are our brothers : they were once a brave and chivalrous people ; and as the Avesta introduced a spiritual fight into our religion, so the Shah Nameh brought it down into our nursery tales and folk-lore.

The second manifestation of the Aryan element is in the popular stories of modern Persia. The reader will remember that a few of them originated in India, principally the geographical story of Sindbad the Sailor. They were translated and enlarged in Persia. With a little thought the reader can separate the Vedic and Mohammedan features. They have Peris who are the seven great Genii of the Avesta in reduced circumstances, and who mean the bright clouds of the Veda ; they have demons who are the Divs of the Avesta, the dark clouds of the Veda. They have an earthly paradise, or dark halls of Iblis, from the Shah Nameh ; marvellous talking birds, and human beings turned into beasts, again from the Shah Nameh. But the manners and customs are such as Mohammedans would naturally adopt, as the many wives, the seclusion of the women. The signet ring of Solomon, which gave power over Genii and Divs, was Mohammedan ; but the cup of Djemschid, which revealed all the secrets of creation to him who gazed in it, was from the Shah Nameh, and reappears as the magic goblet in every Aryan family. If the Persian stories differ from the nursery tales which are the common inheritance of every Aryan branch, it is because they did not grow up until after the separation of the families: although starting in India, they received in Persia a coloring which has only lately been understood. These supernatural stories, with their mixed origin, influenced Europe in the Middle Ages almost as much as the heroic ballads, and both have come down to us from the Shah Nameh. In the chapter upon Mediæval Literature I shall speak of the two roads which they took.

There is something else, too, which we owe to modern Persia, that is, the historical novel. Strictly speaking, the epic is confined to poetry. It tells a story of national character, and national fortunes, and it includes national ballads. In fact, it is founded upon them. But, in a broader sense, an epic may be written in prose. Popular traditions of heroes and gods are indispensable to an epic poem; but, later on, faith in the marvellous dies out, and then the story is put into plain prose. If the facts are national, it becomes the historical romance; if the facts relate only to private individuals, it becomes the novel. So the modern Persians could not make a poetic epic, but they invented a prose epic, the historical novel. The first one was founded upon the life of Alexander the Great, and called "The Tale of Iskander." Do we not owe a debt of thanks to our Persian brethren?

The Sanskrit literature contains no history. The mixed element of modern Persia has produced many valuable histories. Within a few years Persia seems to be composing another Aryan form, regaining something of its old vitality. There were never any plays in Zend, or in Persian; but some rude popular dramas by unknown authors are now acted. They have excited much interest among French scholars because they are so very much like the Mystery plays of the Middle Ages, and have been translated within two years into French. They are wholly religious in their tone, and never mention love or daily life, which are the usual subjects of plays.

CHAPTER VI.

COMPARATIVE MYTHOLOGY OF THE GREEK POETRY AND DRAMA.

WE approach in this chapter the third branch of the noble Aryan family, — our brothers the Greeks. Their literature has been so studied and commented upon, so slavishly copied, so blindly worshipped for centuries, that little would remain to be added if we followed the footsteps of the past. But I wish to look at Greek literature in the new light which comparative philology and comparative mythology have thrown over it. Of course it would be impossible, within the limits of one chapter, to do more than mention the names which have rendered Greek literature so famous in epic poetry, lyric poetry, the drama, physics, metaphysics, history, and political eloquence. I do not pretend to exhaust the subject in one chapter. We shall devote our attention to the comparative mythology found in the Greek poetry and the Greek drama.

Every well-educated person expects to have some definite knowledge of books which have been so celebrated. Undoubtedly they have many beauties; but it is not probable that they will again rule the world as they have done. Since these new discoveries, they take a place which is quite different from their old one, but perhaps it is equally important. Instead of being the one standard by which every other literature must be judged, Greek becomes but one of many sister literatures. Books are now considered worthy of attention if they are not exactly like Greek books ; and it is no longer thought sacrilege to suggest that Greek literature may be criticised. For these new sciences have proved that it is but one of many links in the development of the human mind ; and therefore it may be judged by its intrinsic merits.

In judging the Sanskrit literature, we must not for one moment forget that it was absolutely self-developed ; that it grew up without any contact with other nations. The Greek literature is not so independent a manifestation of human thought. It is true, that it inherited no forms ; it copied no models, but it is greatly indebted to the mind of Egypt and Assyria. From a modern and Christian stand-point it seems far less beautiful than those early spontaneous writings ; for Sanskrit literature seems spiritual, pathetic, and noble ; while the Greek seems unspiritual, artificial, and immoral. I may repeat Max Müller's remarks : " The language of the simple prayers of the Rig Veda is more intelligible to us than anything we find in the literature of Greece or Rome ; and there are, here and there, expressions of faith and devotion, in which even a Christian can join without irreverence." Saint Augustine, even when a Pagan, never loved the Greek literature ; and Bossuet, the greatest French preacher, complained of " le grand creux " which he found in all classical antiquity.

The different authorities have not yet settled whether the Pelasgi of Greece were Aryan or Turanian. It is only a question of pushing a little farther back the Aryan invasion ; for we know that the original inhabitants were

a Turanian race. We do not know when the powerful
Aryans entered Greece, but they conquerd the Trojans
1184 B. c., and from this date they became masters of
Greece. For three centuries after, history is a blank.
But the Grecian Aryans developed the germs they had
brought with them from the common home. Unconsciously they went through the same mental processes
which every other Aryan nation has gone through ; and
from these ideas of the undivided Aryans resulted the
Greek mythology. It is only a completer development
of these intuitions which we have already examined in
the Rig Veda. But we must not for a moment think
it was borrowed from there. India was unknown to
them : even the cradle of their undivided race had long
been forgotten. The Greek mythology is much more
complex and puzzling than the Sanskrit ; it was never
understood until lately. A thousand explanations of it
have been made, but the new light thrown upon it by
the Rig Veda has given its true and final interpretation,
for the gods of all the Aryan mythologies are now considered to be nature personified. Its powers, such as
the sky, the sun, the wind, the dawn, become real
persons. In Greek mythology, each different aspect of
nature had many different names, because a few simple
elements crystallized into many different forms. This is
why there are so many gods and goddesses.

There are books in Greek which tell us these stories
of their gods and goddesses ; but there is no book like
the Vedas, or the Avesta, full of prayers and hymns and
thanksgivings, — full of a spiritual life ; in a word, there
are no sacred books, and this is a sufficient comment
upon the Greek character. They seem to have had

originally the usual Aryan form of worship. They poured
out libations of wine, and offered part of the food, at
every meal; they sacrificed animals upon an altar; each
head of a family was his own priest, and performed his
own sacrifice. Agamemnon was priest and king himself.
Afterwards they erected altars; then temples to every
god, — the bad as well as the good, — even to the god of
thieves, Hermes. But a Greek temple did not contain
a congregation of worshippers, like a Christian church;
at first, it was only large enough to hold the statue and
altar of some god. Art has preserved to us a feature
of distinctively Greek worship : a long procession led
by naked men, who danced and sang in honor of the
gods. It is true that they had solemn and dreadful
mysteries in honor of Kybele, and Dionysos, which are
supposed to have been brought from Egypt by the
Turanian aborigines, and to have survived the Aryan
conquest. These horrid festivals had some hymns and
poems called Orphic sayings, but they do not belong to
united Greece : they only represent that Turanian element which was not entirely crushed out. The oracles
of the gods spoke occasionally at the temples, but gave
no connected utterance. Of religious literature, such as
other nations possess, there is none. That sense of sin,
which weighed down the thoughtful Hindu, that clear
distinction between right and wrong which nerved the
Persian to spiritual struggle, can scarcely be said to
have been present to the Greek mind.

We have seen that the first utterance of the human
mind is a hymn to a god; the next, a code of religious
laws and duties. The Greeks seem not to have gone
through these two periods of mental growth : at any rate,

there is no trace of them left, because the first collected book in Greek is the Iliad. And what is that? Everybody knows that the Iliad is a poem which tells two stories ; — of a war between the Greeks and Trojans to recover a Grecian woman named Helen, who had run away from her lawful husband with a Trojan hero named Paris, and carried a great treasure with her ; also, of the anger of Achilleus, a Grecian hero, and the dreadful consequences it brought upon the Grecian army, encamped upon the plains around Troy.

The latest investigations have succeeded in proving that the Iliad is a collection of heroic ballads ; and that there were, in early Greek literature, hundreds of these heroic ballads, of which the Iliad and the Odyssey are the only ones which have survived to us, though not necessarily the best. There are said to have been several versions of these stories ; but they were finally collected by Peisistratos and Solon, 600 b. c., and in this authorized form they have come down to us. They were sung by minstrels, called rhapsodists, at public assemblies.

The Odyssey is the second book collected. It tells the story of a Greek warrior, Odysseus, and his wanderings after Troy was captured, until he reached Ithaca, his home, during ten years. Both of these belong to the third period of mental growth, the ballad age. It was once believed that they were the unaided work of one mighty mind, the poet called Homer ; but along with the ballad theory, which is now an accepted fact, comes another, not yet accepted fully, — that these ballads were composed by several different poets. In a few years the question will be definitely settled ; the most advanced thinkers maintain the theory. It is from these Homeric poems, these two, that we get our first ideas of the Greek gods and goddesses. They take part in the siege of Troy ; they take sides in the quarrel ; they act like human beings, and very weak and wicked human beings too. There is nothing noble or elevated in the mythology of the Homeric poems.

It is a relief to turn aside from them to the poems of Hesiod, where we find almost the only pure morality of Greek poetry. Some religious feeling breaks out in the poem called " Works and Days." It is an agricultural poem, which tells what work in cultivating the ground should be done upon certain days ; also which days are lucky or unlucky. " On the fourth day of the month lead home a bride." " The first ninth day of a month is wholly harmless to mortals ; but avoid the fifth days, for they are mischievous and hurtful." Here is the . finest passage of Hesiod : —

"Now the gods keep hidden for men their means of subsistence ; else easily mightest thou in one day have wrought so that thou shouldst have had enough for a year, even though being idle. Badness you may easily choose ; easily in a dead level is the path, and right near. But before virtue the immortal gods have set exertion, and long and steep and rugged is the way at first to it ; but when you shall have reached the summit, then truly it is easy, difficult though it may have been before. . . . . And with him gods and men are indignant who lives a sluggard's life, like in temper to stingless drones, which lazily consume the labor of bees by devouring it. Now work is no disgrace, but sloth is a disgrace."

The descriptions of the proper times for beginning work are quite poetical.

"Mark, too, when from on high out of the clouds you shall have heard the voice of the crane uttering its yearly cry, which brings the signal for ploughing, and points the season of rainy winter; then truly feed the crumpled-horned oxen, remaining within their stalls."

"When the artichoke flowers, and the tuneful cicada, perched on a tree, pours forth a shrill song ofttimes from under his wings, is the season of toilsome summer."

It is dull reading to moderns, but it is the model from which many poems have been copied, the Georgics of Virgil being one. Its chief importance in the history of ideas is, that it contains, in one of its episodes, an account of the origin of mankind, and thus tells us what the Greeks thought on this matter. It has also that idea, which we found among the Brahmans, of an early age of virtue; and of the degeneracy of the race. It describes four ages: first the golden; then the silver; then the brazen, an age of heroes; then the iron, in which we are living, — an age of toil. Its idea of the origin of evil in the world seems too frivolous to be connected with so awful a subject. It is the story of Pandora. These three episodes belong to the "Works and Days."

It has been said, that Hesiod also means a class of poets, not one man; and it is not unlikely, for it seems impossible that the same mind which thought out the pure morality of the "Works and Days," could have written down the shocking stories contained in the "Theogony." It gives the Greek ideas of the origin of the universe and of the gods; — not of mankind; that was contained in the "Works and Days." It is an endeavor to make a connected system, and until the Rig Veda was discovered it was the fountain-head for all mythology. But Max Müller says, "The Rig Veda, and not the poem of Hésiod, is the real theogony of the Aryan race." We have been accustomed to speaking of the Greek gods by their Latin names, but I shall use the Greek names, because they are nearer to the Sanskrit: so the connection can be more easily traced. There are contradictory accounts in the different theogonies; but the gods described in them are a most unpleasant and disreputable set. The genealogies are in inextricable confusion. Brothers marry sisters, mothers marry their sons, and fathers eat up their own children; and over them all brooded a dark fate, which the gods themselves were unable to avert. No wonder that the noblest minds among the Greeks turned from these wicked and powerless gods in despair. But the new science of comparative mythology comes to our aid. It enables us to take a more encouraging view of the Greek nature, for all these shocking, repulsive stories lose their bad qualities when understood to be only the personifications of the appearances of nature.

Hesiod says that Ouranos, the surrounding heaven, married Gaia, the earth; one will recognize the Sanskrit Varuna, the all-surrounder. One of their sons was Kronos, who ate up his children as soon as they were born. Kronos is time; our word chronology comes from the same root, and time devours the days which spring from it. But Ouranos has not the prominence of Varuna in Sanskrit. He soon loses his power, and yields his characteristics to his mighty grandson, Zeus.

Zeus is the same as the Sanskrit Dyaus, and the Dyaus Pitar of the undivided Aryans, the god of the

bright sky. He reigns undisturbed in the cloudless
ether, far above storms and conflicts, the king of gods
and father of men. As such, the only spiritual element
in Greek mythology belongs to him. He represents the
only perception they had of one god; and thus he retains those characteristics of Dyaus Pitar which the
Greeks had brought with them and developed. He
has two characters : sometimes he is spoken of as the
righteous judge, who distinguishes good from evil and
punishes wrong-doing. Hesiod speaks of him very
beautifully in this way; and in times of extreme distress, the Greeks called upon him : the prayers of the
heart always went up to Father Zeus. But usually he
is governed by most ignoble motives in his actions : he
cannot bear any comparison with the majestic deities
whom the Hindus and Teutons and Persians reflected
from their own natures and worked out from their own
instincts. We can have but a low idea of the Greek
mind, when it imagined such a god. Zeus is married to
many different wives ; when we look upon him as a
nature myth, and see that the bright sky must look
down on many lands, his visits to different countries
are explained.

Phoibos Apollo was very widely worshipped in Greece,
as the god of wisdom. His temples were found everywhere, and he had great influence in forming the Greek
character. Phoibos means the lord of life and light;
he is therefore the sun, whose light penetrates everywhere, sees and knows everything, so he becomes the
god of wisdom. He was the child of Leto, the darkness, the same word as Lethe, forgetfulness ; he was
born in Delos, the bright land. He has another name,

Apollo, the destroyer; he has that same irresistible weapon which appears so many times, and always marks the solar myth. He slays the children of Niobe, the mist: they are the clouds which the sun melts away. He also kills a more important person, the awful serpent, the Python, which was shutting up a spring of water. His meaning must be transparent by this time; the sun drives away the dark clouds, the rain comes down, and the land is delivered from the drought. Athene is the dawn myth, and shares the worship paid to Apollo. As the dawn, she too, has the penetrating power of the light. She springs from the forehead of Zeus, like Ahana in the Rig Veda, as the light of the dawn often flashes out with a sudden splendor, at the edge of the sky. Hera, the lawful wife of Zeus, is the bright air of the upper regions, above the changes of the middle air. The moon is Selene; she moves across the sky in a chariot, drawn by white horses, or she is a huntress roving over hill and dale. She comes to gaze upon the sun, just as it sets, plunging apparently into the deep sea, or going into the unknown land of Latmos, the darkness. Then the sun is called Endymion. The goddess of love is Aphrodite. She is but another name for the dawn, as it springs out of the sea with dazzling radiance. The god of war is Ares, the same root as the Maruts of the Rig Veda, the storm-winds.

There are in Greek a few hymns, called the Homeric hymns, addressed to the different gods; but nobody knows who wrote them, or when, or where they grew up. There is nothing spiritual in them; therefore, they are not at all what we think of when we use the word Hymn. They are descriptions of the different gods, and one of them, the Hymn to Hermes, is the most amusing book in Greek literature. I shall quote part of it, partly because it is not so hackneyed as the Iliad, but chiefly because it is so perfect a description of the wind, in two characters; first as the harper, then as the master thief of all Aryan literature. Hermes is born in a cave. Before the babe is an hour old, he leaves the cradle, and manufactures a harp or lyre, from which he draws soft, soothing music. His strength grows rapidly; at noon he is a strong man; he steals the cattle of Phoibos because he is hungry. He drives them backward and forward, but he covers his feet with leaves so that his tracks cannot be seen. Then he reaches a forest, rubs the dried branches together till he kindles a flame. At daybreak he steals back again, turns himself into a baby, goes through the key-hole, and lies down in his cradle. We can follow all this. The wind is silent at morning, then makes a soft harping, then with mighty strides it drives the clouds along, and strews the roads with leaves and trees. It blows the boughs together, till fire comes; then, tired out, the wind sinks down into a faint breeze, and penetrates through the key-hole. Phoibos Apollo suspects him, and accuses him. He replies: —

> "'What a speech is this!
> Why come you here to ask me what is done
> With the wild cattle, whom it seems you miss?
> I have not seen them, nor from any one
> Have heard a word of the whole business;
> If you should promise an immense reward,
> I could not tell you more than you now have heard.
> An ox-stealer, I should be both tall and strong,
> And I am but a little new-born thing,

Who yet at least can think of nothing wrong.
My business is to suck and sleep and fling
The cradle clothes about me all day long,
Or, half asleep, hear my sweet mother sing ;
And to be washed in water clear and warm,
And hushed and kissed and kept secure from.harm.
O, let not e'er this quarrel be averred.
The astounded gods would laugh at you, if e'er
You should allege a story so absurd
As that a new-born infant forth could fare
Out of his house, after a savage herd.
I was born yesterday. My small feet are
Too tender for the roads so hard and rough.
And if you think that this is not enough,
I swear a great oath, by my father's head,
That I stole not your cows, and that I know
Of no one else who might, or could, or did.
I do not even know what things cows are,
For I have only heard the name.' — This said,
He winked as fast as could be ; and his brow
Was wrinkled, and a whistle loud gave he,
Like one who hears a strange absurdity.
Apollo gently smiled, and said, 'Ay, ay,
You cunning little rascal, you will bore
Into many a rich man's house, and your array
Of thieves will lay their siege before his door,
Silent in night ; and many a day
In the wild glens rough shepherds will deplore
That you, or yours, comrades of the night,
Met with their cattle, having an appetite !
And this among the gods shall be your gift,
To be considered as the lord of those
Who swindle, house-break, sheep-steal, and shop-lift,
You are the master thief.' "

But when Hermes plays upon his sweet harp, Apollo,

entranced, forgives him all his misdeeds. They swear eternal friendship, and Apollo allows him to wear his own swift sandals. He can go everywhere that Apollo goes, except to the deep ocean. This means that the wind cannot penetrate into the ocean, although the light can. The poem closes by saying that Hermes loves Apollo more than he loves mankind; that is, the wind will do more mischief at night, while the sun is gone. Certainly, the poem is exquisitely pretty, and describes perfectly the wind as that harper and as that thief whom we find in every Aryan literature. Hermes had another office; he was the Psycopompos, and carried the souls of the dead to the underworld. This idea comes into each mythology. In Anglo-Saxon, the expression is used, "Beowulf curled to the clouds." The smoke was supposed to be the soul of the dead; this is why they burned the body on a funeral pile, — that the soul might more easily be set free; and naturally the wind would carry it away. There was always a river to cross. In Sanskrit it was guarded by two dogs; the unburned or unburied ghosts could not cross the river, but wandered disconsolately about. Here is the origin of the superstition, that ghosts cannot cross running water. The happy dead among the Greeks sought the islands of the blest: this idea of Paradise recurs in the Keltic mythology; the unhappy ones were sent to the dark underworld of King Hades.

Now this is just the thought of the Teutonic mythology. There is no idea of the devil, or punishment, connected with King Hades, any more than with Queen Hel; both were persons, not places, and very respectable persons, and mean darkness, the unseen, the under-

world. King Hades is sometimes called Ploutos, as being the guardian of the mineral treasures underground.
He is connected with the purest and sweetest of all the
myths, which tells of Demeter mourning for her lost
daughter. It was repeated among the Romans, where
it is called Ceres and Proserpine. The lovely maiden
is carried away by the dark king of the underworld, and
her despairing mother seeks her everywhere. The earth
is dried up : no grain or fruit will flourish while Demeter
neglects her care of them. So Persephone is the summer, carried away by the dark winter, and Demeter,
the earth, will not yield fruit or flower till the summer
comes back. But Persephone must spend half the year
with King Hades ; so the summer must give half the
year to darkness and winter.

Besides all the great divinities, every spring and river
had its protecting Nymph (the word means water) ;
every tree had its gentle Dryad, which bled and spoke
when the tree was broken. Each production of nature
was a living being to them ; the earth was filled with a
joyous and kindly life, which is the pleasantest side of
the Greek mythology. It is not peculiar to that alone,
for it is found in the Sanskrit and Teutonic mythologies
as well.

Viewed from our standard of character, the Grecian
heroes are no more satisfactory than the Grecian gods.
In the Homeric poems they behave very much like a
parcel of schoolboys ; the king, Agamemnon, is tyrannical and vindictive ; the great hero Achilleus sulks in his
tent like a child, deprived of a favorite toy. His treatment of Hektor's dead body is simply brutal. He drags
it round the walls of Troy, till no shape is left to its

bruised form. Odysseus uses poisoned arrows, and tells lies, and stabs his enemies behind their back. Hektor, the Trojan, is the noblest character, but even he countenances Helen. Hektor's wife, Andromache, is pure and lovely, and the parting scene between them is as fresh and beautiful to the human heart as when it resounded in the cars of the Greeks. Priam's grief over Hektor's dead body is most touching, and Helen's lament over it is very natural and real, although her grief is purely selfish. She pities herself for losing such a friend. Yet it is not strange that the Homeric poems should have lived so long. They are full of poetry, and vitality, and movement. It is not likely that they will ever die. If they seem unsatisfactory, and unworthy of their great fame to a modern and a Christian mind, there is a way of looking at them in which they gain. They too can be subjected to the tests of comparative mythology, and then their characters become copies of the gods and goddesses, personifications of the aspects of nature.

Achilleus is child of the sea goddess; so the sun often appears to rise out of the water. His bride is torn from him, and he sulks in his tent; so the sun must leave the dawn and be hidden by dark clouds. He lends his armor to Patroklos, except the spear; none other can wield the spear of Achilleus; so no other thing can equal the power of the sun's rays. His mother gives him new armor: it bears up the hero like a bird on the wing; the helmet gleams, the shield flashes like a beacon light; but no earthly armor could produce such an effect; only the sun. Then he goes forth to battle, but he fights in the cause of another; so the sun breaks forth from the gloomy clouds, conquers the darkness, and blesses the waiting earth. Achilleus tramples on the dead body of Hektor ; but Hektor is of dark powers, though noble in himself: so a blazing sunset tramples down the darkness. Finally Achilleus is slain by an arrow from a Trojan. He is vulnerable only in the heel, but the arrow finds him there. So the sun is conquered by the darkness, in his turn, and disappears, a short-lived brilliant thing.

A critic has said, that the " monstrous shapes and strange adventures of the Odyssey differ from the probable events of the Iliad ; it is a land of magic and glamour." But it affords still more striking evidence as to the theory of the nature-myth. It is delightful to trace the details, and to interpret them, through so rich a field. Odysseus is the sun in another character, as a wanderer ; and his adventures describe the general phenomena of day-time, from the rising to the setting of the sun. He leaves the bride of his youth, that is the twilight, and journeys in darkness and silence, that is the night, to the scene of the great fight. Ten weary years go on during the fight with the powers of darkness, then the victory comes ; that is, the night passes, and light comes again. Yet the hero has fought in another's quarrel ; he serves the Grecian king and army, beings meaner than himself; so the sun benefits others. Odysseus uses poisoned arrows ; so the rays of the sun are like poison in the veins on the burning plains of Troy ; but the victory cannot be gained by any other weapon. Then he journeys for ten weary years, before he can return to his beloved bride. That is, the sun cannot meet the twilight again till the day is done. " His journey is full of strange changes of happiness and misery, successes and reverses, like the lights and shadows of a gloomy day," Mr. Cox says. He reaches the land of the lotos-eaters, that is, the clear, cloudless, deep blue heaven. Then he meets the Kyklops and slays the one-eyed giant; these are the vast shapeless storm-clouds; like all other giants they are killed and outwitted by the keen-eyed sun. Then he meets the cattle of Helios; they were in seven herds, fifty in each herd; his companions kill these sacred cattle, and then are killed in return. Helios means the sun; his three hundred and fifty cattle are the days; and the companions of Odysseus do not return to him, because they wasted their time till too late, they killed the days. Twice Odysseus is brought under the enchanted spell of women; each time he breaks away. Now Kirke and Kalypso are the same, — the beautiful night, which veils the sun from mortal eyes in her cave, flashing with jewels, which are the stars. Hermes comes to deliver him; that is, the morning wind, which blows away the darkness. Then he reaches the Phaiakian land, and sees with delight their gorgeous golden towers and palaces; and the kindly Phaiakians give him a ship which may bear him home to Ithaka. These mysterious vessels have neither rudder nor oar, but they know the minds of man, and go wherever he wishes. These mysterious ships come into every mythology; the good ship Skidbladnir in Teutonic, the ship which bears Arthur in Keltic mythology: they sail, and they sail without rigging or tackle, and they reach their destined haven. You may see them yourselves, when you look up into the sky and watch the clouds as they sail. Odysseus conquers all obstacles by his marvellous sagacity,

which pierces every plot. Sometimes, alas! he seems
full of craft and cunning. This is the sunlight peering
into every nook, and piercing through every disguise.
In his early home, Penelope, his wife, weaves and ravels
her web, till Odysseus may have time to return. The
suitors trouble her, and eat up her fortune. So the
dawn must see her gold-colored clouds scattered by
dark mists ; but she must weave and ravel their graceful
net-work over and over again ; for she is the twilight
as well as the dawn, and she knows that her hero must
return to her at night. He comes back alone in beggar's
rags, and the suitors jeer at him. Then he seizes the
mighty bow which none could bend while he was away ;
one by one, the suitors fall before him, till the vast hall
swims in red blood ; it is a slaughter-hall. Then his
youthful vigor comes back to him, the brightness of his
eyes, the golden glory of his hair, and his bride recognizes
him, and he puts on his royal robes, and he shines forth
in splendor. So the sun comes to its setting, wrapped
in dark clouds, but it bursts out in all its early glory,
and every dark cloud is dispersed by its rays, and its
career closes in splendor. The bright red clouds, which
often surround the setting sun, and stream out in every
direction, to form a red sunset, are turned into the red
blood of the slain. I beg the reader particularly to remember this slaughter-hall, swimming in red blood, and
these beggar's rags. Mr. Cox says, "'The victory of
Odysseus in his beggar's rags is the victory of the poor,
despised outcast over those who pride themselves on
their grandeur and strength." We must not be surprised when we find him in any nursery tale ; he will
be always the sun breaking through dark clouds.

The physical explanation has been carried still further, and applied to the siege of Troy itself. Professor Max Müller says, " The siege of Troy is a repetition of the daily siege of the east, by the solar powers that are robbed of their brightest treasures in the west." This is not quite plain ; let us go on to hear what Mr. Cox says : " Few will venture to deny that the stealing of the bright clouds of sunset by the dark powers of night, the weary search for them through the long night, the battle with the robbers, as the darkness is driven away by the advancing chariot of the lord of light, are favorite subjects with the Vedic poets."

But whether the germs of the Iliad and the Odyssey exist in the Rig Veda, or not, the mythical history of Greece exhibits a series of movements from the west to the east, and from the east back again to the west. These movements are for the purpose of recovering a stolen treasure, and the heroes who have been robbed return with the prize, which they have regained after a long struggle. Now this stolen treasure is the light of day, carried off by the darkness, and brought back again in the morning, after a long struggle. Let us apply this to the siege of Troy. Helen and her treasure, that is, the golden light of day, are carried away by the Trojans, the darkness and night. The Greeks, the bright powers, go after her from the west to the east. The weary voyage, the ten years' siege, are the long night, the long absence of the sun. The Greeks cannot conquer until Iphigeneia has been sacrificed. She is the dawn, which must completely fade away before the day can come back. In the Odyssey, the Greeks return with the treasure and the woman ; so the light

journeys back from the east to the west, whence it started.
Mr. Cox takes another step and says: "If such a
war took place, it must be carried back to a time preceding the dispersion of the Aryan tribes from their
original home; and the scene can be placed neither in
the land of the seven rivers, nor on the plains of Asiatic
Troy; not in Norway nor Germany nor Wales. Carrying us back one step farther, these legends resolve themselves into phrases which once described, with force and
vividness never surpassed, the various phenomena of
the earth and heavens. These phrases furnish an inexhaustible supply of themes for epic poetry; and the
growth of a vast epical literature was inevitable when
the original meaning of the phrases was forgotten."

That the Iliad and the Odyssey are taken from the
vast stores of mythical tradition common to all the
Aryan nations, may be corroborated by evidence taken
from other poems. Even in Greek literature, there are
several other voyages, singularly resembling each other
in their objects and their details; something bright is
taken away, and a collected body of chieftains go in
search of it. The story was first told in the voyage of
the Argonauts for the golden fleece. In Sanskrit, Indra
is often called a bull, who carried away Dahana, the
dawn. In Greek, the sun becomes a ram with a golden
fleece; he carries away Phrixos and Helle, who are the
children of Niphele. This is the same root as Niobe,
as Niblungs in Norse, and our word "nebulous"; it
means the mist. Phrixos and Helle are the twilight,
children of the darkness, who carries away the golden
sunlight. So Jason collected a band of bright powers,
all chieftains; they are solar heroes, seeking for the

light on which their life depends. They sail in the good ship Argo, which like Skidbladnir in Teutonic mythology, contracts or expands as necessity requires. This is another of those cloud-ships which we found in the Odyssey. They have a weary voyage, with many dangers. Jason is aided by the wise Medeia. She means the dawn, which penetrates everywhere, sees and knows all; for wisdom is always the attribute of the light, as we saw in Phoibos and Athene. She even brings the dead to life in her magic caldron. This is exactly what is said in the dawn hymns of the Rig Veda. "She awakens the sleeping to a new life." The myth is still true to itself. Jason, the sun, conquers and gets back the golden fleece. But on their journey home, like Odysseus and his companions, perils and dangers attack them. Finally, he abandons Medeia, the wise woman. So the sun must leave the dawn, and go on to another land, and a checkered career. But the wise dawn becomes also cruel, and sends to Jason's new bride, Glauke, a glittering dress, which burned to her bones when she put it on. It is here, that same shirt of flame which enwrapped, and ate into, and killed Herakles, — another name given to the glittering, flame-colored clouds of sunset. How strikingly this resembles the Odyssey! I will not describe the other voyages: these are types of all.

There are also expeditions of single heroes who have been robbed of a rightful inheritance, and go in search of it. This inheritance is the bright land where the sun sinks to rest after his journey through the heaven. Every city of Greece had its own hero, whose tale was told in those other ballads lost to us. Let us take

Theseus, the hero of Athens, and see what features of the solar myth are prominent in him. Before his birth it was foretold that he should kill his father. So he is banished when born, and lives poor and unknown. But he has a hero's soul, and he longs to do some great work. An awful monster called the Minotaur ate up every year seven youths and seven maidens, and Theseus wishes to slay him, but he has no weapons. Under a stone lie marvellous weapons, but all the noble youths of the court have tried in vain to lift it. But Theseus raises it, and puts on the sword and sandals, which are of course the rays of the sun. The monster is enclosed in a labyrinth ; but Ariadne gives him the clew, and he penetrates within. She is the wise dawn. When he has killed the monster, he abandons Ariadne. But we will no longer blame the faithless Theseus : he is only fulfilling the instincts of the sun to journey on. When he sails back, he forgets to put up a white sail in place of the black one which always accompanied the fated vessel which carried the dreadful tribute to the Minotaur, and the king, thinking he has been conquered, throws himself into the sea. Then it is discovered that Theseus was his unknown child, and had ignorantly killed his father, according to the prophecy. So the sun of one day must destroy the sun of yesterday.

But the story of Perseus is the most complete and the most beautiful of all. He is the hero of Argos. It was foretold to the king that his daughter Danaë should bear a son who should destroy him. The same story is told of Krishna in Sanskrit, of Cyrus among the Persians, of Romulus among the Romans. So the king shut up Danaë in a tower. Now this is the same tower which comes into the Sleeping Beauty, or any other tale : it means the darkness of night. Danaë is the dawn, and Zeus in the form of a shower of gold married her; that is the daylight streaming in. So Perseus is the grandchild of the night, the child of the dawn and the bright day. But Perseus and his mother were set adrift by the cruel king, in a little boat. This boat comes into the Anglo-Saxon story of Beowulf; it is the sun rising on the water. They are carried to a new land, where Perseus grows up beautiful and strong, but unknown, and living in a stranger's house. This is the youth also which is given to Sigurd the Volsung in Teutonic mythology. But his mother tells him of his birth, and he goes forth to seek his rightful inheritance. Athene gives him weapons, the penetrating light for a sword, the swift-moving light for sandals. He kills the gorgon Medusa: she is simply the darkness. The snakes of her hair are those same snakes which appear so many times : they bit Eurydike, and she died ; Medusa's snakes turn all to stone, but she is only the night. In the story of Perseus, the myth is carried to another stage of development. A victim is rescued, who is a woman ; she can be traced back to the Rig Veda. Vritra, the black snake, not only stole the cows, but also the maiden Sarama, and shut them up in his cave. Then came Indra, and set free the cows — that is, the bright clouds — and the maiden, the dawn. Here arose the distressed damsel, wherever she may reappear. So the noble Perseus rescued Andromeda, the dawn, from the dark monster, the night. Then with Andromeda he sought the court of the king, his grandfather, who received and acknowledged him. But the prophecy was fulfilled; for when he was shooting in the games one day, an arrow glanced aside and slew the king, his grandfather, the night.

Certainly every characteristic of the solar myth is reproduced in the lives of Achilleus, Odysseus, Herakles, Theseus, Perseus: and it explains, in a perfectly satisfactory manner, as nothing else does, the characters and the actions which are so contrary to our standard of right and wrong. Whether the theory be true or not, any one who has read the hero stories must long ago have noticed how very much they resemble each other: one hero is so much like another, that it would be easy to construct a thousand of them. Yet this is the very strongest argument to prove that they all originated in a common source.

There is another kind of poetry which may be considered the representative poetry of Greece pre-eminently; not only because it arose spontaneously, but also because it reached its highest development there. The lyric poetry of Greece has been copied in every language; but it is doubtful if any others have sung so well of love as Sappho, of wine as Anakreon, of victory as Pindar. For their songs were true to these poets, a genuine and natural expression of a genuine feeling, and they bear that stamp of reality which cannot be counterfeited. The song was accompanied by the music of a lyre, — thence its name; and it expressed feeling, instead of action, either of an individual or of a whole nation. The greatest stress was laid upon the metre in which it was written: a different measure being adopted for love and for war songs. Milton says, " Wrap me in soft Lydian measures"; and the words made music, even without the instrument. There were nine lyric poets; but these three were greatest. Anakreon's style is so charming that for a moment one forgets how utterly his poetry should be condemned; the English poet Cowley may be considered his best imitator. He was born 560 B. C. Sappho, 620 B. C., has been much calumniated. The German investigators say that she did not throw herself from the Leukadian rock for love of Phaon. The Greek comic dramatists introduced her on the stage in an unfavorable character. This, and a literal interpretation of her impassioned poetry, have given her a false reputation. She was a rich and respectable widow, with one child, to whom she wrote a charming little ode, which I shall copy; it is less familiar than the Odes to Aphrodite and The Beloved.

> " I have a child, a lovely one,
> In beauty like the golden sun,
> Or like sweet flowers of earliest bloom,
> And Cleis is her name; for whom
> I Lydia's treasures, were they mine,
> Would glad resign."

But Pindar's lyrics are different. They were written to celebrate the victor at those four famous games which were the great national festivals of Greece. There were chariot-races, and athletic games on foot, and contests in music. The victor was crowned before assembled Greece, but with a wreath of leaves only. The heralds proclaimed his name, that of his father, and his city. When he returned to his city, a singing and dancing procession of his fellow-citizens met him, and a breach was made in the walls, through which he

entered; he was considered to have bestowed enduring
honor upon the state. These Odes of Pindar were
sung by a chorus in these processions; but they are not
religious hymns: they are exulting songs of triumph,
and even through a translation their lofty music stirs
one's blood. It is not that they touch the heart, but
they awaken a high enthusiasm and a proud love of
country. At first reading they are hard to understand,
because so disconnected. They begin with an invoca-
tion to some god: this is sincere and deeply felt; for
Pindar was a religious man, and meant what he wrote.
Then mythological stories are dragged in. In Pindar's
time, belief in the gods and heroes had not died out.
He regarded the victory as the necessary result of the
whole previous life of the victor and his ancestors;
because in Greece man was regarded not so much as an
individual as a part of his family or state: so Pindar
traced the good qualities which gained the victory, back
through his ancestors, to some hero of ancient Greece.
Or if the man came from the lower ranks, and had no
ancestors, he compared his good traits to those shown
by the ancient heroes, and thus made a relationship of
character instead of blood. Then again the thread
seems to be lost by moral reflections and precepts; but
these are meant to induce others to copy the virtues
of the victor, because good deeds will be rewarded
and bad ones punished in a future existence. This
is so familiar a thought to us that we hardly realize how
original it is in Pindar. Here is the greatest merit and
highest praise of this lofty poet. Instead of the resistless fate that runs through Greek mythology and poetry,
he teaches a sovereign law of right and wrong over all.

He says, "King of all mortal and immortal things, Law establishes with an omnipotent hand the absolute power of justice." Villemain says, if he sung the praises of kings, it was because they represented to his mind that idea of law and order and justice which was his highest ideal; not because they were rich and powerful.

His life is interesting too. He was born at Thebes, 518 B. C. He is the sole representative of Doric literature: what we call, rather vaguely, Greek literature includes only that of Ionia, Athens, and, later, of Alexandria. He was educated to be a musician. He wrote hymns to the gods, and funeral odes, but only his triumphal odes have been preserved. These made him venerated throughout all Greece. A portion of the people's first-fruits was laid aside for his support; an iron chair for him was erected in the very temple of Phoibos Apollo. He was courted by the rulers and people of other lands: wherever the Greek language was known he received rich gifts and heart-felt homage. In later times, when Thebes was captured by a foreign foe, the house which he had inhabited was twice spared by the conquerors. In one of his odes he praised Athens so much that his own city, Thebes, became jealous, and ordered him to pay a fine of ten thousand drachmas. The Athenians paid back double the sum, and erected a statue to him in Athens beside. Poets were royally treated in those days. The finest odes are, to my mind, the 1st, 2d, and 12th Olympic; the 1st and 4th Pythian; the 7th Nemean; and the 3d and 8th Isthmian. Their perfect music gives them a charm even in these later days when their thoughts seem so remote. The religious feeling of Pindar can never cease to make us admire and wonder, yet I doubt if that would cause him to be read without the matchless charm of his style. Matthew Arnold quotes him and his best imitator, Gray, as examples of the power of mere style to thrill us. Gray's Ode on the Progress of Poesy was suggested by the 1st Pythian.

The Greek ode leads directly up to the Greek drama; for scholars agree that it is only a development of the singing and dancing chorus so typical of Greece, in which the ode was sung by many individuals, instead of one. One writer says: " Greek drama sprang from the worship of Dionysos (Bacchus), in all probability the indigenous religion of the country, and, as it gathered development, absorbed the creeds of all the other tribes, till the very form of tragedy, as it existed in the days of Aischylos, had a deeply religious and ethical signification." Then there was a dialogue between the chorus; that is, it became antiphonal. Then one actor was introduced. Then Aischylos, 521 B. C., took a great step, and is therefore called the founder of the drama. He introduced two actors upon the stage at once, who spoke in prose, and reduced the importance of the chorus. It sung when one actor left the stage; but it became usually a listener to the dialogue, or an intermediary between the actors and the audience, a running commentary. It is supposed to express the real sentiments of the author. It is sometimes an echo; and when the situations are tragic, the wails and groans of the chorus are very effective. It is only fair to say, that, while the nation was still full of belief and patriotism, the choruses had noble thoughts, expressed in grand lyric poetry. Aischylos was a contemporary of Pindar. Some of his choruses are as religious and patriotic as Pindar's odes. Also the chorus uttered reflections: sometimes it is very *naïve;* its reflections being full of worldly wisdom, and its anxiety to keep on the winning side very apparent.

Any national, self-developed growth has a certain interest which it can never lose; but it is incomprehensible that any one who can read Shakespeare can for a moment suggest the Greek drama as a model to be copied. The blind reverence, the extravagant admiration, the devotion of a lifetime, which these plays have received, are simply amazing. It must have been caused by the charm of form, by the resounding poetry of their choruses; and this no translation can adequately render. They resemble our idea of poems far more than of plays; and to understand them we must put away every association with the word drama which we have in our modern minds. The theatre was utterly different. A vast space was enclosed, and a stage built with seats rising from it in the shape of a semicircle; a stage not deep like ours, but broad and shallow, so that the actors grouped themselves like a bas-relief, like statues; all this in the open air. Imagine to yourselves the blue and sunny sky of Athens above, the white marble temples gleaming through the olive groves in the distance; and on the stage figures which seemed more than human, pacing with a slow and stately step, speaking in a solemn and measured voice, with a distinct rhythm, which we should irreverently call sing-song. There was a reason for this: the Greeks did not aim at fidelity to real life; their object was the ideal life. They did not wish to draw upon the sympathy of the audience, so much as upon their religious feeling. Aischylos and Sophokles really wished to make the drama a religious teacher. To this end it was necessary to merge the individuality of the actor: a mask increased the volume of his voice; a cothurnus gave him height; padding gave him size, and the monotone in which he spoke, solemnity. Of course, he would be obliged to move slowly, so that all action on the stage was impossible. It took place behind a scene, and was described in long, tedious speeches. There was no gradual development of character as with us. The people in the play had no mental struggles, they immediately proceeded to act. A critic says: "Tragic representation was divorced from every-day life: so delineation of mental conflict became impossible, and the dialogue was retrospective." The plays were not divided into acts, but went on in one unbroken stream of song from the chorus and prose from the actors. This was because the unities must be observed, of time, place, and action. The time must not exceed a few hours; the place must be always the same; the action must be performed by one set of characters alone, while in our plays there are often two or three plots, each with its own set of characters. There was no plot: if any difficulty came up, it was not removed by the energy and wit of the characters, but a divinity from Olympos came down, and put an end to it by his supernatural powers. The Greek drama deals only with kings and heroes; the lower classes are never distinctly drawn, or clearly individualized. This may be because they are more conspicuous examples of that idea of retribution which is the key-note of the drama.

"The prevailing idea of the Greek religion was harmony," one critic says : " an act wrought in violation of this harmony was invariably followed by retribution ; the gods became simply the instruments of revenge." This idea of a dark and dreadful fate runs through all the plays. It hangs over some family, — the gods themselves cannot avert it; but the sins of the fathers are visited upon the innocent children ; they struggle in vain against this relentless destiny. One play did not close the theme ; there were usually three, called a trilogy, continuing the same subject, or the fortunes of the same family. They never mix tragic scenes with comic, or every-day life scenes, as we do : one dreary monotony of gloom runs through the whole play. It is plain, therefore, how very simple and undramatic they appear to a modern mind. The stories are simply horrible ; they were drawn from those ballads which preceded the Iliad and the Odyssey, and which are lost to us. They are told over and over again by the three great dramatic poets, and the same characters reappear in the three different authors. In fact, they are so horrible that they cease to be natural ; they seem taken out of the range of all human interest.

But here again the new science of comparative mythology comes to our relief, and enables us to give to these sickening stories a different tone. Of course, at the close of one short chapter, I cannot examine every play in detail ; but we will take up the only trilogy of the vast, vague, sombre Aischylos which remains to us. It tells the fortunes of the house of Pelops, sometimes called the house of Atreus. Agamemnon, a descendant of Pelops, returns from the siege of Troy. He is wel-

comed by his wife, Klytaimnestra, and enters his palace
with her. He has brought back with him as a captive the
Trojan maiden Kassandre, who has the gift of prophecy.
As he disappears in the palace, Kassandre bursts into
wails of woe. She describes in magnificent poetry the
awful deeds of the Atreidai in the past. Tantalos and
Thyestes had both cut up their children, roasted them,
and served them at table, where they had been eaten.
Thyestes unconsciously had eaten up his own son. The
mother committed suicide; and Thyestes ran away
with his brother's wife. Then the prophetess proclaims
what is even now going on in this house of blood;
Klytaimnestra is murdering Agamemnon in his bath;
and in a moment Klytaimnestra herself appears, and
proudly justifies the awful deed, because Agamemnon
had killed his own daughter, the lovely Iphigeneia.
Then she marries her husband's cousin Aigisthos, who
had aided in the murder. In the second play, Orestes,
the young son of Klytaimnestra, returns from a distant land, whither he had been banished; murders his
mother and Aigisthos; but he is haunted by the awful
Furies with gory locks, and in the third play he seeks
the temple of Apollo. There by rites of expiation he
is purified, absolved, and the curse is lifted from the
house; which seems a very insufficient atonement. But
we shall be much more interested in this unnatural tale
when we learn that Tantalos and Thyestes are only the
sun, which dries up with its heat the fruits of the earth.
Agamemnon again is the sun, who had killed the dawn,
Iphigeneia; he in turn is killed by the darkness as he
sinks into the water. Orestes also is the sun, again
coming back from the west into the east. He is one

of those heroes who travel back to regain a rightful heritage. He murders his mother, the dark night. He is pursued by the Erinnys; now this word comes from the Sanskrit Saranyu, the dawn which creeps along the sky: they are therefore the light which sees and knows everything. Later in the development, they become avengers, but when appeased by rites of penance and expiation, they are gentle and kind; then they are the Eumenides, the gentle twilight.

The idea of fate was probably derived from the resistless course of nature, the Kosmos; or from time, which seems hurried on by a power beyond itself. The thought often occurs to a modern mind even, for nature seems bound by stern necessity now as then. It comes out very strongly in the tale of the house of Labdakos. We will take the account which is given in Sophokles's sweet and polished dramas. They are more interesting to most people than those of Aischylos; the speeches are shorter, there is more dialogue, — he introduced three actors on the stage at one time. The choruses are exquisitely poetical, and perfect in form, and have a religious spirit. They teach that the sins of the individual in addition to the curse of race brought punishment; and that the great invisible powers will finally do justice. The first play is Oidipous, the king of Thebes. He came a stranger to Thebes, and found the city in despair. A dreadful monster called the Sphinx sat on a cliff, near the city, and shut up all access to the springs of water. She roared and muttered a riddle, and could only be overcome by whoever could solve the riddle. Oidipous solved it; the Sphinx threw herself from the cliffs, and the imprisoned waters gushed forth. The queen's husband had just been killed, so he married the queen, Iokasta. Now it had been foretold long before to the queen and king, Laios, that their son should destroy his father; so the babe had been exposed to die on the side of a mountain. One day Laios was driving in his chariot, when he was met and killed by a youthful stranger. And by and by it comes out that Oidipous was this youthful stranger; still more, that he was the babe who had been exposed on a mountain, nourished and brought up by a kind shepherd. Horror-stricken, Oidipous discovers that he has married his own mother. He puts out his eyes; she commits suicide. In the second play, Oidipous wanders to Kolonos, accompanied by the loveliest heroine of Greek literature, Antigone, his daughter. There he dies; but he passes away in a storm, and unseen by mortal eyes. In the play of Antigone, the sweet and noble heroine is condemned to die, because she persists in giving burial to the body of her brother. She bids farewell to the light and life, and then the " last lone scion of a kingly race," she is dragged away to die in a cave; so she expiates the curse, and dies through her own self-sacrificing heroism. The explanation becomes plainly perceptible. The babe exposed to die on a mountain is the same as Feridun and Cyrus, the sun rising behind a mountain. The Sphinx is of course the drought; its mutterings, the rumbling of the thunder, like Vritra in the Rig Veda; the waters are set free, the rain comes down, as the sun pierces the dark clouds. Laios, his father, is the night; Iokasta, his mother, is the dawn. Like other solar heroes, Oidipous has a mysterious death; in storm and thunder he passes away, —

the sun setting amid storm and thunder. Antigone is the twilight, the pale light which springs up opposite the setting sun ; a cave always means the darkness : here the twilight dies away in the darkness.

Philoktetes is really a most beautiful poem ; it is nearer to a modern standard, because it has one complex character, Neoptolemos, and mental struggle, and so it is interesting : but it deviates from the typical Greek drama. When Herakles lay dying, he gave his unerring bow and poisoned arrows to Philoktetes, whom he loved. Philoktetes sailed for Troy with seven ships of his own. Landing at an island, he rashly entered the sacred ground of a nymph, and was bitten by a serpent. The stench of the wound and his groans annoyed the Greek chieftains, and they sent him to a lonely island, and left him alone in a cave. After nine years it was foretold that Troy could not be taken without Philoktetes's poisoned arrows. So Odysseus and Neoptolemos, son of Achilleus, were sent to seek him. They deceive him with fair words, and get away his bow, and seek to carry him by guile to Troy. Then Neoptolemos repents, gives him back his bow, and promises to carry him to his old home, knowing that, nevertheless, Troy cannot be conquered without him. In all this perplexity Herakles, a deity, descends, and induces Philoktetes to go to Troy of his own free will. Thus all ends well, and Neoptolemos wins our highest admiration. Now, this is a very interesting manifesta- tion of the solar myth. Philoktetes is bitten by the snake of darkness. During the long night he suffers ; but since he is the sunlight, Troy, the dark power, cannot be conquered till he returns and shoots his arrows of light. The two chieftains who seek him are also solar powers. They too must aid, or Troy cannot fall. Philoktetes dwells in a cave, for darkness has overcome the bright sun. It is supposed that Sophokles was influenced in composing this drama, so different from his others, by the new and rising genius Euripides, and the tone he introduced.

Aischylos, born 521 B. C., fought against the Persians in the battles of Marathon and Salamis. Sophokles, 495 B. C., when sixteen years old, led the chorus which celebrated these victories, and in middle age became a general of the Athenian army. But Euripides, 480 B. C., studied with the Sophists, and learned to argue on both sides of the same question. Naturally his plays would have a different spirit. He seems prosaic and argumentative, after the vague grandeur of Aischylos and the finished harmony of Sophokles. His characters are not so noble as theirs, but he has his own good points. There are reality and pathos in his plays; they are interesting too; they have more development of character and dramatic action; three or four actors are introduced upon the stage at one time. But this is directly opposed to the legitimate Greek drama, and critics say that he was not sufficiently imbued with poetry to enable his chorus to take its proper position, and fill out the action by appropriate illustrations. In Aischylos and Sophokles the choruses and the tragedy were perfectly connected; in Euripides they are not, although they are occasionally poetical and beautiful. There are many plays, and they are very unequal. It is becoming the fashion to praise them. One critic says, " He was the first to make his characters play a sustained dramatic part." And in spite of all critical objections, his plays go straight to the heart. But when we demand from him faith and reverence towards the invisible powers, and in the final triumph of justice, we feel his limitations. He said plainly, that, if the gods are righteous, the stories of the poets are wretched falsehoods ; if the stories of the poets are true, and the gods do such things as the poets ascribe to them, they are not gods at all. He is intensely sceptical, and the gods in his plays are as jealous and tyrannical and spiteful as human kings. They argue and reason like sophists.

Of the plays, the Iphigencia in Aulis is most complex and interesting, with dramatic action and a most pathetic and noble heroine. You have already learned from comparative mythology what she is. Euripides is remarkable for his noble and self-sacrificing women. We find another of them in the Alkestis. It is like a modern play : it has a comic vein and every-day life scenes. We will take up this best known and loveliest of his plays, the Alkestis, and look at the comparative mythology to be found in it. Admetos, the king of Thessaly, is dying of a fever. Apollo, remembering some kindness shown by Admetos to him, says that he may recover if some one will die in his stead. His aged father and mother refuse his request; but his sweet wife, Alkestis, says that she will willingly die that he may live ; and she expires. While the whole family, plunged in grief, are celebrating her funeral rites, Herakles arrives. Admetos entertains him, hospitably trying to conceal his grief. But some servant tells the whole story to Herakles, and he is so much pleased with Admetos's hospitality under such trying circumstances that he goes down to the kingdom of Hades, and brings back Alkestis. But what can be said for that poor creature, Admetos? Simply that he is a solar myth, the sun; and Alkestis is the beautiful twilight, who must die if he is to live again, and gladden the world with his light. She must die too, and be carried away by the dark night, if she is to live again herself, and stand before her husband in her ancient beauty; for she is also the dawn, brought back from the apparent death of darkness and night by the brave Herakles, the triumphant sun. The story must be a primitive Aryan myth, for it is found with a little variation in the Maha Bharata, where Yima carries away the husband to die, and the wife, Savitri, follows him until he restores her husband to her, on her promising to die in his stead. This is the strongest proof of its mythical element.

14

CHAPTER VII.

GREEK PHILOSOPHY AND HISTORY.

THE gods of the poets and dramatists had ceased to satisfy the thoughtful minds of Greece, and the philosophers had long been endeavoring to build up gods for the people. Buddha in India, before the rise of the second school of philosophers in Greece, the Eleatics, had pronounced all metaphysical discussion to be vain and useless: Goethe says, "Man is not born to solve the mysteries of existence." Mr. Lewes, in his history of philosophy, acknowledges that human reason alone cannot solve the problems of metaphysics. But I hope it is not presumptuous to try to get a few distinct ideas about the principal steps the Greeks took in their struggles towards clearness and precision in these matters.

The philosophy of Greece ruled the ancient world and Europe for centuries; yet it is neither more original nor more profound than the Sanskrit metaphysics, which arose before it and existed contemporaneously, though only made known to us within the last fifty years. The Greeks unconsciously went over the same ground, and the Germans are going over it in our day, and the questions are still unsettled. I want particularly to express that we moderns divide philosophy into two branches, and we are correct in doing so: metaphysics, or the philosophy of the mind; physics, or science, the philosophy of external nature. But the Greeks made no such division. It is curious that their first speculations belong to what we very properly call physics. The first problem which the Greeks sought to solve was the origin of the world and of mankind. Thales of Miletos, 600 B. C., is the father of Greek philosophy, and he taught that water is the beginning of all things. Some one has said: "The schoolboy wonders why this should be called the beginning of philosophy. Because it was the first bold denial that the gods had made the world, the first open protest against the religion of the crowd. It had to be repeated again and again before the Greeks could be convinced that such thinkers as Herakleitos and Xenophanes had as good a right to speak of the gods as Homer and the itinerant singers." The next philosopher taught that air is the beginning of all things, and these philosophers wrote in poetry, in hexameter metre. Herakleitos declared that religion is a disease arising from the sick heart of man (600 B. C.); which was repeated by the German Feuerbach, when he said that "religion is a radical evil inherent in mankind." Herakleitos was the first Greek to write in prose; he said that fire is the beginning. Then another proclaimed the atomic theory, which is so fashionable to-day, — that an innumerable quantity of the smallest atoms is the beginning. But Anaxagoras said that there was something more than matter, there was mind, in this creation: so he was the first to recognize a Supreme Intelligence. So they struggled on: discovered independently the sun-dial, the geographical map; wrote books on astronomy, geometry, and music (music being an important part of their worship). Then came the theory that the beginning is a kind of chaotic matter, called Infinite Substance, containing within itself a motive power. Then Pythagoras, a most interesting character, taught that this Infinite Substance is one, therefore number is the beginning.

Finally Xenophanes, a rhapsodist who wandered over many lands uttering the thought that was in him, in wild, vague poetry proclaimed that this one of Pythagoras was God, self-existent and intelligent; that he was far above the gods of the poets, whom Xenophanes denounced. His wild and turbulent verse was developed by others into a system of what we very properly call metaphysics. It belongs to the idealist school named the Eleatic, from the city of Elea. Then followed arguments against this and the realist, or Ionic school, by the Sophists. They argued equally well on both sides, and taught that we really know nothing, and that there is no such thing as right or wrong by nature, only by the customs of society. Mr. Lewes says: "While the brilliant but dangerous Sophists were winning money and renown by protesting against metaphysics and teaching the word-juggling which they called disputation, and the impassioned insincerity they called oratory, there suddenly appeared among them a strange antagonist. He made truth his soul's mistress, and with patient labor and untiring energy did his large wise soul toil after communion with her."

Sokrates was born 469 B. C. His early studies were devoted to science, but left him unsatisfied. He fought in three battles, and served in the Senate before he

begun to teach, which was about the middle of his
career. He did not give lectures, nor write books; he
only argued. "He would seize on a person whom he
met in his walks, and by searching argument and
homely illustration constrain him into contact with the
truth." His rules were: "Before speaking or acting,
know what you propose. If you speak, know what
you speak; if you believe, know what you believe.
Ascertain what your own mind in verity is, and be
that." His method was to ask questions until the antagonist had accurately defined what he thought; from
these definitions Sokrates reasoned to a conclusion.
He used very homely illustrations from every-day life.
In a history of philosophy he would be said to have
invented, first, abstract definitions; second, inductive
reasoning; and he owes his position in metaphysics
wholly to this invention of a method. But his peculiar
work lay elsewhere. He turned away from metaphysics to morals, and invented what we call moral
philosophy, — the distinctions between right and wrong.
Before Sokrates, the religion of the Greeks consisted
in offering sacrifices to each particular god: to propitiate his anger or win his favor was the only needful
thing. But Sokrates insisted that our conduct, our
own actions, were the necessary things to make us
happy here or in the future life. To the Athenians,
mad in the pursuits of luxury or ambition, he proclaimed that these would be their ruin; that truth,
wisdom, and temperance were the only treasures. No
wonder that the Athenians hated the man who so boldly
rebuked them. He condemned the gods of the poets,
and taught that there was one God. Now, this was the

heresy of that day; so he was accused of corrupting the youth of Athens, and made to drink poison. " His heroic death, his moral teachings, and his invention of a method in metaphysics, are his titles to fame." Mr. Lewes says. He taught and believed that, on critical occasions, he was guided by a dæmon, who always accompanied him. Probably he was a very religious man, and believed in spiritual communications.

Plato (B. c. 429) is the culminating point of all Greek philosophy : its various and conflicting tendencies were harmonized in his mighty mind. The two schools met in him. This is an interesting summing up of them : —

THE ELEATIC, OR IDEALIST.	PLATO.	THE IONIC, OR REALIST.
The One.	The One in all.	The All.
Unity.	Unity and Variety.	Variety.
Being.	Life.	Motion.
Pantheism.	Divine in Nature.	Naturalism.
Substance.	Substance and Manifestation.	Phenomena.

Plato's fame is world-wide; but some of the ideas about him are erroneous. I was amazed to find that Plato is not eloquent, his style not poetical. It is simply the most exact definition of what you think; then the closest reasoning, step by step. " His writings are dialogues where each character states his opinions, which are refuted with sarcasm or good-natured banter." His illustrations are drawn from familiar life, — are very homely; the dialogues are highly dramatic, therefore, and full of animation, and bring the manners of Athens before us. Lewes says : " In truth, Plato is a very difficult and somewhat repulsive writer. He is an inveterate dialectician, a severe and abstract thinker, a great quibbler. His metaphysics would frighten away any but the most determined student; but he is occasionally eloquent and poetical." His descriptions of natural scenery in his first work, the Phaidros, are beautiful : in that the soul is compared to " a chariot, with a pair of winged horses and a driver. In the souls of the gods, the horses and driver are entirely good ; in other souls, only partially so, — one horse excellent, the other vicious. So the business of the driver is difficult and troublesome." His education was excellent. In gymnastics he was sufficiently skilled to contend in the Pythian and Isthmian games. He first studied poetry; next. philosophy with Sokrates, whom he attended through his trial till his death. Then he travelled, and returned to Athens to found the Academe in the olive groves near Athens. Plato based his argument for immortality upon the theory that ideas are eternal. Humanity has in it. mingled with much that is evil, the remnants of another and better nature. So he said that all our ideas are but reminiscences of another existence, — an existence of which we had lost all memory and almost all the glory ; that the soul had lived in another sphere, pure and undefiled ; that in the transition it had lost much of its higher nature, and the little left was tarnished by union with the body and contact with this world. " But the immortal soul is stung with resistless longings for the skies, and solaced only by the reminiscences of that former state." Wordsworth has this very idea in his Ode to Immortality ; and Goethe says, " The soul of man is highly endowed on its arrival, and we by no means learn everything. We bring much with us." Sokrates be-

lieved and taught the immortality of the soul, but Plato
"established the doctrine by solid arguments." We
cannot take Plato for a typical heathen; for he also
taught the existence of one God, with attributes much
like those we believe in. He made this idea the starting-
point of his whole system. He supported it by the
favorite modern doctrine that God is proved to exist
by the need we feel for him, by the very affinity to his
nature which stirs within our own souls. He first used
the inductive method of Sokrates; but his later discoveries were made by the deductive method, which
assumes a theory to be true, and proves it afterwards.
Plato, too, tried to make men better; but he utterly
ignored their instincts and their passions. He said, if
people did wrong, it was only because they did not
know what was right. We must admire his pure, clear
intellect, and his spiritual insight; but there is an unpleasant side to him. He is terribly wanting in humanity. Mr. Lewes says: "The thinker predominated
over the man. He was intensely melancholy; he had
many admirers, but no friends. His Republic, where
he paints his ideal of society, is not suited to human
beings, only to logicians." The Republic taught that
wives, children, and property should be held in common: they belonged to the state; and children should
be taken from their parents, and educated by the state.
He banished all poets, because they enervated the soul
and taught a life of pleasure: they also told fictions
about the gods. Here you see his dissatisfaction with
the Greek gods. He banished all musicians who were
plaintive and harmonious: only the Dorian music,
which was warlike, or the Phrygian, which was calm,

was admitted.   The most celebrated and interesting dialogue is the Phaidon, on the immortality of the soul. The thoughts are all Plato's, the characters being simply mouthpieces for him, *dramatis personæ.* This is a little confusing, when one takes up Plato for the first time. I have not alluded to his metaphysics; for its vast, vague speculations are difficult to comprehend. Our chief interest is in the man who proved one God, and immortality. Plato's position has been admirably defined as follows : —

"The belief in immortality was almost unknown to the Greek religion. The Iranians founded on their ethical dualism a positive and intelligible theory of immortality; a theory which, passing first into Judaism, then into Christianity, has played so great a part in the religious history of the world. The Teutonic tribes so conceived the future as to reduce death to a 'home-going,' — 'a return to the Father.' The Kelts believed in a metempsychosis which made the future life as active as the present. The Hindu Aryans evolved from their early naturalism a religion whose distinctive characteristic was the continued existence of the transmigrating soul. The causes of this peculiarity in the religious development of Greece are, first, the national mythology crystallized into permanent form before the national mind attained to full religious consciousness ; second, religious thought did not develop within, but without, this mythology. The functions of religion passed in Greece to poetry and philosophy. The poets became the true priests of Greece, embodying, in epic or ode or tragedy, the ideas of moral law and order, and judgment. The philosophers became her true prophets, revealing mind in nature, — the supreme Good within, above, and before man. But the words God and Creator were not to the Greek synonymous, as to the Hebrew. Plato was the true prophet of this belief to the Greeks."

When we come to Aristotle, 384 B. C., we are in a different world.   He wrote metaphysics, and for centuries it divided the world with that of Plato.   It has been said that every man is born a disciple of Plato or of Aristotle, such opposite types do they represent. But we do not now value Aristotle for his metaphysics. He may justly bear the proud title of Father of Science. (The Sanskrit scientific writings are valuable ; but they have not yet exercised any influence over the world.) He observed and wrote down the facts of external nature.   Alexander was his friend, as well as pupil ; and during all his campaigns in Asia he sent to Aristotle the birds, plants, and animals of different countries. Besides, he gave Aristotle a sum of money equal to a million dollars of our money to expend upon his " History of Animals and Parts of Animals," and several of the most astonishing discoveries of modern naturalists have since been found distinctly described by Aristotle. Even on subtle questions in natural history, scientists are often forced to come back to Aristotle's classifications.   His discoveries were wonderful, and made by the inductive method ; in which the facts are carefully collected and studied, then a theory is reasoned out, based upon these facts ; it was the method invented by Sokrates, abandoned by Plato, perfected by Aristotle. Naturally, therefore, he would consider reasoning, or logic, to lie at the foundation of all knowledge.   He invented logic, and considered it the fundamental science.   He also invented grammar ; and the categories or principles, the fundamental forms of thought, for these two sciences, have never been superseded.   Mr. Lewes thinks him " the greatest intellect of antiquity ;

at once comprehensive and subtile patient, receptive, and original." He is not an interesting writer. Mr. Maurice says: " A student passing from the works of Plato to those of Aristotle is struck with the entire absence of that dramatic form, those living human beings, with whom he has been familiar. But there is ample compensation in the precision and dignity of the style." He wrote an astonishing number of books, three fourths of which have been lost. In another chapter, I shall speak of the curious path by which the remaining books reached us. He lectured whilst walking up and down a shady grove, attended by his eager listeners : so his school at Athens was called the Peripatetic, or walking school. His father was a rich and eminent physician of Stagira ; but Aristotle came to Athens when only seventeen, that he might study with Plato. He was rich enough to buy books, which was a great advantage ; and before making up his own opinions he faithfully studied those of others.

We cannot leave Greek metaphysics without speaking of two other forms whose names are well known to us, although both views have been often misunderstood. Epikouros was born in the decay of Grecian glory, 342 B. C., and founded a school at Athens. He taught in a garden, and made a system of his own. He said the object of philosophy was not to learn the truth, but simply to learn how to live. Philosophy was the power by which reason conducted men to happiness, and happiness was the object of life. Happiness consisted in avoiding pain, so it is not the enjoyment of the present moment only that we must seek, but the enjoyment of the whole life. Therefore you must be temperate to-day if you would be comfortable to-morrow. But the pleasures of the body are less than those of the soul; so you must be virtuous if you would be happy, because virtue gives more lasting enjoyment than vice. This does not seem a very elevated motive to appeal to, yet Epikouros led a simple and modest life, and was always poor and temperate. He despised metaphysics, because he considered that they were useless and contributed nothing to happiness. But we cannot greatly admire a goodness so founded upon self-interest and prudence; and his doctrine possessed one fatal error. He taught "that a total secession from public and civil business was the fundamental principle of a wisely regulated mode of life." In a state like Athens, where every citizen had once considered it his proud privilege to discuss public affairs, to criticise the generals of the army, — where the actual labor was performed by slaves, and the free citizens passed most of their day in talking, — where the life was spent out of doors, and the philosophers taught in a grove or in the market-place walking about among the people, — the change was radical. If they did not discuss government and politics, they gave up the privilege of freemen, and allowed themselves to be governed by demagogues. Such indifference would ruin any country, and the Stoics endeavored to recall the Greeks. Mr. Lewes says, "Greece was falling to decay, and there was nothing to counteract scepticism, indifference, and Epicurean softness, except the magnificent but vague works of Plato, or the vast but abstruse system of Aristotle."

Alarmed at the scepticism which inevitably followed metaphysics, Zeno, the Stoic, fixed his mind also upon the art of living; but he made virtue, and not happiness, to be the object of life; and virtue was not in a life of contemplation and speculation, but of activity. "O Plato, man was not made for speculation only; wisdom is not his only pursuit! O Epikouros, man is not made for pleasure alone; he was made to do somewhat, and to be somewhat. Philosophy is a means, pleasure may be a means; but the aim is to lead a virtuous life." Now this is a noble and energetic doctrine: it recalls the morals of Sokrates, the manly energy of the early days of the Greek history; but it assumes that man is all intellect. The pleasures and pains of the body are not to be tolerated; they are to be absolutely despised. It is man's duty to surmount his passions and his senses, that he may be free, active, virtuous; only the pains and pleasures of the intellect are worthy to occupy man. There is something noble in this doctrine: as a reaction against the low state of society it accomplished something, the noblest Greeks and Romans became Stoics: but it is a one-sided doctrine, and hardens and deadens the heart. The struggle was vain, moreover, and scepticism settled down over the world.

Of the Aryan races, the Greeks may be said to have invented history; for the Hindus did not write it at all, the Persians not until very much later. The transcendent ability of the Greek historians has rendered them the models of the civilized world for more than two thousand years. The philosophical school in history has outgrown them; but for a simple recital of actual facts, they are still unsurpassed. The first in time is the delightful Herodotos; one is tempted to call him the greatest. He used to be called the Father of Lies; but late discoveries have proved that his stories mostly are true. He was born 484 B.C. He travelled far, into Egypt and Persia. He read his books which describe the Persian wars before the assembled Greeks at the Olympic Games. What an inspiring audience for the historian! What admiring love the people must have bestowed upon the man who could so well describe their national glories! His work is a faithful chronicle of what he saw; very long-winded, and full of episodes and amusing gossip. He must be hard to translate, because the connection is obscure. In the middle of one story, an episode is suggested to him by a name; so he rambles off, and long after returns to the original thread. But everything seems real; his personages live and breathe, and seem like our own acquaintances: we feel sure that they must be on our visiting list. There is a simplicity and *naïveté* in the early writings of a literature which are more charming than all its later glories. Herodotos is like Homer, childlike, artless, and real; and these qualities are so rare that we know how to value them when we find them. He does not philosophize about causes, or argue about principles: he simply tells what he has seen with the confidence of a child, who is sure that you will be interested. It is pleasant to find in him the stories we have always known; such as the visit of Solon to Kroisos; the ring of Polykrates; the birth, life, and death of Cyrus the Great; the battles of Salamis and Thermopylai. His account of Xerxes is extremely interesting, delightfully told, with little *naïve* touches of personal gossip. He was among the first to use prose; his is a prose epic. Macaulay declares that he is and ever will be charming; and Taine speaks of "les périodes enfantines d'Hérodote."

There is no more enchantment when you come to the pages of Thoukydides, 471 B. C.   He is reasonable and calm and unimpassioned.   The opening of his history is very dignified and simple :   " Thoukydides, the Athenian, has written the story of the war between the Peloponnesians and the Athenians."   And with a certain consciousness of power and self-respect he says : —

" My relation, because quite clear of fable, may prove less delightful to the ear ; but it will afford sufficient scope to those who love a sincere account of past transactions, — of such as in the ordinary vicissitudes of human affairs may occur again, or at least be resembled ; I give it to the public as an everlasting possession, and not as a contentious instrument of temporary applause."

His expectations have been justified : his work has indeed been " an everlasting possession " ; for it is history that he gives us, — a recital of actual facts.   Even more, like a modern historian, he sifts his information ; he does not blindly swallow it, like the delightful Herodotos ; and he endeavors to seek out the causes of the events.   We must not expect to find him as critical and philosophical as modern historians ; but it was a very great step that he should have attempted to be either, for he had no predecessor to invent a method, or even teach him how to use prose ; he is so utterly unlike Herodotos that he cannot have been modelled upon him. There is a tradition that, when he was very young, he heard Herodotos read aloud his history of the Persian war, at the Olympic games, and wept because he could not write history.   Some authorities doubt the tradition. Dr. Arnold speaks of the " simple sweetness of Herodotos, the pithy conciseness of Thoukydides."   His subject put him at a disadvantage with Herodotos. The fight of Athens and Sparta for power during twenty-seven years, which he describes, is far less interesting in itself than that struggle of united Greece against the Persian invaders which Herodotos makes real to us. The most interesting part of Thoukydides is the tale of the Athenian expedition against Syrakousai in Sicily, told in the sixth and seventh books. Its defeat caused the decline and fall of Athens ; yet Thoukydides is wonderfully impartial, and praises or blames friend and foe alike. His account of the night attack where " Greek met Greek," when the Spartan allies of the Syrakousans fought against the Athenians, is vivid ; in his description of the last naval battle between the Greeks and Syrakousans he shows some excitement ; but when he relates the parting between the retreating Greeks and their dying whom they left behind, or when he tells of the sufferings of the Greeks sold as slaves, he writes clearly indeed, but in the most cold-blooded manner. Thoukydides is dull, except in those brilliant orations which he puts into the mouths of his characters. The most beautiful of these is an extract from Pericles's funeral oration in commemoration of those who had fallen in battle.

"They gave their lives for their country, and gained for themselves a glory that can never fade, a tomb that shall stand as a mark for ages. I do not mean that in which their bodies lie, but that in which their renown lives after them, to be remembered forever on every occasion of speech or action which calls it to mind. For the whole earth is the grave and monument of heroes: it is not the mere graving upon marble in their native land which sets forth their deeds ; but even in lands where they were strangers, there lives an unwritten record in every heart, felt though never embodied."

Thoukydides does not pretend that these speeches are genuine ; they were simply ornaments to the narrative ; so he argues on both sides of the same question. He studied rhetoric, the fashionable study of the time ; and these speeches give evidence of it : for they are the work of an advocate, not an enthusiastic believer. We do not read Thoukydides with delight, but we must acknowledge his great intellectual power in an unbroken field. Dr. Arnold speaks of "those brief touches of a master hand, by which Thoukydides has furnished matter of thought for twenty centuries."

Xenophon, 431 B. C., took up Greek history where Thoukydides left it, in the Hellenics. He wrote many books, — among them an account of Sokrates's conversations ; he was a pupil of Sokrates. His Kyropaideia is a life of Cyrus the Great of Persia : it is entirely different from the life which Herodotos gives ; this discrepancy, puzzling to youthful students who attack Greek literature, is reconciled by discovering that Xenophon's book is simply a treatise giving his views on education : it is in fact the first historical novel ; not true at all. The real Cyrus is found in Herodotos ; yet one cannot help hoping that the beautiful stories of Panthea and Abradatos, of Tigranes and the Armenian princess, may be true after all. The book by which Xenophon takes his own place as the third Greek historian is the Anabasis. This is an account of the march and return of ten thousand Greek mercenaries, who joined the younger Cyrus in his revolt against his brother and king. It was not, therefore, a patriotic expedition on either side ; and there is no lofty feeling to ennoble the physical sufferings. The expedition lasted

15

one year and three months. Xenophon, at first a mere follower, became at length the general who conducted the retreat. He shared every peril, and wrote his account afterwards. He describes the whole expedition in a very straightforward, matter-of-fact manner, without any comments, whether philosophical or enthusiastic. Only when the Greeks reach a hill-top from which they behold the sea, and cry out, "Thalatta!" does he show the slightest emotion. The story tells of physical sufferings, endured with courage and patience by the soldiers; and of wise, persuasive speeches, models of skilful oratory, made by their leader, Xenophon. By them he was wonderfully successful in governing the minds of his soldiery. The soldiers were pious according to their light: they offered sacrifices and sang the pæan before going into every battle : and when the wind blew very hard, they offered a sacrifice to the god of the wind, which soon after abated. The style of Xenophon is good, because so simple and unpretentious ; it is considered a model for every-day familiar Greek. His style is his strong point ; for Xenophon is not great, like Thoukydides, nor charming, like Herodotos. It is undoubtedly true that the reading of the Anabasis inspired Alexander the Great with his design of subjugating Greece, and conquering Persia, and thus changing the destinies of the world. While Cyrus the Younger failed, Alexander succeeded.

Among the very first writings of the Greeks were the laws of Lykourgos in Sparta. Mr. Fergusson says : " These are a characteristic effort of a truly Aryan race, and conferred on the people who invented them that power of self-government and that capacity for

republican institutions which gave the Spartans such
stability at home and such power abroad." At Athens
we find also a code of laws made by Solon, somewhere
near 600 b. c. The struggles of the small states which
composed Greece are so frequent, and the states are so
small, that it is difficult for an ordinary mind to keep
a clear recollection of them all. But when we realize
that they were owing to the very energy and individualism of the Aryan character, we are at once interested;
for we feel that the Greeks are our brothers. In the
second stage of every Aryan civilization, we find codes
of law, and political eloquence ; and they grew into great
perfection in Greece. Among the many statesmen and
orators who glorified Greece, we shall mention only
the greatest ; — Perikles, 495 b. c., as a statesman, because he gave his name to that astonishing literary
period which extended beyond his own actual life, when
Athens became the literary centre of Greece ; and
Demosthenes as an orator, 385 b. c., the last great
name of Greece as a nation. His strong orations are
still read and honored through the civilized world ;
but Philip and Alexander subjugated Greece in spite of
them. Demosthenes died in 322 b. c., one year later
than Alexander : the political and literary glories of
Greece perished with them. All that Greek literature
which has enslaved the mind of man is the product of
three hundred years, from Solon to Alexander. Henceforward Greece was but a province of the Macedonian
empire, its nationality gone. But its literary glory revived elsewhere.

In 332 b. c. Alexander the Great founded the city of
Alexandria in Egypt. A splendid court grew up there.

Greek was the language spoken. Literature was patronized and aided by every appliance which wealth and power and peace could furnish. There were libraries for poetry, which contained copies of all books. When the Athenians were starving, Ptolemy Philadelphus refused to send them food until they had given him copies of Aischylos, Sophokles, and Euripides; then, in addition to food, he sent them fifteen talents of gold. There were museums and perfect instruments for science: her scientific instruments and discoveries are the real goods of Alexandria. The mathematicians Euclid and Archimedes throw a glory around this last stronghold of Paganism. Science and metaphysics lived and grew in the atmosphere of a court; but grand poetry, earnest history, political eloquence, were dumb: freedom and virtue are necessary to them.

Not that there were no poets: there were many. The most original of them is Theokritos, 272 B. C. He charmed the pompous court by inventing the idyl, — that form of poetry which describes, from a spectator's point of view, the pleasures of a country life. And, since great ladies have always loved to play at shepherdesses, Theokritos was immensely admired. He used the Doric dialect instead of the court language; and this gives him a rustic sweetness and romantic simplicity, which may be the very perfection of art, but are far removed from the genuine simplicity of nature. Perhaps no Greek poet has been more copied than Theokritos; for the idyl, that very artificial style, was fashionable in Rome, and all over Europe after the Renaissance, though no one wrote it with the grace and tenderness of Theokritos, their master.

CHAPTER VIII.

COMPARATIVE MYTHOLOGY OF THE LATIN AND KELTIC LITERATURES.

WHEN we reach our Latin brethren, the beginnings are even more darkly hidden than in
India, Persia, Greece; for we cannot even find that
Turanian race whose remains exist elsewhere. Most
writers class the Etruscans as Turanians; but Mommsen, in his history of Rome, puts them positively into
the Aryan family. If the Etruscans be not Turanians,
there are none in Italy; but the question cannot be
regarded as settled. In all the other Aryan countries
are memorials of a primitive race, Turanians unquestionably; but Italy is singularly deficient in those
implements of stone or bone, those peculiarly formed
skeletons, which mark the primitive period. Mommsen
says there can be no doubt that the migration of the
Aryans into Italy took place by land: they came over
the Apennines; but how or when remains a mystery still.
The Romans, however, conquered all their brethren,
Aryans though they were, and remain the representatives of the Aryans in Italy.

They possessed some of the noblest characteristics of
their race, but are peculiarly wanting in others. The
spirituality of India, the gayety of Greece, are not natural traits of the Romans. They are a stern and serious
people; but they had a deep reverence for moral worth

in their early days, which reminds us of Persia. In the noblest Romans there were a manly energy, a stern simplicity, a passionate patriotism, which kindle our enthusiasm as we read of them. Their aim was to conquer nations abroad, and build up a powerful state at home. Their genius expressed itself in a practical manner: in roads, bridges, aqueducts; in laws for the protection of life and property. The farthest forests of Gaul and Britain were made accessible by Roman roads, and habitable by Roman laws.

Their gods are a reflection of their own minds, — useful and practical beings; narrow and prosaic, each with some official work to perform. The oldest of them show that the Romans were originally an agricultural people: " The gods are of the homeliest simplicity; sometimes venerable, sometimes ridiculous." The act of sowing becomes the god Saturnus; field labor becomes the goddess Ops; the ground, the god Tellus. The second gods to take shape were also brought into existence by the habits of Roman thought. Increase of riches was what the Roman desired; not only by flocks and herds, but afterwards by commerce and seafaring. So he prayed to Mercurius, the god of traffic; to Fortuna, the goddess of good luck; to Fides, the goddess of good faith and honesty in dealing. All these arose before contact with the Greeks. The double-headed Janus is the most original of their gods; as the sky of morning, he is the tutelary spirit of all beginnings. He first opened the day: next he opened all gates and doors, and was invoked therefore at the beginning of every act, — the god of all openings.

There were many gods: the ruler of them was Jupiter, that is, the Dyaus-pitar, whom they brought with them from their early Aryan home. No mythical tales have clustered around him, as in Greece ; but he takes up many different occupations. As Jupiter Pluvius, he is the heaven, giving rain ; one of Indra's characteristics, the reader will remember. As the father who protected the boundaries of a nation, he is Jupiter Terminus : his statue was set up at the termination of every Roman road, and was moved as the road extended : to carry the statue of the god Jupiter Terminus was one of the duties of every Roman army. There is a quaint and artless side to their religion when we know that there was also a Jupiter Pistor, whose business it was to take care of bakers ! Juno is simply the feminine form of Dyaus. The name was first Zeus, then Zenon ; the Latin deities Janus and Diana are the same word, and mean the sky of morning. Venus, the Latin goddess of love and the patron deity of the Romans, comes from the same root as our words venerate and winsome. Neptune, the god who dwells in the waters, is the same as the Greek Nereus. Pluto is a very respectable person. He is the same as the Greek Hades, or Ploutos, the dweller in the dark underworld ; the guardian of that hidden treasure, the light of day. Mars, their god of war and killing, who hurls the spear, comes from the root of the Maruts, the storm-winds of the Rig Veda.

The most interesting discovery is about the Latin Minerva. She comes from the same root as our word mind. It is therefore thought or wisdom : the piercing, penetrating power of the dawn, which sees and knows all. She can be easily identified with the Sanskrit

Ahana and the Greek Athene, dawn goddesses; for she has another Latin name, Matuta, the same root as the French *matin* and our matutinal. The Latins had another dawn goddess, Aurora; but she is less noble. She is the same root as Eos in Greek, Ushas in Sanskrit; also, as *aurum*, gold, and *urere*, to burn. This is the golden color of the dawn burning along the sky. The Latin god Vulcan, the fire, comes from the Sanskrit *ulka*, a firebrand. He reappears in Anglo-Saxon, where we shall trace him further.

But the noblest as well as the most important of the Latin deities was Vesta, the same as the Greek Hestia. Her shrine was the sanctuary of peace and honorable dealing. Men were obliged to keep the word which they had plighted on the altar of Vesta, where burned the sacred fire: for everything most sacred was associated with this fire. Each town had a hall where its chief men met, and the fire on this public hearth was never allowed to go out. When a colony started, it carried a portion of the sacred fire of Vesta with it, in order to keep up the bond of union with the parent state. Vesta was also the guardian of the family, as well as of the state, among the Romans. There was a household altar for each family, which could only be lighted by the head of the family. Our word family comes from altar, — *thymele* in Greek, *familia* in Latin; for the sacred centre of fire was also the centre of the family. In addition to the public gods we have just described, each family worshipped its own Lares and Penates, — the spirits of its deceased ancestors. They had the same form of worship which we found in the Vedas, — libations poured upon the ground, and sacrifices on the altar. This form, which scholars were once obliged to imagine and reconstruct from hints scattered through Greek and Latin books, has been so explained and illustrated by the hymns of the Rig Veda that it is now proved to belong to each Aryan family. The family worship paid to Agni in Sanskrit is precisely what we find given to Vesta among the Romans. It is acknowledged that they preserved most faithfully the old Aryan family type. We do not find this reverence of the sacred fire so all-important among the Greeks, Kelts, or Teutons. But even the Romans finally erected temples to other gods than Vesta. In this they copied the Greeks, who paid more sacrifices and libations to the bad gods than to the good ones. The Latin branch of the Aryans had one belief which we do not find among the Hindus or the Greeks. They taught that every existing thing had a tutelary spirit called a Genius, from whom its power and success came; probably we get our guardian angel from this. It is not precisely the same being as the Fravashi of the Persians, the Fylgia of the Norsemen ; for every plant, every nation, even every building, had its genius, which arose and perished with it : so new ones were constantly arising.

The Romans have what may pass for a sacred book. It is a very short chant sung by the Arval brethren, who were the twelve priests who invoked blessings upon the growth of the grain. It is a hymn to Mars. but is far from the exquisite poetry and spirituality of the hymns of the Vedas. These early Latin chants are simply incantations to call down rain, or drive away lightning from the growing seed ; thus giving another proof that the first thoughts of the Latins were agricultural. These chants had a peculiar metre of their own, called the Saturnian, the same root as the god Saturnus. The pipe was the national instrument of the Romans, as the lyre was of Greece. The first poetry which we should call lyrical was the funeral chant, which was sung by some woman accompanied by a piper, who followed the body to its burial-place.

Next came lays in praise of dead ancestors; and these were sung by boys at banquets. They descended by memory and tradition from father to son: but instead of developing into the glorious epics of India, Persia, Greece, Scandinavia, or Wales, these songs remained barren and bare; no cycle of legends grew up around them; the prosaic nature of the Romans crushed down poetry. No national god of song arose; and the old Latin language contains no word for poet. The word *vates* belongs to a religious ritual; it meant a leader of the singing; when afterwards applied to poetry, it retained the idea of divinely inspired singer, the priest of the Muses. The singing and dancing were at first religious, both in Greece and Rome; in Greece, they remained reputable employments; but in Rome they became insignificant first, disgraceful afterwards.

Yet these banquet songs, sung by the boys of the clan, are all we have of old Rome. The old Roman families kept them alive long after the current of thought had changed, and we are indebted to them for the most interesting, as well as the most original, Roman characters. The tales of Romulus and Remus, the Sabine women, Lucretia, and Coriolanus belong to this early period. We shall only stop to inquire into that of Romulus and Remus: they are the same twin deities

whom we find in each literature, as the Aswins in Sanskrit, the dawn and the twilight always; Romulus gradually becomes the most important, and the story told of
him is so like that of many other heroes that we are
tired of repeating it.   His grandfather was warned that
the babe to be born would destroy him; so the child
was exposed to die, nursed by a wolf, and brought up by
a shepherd.   He grew up strong and beautiful, and was
discovered by his princely bearing.   All unconsciously
he killed his parents, and himself did not die, but disappeared in a storm.   All these circumstances apply to
Romulus in Latin, as they did to Feridun in Persian,
and Oidipous in Greek.   Romulus's wolf has so many
brothers that we see at once that Romulus is one of
those beings invented to account for the name of a city.
There is no other original Roman literature.   To conquer and subdue the outside world left the Romans no
time for the world of the human mind.

But when, after five centuries, they had conquered
Greece, they were conquered in their turn.   The Greek
religion and literature gained an entire ascendency over
their minds.   The young noblemen of Rome were sent
to Greece to be educated, and spoke Greek in preference
to their native Latin.   Then arose a religion and a
literature that are simply copies of Greek literature;
like all copies, elegant and finished, but not fresh and
living.   The Greek philosophers and sophists were at
first expelled by the Roman Senate, as corrupting the
morals of the youth; but as orators, artists, and physicians, they soon returned and ruled Rome.   Cicero
introduced the Greek philosophy and literature to his
countrymen, and the ambitious young politicians soon

made use of Greek oratory and sophistry. The Emperor Augustus endeavored to patronize literature, and gave his name to a period, the Augustan age, when Virgil and Horace were personal friends of the Emperor. They tried to be patriotic and write upon Roman themes, in Greek metre; but the Greek metres were not congenial to the true Roman spirit. That was, at first, rural and agricultural. The old Roman loved his plough, and his great dark-eyed oxen, and his fertile field; and so Virgil, with his Bucolics and Georgics, and the second half of the Æneid, is the most national poet.

One of the stories in the Æneid puzzled scholars, but has lately been explained by M. Bréal, a French *savant;* that of Hercules and Cacus, in which Cacus, a strange monster, stole the cows of Hercules, dragged them backwards into a cave, and vomited forth smoke and flame when Hercules tried to attack him: but Hercules killed him with his unerring arrows. Herculus was an original Latin god, — the god of fields and fences; but the Romans seem to have confounded him with the Greek hero, Herakles. So Hercules, the Latin, is another form of the hero who fights with a monster. Cacus is the same as the snake Vritra in Sanskrit, Azhidalaka in Zend, the Python in Greek, the worm Fanir in Norse. The cows are the same bright clouds, the smoke and flame are the same lightnings. Is it not pleasant to meet him again among our Roman brethren? Light and darkness, good and evil, are all over the world. It is plain too that Virgil's Æneas is a distinct form of the solar myth. His mother was a goddess, the dawn; he is parted twice from women whom he loves, Creusa and Dido. He travels from land to land;

he labors for the good of others ; finally, he does not die, but disappears mysteriously from the sight of men, beneath the waters of the Numician stream, — the sun setting beneath the water.

It is interesting to notice within how short a period the great names of Latin literature are confined, — but little more than one hundred years, — which proves that the Romans were not a literary people. Their prose stands higher, relatively, than their poetry. Yet there is something fine in their literature, — the lofty patriotism which runs through it all. The humblest soldier could forget himself and die for Rome ; and the writers show some spark of the same spirit.

The most fatal influence which Greek literature exercised was through the philosophy of Epikouros. The same results followed which we saw in Athens : the best Romans became Stoics, and endeavored to avert the ruin they foresaw from the neglect of public duties. Marcus Aurelius the Emperor, 121 A. D., and Epictetus the slave, 90 A. D., were Stoics ; and taught that true philosophy consisted in the practice of virtue, not in speculation. Prompted by Alexandria, both neglected their native tongue to write in Greek. Alexandria had become a great commercial city. The mysteries of the Egyptians, the fire worship of the Persians, the theocracy of the Jews, the philosophy of the Greeks, were practised in this cosmopolitan city. It even invented a new school of metaphysics, and for a while paganism revived and flourished there, and influenced Rome again.

Byzantium is the third great literary centre after Alexandria and Rome ; but the greatest pagan work of Byzantium was the splendid code of laws which still forms the basis of the civil law of Europe. Tribonian, the great lawyer, codified and formed the whole Roman law. It is a true manifestation of an Aryan spirit, undoubtedly the best and greatest legacy which Rome has bestowed upon the world. The last great pagan writer was Boëthius. He wrote upon the consolations of philosophy, A. D. 470, and is interesting to us because he was translated into Anglo-Saxon by Alfred the Great. With him and Theodoric the Ostro-Goth closes antiquity, and open the Middle Ages. But before we can go on to the Middle Ages, we go back to trace the rise and growth of two other pagan races, our brothers still.

The next race in the development of the Aryan families is the Keltic, a great primitive race which once occupied all Central Europe. The Keltic tribes are supposed to have been the first to leave the common home, and are said to have entered Europe as early as 1900 B. C. They came by the northern slope of the Balkan and Carpathian Mountains. Conquering and moving onwards, they finally made a permanent settlement, and occupied France, where they were called Gauls; a small part of Spain; and England, Scotland, Ireland, and Wales, then called Britain. We meet them in history; for the Gauls attacked Rome itself, 390 B. C., and inhabited Britain when the Romans invaded it. The wild Keltic tribes were overcome and pushed back everywhere. In France they were driven to the sea-coast, to what is now the province of Brittany, with the language called Bas Bréton; in England they sought the sea-coast of Cornwall and the mountains of Wales, where their language is called Kymric;

the Highlands of Scotland, where it is called Gaelic; Ireland, where the language is Erse; the Isle of Man, where their Manx language is still a spoken tongue. Philology has taught us much of our knowledge about them; for Matthew Arnold says: "Philology, that science which in our time has had so many successes, has not been abandoned by her good fortune in touching the Kelt." The word Wales means simply a foreign country; Welsh means a foreigner. The Romans applied these words to the Kelts and the country where they took refuge. The words Gaul, Gael, and Scot are the same at bottom; they mean a violent, stormy people. But the discoveries to which the Erse language contributed have the most general interest. The Keltic races were discovered to belong to the Indo-European family by two Erse words: *traith*, the sea, has the same root as the name of a Sanskrit deity, Tritona; of a Zend hero, Thraetaoma; of the Greek goddess Amphitrite; of the Latin god Triton; — all connected with the sea; and the key to the riddle of the whole was the Erse word for sea, *traith*. The Keltic languages are still spoken, except in Cornwall. You may recognize them by the two vowels coming together, and yet not forming a diphthong, — Ploërmel, Coëtlogen, and such words.

It is curious to know that the Kelts as a race are deficient in two characteristics of their Aryan race, — a respect for women, and codes of well-organized law. Perhaps the reason that they were pushed back and crowded down by the Romans first, and the Teutons afterwards, was this very absence of organization, law, and order. They have one growth which is peculiarly their own, — the wildly beautiful music of the Gaels in Scotland, and the Erse in Ireland. "The law forbade the seizure by justice of a Gael's sword, harp, and one book ; the harp and book being as precious as the sword."

But the most important thing about them is that they, among the surrounding nations who had long forgotten their noble origin, preserved unchanged the primitive religion they had brought with them, which we found explained in the Rig Veda. The first knowledge we have of them is from the testimony of educated Romans, — Cæsar, Strabo, and Lucan. These all agree that the Keltic tribes worshipped one God, called Teutates. This is a form of Dyaus, Zeus, Theos, Deus, — the bright sky deified and personified. The word was traced by a French *savant*, M. Leflocq. He says : "The poetic naturalism of the Veda and the Edda is found in the few remains of Gaulish mythology : it is a remembrance of a primitive worship, anterior to all paganism." He is my authority for the meaning of the word. The Romans also agree that the Kelts in Gaul and in Britain taught the pre-existence and the immortality of the soul. You may imagine what a marvel this must have seemed to the Romans, who were not at all certain about these things ; but to us who have found them in the Rig Veda it is only natural that the Kelts should believe them. They taught that a noble action raised the soul to a higher condition of body, a bad action made it sink to a lower; which is simply transmigration. They had priests and bards, who were called Druids. Here is a song of Taliesin, their greatest bard, which describes transmigration better than any other poem known, and most poetically also.

" When my creation was accomplished, I was formed by the earth, by the flowers of the nettle, by the water of the ninth wave. By the wisest of the wise I was marked, — I was marked in the primitive world when I received existence. I played in the night ; I slept in the dawn ; I was in the bark with Dylan when the water, like the lances of an enemy, fell from heaven into the abyss. I have been a spotted serpent on the mountain ; I have been a viper in the lake ; I have been a star among the chieftains ; I have been a dispenser of liquids, clothed in sacred robes, bearing the cup. Much time has slipped by since I was a shepherd. I wandered long over the earth before becoming skilful in science. I have wandered ; I have slept in a hundred isles ; I have moved in a hundred circles."

The Druid priests were allowed to spend twenty years in learning the sacred hymns ; but, as they never committed anything to writing, the hymns are lost to us. We need not regret this, since we have the Vedic hymns, which are sufficient to prove all our conclusions ; but we shall at once be reminded of the customs in India. It was formerly believed that the cromlechs and dolmens of Brittany and Stonehenge were the Druid temples ; but the latest researches declare that they were built before the Kelts left Asia. But it is certain that the Kelts had altars erected in groves ; which therefore became sacred, like the altar groves of the Greeks and Teutons. Here originate all the enchanted forests of the Middle Ages. Oaks were sacred among the Kelts, as among the Teutons. Our ideas of Druids were based upon the opera of Norma ; it is pleasant to find the truth about them so much more valuable and interesting. These Druids were also teachers and judges and physicians. Finally their power was so great, like the Brahmans in India, that the warriors arose and reduced them to submission. But the bard retained his power for centuries. Each Keltic king, who was simply the chief of a clan, had his domestic bard attached to his petty court. The bard carried a harp presented by the king, wore a gold ring presented by the queen. His business was the same as in other nations; but these bards seem to have wandered less. They sang the deeds of national heroes, the genealogies of families, and the victories of tribes or single chieftains. Here are the laws relating to them: —

"The domestic bard shall receive from the family one beas out of every spoil in which he shall be present; and, if there should be fighting, the bard shall sing in front of the battle, 'His land shall be free'; and he shall have a horse from the king, and a man's share, like every domestic. The domestic bard, and the physician, shall be in the lodging of the master of the family. At the table he sat below the salt, with the domestic chaplain. But the great president of all the bards, who has won the prize in contests, shall sit at the royal table."

They exercised such power that the Romans punished them, and they fled to Wales. When the Romans left Britain, 426 A. D., the Kymry recovered power for a short time, and the bard flourished in his greatest glory. This was a brilliant period for the Kymry. They had intelligent princes, fond of fighting, and the songs of their bards of the sixth century are full of fire, or genuine pathos; they were written in triads of three lines, instead of four, peculiar to the Welsh bards. Then came in the Saxon invasions; and the Kelt and the Teuton fought and hated each other for centuries. The cattle-

stealing, the border warfare, which are perpetually crop-
ping out in Scott's ballads, began here in the sixth
century. It is proved by the fact, that the title Jarl is
frequently given to the Kymric princes; it is stolen
bodily from the Saxon invader.

THE BATTLE OF MENAO, 560 A.D.

This year, a chief, lavish of wine, gold pieces, hydromel,
and full of courage without barbarity, broke over the borders,

And followed by a swarm of lances, and his united chieftains,
and his brilliant nobles, all well disposed, he went to battle ;

And, mounted upon his horse, he endured the battle of
Menao, kindling the bardic Muse.

What abundant booty for the army ! eight times twenty
beasts of one color, cows and calves.

Milch cows and oxen, and riches of every kind!

Oh, I should have ceased to be cheerful, if Urien had perished !

He has been cut to pieces, that chieftain of a different language ; trembling, shuddering, the Saxon has had his white hair
bathed in his blood. They carried him away on a litter, his
brow bloody, ill defended by the blood of his own people.

This brave and insolent warrior left his wife a widow.

I have wine from my chieftain ! I often have wine, thanks
to him! It is he who inspires me, he who supports me, he
who guides me ; no one equals him in greatness!

But the enemies are fighting. Keeper of the door, listen !

What a noise ! is it the earth trembling? Is it the sea rising,
breaking over its habitual circle, as for the feet of men ?

If a groaning arises in the valley, is it not Urien who is
striking ?

If a groaning arises on the mountain, is it not Urien who
is conquering ?

If a groaning arises on the hill-side, is it not Urien who is
crushing ?

If a groaning arises in the citadel, is it not Urien who makes it to be uttered?

Groaning on the road, groaning on the plain, groaning in all the mountain passes!

There is nobody who can make these groanings cease! there is no refuge against him!

There is no famine for those who plunder in his land!

When he fights, clothed in his armor, enamelled with dazzling blue, his blue lance is the lieutenant of death, in the carnage of his enemies.

Ah! until I lose myself, growing old, until the rude anguish of death arrives, I shall not smile unless I celebrate Urien!

This is certainly very poetical and exciting. I translated it from the French collection. The ballad proves that the chiefs lived by plunder, by cattle-stealing. The bard congratulates himself on serving a chief who can pay him so well. The "chieftain of a different language" is not the Roman at all, but the invading Saxon; the Romans had been driven off. These ballads of the sixth century were not written down until the eleventh and twelfth centuries. But there is no doubt that they were composed in the sixth century, their form, their technical part, is so much better than that of the other mediæval ballads. This correctness of form proves that there had been an early period of great poetical development; and there is also a stream of continuous testimony from historical writers who were Christian monks, to prove that this older national literature existed in the sixth century.

I dwell so strongly upon this point, because, when it is granted, unlooked for consequences will appear. King Arthur, the very flower and model of chivalry,

Arthur, the Christian knight, the blameless king, was first a Keltic hero, sung by the Druid bards. Shall I say more, or is it already guessed that Arthur, like so many other Aryan heros, is only the sun and its course personified in a human form? It is beyond doubt that Arthur lived, a date is even fixed for him at 542 ; but the mind of his race could not invent new facts about him. Those very circumstances which happen to each Aryan hero fasten themselves upon him, with a monotony which would become wearisome had it not a great principle lying underneath it. Certainly, if the Kelts had imagined a hero, they would have found some new thing for him to do. That they did not, proves that they simply formulated the thoughts which lie dormant in each branch of the race, brought from its home.

A cycle of ballads has grown up around him, but the different heroes are but reflections of Arthur. We may digress for a moment to remark that each literature has these secondary heroes, who are but faint reflections of the glory of the chief hero. In Sanskrit, Arjuna is the reflection of Krishna ; in Greek, Patroklos of Achilleus, Telemachos of Odysseus ; Remus of Romulus, in Latin. We will therefore separate Arthur from the knights who surround him, and look at his story. His birth was supernatural : as soon as he was born he was wrapped in gold-colored glittering raiment, and taken away from his mother. He was brought up by a kind old knight, from charity, and knew nothing of his royal birth. Then the king died, and all were striving for the crown. The lords came into a church-yard, and there "stood an anvil of stone, and stuck therein a fair sword, naked at the point, and letters of gold were written about the stone, that said this : 'Whoso pulleth out this sword out of this stone and anvil is rightwise born king of England.'" All the great lords try, but of course none can pull out the sword but Arthur. This is exactly the story of the sword in the Volsung Saga, and somewhat like that of the sword of Theseus in Greek. The beard and hair of Arthur shine like gold, and the nobles are forced to make the beautiful youth their king. Then enemies attack the land, but Arthur draws the "sword that flashed in the eyes of his enemies like thirty torches," and kills them all. Finally, in battle, this sword snaps, like the sword in the Volsung Saga. Then a maiden out of the water, like Thetis in Greek, like Hiordis in Norse, brings him another sword : while she keeps the scabbard, his life is safe ; he can neither bleed nor die : Arthur thus becomes another of the invulnerable heroes. He has miraculous powers over nature ; an owl, a blackbird, and a stag talk to him, and do his bidding ; these are the same talking animals which we meet in other Aryan literatures. Then Arthur marries the queen of the Orkneys, whom he soon leaves. She is the mother of Sir Mordred, who afterwards seeks to kill him ; and she is his sister, although he does not know it. Merlin warns him that he will be destroyed by his sister's son, who will be born on May-day; and he orders all the children born on May-day to be drowned. But Mordred escapes, and grows up to kill his father. This brings Arthur still more closely within the mythical framework. It is the old story of the sun marrying the dawn, — of one day destroying the day which preceded it ; and shows very clearly that

Arthur was a pagan demigod before he became a Christian king.

The Kelts in Wales, the Kymry, embraced Christianity very early from their Roman invaders, and with a passionate enthusiasm which was highly edifying to the Christian monks. And this Christian influence makes Arthur fight against the invading Saxons, because they are pagans. It is the old contest between good and evil. It is most perceptible, however, in the modifications it gives to the story of Lancelot and Gwennivar. Arthur weds her, although Merlin tells him she is not a wholesome wife for him. She brings with her a rich dowry, the round table; now this is the bardic table of the Druids, the round emblem which appears so often, and is always a symbol of riches; and Gwennivar and her riches play the same fatal part that Helen played in Greece. She is the destroyer of her country The invading kings ravage the land again, scarce one month after Arthur is married: and he cries out like the wanderer, "Never have I had one month's rest since I became king of the land." So Arthur's life goes on in fighting; finally Lancelot plays the part of Paris in the Iliad. He makes Gwennivar untrue to her husband, and a last great battle comes between the forces of the two. Here the myth brings in the snake. There was to be no fighting until a sword should be raised; but a snake bit one of the knights; he raised his sword to slay it, and the two armies, supposing it to be the signal, came to battle. His son, the traitor Sir Mordred, wounded the bright king, because the scabbard of his sword had been stolen. Yet Arthur cannot die till the sword has been thrown into the water, for the sun must set in the waters. But Arthur is one of those heroes who does not die. The three mystic queens, like the three fates, or three furies, bear him away in the ship of the dead, — but he will return. All Wales and Brittany look for his coming. He has only gone to the land of Avalon to be healed of his grievous wound. Now the word Avalon means the island of apple-trees. The paradise of the Kelts was always an island far over the blue seas, beneath the setting sun. And if he return, so will the heroes of other lands, Sebastian of Portugal, or Endymion, who sleeps in his Latmian valley; the sun must return when healed of the wound the darkness had given it, for the sun cannot really die. Then Gwennivar's career closes in prayer. She leaves Arthur, as Helen left Menelaos; but she does not follow Lancelot. Her treasure, the round table, is destroyed, but she seeks to atone for the wrong she has done to her country: unlike Helen, who coolly goes back without the slightest consciousness of wrong-doing, carrying her treasures with her.

And the story is repeated in the tale of Tristram and Iseulte, with the pagan tone remaining more visible. Many single incidents are repeated in relation to the knights. Sir Galahad finds his sword, just as Arthur found his; but one hero is the type of all.

Nothing can be more interesting than to trace the road which these ballads took, in coming down to us. Disheartened by the successes of the invading Saxons, many Kelts fled from Wales into Brittany in the sixth century, and carried their native hero, Arthur, with them. For several centuries Wales and Brittany were practically one, (this intercourse of nations makes history

very living to us,) and Arthur was their own king,
dearer than the other knights : so he became the national hero of Brittany : ruins bear his name, rocks the
impress of his horse's feet, and the haunted forest of
Broceliande, where Merlin slumbers, waves its boughs
in the enchanted air of Brittany too. These tales of
Arthur and his knights of the round table were sung
in Brittany by the poor homesick exiles, and thence
they passed to the court of the Franks. These bold
Teutons had played the same part as the Saxons in
England ; had invaded Gaul, and pushed the Kelts into
Brittany ; and in 513 A. D. the Welsh bards were singing
to Childebert. From his court this ballad cycle spread
over Europe, because bards of different nationalities met
there ; each sang in his native tongue, and the rude
king made them welcome, though he could not understand them. Several centuries went by : in 1077 Rhys
ap Tudor, a Welsh prince, was sent to his kindred in
Brittany to be educated ; when he returned to Wales, he
brought with him the ballad cycle of Arthur and the round
table, which had been forgotten in his native land, and
restored them as they had been " sung at Caerleon upon
Usk, at the time of the sovereignty of the Emperor
Arthur and the race of the Kymry over the island of
Britain and the adjacent islands." So the Welsh bards
began to sing again of Arthur. There was in the
twelfth century another great burst of bardic poetry in
Wales ; but these later ballads are extremely stupid ;
they are composed according to fixed rules ; even when
read one at a time, they are not inspiring, like the
grand ballads of the sixth century. The bards espoused
the cause of the Plantagenet kings as against the Anglo-

Saxons. The old hatred reawakened, and they declared the Plantagenets to be the rightful possessors of the crown, on account of a prophecy of Merlin, which I will quote, it is so poetical.

"From Neustria [Normandy] will come a people mounted upon coursers of blood, clothed with iron, who will draw vengeance down upon the wickedness of the invaders. They will give back their dwellings to the former inhabitants, and will ruin the strangers. They [the Anglo-Saxons] will bear the yoke of an eternal slavery. With the hoe and the plough they will tear up the bosom of their mother [the earth]. That day the mountains of Cambria [Wales] will tremble with joy; the fountains of Brittany will gush out; the oaks of Cornwall will grow green again."

So of course the Plantagenet kings honored them, and Henry II. went to Wales expressly to hear them. It is now said that Edward did not cause the bards to be massacred when he conquered Wales in 1284 A. D.; so that Gray's splendid ode is founded upon a mistake. But they were suppressed and silenced, for they fostered political discontent. About a hundred years ago their poetical contests, called Eisteddvods, were renewed. Their ballads about Arthur were translated into Latin by Geoffrey of Monmouth, a Welsh monk, and he is one of the sources from whom we get the ballad cycle. Without him that form of it might have perished with the Welsh nationality.

But there is quite another source from which we have derived our story of Arthur, flower of kings. In the twelfth century, 1155 A. D., a Norman Trouvère named Robert Wace found these ballads ready made to his hand. He took the same names, the same story; but

he threw over it an utterly different spirit, — the spirit
of his age, — and as such Arthur has come down to
us. He was no longer a brave warrior fighting against
pagan Saxons; he is the brightest expression of the
noble chivalric spirit, truly Christian throughout his
whole career; filled with an exalted tenderness, a re-
fined sentiment, far removed from the Keltic demigod's
sensual life. Of course the Trouvères carried this version everywhere. They brought it to England, to the
court of the Norman kings; and it was carried back
again by their French wives to Anjou and Aquitaine,
to Poitou and Guyenne, — thus spread still further in
Europe. The French dwell with the greatest pride and
delight upon their Keltic ancestors, and have done far
more to make known the literature of Brittany than the
English for all their Keltic possessions. I am indebted
to the very learned and careful works of M. le Vicomte
de la Villemarqué for tracing the movements of the
ballad cycle of Arthur. And I have described it so
minutely only because it explains how many other ideas
found their way into mediæval literature.

With this ballad cycle of Arthur has been connected
the story of the Holy Grail; but it was originally
separate and distinct from that. Perhaps the most
interesting discovery of comparative mythology is that
which connects this sublime mystery of Christianity
with the early pagan thought of humanity. The Druid
bards taught the existence of a great earth mother,
like the Demeter of the Greeks. They called her
Keridwen, and worshipped her with mysteries, and
taught that she had a mighty caldron or bowl containing a drink which inspired them to utter their songs.

From the bardic songs this idea passed into the popular tales of the Welsh; their collection is the oldest of all the Keltic folk stories, and is charming indeed. Matthew Arnold says: "It breathes the very breath of the primitive world; it belongs to the sixth-century period, all pagan and mythological. Through it shine plainly those old myths which wandered westward with this oldest emigrant of the Aryan race." If it paints the feeling of the times, it proves the brilliant civilization of the Kymry in the sixth century; for these tales were told to amuse and instruct the young chieftains. They show a high morality, great generosity to friends, and a strong love of literature; but all the marvels are performed by supernatural power, and these fairy tales of the Mabinogeon are the foundation of nine tenths of the romances of the Middle Ages. It is amazing to find here the familiar figures, and delightful to be able to understand just how they came into Europe. Here reappears the knight delivering distressed damsels from monsters ready to devour them. One character is peculiarly Keltic: a hero kills a serpent which tormented a lion, and the grateful lion follows him about like a pet dog: this troublesome pet often comes into the mediæval stories. We must be thankful to the Mabinogeon for something more satisfactory still. We owe to it Shakespeare's Cordelia, who is the lady Creiddylad. King Lear is King Ludd. But we will confine ourselves to one particular tale.

Péredur leaves his home to seek for a great basin or caldron, which is called in Kymric a graal; and the exiled Welsh carried with them to Brittany the story of the search for the graal. Of course it lived and grew,

like the ballad cycle. Now it is evidently the same
round vessel which appears, in countless forms, in each
literature : the cup of Djemschid in Persian ; the enchanted cup from which Odysseus drinks in Kirke's
palace ; the horn of plenty of the Greeks ; the purse of
Fortunatus, always full ; the lamp of Aladdin, which
bestows treasures. It is the round table which Gwennivar brought as her .dowry, the caldron of Keridwen.
It is an emblem of the fertility of the earth, and it
always yields exhaustless riches to its possessor ; so
that the search for the graal is that same voyage for
treasures which appears in the Greek voyage for the
golden fleece. In the poetical activity of the twelfth century, a Trouvère named Chrétien de Troyes, 1160 A. D.,
rewrote this pagan tale : he made it into a poem full of
the tone of chivalric Christianity. The San Greal could
cure all wounds, raise the dead to life, and supply its
possessors with food and drink forever, — meats more
delicate than mortals had ever tasted before ; but the
reason it could do all these miracles was because it
contained the blood of Christ, caught as it dropped
from the cross. And then another difference : the
magic graal of the pagans fed good and bad alike ; but
the Holy Grail yielded its delicious food only to the
pure in heart. More, it even became a talismanic test.
The foul with sin could not even see it. A vision came
to a knight of Arthur's court. He saw a herd of black
bulls, — among them, two snowy white, and one white
spotted with black. And the interpretation was that
the black bulls were the knights black with sin, who
had not repented and confessed to a holy priest ; the
snow-white were Sir Galahad and Sir Perceval, all pure

and good ; the spotted one, Sir Lancelot, with one sin
marring his snowy purity. And the fair meadow where
they fed was humility and patience, which were to be the
starting-point of their search for the Holy Grail. So
all the knights go forth to seek this heavenly treasure.
It would be too long to tell you of their adventures.
Wagner's new opera, soon to be published, " Parsifal,"
tells the story. The sinful knights seek in vain. Lancelot dimly sees it ; but it dashes him senseless to the
ground. Sir Galahad and Sir Perceval taste its delicious food : then it is borne up into heaven. They
linger a little while in the cell of a holy hermit : then
they follow it to heaven. The lovely story is familiar
to us all : for that very reason we more enjoy watching
its development. M. de la Villemarqué is my authority
for the meaning of the word graal.

The Keltic spirit has affected our literature indirectly
as well. Matthew Arnold says that it owes to the
Kelts its capacity for style, for poetic form, — for in
this the Teutons are extremely deficient, and the Welsh
bards pre-eminent, — its sensibility to beauty, and its
power of catching and rendering the charm of nature ;
— in a word, the dash of genius comes from the Kelt.
In the Mabinogeon, Math made a wife for his pupil out
of flowers, " and four white trefoils sprang up wherever
she trod." Is not this poetic? A twelfth-century bard
wrote : —

> " See her the earth elastic tread ;
>   And where she walks with snow-white feet
>   Not even a trefoil bends its head."

Our language owes to its Keltic element some popular
words : basket, kick, twaddle, fudge, hitch, and muggy.

The next Keltic literature arose in Brittany. The earliest written document in Bas Bréton is in the ninth century; but there were unwritten ballads before then. The Bretons have a ballad literature which is positively beautiful, not relatively so: for it will bear comparison with any other. These ballads have been handed down from father to son, by recitation among the peasants, since the tenth century. They have kept alive the national faiths and glories and manners in this nook of France. Some of them are distinctly historical; more so than the English Chevy Chace and the Scotch Border Minstrelsy. One ballad is now repeated which actually was sung at the time of William the Conqueror, 1066 A. D. Here is one of the historical ballads, which is quite unlike anything we are accustomed to.

THE EVIL TRIBUTE OF NOMÉNOË.

[Noménoë is the Alfred of the Brétons, their deliverer from the Franks, — a strictly historical personage.   871 A. D.]

FYTTE I.

" Good merchant, farer to and fro,
Hast tidings of my son, Karó ? "
" Mayhap, old chieftain of Aré :
What are his kind and calling?—say."
" He is a man of heart and brains,
To Roazon [Rennes] he drove the wains ;
The wains to Roazon drove he,
Horsed with good horses, three by three,
That drew, fair shared among them all,
The Bréton's tribute to the Gaul."
" If thy son's wains the tribute bore,
He will return to thee no more.

When that the coin was brought to scale
Three pounds were lacking to the tale.
Then out spoke the Intendant straight,
' Vassal, thy head shall make the weight.'
With that his sword forth he abrade,
And straight smote off the young man's head ;
And by the hair the head he swung,
And in the scale for make-weight flung."
The old chief, at that cruel sound,
Him seemed as he would fall in swound.
Stark on the rocks he grovelled there,
His face hid with his hoary hair ;
And, head on hand, made heavy moan,
" Karó, my son, my darling son ! "

FYTTE II.

Then forth he fares, that aged man,
Followed by all his kith and clan;
The aged chieftain fareth straight
To Noménoë's castle gate.
" Now tell me, tell me, thou porter bold,
If that thy master be in hold.
But be he in, or be he out,
God guard from harm that chieftain stout."
Or ever he had prayed his prayer,
Behold, Noménoë was there !
His quarry from the chase he bore,
His great hounds gambolling before ;
In his right hand his bow unbent,
A wild boar on his back uphent ;
On his white hand, all fresh and red
The blood dripped from the wild boar's head.
" Fair fall you, honest mountain clan,
Thee first, as chief, thou white-haired man.
Your news, your news, come tell to me,
What would you of Noménoë ? "

" We come for right : to know in brief
Hath heaven a God, Bretayne a chief."
" Heaven hath a God, I trow, old man,
Bretayne a chief, if aught I can."
" He can that will, thereof no doubt ;
And he that can the Frank drive out
Drives out the Frank, defends the land,
To avenge and still avenge doth stand, —
To avenge the living and the dead,
Me and my fair son foully sped ;
My Karó, whose brave head did fall
By hand of the accursed Gaul.
They flung his head the weights to square :
Like ripe wheat shone the golden hair."
Herewith the old man wept outright,
That tears ran down his beard so white,
Like dew-drops on a lily flower
That glitter at the sunrise hour.
When of those tears the chief was ware,
A stern and bloody oath he sware :
" I swear it by this wild boar's head,
And by the shaft that laid him dead,
Till this plague 's washed from out the land,
This blood I wash not from my hand."

FYTTE III.

Noménoë hath done, I trow,
What never chieftain did till now, —
Hath sought the sea-beach, sack in hand,
To gather pebbles from the strand, —
Pebbles as tribute-toll to bring
The Intendant of the bald-head king.
Noménoë hath done, I trow,
What never chieftain did till now.
Prince as he is, hath ta'en his way,
The tribute-toll himself to pay. . . . .
17

"Fling wide the gates of Roazon,
That I may enter in anon.
Noménoë comes within your gate,
His wains all piled with silver freight."
"Light down, my lord, into the hall,
And leave your laden wains in stall.
Leave your white horse to squire and groom,
And come to sup in the daïs room :
To sup, but first to wash, for lo !
E'en now the washing horn doth blow."
"Full soon, fair sir, shall my washing be made,
When that the tribute hath been weighed."
The first sack from the wains they pight,
(I trow 't was corded fair and tight,) —
The first sack that they brought to scale,
'T was found full weight and honest tale :
The second sack that they came to,
The weight therein was just and true :
The third sack from the wains they pight,
"How now, I trow, this sack is light !"
The Intendent saw, and from his stand
Unto the sack he reached his hand, —
He reached his hand the sack unto,
So that the knot he might undo.
"From off the sack thy hand refrain :
My sword shall cut the knot in twain !"
The word had scantly passed his teeth,
When flashed his bright sword from the sheath.
Through the Frank's neck the falchion went,
Sheer by his shoulders as he bent ;
It cleft the flesh and bones in twain,
And eke the links o' one balance chain.
Into the scale the head plumped straight,
And there, I trow, was honest weight !
Loud through the town, the cry did go :
"Hands on the slayer !   Ho, Haro !"

He gallops forth out through the night :
" Ha ! torches, torches ! — on his flight ! "
" Light up, light up, as best ye may !
The night is black, and frore the way.
But ere ye catch me, sore I fear
The shoes from off your feet you 'll wear, —
Your shoes of gilded blue cordwain : —
For your scales, — you 'll ne'er need them again !
Your scales of gold, you 'll need no more,
To weigh the stones of the Breton shore.
                              To war ! "

You will find evidence in this of that form of government by clan which was once supposed to be peculiar
to the Highlands of Scotland ; but since the discovery
of Sanskrit literature this clan government is found to
have existed among the undivided Aryans. So the
Kelts, who were the first to leave the common home,
are also those who have longest kept their original simplicity of government. But there are other ballads,
spirited war-songs, tender love-songs, and touching funeral dirges. These dirges are perhaps the most beautiful, but it is difficult to decide when all are so lovely.
One ballad tells of a phantom army sweeping by, like
Odin and his warriors. It is written in triads, the Keltic
metre.

Here is a mythological ballad of the sixth century.
It contains familiar characters. The wife is the dawn
and the twilight ; the Corrigaun is the same wicked
enchantress who beguiles Odysseus, the darkness, sister of Kirke and Kalypso.

THE LORD NANN AND THE FAIRY.

[The Corrigaun is identical with the Scandinavian elf.]

The good Lord Nann and his fair bride
Were young when wedlock's knot was tied,
Were young when death did them divide.
But yesterday, that lady fair
Two babes as white as snow did bear :
A man-child and a girl they were.
" Now say what is thy heart's desire
For making me a man-child's sire ?
'T is thine, whate'er thou mayst require.
What food soe'er thee lists to take,
Meat of the woodcock from the lake,
Meat of the wild deer from the brake."
" O the meat of the deer is dainty food !
To eat thereof would do me good,
But I grudge to send thee to the wood."
The Lord of Nann, when this he heard,
Hath gripped his oak spear with never a word :
His bonny black horse he hath leaped upon,
And forth to the greenwood he hath gone.
By the skirts of the wood as he did go,
He was 'ware of a hind as white as snow.
O, fast she ran, and fast he rode,
That the earth it shook where his horse hoofs trode.
O, fast he rode, and fast she ran,
That the sweat to drop from his brow began,
That the sweat on his horse's flank grew white :
So he rode, and he rode, till the fall of night,
When he came to a stream that fed a lawn
Hard by the grot of a Corrigaun.
The grass grew thick by the streamlet's brink,
And he lighted off his horse to drink.
The Corrigaun sat by the fountain fair,

A-combing her long and yellow hair,
A-combing her hair with a comb of gold
(Not poor, I trow, are these maidens bold) :
" Now who 's the bold wight that dares come here,
To trouble my fairy fountain clear ?
Either thou shalt wed with me,
Or pine for four long years and three,
Or dead in three days' space shalt be."
" I will not wed with thee, I ween,
For wedded man a year I 've been ;
Nor yet for seven years will I pine,
Nor die in three days for spell of thine;
For spell of thine I will not die,
But when it pleaseth God on high,
But here, and now, I 'd leave my life,
Ere take a Corrigaun to wife."
" O mother, mother ! for love of me
Now make my bed, and speedily,
For I am sick as a man may be.
O, never the tale to my lady tell !
Three days, and ye 'll hear the passing-bell :
The Corrigaun hath cast her spell."
Three days they passed, three days were sped,
To her mother-in-law the lady said :
" Now tell me, madam, now tell me pray,
Wherefore the death-bells toll to-day.
Why chant the priests in the street below,
All clad in their vestments white as snow ?"
" A strange poor man, who harbored here,
He died last night, my daughter dear."
" But tell me, madam, my lord, your son, —
My husband, whither is he gone ?"
" But to the town, my child, he 's gone,
And at your side he 'll be back anon."
" What gown for my churching were 't best to wear, —
My gown of red, or of watchet fair?"

" The fashion of late, my child, hath grown,
That women for churching black should put on."
As through the church-yard porch she stept,
She saw the grave where her husband slept.
" Who of our blood is lately dead,
That our ground is newly raked and spread ? "
" The truth I may no more forbear,
My son, your own poor lord, lies there ! "
She threw herself on her knees amain,
And from her knees ne'er rose again.
That night they laid her, stiff and cold,
Beside her lord, beneath the mould :
When lo, a marvel to behold !
Next morn from the grave two oak-trees fair
Shot lusty boughs high up in air ;
And in their boughs, O wondrous sight !
Two happy doves, all snowy white,
That sang, as ever the morn did rise,
And then flew up — into the skies !

This is certainly far the most beautiful of all the
ballads which tell the story of trees and rose-bushes
rising from the graves of dead lovers, and Lord Nann
the very model of men.

There are also Bréton folk-stories. One of them is
about a city drowned for its wickedness, — completely
submerged : this same story comes into the Maha
Bharata ; but there is no idea of punishment in that.
On Christmas night the stones of the cromlech go down
to the river to drink, leaving vast treasures uncovered.
Whoever can, may seize them, but must take care to
get out before the stones come walking back. This is
like the cave of Aladdin, which opens for a moment
only.

Dwarfs are the specialty of Brittany, as giants are of Ireland. Every faithful reader of folk-stories will recognize an Irish giant as a familiar friend; and the huge cliffs on the west coast of Ireland are called the Giants' Causeway. There is an immense literature in the Erse language in Ireland. There are ballads and stories about voyages and battles and elopements and cow-spoils, and other equally exciting themes. From the mere title - cow-spoil, can you not see the Irish chieftain eager for a fight, starting out to steal the cows of his neighbor, to feed his own hungry dependents? A collection of the Erse folk-stories would be the most amusing of all, if the genuine Keltic wit of the Irish peasant could be preserved. The ballads in Erse re-late at length the doings of the Feane, — a body of men and their chieftain, Fionn: of course, our word Fenian is the same. They are perpetually fighting against the Norsemen and Saxons; here is the same old struggle between Kelt and Teuton. Then the Erse went over to Scotland, — Ireland and Scotland were practically one, — and carried their heroes with them; and the Gaelic bards, the latest of all, wandered about in kilts, and sang of Fionn and his chief knight, Diar-maid: a witch from Norway was the foe whom they dreaded most. We have no time to go into the contro-versy as to whether Ossian's poems published by Mac-pherson are the genuine remains of the Erse and Gaelic bards, or not. The latest authority says that the ballads are the germs of Macpherson's Ossian, but that he has entirely altered their character. "Mac-pherson's Ossian is distinguished by a peculiar vein of sentimental grandeur and melancholy; and the popular

manners of the time do not at all accord with such a
spirit. Short, wild, martial, stirring songs, political
ballads, or love-songs, would suit the taste of grim soldiers; but a long melancholy epic would put them to
sleep." Here is a real Gaelic ballad. It presents nothing indistinct, but sharply drawn figures of a graceful
hero, and nymphs gazing at him (the word nymph
means water), and the cave of darkness ready for him.

ODE TO THE SETTING SUN.

Hast left the blue distance of heaven,
Sorrowless son of the gold yellow hair?
Night's doorways are ready for thee,
Thy pavilion of peace in the west.
The billows come slowly around
To behold him of brightest hair:
Timidly raising their heads
To gaze on thee, beauteous, asleep,
They, witless, have fled from thy side.
Take thy sleep within thy cave, O sun!

Mr. Campbell thinks that the Ossianic heroes were the
ancient Keltic gods. Formerly the most ancient Scotch
ballad known was Sir Tristrem; and he, like all the
others, slays a dragon and delivers a damsel. But Mr.
Campbell's researches have recently discovered another
character who joins the army of invulnerable heroes.
Diarmaid can be wounded only in a mole which is on the
sole of his foot. He has bright golden hair. He carries a sword, — the white sword of light, which tells its
own story. His battle-flag was called the sunbeam. He
ran away with the beautiful wife of King Fionn, just as
Lancelot would have gone with Gwennivar, if the myth

had not been Christianized, — just as Helen goes with Paris. He killed a wild boar, and the king, to revenge himself for the abduction of his wife, forced Diarmaid to step on the boar. A bristle entered his foot and killed him. This is again Adonis killed by a boar, — the only time the boar reappears in this connection. The darkness kills the sun, or winter kills the summer. Diarmaid can be set up as the Gaelic hero, and the Clan Campbell in Scotland claim to be descended from him. A boar's head is their crest. The Scotch ballads would be interesting to examine; but we will devote our time to a subject less familiar, the Gaelic folk-stories. Mr. Campbell went about among the peasants of the Scotch Highlands, just as M. de la Villemarqué had done in Brittany, and in 1859 took down from the lips of living men and women these tales. He says, "After working for a year and weighing all the evidence that has come in my way, I have come to agree with those who hold that popular tales are pure traditions preserved in all countries and all languages alike; woven together in a net-work which seems to pervade the world, and to be fastened to everything in it. Tradition, books, history, and mythology hang together." In one of the tales, impossible tasks are given; one of them, the clearing out of a stable, comes into Norse folk-stories, and was one of the labors of Herakles, the Greek hero. In another, a maiden marries a monster, who becomes a prince by night, and loses him by her own curiosity; just Psyche over again. There are several resemblances to the adventures of Odysseus. Conall is shut up in a cave by the Glashan, a giant, and gets out exactly as Odysseus did, by tying himself under the sheep. He induces the poor, stupid Glashan to scald himself; and when his comrades return, and ask who did it, he says, "Myself did it,"— just like Polyphemos in the Odyssey. Conall kills a giant by putting a red-hot stick through his heart.

We must not overlook dear Cinderella; she is the dawn, dark and gray, when away from her prince, the bright sun, obscured by envious sisters, the dark clouds ; for her story is found in Gaelic also, with some witty additions. When the prince asks her where she comes from, she says, first, from "Towel land"; she has been a laundry maid : the second time she says, "from the kingdom of Broken Basins"; she is a cook. We find among the heroes one with a horse who talks like the horses of Achilleus in Greek. He fights with a monster, and sets free a distressed damsel ; but the monster swims about in a Highland loch, and his Andromeda is fastened to the lake shore.

The local coloring applies also to the talking birds and animals. In all the Keltic stories, fish play the most important part ; salmon and otter and trout do the talking in the Gaelic tales. In all the Aryan stories, no animal is ever mentioned which dwells outside of any Aryan country. Apples are the magical possessions most valued. There is apparently no reason why Paris should have given an apple to the goddess, rather than a pear or a peach ; but this magic apple appears in Gaelic as well as in Greek, and even gives the name to the Keltic paradise, Avalon, the island of apples. It is because apple was the generic name for all fruits.

CHAPTER IX.

COMPARATIVE MYTHOLOGY OF TEUTONIC LITERATURE. — SCANDINAVIAN FAMILIES.

OUR subject in this chapter is the Edda, the sacred book of the Scandinavian branches of the Teutonic family. The name Teuton is the Latin form of Deutsch, and the history of the Middle Ages of Europe is little more than a record of the deeds of the Teutonic family; for it includes the Goths, of different names: the Mœso-Goths near the Danube; the Visigoths in Spain; the Ostro-Goths, who culminated under Theodoric in Italy; the Franks, whose name means " free men"; the Lombards, who founded a second kingdom in Italy after the Ostro-Goths were driven out by the Eastern Emperor; the Saxons, whose name means " swordmen"; the Angles; — all whose races and languages have gone into other forms. It includes also the Norwegians, Swedes, Danes, Icelanders, Germans, Dutch, and English, whose languages are spoken to-day. It is only one hundred years ago, only since the Sanskrit language was recovered, only since philology has touched them with its revealing magic, that we have learned how near all these nations are to us.

It is not known when the Teutonic family of the Aryan race entered Europe. The Greeks and the Latins sought the extreme South, the Kelts swarmed

over the centre of Europe · but the Teutons are supposed to have passed through Russia to the extreme
North; and though it seems unaccountable to us that
they should have sought so cold a climate and so
barren a soil, we must disconnect ourselves from our
standard, and remember what these people wanted.
The explanation is simple. This family did not care
for cultivating the ground, but preferred hunting and
fishing; and game and fish abounded in Norway.
And, most important of all, they found in Sweden an
inexhaustible supply of what were to them the first
necessities, — wood to make and iron to point the
arrows and spears with which they killed alike fish, or
beasts, or men. Many of these spears and arrows
would be lost in every hunt and every battle; so more
wood and iron would be needed for new ones. The
native climate of the Aryans was cold; so this cold was
no objection to them. From there they spread south-
ward; but for centuries they were unknown, unlike
the Kelts. Of the Teutons we hear nothing until
Tacitus, the Roman historian, found them settled in
Germany, in the first century of our era. In the Goths,
Burgundians, Franks, Lombards, who invaded the
Roman empire at so many different points; the Angles
and Saxons, who invaded Britain; the Norsemen,
who invaded France; the Normans, who invaded England and Sicily; the Varangians, who formed the
body-guard of the Greek Emperors at Byzantium, —
we recognize them, — restless, migrating, conquering
Aryans. But to Iceland we must go to learn what they
believed and felt before they were brought into contact
with Christianity.

In the year 874 A. D., a body of people left Norway because they would not submit to the tyranny of Harold Harfager, or Fair Hair, and settled in Iceland. They carried with them the religion, the poetry, and the laws of their race; and on this desolate volcanic island they kept these records unchanged for hundreds of years, while other Teutonic nations gradually became affected by their intercourse with Roman and Byzantine Christianity. In 1639, about two hundred years ago, these books were discovered. The first publication was in 1777, and thus the nature of the whole Teutonic family was laid bare to us. Of course the consequences of this discovery are not so universal nor so revolutionary as those following the discovery of Sanskrit; but they are exceedingly interesting in two ways: first, this literature of the Scandinavian peninsula gives a key to the literature of all the Teutonic families, including our immediate ancestors; second, its ideas agree so wonderfully with the Sanskrit ideas, that it is another witness to the brotherhood of the different families of the Aryan race. The word Scandinavia means the watery land, *apia* being the root, and the Scandinavian peninsula has received from these discoveries in Iceland a prominence it never had before. Modern poets have gone to it for their subjects; modern musicians, for their libretti; everybody is discussing the sagas; in short, Scandinavian, like Sanskrit literature, is the fashion. The ancient literature of the four nations who inhabit the Scandinavian peninsula is practically one. In this chapter we shall speak only of the Swedes, Norwegians, Danes, and Icelanders.

In Icelandic are complete remains of Teutonic heathendom. "The characters come out in full pagan grandeur." As a language, the Mœso-Gothic is older, but it has no pagan literature; its only book is the translation of the Bible by Bishop Ulphilas: so here is our last glimpse of an original pagan view of this world and the other. The Norsemen were converted to Christianity so much later than any other European nation, that their cosmogony and mythology have been preserved to us in a perfectly unaltered condition. But even if they were pagans, we may be proud of our ancestors; for their literature is both grand and poetic, and through it all runs a vein of grim humor, (quite different from the Keltic wit,) which is lacking in the other Aryan literatures.

Their sacred books are the two Eddas, one poetic, the other prose, written in that old Norse tongue which was once spoken by the four families throughout the Scandinavian peninsula. The word Edda means great-grandmother, because the poems were handed down from the grandmothers by repetition. The poetic Edda, which is the older of the two, is a collection of thirty-seven ballads, called sagas. Some of them are religious, and give an account of the creation of the world, of the gods, and of men; some of them historical, telling of the heroes of the nation; one of them gives a series of moral maxims. But they are quite different from the Vedas or the Avesta; the Edda has none of those prayers and hymns and thanksgivings which make the Vedas and the Avesta so beautiful. The ballads were written before the sixth century, but they were collected together, in 1086 A. D., by a Christian priest named Sæmund. Some scholars think Sæmund was a name given him, in reference to this, for it means the mouth which scatters seeds. It is only a very small book, but we look at it with reverence, for it contains the thought of a whole people. The prose Edda was collected about 1200 A. D. It explains the mythology and the history of the poetic Edda, which, indeed, could hardly be understood without it. It would be difficult to gather a system of belief, even a connected story, from utterances so vague, incoherent, and disjointed as those of Saemund's Edda, especially the mythological part: the heroic portion is more connected and comprehensible. But nevertheless there is a wonderful charm about the Edda, — a vague breadth in the thought, a delicious simplicity in the expression.

Of course there is first the cosmogony, or creation of the world; and there is an amazing resemblance between this and the Greek cosmogony told in Hesiod. The same ideas reappear in the Edda, — those ideas which have been manifested by every Aryan race. There are two worlds. Niflheim, the home of mist and cold, — the same word as *nebula*, a cloud, and our word nebulous, — and Muspelheim, the home of fire ; between them a vast empty abyss.

> " There was in times of old
> Nor sand nor sea,
> Nor gelid waves ;
> Earth existed not,
> Nor heaven above.
> 'T was a chaotic chasm,
> And grass nowhere."

Then the supreme ineffable Spirit willed, and a formless chaotic matter was created. This will immediately

suggest that wonderful hymn of the Rig Veda, quoted
in the fourth chapter, where the same thought is expressed more spiritually. From this matter gradually
issue all creations : first the ice giants, called Jötuns ;
they are the evil beings of Norse mythology ; the cold,
the frost, the mist, are devils here : they are like the
Titans of Greek cosmogony. Then a second race is
created by the Supreme Spirit, called Æsir, or gods ;
the singular is Asa ; it is the same root as Asura in the
Vedas, Ahura in the Avesta. They are the good powers
constantly warring with the Jötuns ; they conquer and
drive away these ice giants. For there was struggle
here in this wild climate, just as in Persia, — a perpetual warfare between heat and cold, which were
good and evil to them ; a warfare unthought of in the
temperate climate of Greece, and totally reversed in the
burning heat of India, where the frost and cold would
have been welcome friends, and the heat and drought
were the dreaded enemies. Then the Æsir, or gods,
create heaven, and the earth, and the deep ocean ; they
make subordinate spirits of several kinds : elves, who
dwell in the air, and plants on the earth's surface ;
dwarfs, who dwell under ground and work in minerals ;
nixies, who dwell in the water. All these, you will understand, are the forces of nature working. Then when
all the elves, dwarfs, and nixies had worked and made
ready the earth and the sea, the Æsir created mankind.
Each creation has a world of its own. Muspelheim is
the highest heaven, — the home of light and warmth ;
Asgard, the home of the Æsir, or gods ; Midgard, the
middle-world, home of men ; Utgard, or Jötunheim,
uttermost boundary of the world, home of the Jötuns or

giants ; last, the dark Niflheim, home of mist and cold,—
a frozen under-world, which corresponds to the Greek
Hades, that dark under-world. There was the home of
Queen Hel. In a bitterly cold place she received the
souls of all who died of sickness or old age ; as no
Norseman would wish to die, "Care was her bed, hunger was her dish, starvation was her knife." But there
is no idea of punishment connected with her. She is
not an evil spirit, though stern and severe. She received those who were unfortunate, not wicked ; those
who died before they were killed, —the cowards. There
are many more personifications, full of meaning ; and
we feel that the Teutonic mind was deeply poetical
to have expressed the actions and the manifestations
of nature in such lovely conceptions.

In Teutonic mythology women occupy a more honorable place than in any other. There were three Fates,
just as in Greek : these are called Norns ; they govern
the past, present, and future. Their names are Urd,
Verdand, and Skuld. Our word *weird* is the same as
Urd, and the three witches in Macbeth are unconsciously
expressions of the same idea. The Vala, or prophetess,
was supposed to possess knowledge of the past and the
future ; to be inspired by the Norns, and to express
their decisions. The first poem of the Edda is the
"Wisdom of a Vala," called the Voluspa Saga ; and
from the words of this Vala comes all we know of the
Teutonic creation of the world.

It is curious to see how this branch has described its
gods and goddesses, — how expressed the mythology of
its race. High on a throne, above all the Æsir and
men, sits Odin, the father and ruler ; like Dyaus in

18

Sanskrit, or Zeus in Greek, or Jupiter in Latin. Two ravens sit on his shoulder, who fly over the world and come back to tell him all that has happened. They are named Hugin and Munin ; that is, thought and memory. Two wolves sit at his feet. He is a stately figure, wrapped in a garment of cloudy blue ; this is, of course, the blue sky. He often wears a broad hat, which symbolizes the broad expanse of the sky. He is always described as having but one eye. The other he left as a pledge when he went to drink at Mimir's well. Here he changes his character and represents the sun, which becomes one round eye only, when reflected in any well. It has been difficult to trace the derivation of his name, but now it is considered to come first from the word Atman, another Sanskrit name for the Supreme Spirit, which we examined in the fourth chapter, which means the spirit simply existing : next, from the verb *wotan*, which means to move. And Odhinn is one of the forms of this verb. Wuotan, the German deity, is another, and means the Supreme Spirit in motion, creating and working, penetrating, and circulating everywhere. So Odin is also the air and the wind. We meet exactly this distinction in Sanskrit between Brahman and Brahmā. It is rather hard to understand, but becomes easier if we remember that every new action of a deity gives him a new name. This derivation has been traced by Grimm, and is considered a great triumph of scholarship. Odin performs many different actions and has many names. He marries Frigg, the earth, and they are parents of Thor, the thunder ; Baldur, who is sometimes the summer, sometimes the sun ; Hödur, the blind god, who is the dark winter, or the night. But Odin marries many other wives, like the Greek Zeus, and is the father of Bragi, the god of eloquence and poetry, from whom comes our word brag ; of Saga, goddess of history, — hence our word say ; of Tyr, the war god, whose name we have preserved in Tuesday, originally Tyr's day.

Odin has other warlike deities under his rule. The sternly beautiful Valkeyrie are white maidens that ride through the air ; dew and hail fall from the manes of their horses ; these are distinctly the clouds. They visit every battle-field and choose from the dead corpses the heroes, whom they carry to Valhall, the hall of Odin's palace at Asgard. Odin often accompanies them, that is, the wind blows along the clouds. He is sometimes called Valfadir. The same root Val occurs in three words ; it means to choose : Valfadir, the father who chooses ; Valkeyrie, the choosers ; Valhall, the chosen hall. But no man ever went to Valhall unless he died fighting, so the Norseman dying would be carried from his bed to the field of battle, or leap from a rock into the sea, or fall upon his own sword. And in Valhall the warriors fight and get bloody wounds every day, and feast and drink mead every evening, and wake up every morning as good as new, healed of their wounds, and begin the same sport over again. It is not such an ignoble Paradise as the Mohammedan, certainly. All cold was banished from Valhall: " huge logs blazed and crackled for the brave and beautiful who had dared to die on the gory battle-field, or sunk beneath the waves ; while Queen Hel ruled in her frozen regions over the cowards." It has lately been discovered what became of Queen Hel's subjects, — of all the other

Norsemen, and of all the Norse women, after they died and sought Queen Hel's regions. Finn Magnussen says: "The pagan Norsemen held, in common with the Druids (Keltic priests) and the Brahmans (Hindu priests), the doctrine of transmigration. They believed that, by giving a child the name of a distinguished man, especially of his own forefathers, the soul of the name father was transferred into the child." The soul would be born again, incarnated into another body. Perhaps from this came another idea, which suggests the Persians. Each individual had a Fylgia, a spiritual body, which appeared sometimes to the individual himself, sometimes to his friends.

Odin wanders about, and has many adventures: of course the wind must always wander. He shows simply great physical strength and a keen wit, — nothing disreputable, like the Greek and Latin gods. His greatest benefit, however, was the invention of writing. The Norse alphabet had sixteen letters, combined into sentences called runes, which had a magical power, and were carved on sword-blades, called runes of victory; on drinking-horns, called love-runes, to make maidens love the hero. Storm-runes were carved on the mast and rudder of vessels to make them sail safely; herb-runes, on the bark of the tree to cure diseases. Speech-runes were used to defeat an enemy in the parliament called the Thing; they are described in one of the sagas of the Edda, and they are constantly referred to in all Norse literature. There were even strange and awful runes, which could raise the dead to life, when uttered by a Vala.

Our word Thursday comes from the god Thor, from

the same root as tender and thin and thunder. Thor
had originally no reference to noise ; it meant to ex-
tend, to stretch, — an extension of anything, sound included. Thor is the greatest god after Odin, his eldest
son, the inheritor of his power. He is sometimes called
Ving Thor, the winged. He has a fiery red beard : this
is the lightning ; and he carries a mighty hammer,
Miolnir, the crusher, the pounder. With this hammer
he slew the frost giants, just as Indra slew the drought
in India. His hammer is the thunder : he is the god
of the rain, the thunder, the lightning, like Indra.
Just as Indra assumed some of the characteristics of
Dyaus, so does Thor take those of Odin, his mighty
father, and is sometimes worshipped as the Supreme
God. He is scarcely ever at home at Asgard among
the Æsir, but visits the giants, his enemies, in Jötunheim, where he has many amusing adventures. He
is girded with a belt of strength, and is a famous
wrestler. He is not very clever, but, in spite of his
enormous strength, is very good-natured. He is perpetually losing his hammer by his stupidity, but it invariably comes back to him, no matter how far he may
have hurled it.

THE LAY OF THRYM ; OR THE HAMMER RE-
COVERED.

1. Wroth was Ving Thor
when he awoke
and his hammer
missed :
his beard he shook,

his forehead struck,
the son of earth
felt all around him :
2. And first of all
these words he uttered :

"Hear now, Loki!
what I say,
which no one knows
anywhere on earth
nor in heaven above,
the As's hammer is stolen!"

3. They went to the fair
Freyia's dwelling,
and he these words
first of all said :
"Wilt thou me, Freyia,
thy feather garment lend,
that perchance my hammer
I may find?"

FREYIA.

4. That would I give thee,
although of gold it were,
and trust it to thee
though it were of silver.

5. Flew then Loki —
the plumage rattled —
until he came beyond
the Æsir's dwellings,
and came within
the Jötuns' land.

6. On a mound sat Thrym
the Thursar's lord,
for his greyhounds
plaiting gold bands,
and his horses'
manes smoothing.

THRYM.

7. How goes it with the Æsir?
How goes it with the Alfar?

Why art thou come alone
to Jötunheim?

LOKI.

8. Ill it goes with the Æsir.
Ill it goes with the Alfar.
Hast thou Ving Thor's
hammer hidden?

THRYM.

9. I have Ving Thor's
hammer hidden
eight rasts
beneath the earth :
it shall no man
get again
unless he bring me
Freyia to wife.

·   ·   ·   ·   ·

13. They went the fair
Freyia to find ;
and he these words
first of all said :
"Bind thee, Freyia,
in bridal raiment,
we two must drive
to Jötunheim."

14. Wroth then was Freyia
and with anger chafed,
all the Æsir's hall
beneath her trembled ;
in shivers flew the famed
Brisinga necklace.
"Know me to be
of women lewdest,
if with thee I drive
to Jötunheim."

15. Straightway went the Æsir
all to council,
and the Asymirs
all to hold converse :
and deliberated
the mighty gods,
how they Ving Thor's
hammer might get back.
16. Then said Heimdall
of Æsir brightest :
"Let us clothe Thor
with bridal raiment,
let him have the famed
Brisinga necklace.
17. Let by his side
keys jingle,
and women's weeds
fall round his knees,
but on his breast
place precious stones,
a neat coif
set on his head."
18. Then said Thor,
the mighty As :
"Me the Æsir will
call womanish,
if I let myself be clad
in bridal raiment."
19. Then spake Loki,
Lanfey's son :
"Do thou, Thor ! refrain
from such like words ;
forthwith the Jötuns will
Asgard inhabit,
unless thy hammer thou
gettest back."

20. Then they clad Thor
in bridal raiment, etc.

. . . .

21. Then said Loki,
Lanfey's son :
"I will with thee
as a servant go ;
we two will drive
to Jötunheim."
22. Straightway were the goats
homeward driven,
hurried to the traces ;
they had fast to run.
The rocks were shivered,
the earth was in a blaze.
Odin's son drove
to Jötunheim.
23. Then said Thrym
the Thursar's lord :
"Rise up, Jötuns !
And the benches deck.
Now they bring me
Freyia to wife."
24. "Hither to our court let
bring
gold-horned cows
all-black oxen,
for the Jötuns' joy.
Treasures I have many,
necklaces many,
Freyia alone
seemed to me wanting."
25. In the evening
they early came,
and for the Jötuns
beer was brought forth.

Thor alone one ox devoured,
salmons eight,
and all the sweetmeats
women should have.
Sif's consort drank
three salds of mead.

26. Then said Thrym
the Thursar's lord :
" Where hast thou seen brides
eat more voraciously?
I never saw brides
feed more amply,
nor a maiden
drink more mead."

27. Sat the all-crafty
serving-maid close by,
who words fitting found
against the Jötun's speech :
" Freyia has nothing eaten
for eight nights,
so eager was she
for Jötunheim."

28. Under her veil he stooped
desirous to salute her,
but sprang back
along the hall.
"Why are so piercing
Freyia's looks?

Methinks that fire
burns from her eyes."

28. Sat the all-crafty
serving-maid close by,
who words fitting found
against the Jötun's speech :
"Freyia for eight nights
has not slept,
so eager was she
for Jötunheim."

. . . .

31. Then said Thrym,
the Thursar's lord :
" Bring the hammer in
the bride to consecrate :
lay Miollnir
on the maiden's knee."

32. Laughed Ving Thor's
soul in his breast,
when the fierce-hearted
his hammer recognized.
He first slew Thrym
the Thursar's lord,
and the Jötuns' race
all crushed.

So got Odin's son
his hammer back.

The bad god is Loki ; he comes from the word *lukos*,
bright, and at first he meant mild warmth, and was
all good. But he is a kind of fallen angel, mischievous rather than bad, always playing tricks upon the
Æsir, like Hermes in Greek. And here comes in the
grim humor so characteristic of the Teutonic branch.

Thor's wife, Sif, had lovely bright hair; but Loki cut it all off for mischief. Then Thor threatened to crush every bone in his body with the hammer, if he did not force the elves to make Sif a head of hair all of gold: so the dwarfs made it. Sif is the uncultivated earth, her hair the grass; the fire burnt it up: then the powers of nature working under ground made beautiful, bright, green grass spring up again. Loki becomes crafty, like the creeping fires under the earth; or devastating, like the fire of the volcano. He lives under ground; his daughter is Hel, queen of the dark under-world. Loki is a great eater, and is perpetually wandering about in search of adventures.

But the most bright and beautiful of the Æsir is Baldur. His story is well known, but has been so perfectly explained by comparative mythology that I must allude to it. Every living thing has sworn never to injure the beautiful, beloved Baldur, except the mistletoe, — all plants, stones, beasts, and birds. Then the Æsir were playing together and shooting at Baldur in Asgard. And the blind god Hödur took a mistletoe wand, not knowing what he did, which killed Baldur. This was the most deplorable event which had ever happened to gods or men. Now Odin had a son Vali, whose mother was an obstinate princess named Rind. And when the son of Odin and Rind was only one day old, unwashed and uncombed, he was so mighty that he slew the blind god Hödur, and avenged Baldur. Nothing could be prettier than the explanation. Baldur is the summer, beloved by all; Hödur, the blind god, is the dark winter. The mistletoe is not like other plants, which die with the summer: it outlives the summer, and is green all through the winter, not killed by the winter's cold. The obstinate princess, Rind, means the hard-frozen winter earth, the stiff outside, just what our English word rind means. Her son Vali, who grows so fast that he can kill Hödur, the winter, when only a day old, is the bright spring day: the sudden transition of the year from the winter to spring, and his miraculous growth, is exactly what is told of the Maruts, or Hermes.

Of the summer, Iduna, the same story is told as of Persephone in Greek. She is stolen away with her apples, and all the Æsir mourn; the trees shed frozen tears, and the sun withdraws his face, until Loki brings her back in the form of a quail. In Greek mythology Delos, the brilliant birth-place of Phoibos, is also Ortygia, the land of the quail. Freya is the goddess of love and beauty and plenty. Her chariot is drawn by cats, and also she travels far and wide. She has a lovely necklace: this corresponds to the girdle which Aphrodite wears in Greek. All these round ornaments have one meaning: they are a symbol of the earth. Her name comes from a root which means joy and abundance; and the German word Frau, applied to high-born women, comes from the same root.

The idea of the rainbow is poetical. It was Bif-röst, the trembling path; and it was the bridge from Midgard, the habitation of men, to Asgard, the home of the gods, over which the gods passed. One of the possessions of the gods is the good ship Skidbladnir, which can enlarge itself to carry all the Æsir, or shrink till it is folded into one's hand, like the ship Argo in Greek literature, which bore the Argonauts.

By degrees, worship became more material. Tem-

ples were raised to Odin and Thor, and the most acceptable sacrifice was a horse. The reader will remember
that in India the same idea existed : the Aswemedha,
or horse sacrifice, was the chief gift of some powerful
king. Each chief of a tribe, even each head of a family,
could perform the sacrifice among the Norsemen. Their
temple was at Upsala in Sweden ; the grove that surrounded it was sacred, like the Greek and Keltic
groves. It was dedicated to Odin, and the bodies of
the slain were buried in it, for our Norse ancestors
went farther than other Aryans : they sacrificed human
beings, even kings, in tīmē of great calamity. Yarl
Hakon sacrificed his only son. But in spite of this
darkest stain, Norse mythology has a spiritual idea in
it, — that of the twilight of the gods, called Ragnarok.
Odin and the Æsir are mortal ; they will be overthrown,
a new heaven and a new earth will arise. The Mighty
One will sit in judgment, the good be rewarded, the evil
punished ; strife will be over, peace will prevail. And
in this are implied the most religious of all beliefs, —
the immortality of the soul, the final triumph of good,
and the existence of a mighty spirit, the overruling Deity
of the universe, too sublime to be enclosed in temples
made with hands, or to be represented in human form,
— too lofty almost to be named. The Edda says : —

> " Then comes the mighty one
> to the great judgment,
> the powerful one from above
> who rules over all.
> He shall dooms pronounce,
> and strifes allay,
> holy peace establish,
> which evermore shall be."

It would seem impossible that such an idea could have originated without some Christian influence, were it not that we have met something like it in the Persian religion. It has been said, that " in the Norse gods we find a picture of the Norseman himself, — his bravery and endurance, his dash and spirit of adventure, his fortitude against the certain doom, — ' the twilight of the gods.' " Christianity, with its teaching of an ever-living God, filled them with comfort and joy, and easily supplanted their dead gods. But a curious transformation took place : these did not lose their power; but, instead of being kindly and genial, they became powerful for ill, — malignant demons, just as they had in Persia ; and this is the second way in which evil spirits got into Christianity. Queen Hel, for instance, became a place, and her cold, dark world became a place of torment, where these demons lived.

Not only has the old Norse language its gods, but it has also its heroes, — mighty men they are. The greatest of them is Sigurd the Volsung. His story is told in several of the ballads of Sæmund's Edda, but in so disconnected a way that we could not understand it unless many additions had been made and many gaps filled up. It is a fierce and cruel story ; but it is the epic poem of the Teutonic branch. Wagner has taken it for the libretto of his great trilogy, and William Morris has expanded it into a long and lovely poem. I think that no profane hand will venture to touch it after him, but the Teutonic epic will go down to posterity in the perfect form which he has given it. It is a story within a story, — the history of a family, the Volsungs. Mr. Cox says, "The real difference between the Greek and the Teutonic epics is the greater compass of the Northern poems." The Iliad relates the incidents of only a single year in the Trojan war, but the Volsung sagas have three distinct stories. The first part is the history of Sigmund, — an awful tale of evil passions and revenge and blood, too wild and horrible to have any reality about it. I shall allude to only a few of its incidents. The first is the miraculous way in which he gains his sword, like Arthur's sword, which was stuck into the anvil, or Theseus's sword, hidden under a heavy stone ; and the weapon is another of those resistless swords which every hero uses.

" There was a dwelling of kings ere the world was waxen old.
  Dukes were the door-wards there, and the roofs were thatched
    with gold ;
  For amidst of its midmost hall floor sprang up a mighty tree.
  They call that warduke's tree, that crowned stem, the Bran-
    stock. . . . . .
  Then into the Volsung dwelling a mighty man there strode,
  One-eyed and seeing ancient, yet bright his visage glowed.
  Cloud blue was the hood upon him, and the kirtle gleaming
    gray
  As the latter morning sun-dog when the storm is on the way.
  So strode he to the Branstock, nor greeted any lord ;
  But forth from his cloudy raiment he drew a gleaming sword,
  And smote it deep in the tree bole. . . . . .
  ' Earls of the Goths and Volsungs, abiders on the earth,
  Lo there amid the Branstock a blade of plenteous worth.
  Now let the man among you, whose heart and hand may shift
  To pluck it from the oak-wood, e'en take it for my gift.' "

Sigmund and his son become wolves at night, and kill all that cross their path, and then take on their human form again. The gods do this in all mythologies; the power extended to men in many different legends: the were-wolf is found among the Anglo-Saxons, the Brétons, and the Slavs. The superstition came from a confusion between two words, — *leukos*, bright, and *lukos*, a wolf. This is shown most plainly in the Greek mythology. One of the names of Phoibos Apollo is the Lykeian, the god who slew the wolves. The myth is very near its primitive form: there it is the bright day overpowering the darkness, but since then has come down to a very humble shape. For it is the same wolf which eats up little Red Riding-Hood, — the darkness eating up the red light of the day. Sigmund has many adventures, and a long life. He marries when he is old a wise and lovely woman; but he is forced to leave her and go to battle. In the thickest of the fight, while he is slaying hundreds of enemies with his single arm, Odin comes to him: the arm falters that never faltered before; the good sword is shattered. Before he dies he says to his wife: —

> " Lo yonder where once I stood
> The shards of a glaive of battle that once was the best of the good.
> Take them, and keep them surely. I have known full well
> That a better one than I am shall live the tale to tell.
> And for him shall these shards be smithied, and he shall be my son
> To remember what I have forgotten, and to do what I left undone."

He dies, and his faithful queen is cared for in the house of a good king, until Sigurd the Volsung is born. His awful eyes are the eyes of Phoibos and of Odysseus.

" Yet he shrank in his rejoicing before the eyes of the child,
So bright were they and dreadful ; . . . . . .
The eyes of the child gleamed on him, till he was as one who
sees
The very gods arising through their carven images
As he hung o'er the new-born Volsung."

The queen marries the good king, and Sigurd dwells
with his step-father, in a land that is not his. His kith
and kin are dead, his kingdom lost, and he has never
seen his great father. This is the story of Perseus,
whose mother married again, in Greek ; and Karna, in
Sanskrit ; and Romulus, in Latin ; and, having found
the same circumstance so many times, its meaning is
plain. The sun never can see its father, the sun of
yesterday. Now comes the greatest hero, Sigurd, and
the poem which tells us of him is lovely as a dream.
Long days of peace go by, while Sigurd is trained to
every knightly grace. Then he longs for a horse, and
refuses all those his good step-father offers. He goes
forth and gets himself a wondrous horse, called Greyfell.

" Then again gat Sigurd outward, and adown the steep he ran,
And unto the horse-fed meadow ; but lo a gray-clad man,
One-eyed and seeing ancient, there met him by the way. . . . .
Thus spake this elder of days : ' Hearken now, Sigurd, and
hear :
Time was when I gave thy father a gift thou shalt yet deem
dear,
And this horse is a gift of my giving.'
 .   .   .   .   .
And indeed he was come from Sleipnir's blood,
The tireless horse of Odin : cloud-gray was he of hue,
And it seemed as Sigurd backed him that Sigmund's son he
knew."

Then Regin, the dwarf, tries to induce him to do a "deed of awing." He tells him that the dwarfs had collected a mighty treasure, — a heap of gold; but it had been stolen, and was guarded by the worm Fafnir, who lay wallowing upon it. The dwarf's curse is upon the gold because stolen, and whomever shall obtain it; but Sigurd at length promises to win it, and the coat of mail and the helmet, and the ring Andvari, from which drops a new ring, — all of which are part of the dwarf's treasures. The dwarfs who work under ground are peculiar to Keltic and Teutonic mythology: they represent the wonderful properties of the mineral and vegetable kingdoms, and the silent growing and development of life. The treasure which the dwarfs had piled up would be therefore the powers of vegetation, the forces of nature working unseen: the ring of Andvari, from which other rings dropped, is but another form of the same thought, — the reproductive power of nature, — and this ring appears in many other stories. The worm Fafnir, who steals all this, is the same dragon who stole the waters in India and Greece; but the difference of climate gives him a different form. The winter and the cold are the foes to be dreaded in the North, instead of the heat and drought: so the worm Fafnir is simple darkness and cold, — the mere negation of light and warmth and life; he steals away the summer and the growing power of nature, and buries them in the death-like sleep of winter. Sigurd seeks to get himself a sword. Regin makes him two swords, but they shiver at the first stroke. Sigurd exclaims that they are untrue, like Regin and the dwarf race. So he turns elsewhere, and asks from his mother his father's

sword. So his mother brings him the pieces of his father's old sword, like Thetis bringing armor to her son
Achilleus. Regin forges the pieces, and cries : —

> " Before the days of men
> I smithied the wrath of Sigmund, and now it is smithied
> again."

This sword is keen and firm ; the difference between it
and the swords of Regin the dwarf is just the difference
between the subterranean fires and workings of the
earth and the life-giving rays of the sun, which alone
can slay the worm of cold. The sword is called the
Wrath of Sigurd.

> " Now Sigurd backeth Greyfell, on the first of the morrow
> morn,
> And he rideth fair and softly through the edges of the corn.
> The Wrath to his side is girded, but hid are its edges blue,
> As he wendeth his way to the mountains and rideth the
> meadow through.
> His wide gray eyes are happy, and his voice is sweet and soft,
> And amid the mead lark's singing he casteth song aloft.
> Lo ! lo the horse and the rider. So once may be it was
> When over the earth unpeopled the youngest god would pass.
> But never again, meseemeth, shall such a sight betide
> Till over a world unwrongful new-born shall Baldur ride."

He reaches the glittering heath, and finds the loath-
some worm Fafnir wallowing upon the gold. The hero
and the monster are familiar figures ; any differences
between Sigurd and the other heroes can readily be
explained by the differences of climate. So the mighty
Sigurd killed Fafnir, and took the gold, and the ring of
Andvari, and put on the coat of golden mail and the

helm of awing, which dazzled whoever looked at them. The sun had come out in full splendor, conquered the cold, and brought back vegetation. He ate the heart of Fafnir, and got possession of his wisdom; but before his death Fafnir had foretold the future to Sigurd: as the Python, the serpent slain by Apollo, is connected with the Delphian oracle, which foretold the future, and gave wisdom. Sigurd rode away on Greyfell till he came to a mountain-side where there was a wall of flickering fire; but he rode through it, and beyond he saw a stately palace. No one was within it; but on a mound was extended a figure clad in armor. At once, —

> " He draweth the helm from the head; and lo the brow snow-
> white,
> And the smooth, unfurrowed cheeks, and the wise lips
> breathing light,
> And the face of a woman it is, the fairest that ever was born.
> And he looketh, and loveth her sore, and he longeth her
> spirit to move,
> And awaken her heart to the world, that she may behold him
> and love.
> So the edge of his sword he setteth to the dwarf-wrought
> battle-coat,
> Where the hammered, ring-knit collar constraineth the wo-
> man's throat.
> Then he driveth the blue steel onward, and through the mail,
> and out,
> Till naught but the rippling linen is wrapping her about.
> Then he turns about the Warflame, and rends down either
> sleeve,
> Till her arms lay white in her raiment, and a river of sun-
> bright hair
> Flows free over bosom and shoulder."

She speaks : —

" ' O, what is the thing so mighty that my weary sleep hath
   torn ? '
He said, ' The hand of Sigurd, and the sword of Sigmund's
   son,
And the heart that the Volsungs fashioned this deed for
   thee have done.'
But she said, ' Where, then, is Odin, that laid me here alow ? '
' He dwelleth above,' said Sigurd, ' but I on the earth abide,
And I came from the glittering heath, the waves of thy fire
   to ride.' "

She tells him that she is a Valkeyrie ; but for disobedience to Odin the thorn of sleep had pierced her,
and she was doomed to lie there until some knight
should ride the flickering fire and awaken her : then
she would marry the mortal who could ride the flickering fire, and cease to be a Valkeyrie. This is the same
story as the nursery tale of the sleeping beauty, Brynhild, and her riches are but another form of the first
idea, — the earth, sleeping in winter, awakened by the
sun. Brynhild teaches him many wise things ; she has
more than mortal wisdom : they plight their troth to
each other. Sigurd gives her the ring of Andvari,
which has the curse upon it. He promises to come
back that they may be married ; then he rides away
with his treasures to the country of the Nibelungs :
they, with their dark blue garments, are the dark blue
storm-clouds. The queen of the Nibelungs gives him a
magic drink ; and he marries Gudrun, her daughter,
the princess of the Nibelungs. She is outwardly fair
and beautiful, with soft, dark eyes, and long, dark hair,
and wears dark blue garments. So the days of late

summer are fair, but they are near to the storms of
winter, more akin to darkness than to light. Since the
sun must leave the spring, Sigurd leaves Brynhild;
since it must wed the late summer, he marries the dark-
blue clad Gudrun; since it must be covered with clouds,
he dwells among her kin, the swart Nibelungs. Long
days go by. The golden Sigurd has forgotten Brynhild,
for the spell is upon him; and he has given himself and
his treasure to the Nibelungs, and he toils for others.
Then Gunnar, the king of the Nibelungs, desires to
marry the mighty wise woman Brynhild, and they all
go forth to seek her. But neither man nor horse
can ride the flickering fire, except the golden Sigurd.
Therefore he assumes the shape of Gunnar, the Nibelung king, — that is, the sun covers itself with clouds,
— rides the flickering fire, and, wearing the form of
Gunnar, he asks her to be the wife of Gunnar. Brynhild thinks that Sigurd has forgotten her; and so she
promises to marry Gunnar, and she gives to the man
whom she thinks to be Gunnar the ring of Andvari,
which Sigurd had given to her. And Sigurd keeps the
ring himself, instead of giving it back to Gunnar.
Gunnar weds Brynhild; — he is the winter carrying
away the spring; like Ravana, who carried away Sita;
or Pluto, who carried away Proserpine; — and Brynhild comes to dwell in the Nibelung palace.

The spell has passed by; and Sigurd recognizes her,
and remembers the past. But they live on for some
time, till finally the two queens quarrel; and then the
truth is known that it was not Gunnar, but Sigurd,
who rode the flickering fire. Brynhild is full of wrath
at the treachery practised upon her, and so she per-

suades the Nibelungs to murder Sigurd. The Nibelungs are jealous of him and his treasure, — they are
angry; that is, the storm and cold wish to slay the
bright, beautiful sun: it is but the slaying of Baldur
over again. Then Brynhild, wild with misery, can live
no longer, now that Sigurd has left the world, and the
day is dark without him. She kills herself, and she
cries out : —

" I pray thee a prayer, the last word I shall speak, —
That ye bear me forth to Sigurd. . . . .
The bale for the dead is builded ; it is wrought full wide on
the plain ;
It is raised for the Earth's best helper, and thereon is room
for twain ;
Ye have hung the shields about it, and the Southland sayings
speak ;
There lay me adown by Sigurd, my head beside his head.
.   .   .   .   . Draw his Wrath from out the sheath,
And lay that light of the Branstock, that blade that frighted
death,
Betwixt my side and Sigurd's. .   .   .   .
How then, when the flames flare upward, may I be left
behind ?
How then may the road he wendeth be hard for my feet to find ?
How then in the gates of Valhall may the door of the gleam-
ing ring
Clash to, on the heel of Sigurd, as I follow on my king ? "

And she is burned on the funeral pile of her hero. It
is the same familiar tale of a hero torn from the bride
of his youth. He is more beautiful than all the sons of
men. He slays the serpent, and then toils for others
meaner than himself. He is slain by dark powers, and
joined on his funeral pile by the bride of his youth. Of

course the resemblance cannot be accidental, any more than it can have been consciously copied. It is but the same Aryan thought breaking out in new form.

Gudrun flees away, and hides from the sight of men. Seven years go by, and she broods and dreams of her revenge. Then the third tale, Gudrun's vengeance, begins. She marries a great king; but the Nibelung brothers refuse to give up the gold which was once Sigurd's, and should now be hers. Finally she persuades her new husband to insist upon having the gold. She sends for her brethren, and when they have come to her new home she entices them all into her husband's palace-hall, where the Nibelung brothers refuse to give up the gold. Then there is an awful battle in the hall: the doors are closed, and they cannot come forth; but they still refuse to give up the gold. They fight till all the Nibelungs are dead save Gunnar the king, and Hagen. Gunnar is thrown into a pit full of snakes until he shall tell where the gold is. He promises to tell if they will bring him the heart of Hagen, his brother; for no one else knows the secret. So Hagen is killed, his heart is cut out and brought to Gunnar. And Gunnar laughs aloud, and cries: "Now the secret shall die with me. The gold is sunk beneath the water, and none knows the spot." He sings a proud death-song on his harp, and the serpents pause to listen. But at last they sting him to death, and the gold is lost forever; and all the Nibelungs are dead except Gudrun, and she is revenged for Sigurd's death. The husband and his nobles feast together till all are asleep. Then Gudrun sets fire to the hall, and the king and the nobles are burnt to death, and Gudrun is avenged for the slaughter of her kindred; and she plunges into the sea to die in the waters, to seek the gold which is there. It is a gloomy tale of love and sorrow, and falsehood and revenge. The vast slaughter-hall swimming in blood, which no one is allowed to leave, is like the slaughter-hall in the Odyssey when Odysseus shoots down his enemies. But "the fierceness of the Northern tale is the fierceness of the Northern climate." In the Grecian story, the treasure and the woman are carried back to Greece, their home, in joyful triumph. In the tragic North the ending is quite unlike: the treasure is sunk beyond recovery, — lost to both sides of the quarrel. Yet the tale is nevertheless the same: Mr. Cox says, "The Teutonic epics, like the Greek, are the fruit of one and the same tree, which has spread over all the Aryan lands." Here Mr. Morris's poem ends; but in the Edda the story is carried on to follow the fortunes of Swanhild, the daughter of Sigurd and Gudrun. The waves carry Gudrun to another country. There she marries the king, and her daughter, Swanhild, grows up in the house of a kind step-father. She is a solar myth too, and has never seen her great father, Sigurd, because one day cannot see the day before. Gudrun in the Edda sings : —

1. Of all my children
her I loved the best.
Swanhild was
in my hall
as was the sunbeam
fair to behold.

2. I with gold adorned her,
and with fine raiment,

before I gave her
to the Gothic people.
That is to me the hardest
of all my woes,
that Swanhild's beauteous
locks
should in the mire be trodden
under horses' feet.

Swanhild was condemned to be trampled under horses' feet. She opened her bright piercing eyes, — the awful eyes of Sigurd, — and the horses refused to trample upon her. But she was finally killed. This is just the story of another day, and so the saga might go on forever, but here ends the Volsung race; Swanhild is the last. Another saga tells about Gudrun's other children, who are Nibelungs, dark powers, but this will not interest us. The glory has died from the world with the Volsungs, and we care not for the Nibelungs.

Wagner's libretto is not a copy pure and simple of the Volsung Saga, but it is much nearer to that than to the Nibelungen Lied. He has taken the names from the Nibelungen, but the spirit of his libretto from the Volsung: it is steeped in the two Eddas. There is first an introduction, in which the gods and goddesses, giants and dwarfs, and daughters of Rhine, swan-maidens, appear. The names are German: Odin becomes Wotan, Thor becomes Donnor, the thunder; but the characteristics are Norse, of the Edda. There are three parts to the libretto. The stage shows the hall, and the stately Branstock, and the sword fast in it. Siegmund draws it forth, and, after adventures and battles in which he is slain, eight Valkeyrie swarm upon the stage, which must have produced a wonderful effect. Brünhilde is one of them: she has disobeyed Wotan, so the sleep thorn pierces her, and she falls down in her armor, while the flickering fire rises up about her. In the second play, Siegfried is the hero. He is the child of the dead Siegmund; gets the broken pieces of his father's sword, forges them, kills the worm Fafnir, rides the flickering fire, and awakens Brünhilde.

In the third play the three awful Norns form the chorus : thoroughly Norse all this, — the mythology of the Edda put into actual, tangible form. The names are changed to those of the Nibelungen, but the plot is more like the Volsung Saga. He marries Gudrun, who gives him the magic drink herself, and he is slain by an arrow in the back. Then Brünhilde in full armor rides proudly into the fire of his funeral pile. She is even grander than in the Volsung Saga. She is ashamed that she, a Valkeyrie, should love a mortal man, and struggles against the feeling. Yet this is Wotan's punishment for her disobedience, and she must yield. Wotan, in the opera, is the god come down to earth as a wanderer. He is wrapped in a cloak of cloudy blue, and wears the wide hat of Odin. The Siegfried of the opera is rough and rude compared to the golden Sigurd of the Volsung Saga and the knightly Siegfried of the Nibelungen Lied. But this drawback is slight, and it is wonderful that the very spirit of a past age could have been brought before us so vividly. For actual representation, the operas must have been too long, (Wotan becomes intolerably tiresome,) and there is no humanity about them ; they are, however, grand poetical works, where the wild pagan Norseland is embodied.

CHAPTER X.

COMPARATIVE MYTHOLOGY OF THE TEUTONIC LITERA-
TURE. — ANGLO-SAXON AND GERMAN FAMILIES.

IN our last chapter we examined the Edda and its ficti-
tious poems, called sagas. From them we gathered
some knowledge of the gods and heroes of our Teutonic
ancestors. We saw the ideas which had prevailed in
India, Persia, Greece, expressed by the Teuton : the
forces of nature personified by the restless energy, the
defiant individualism, the grim humor, the deep melancholy, of the Teutonic mind. Their gods and heroes
represented themselves. We come now to those sagas
which are partly historical, or which are domestic, and
paint manners and customs.

My words cannot sufficiently say how fresh, vigorous,
and peculiar this whole literature is : the noble Viking
spirit is expressed in fitting words. It was poured
forth in abounding fulness at a time when Europe had
no literature, except ballads and theology in monkish
Latin. For five hundred years, beginning in the sixth
century, these stout fellows wrote innumerable sagas.
On this remote and poverty-stricken island, uninfluenced by contact with any other nation, this free and
noble people developed the soul that was in them. A
love of liberty, a proud contempt of danger, a delight
in labor, a joy in struggle, a consciousness of personal
independence, a respect for woman, a purity of domes-

tic life, breathe through every line. In the sagas everything is spoken of in a figurative manner. A maiden is
called "the linen-folded"; a sword, "blood-drinker";
water, "the swan's bath"; gold, the "worm's bed"
(this evidently comes from the story of Fafnir, the
worm); a king, "shelter of earls"; a ship, "foamy-
necked," "wave-traverser." Some sagas have prose
intermingled with their poetry. The poetry itself is not
much like our idea of what poetry should be. It has
no rhyme, only alliteration; but it is much more difficult to write than our poetry, and had strict rules for
its metre. It has a certain music of its own. Here is
a very perfect specimen of alliteration. Ragnar Lod-
brok is another of their heroes. He killed his serpent,
and delivered his maiden named Thora, like the other
Aryan heroes, and sang : —

> "*H*ewed we with the *H*anger,
> *H*ard upon the *t*ime 't was
> When in *G*othlandia *g*oing
> To *g*ive death to the serpent :
> *Th*en obtained we *Th*ora.
> *Th*ence have warriors called me
> The *L*ing-eel, since I *l*aid *l*ow
> *L*odbrok : at that carnage
> *St*uck I the *st*ealthy monster
> With *st*eel of finest temper."

This is another one, which says that no soldier shall
ever marry a maiden.

> " He, who *b*rand of *b*attle
> *B*eareth, over weary,
> Never *l*ove shall *l*et him
> Hold the *l*inen-folded."

Here is poetry taken from a saga written in prose, but with these snatches of song bursting out. Gunnlaug, the worm-tongue, is the name of the hero, because he is so eloquent, so persuasive, that his tongue slips along like a worm. The "king's walls" are cities built by kings; the "war-lord's son, the wealth-free," is the king, who gives him the gold.

> "My ways must I be wending
> three king's walls yet to see,
> and yarls twain, as I promised
> erewhile to land sharers.
> Neither will I wend me
> back, the worm's bed lacking,
> by war-lord's son, the wealth-free,
> for work done, gift well given."

Gunnlaug and another fall in love with the same woman. Gunnlaug sings; then his rival sings, and addresses Gunnlaug by very complimentary names connected with his great bravery, calling him god of the sword, glory of the goddess of war, a staff which causes death.

> "God of wound-flames' glitter,
> glorier of fight-goddess,
> must we fall a-fighting
> for fairest kirtle-bearer?
> Death-staff! Many such-like
> fair as she is are there
> in south lands, o'er sea-floods;
> so saith he who knoweth."

The following is a lovely song, so simple and heart-felt. The maiden marries the rival, and dies; then the

rival sings. Gold-ring's bearer is the wife, who wears
the gold ring. Being a sea rover, he calls himself the
seeker of the water; and the water he calls the highway
of the fishes.

> " Dead in mine arms she droopeth,
> my dear one, gold-ring's bearer;
> for God hath changed the life days
> of this lady of the linen.
> Weary pain hath pined her;
> but unto me, the seeker
> of hoard of fishes' highway,
> abiding here is wearier."

There are many of these half-historical, half-domestic
sagas, and the defiant Norse nature crops out delightfully in spite of the Christianity they had adopted.
They sang of battles, sea-fights, single combats, feast-
ings, and gifts. Every wealthy house had in the middle
an immense hall, with benches all around it, a table in
the centre, an elevated place at one end, called the high
seat. And when the king and his wife and honored
guests sat on the high seat, the yarls and bonders
around the tables, the skalds chanted their awful
strains. No wonder that the " Berserker rage " fell
upon these stormy Norsemen. They foamed at the
mouth, they clashed their swords, they rushed to their
long, narrow ships, and sailed out to conquer the world.
Each great yarl, or earl, had a fleet of these ships built
expressly to run up the rivers, long and narrow. Sometimes one ship would be the only property of some bold
Viking. He named it with a favorite name, and talked
to it, and loved it as inland knights loved their horse.
A ship manned with rowers was a common present from

one great man to another. Here is the ship belonging
to Frithjof the Bold. It is like the Greek ship Argo.
" This wonder went with the good ship Ellida, that she
knew the speech of men." So the Norseman was sail-
ing, and he saw two Troll wives (witches) riding on
the waves. So he called out : —

> " Ellida, now
> or ever her way stop
> shall sink the backs
> of those asunder.
> Ellida, sail,
> leap high o'er the billows !
> break of the Troll wives
> brow and teeth now."

I copy an extract from a saga which will sound very
familiar. The legend lived among the Norsemen ; it
was told about two other heroes in two other sagas,
which were written down somewhere between 1200 and
1300 ; it is told about a fourth hero, and the Turks
and the Mongol Tartars tell the same story, who are
Turanians. Now, the story of William Tell was not
written down before 1499 ; so we see that this master
shot, this unerring arrow, belongs to all the Aryan
race, and some of the Turanian families even. The
idea is so true in itself, the arrow of the sun is so resistless, that the myth settles upon every hero whom a
grateful country wishes to honor.

" About that time the young Egill came to the king's court.
Egill was the fairest of men, and this one thing he had before
all other men, — he shot better with the bow than any other
man. The king took to him well, and Egill was there a long
time. Finally, the king wished to try whether Egill shot so

very well or not; so he let Egill's son, a boy of three years old, be taken, and made them put an apple on his head, and bade Egill shoot so that the shaft struck neither above the head, nor to the left, nor to the right. The apple only was he to split. But it was not forbidden him to shoot the boy, for the king thought it certain that he would do that on no account. And he was to shoot one arrow only, no more. So Egill takes three, and strokes their feathers smooth, and fits one to his string, and shoots, and hits the apple in the middle; so that the arrow took along with it half the apple and then fell to the ground. This master shot has been long talked about; and the king made much of him, and he was the most famous of men. Now, King Nidung asked Egill why he took out three arrows, when it was settled that one only was to be shot with. Then Egill answered, 'Lord, I will not lie to you : had I stricken the lad with that one arrow, then I had meant these two for you.' But the king took that well from him, and all thought it was boldly spoken."

All the sagas, whether imaginary or historical, are full of revenge and atonement. Life was held cheap. Difficulties were settled by a hand-to-hand fight, and all the relatives of the slain were bound to avenge him. In the saga of Burnt Njal, a revenge was carried out by shutting up the enemies in their own house, and burning them alive. But through this lurid horror shines one lovely gleam. I copy an episode of Burnt Njal. From the artless way in which it is told, it is plain that the Norsemen were not conscious of doing anything wrong : their Christianity was not very deep.

"Then Flosi, the burner, came back to the house, and called for Njal and Bergthora, his wife. And when they came to the window, he said, 'Njal, thou art an old man, and I would not burn thee in-doors. Thou shalt pass out free.' Njal answered,

'I am too old to avenge my sons upon thee, but I could not live in shame : I will stay with them.' Then Flosi said to Bergthora, 'Do thou come out : for I would not have it on my soul that I burned a woman alive.' And he entreated her. But Bergthora said to him, 'I was very young when I was given to Njal, and then I promised him that nothing should ever part us twain. We have lived long together, and nothing has ever parted us, nor ever shall.' So they went back together, hand in hand, into the house. And Bergthora laid her head against Njal's shoulder and said, 'Husband, what shall we do ?' He kissed her tenderly, and answered, 'It is bed-time, dear one, it is time to rest.' So they went into their chamber. A little boy, Kari's youngest son, was lying in their bed, and Bergthora went to lift him up to take him to another room ; for she said to Njal, 'We cannot see the boy die before our eyes.' But the child said, 'Grandmother, I have always slept with you, and I would rather die with you and Njal than live afterwards.' Then they laid them down in their bed, and took the boy between them ; and having signed themselves and the child with the cross, and committed their souls into God's hands, Njal called to his house steward, and said, 'Mark well how we lie, so that thou mayest afterwards be able to tell where to look for our bones ; for we shall not stir hence for any pain or smart of burning. And now take yonder ox-hide from the wall, and cover us therewith.' The steward took the hide, and, having spread it over them, went out. That was the last that was seen or heard of Njal or Bergthora alive."

Then the awful fight went on, and Njal's sons were all burned alive in the house. Some days after, men came to search for Njal and Bergthora's bones. When they had digged a long time, through a great heap of ashes, they came upon the ox-hide, charred and shrivelled. The hide was lifted, and, —

"Lo! the bodies of Njal and Bergthora were bright and fair, and scarce the smell of fire had passed upon them. They lay as though they slept, and smiled in their sleep, and the child in like manner, save that one of his fingers was burnt where he had stretched it forth from beneath the ox-hide."

There was another way of atonement which was sometimes adopted, but not considered so creditable. This was by paying "blood-gold," — a sum of money, the amount of which was fixed by the Thing or parliament. These were local courts of justice; once a year all the yarls and bonders met to settle the affairs of the whole country, and to choose a king. This was called the All Thing. The yarls were noblemen; the bonders were freemen who owned their land; the thralls were slaves, and had no voice in the government. For this defiant individualism did not prevent the Norsemen from submitting to laws; only they must be of his own making. The codes of law in Norse are among the most remarkable writings of their whole literature. The principal one is called the Gragos, or gray goose, because it was written upon goose-skin, and has been translated. It was to resist tyranny that the Norsemen fled to Iceland, and there they developed that capacity for self-government which is almost the noblest characteristic of the Aryan race. They preserved that form which we found among the undivided Aryans: first the family, then the village, then the clan. Each yarl was the head of his clan, and the kings were chosen by them just as in India, in the society described by the Maha Bharata. The king's power was slight; and when one of the kings issued an order which displeased the yarls and bonders, nine of them threatened to throw him into a marshy pool unless he should retract it. So he retracted it.

The literal actual history of these kings was written down by Snorre Sturleson, the same man who collected the prose Edda, and it is most amusing. It is as lively, and entertaining, and gossiping, as any of the celebrated French memoirs. It is called the Heimskringla, or " Chronicle of the Kings of Norway," and Carlyle stole it bodily in his " Early Kings of Norway." This is actual history, not poetry, like the sagas which we have been examining. The sturdy old kings live and move before us. There was much intercourse with Russia. Every discontented Norseman went to Byzantium to join the Varangian body-guard of the Eastern Emperor, and passed through Russia on his way. Gudleif, a great merchant, drove a trade with Russia, and went eastward in summer to Novogorod, where he bought fine and " costly clothes, which he intended for the king as a state dress, and also precious furs and splendid table utensils," And a Swedish princess often married some Russian king. King Olaf the Saint is one of the most interesting kings of Norway.

" In the autumn news was brought to King Olaf that the bonders had a great feast, at which all the remembrance cups to the Æsir, or old gods, were blessed according to the old forms ; and it was added that cattle and horses had been slain, and the altars sprinkled with their blood, and these sacrifices accompanied with prayers for good seasons."

Now, King Olaf was the first Christian king, and he immediately made a royal progress through the country to convert the nation.

"He taught them the right customs. If there were any who would not leave heathen ways, he took the matter so zealously that he drove some out of the country, mutilated others of hands or feet, or stung their eyes out, hung up some, cut down some with the sword, but let none go unpunished who would not serve God."

Is not this *naïve?* But here is King Olaf's crowning achievement during his royal progress. When Gudbrand heard that he was coming to hold a Thing (parliament), he said : —

"'A man is come to Loar who is called Olaf, and will force upon us another faith than that we had before, and will break in pieces all our gods. He says that he has a much greater and more powerful god ; and it is wonderful that the earth does not burst asunder under him, or that our god lets him go about unpunished, when he dares to talk such things. I know this for certain, that if we carry Thor, who has always stood by, out of our temple, that is standing upon this farm, Olaf's god will melt away, and he and his men will be made nothing, so soon as Thor looks upon them.' Then the bonders all shouted as one man : people streamed to them from all parts, who did not wish to receive Christianity. The king went out to meet the bonders, and hold a Thing with them. On that day the rain fell heavily. When the Thing was seated, the king stood up and said, that the people in Lesso, Loar, and Vaarge had received Christianity, broken down their houses of sacrifice, and believed now in the true God, who had made heaven and earth, and all things. Then the king sat down, and Gudbrand replied, 'We know nothing of him whom thou speakest about. Dost thou call him God, whom neither thou nor any one else can see ? But we have a god who can be seen out every day, although he is not out to-day because the weather is wet ; and he will appear to thee terrible and very grand ; and I expect that fear will mix with your very blood, when he comes into the Thing.' In the evening the king asked

Gudbrand's son what their god was like.   He replied, that he
bore the likeness of Thor; had a hammer in his hand ; was of
great size, and hollow within ; and had a high stand upon
which he stood when he was out.   Then they went to bed, but
the king watched all night in prayer.   When day dawned, the
king went to mass, then to table, from thence to the Thing.
Now the bishop stood up in his choir-robes, with the bishop's
coif on his head, and his bishop's staff in his hand.   He spoke
to the bonders of the true faith, told the many wonderful acts
of God; and concluded his speech well.   Thord replied, and
they separated for the day.   Now the king was in prayer all
night, beseeching God of his goodness and mercy to release
him from evil.   When the mass was ended and morning was
gray, the king went to the Thing.   When he came there he saw
that bonders had arrived already ; and they saw a great crowd
coming along, and bearing among them a huge man's image,
gleaming with gold and silver.   When the bonders who were
at the Thing saw it, they started up and bowed themselves
down before the ugly idol.   Thereupon it was set down upon
the Thing-field ; and on one side of it stood the bonders, and on
the other, the king and his people.   Then Gudbrand stood up
and said: ' Where, O king, is now thy god ?   I think he will
now carry his head lower; and neither thou, nor the man with
the horn, whom ye call bishop, is so bold as on the former
days; for now our god, who rules over everything, is come,
and looks on you with an angry eye, and I see well enough
that ye are terrified, and scarcely dare to raise your eyes.
Throw away now, all your opposition, and believe in the god
who has all your fate in his hands.'   The king then stood up
and spoke : ' Turn your eyes towards the east, behold our
God advancing in great light.'   The sun was rising and
all turned to look.   That moment Kolbein gave their god a
stroke, so that the idol burst asunder, and there ran out of it
mice as big almost as cats, and reptiles, and adders.   The
bonders were so terrified that they fled.   Then the king ordered
them to be called back, and said, ' I do not understand what

your noise and running mean. Ye see yourselves what your god can do, — the idol ye adorned with gold and silver, and brought meat and provisions to. Ye see now that the protecting powers who used it were the mice and adders, reptiles and paddocks : and they do ill who trust to such, and will not abandon this folly. Take now your gold ornaments which are scattered about on the grass, and give them to your wives and daughters; but never lay them again upon stock or stone. Here are now two conditions between us to choose upon, — either accept Chistianity, or fight this very day, and the victory be to them to whom the God we worship gives it.' Then Gudbrand stood up and said, 'We have sustained great damage upon our god, but since he will not help us, we will believe in the God thou believest in.' Then all received Christianity. The bishop baptized Gudbrand and his son. King Olaf and Bishop Sigurd left behind them leaders, and they who met as enemies parted as friends ; and Gudbrand built a church in the valley."

There is a realism about this, which almost makes us believe in Thor too. Snorre tells us that after King Olaf the Saint died, his body worked many miracles. The blind, the lame, the sick, were cured by touching it. People could hear a sound over his holy remains, as if bells were ringing. All this happened in 1030. Paganism had lingered until then.

But there is another kind of literature in Norse which has preserved the common traditions more faithfully even than the mythology and the saga. Baldur, the beautiful, bright summer, slain by the dark winter, descended into the hero of the epic poem, and became the golden Sigurd. He went even further, and became Boots, the hero of the folk tales. And these popular tales have now become a study fit for grown minds,

instead of being condemned by severe parents. The
Norse folk tales are many and delightful. In the "Master Maid" is a horse that darts fire and flame from his
nostrils, like the Greek horse. In "East o' the Sun,
West o' the Moon," there is the same maiden wedded
to a monster she does not see, whom we found in Sanskrit as Urvasi, in Greek as Psyche, in English as
Beauty and the Beast. They are separated, and the
maiden travels far to find her lost hero. In the Norse
story, the winds carry her upon their back; they are
rough, but kindly fellows. The evil spirit in these
stories is always stupid; he is called a Troll. He fights
against mankind, just as the Jötuns fought against the
Æsir. Here is the end of a story : —

"As they sat at supper, back came the Troll who owned the
cattle, and gave such a great knock at the door. As soon as
Peter heard that, down he ran to the gate : 'Stop a bit, and
I 'll tell you how the farmer gets in his winter rye.' And so he
told a long story, over and over again, and he went on until
the sun rose. 'O, do look behind you, and there you 'll see
such a lovely lady!' said Peter to the Troll. So the Troll
turned round ; and of course, as soon as he saw the sun, he
burst."

Now this little myth is very plain. The Troll, the
evil spirit, is the darkness, which must burst before the
light of the sun. Most of the stories are like Cinderella
reversed. There are two haughty brothers, and a third
brother who is despised and abused, and called Boots.
He goes off in disguise, and does brave and kindly
deeds ; and at night he comes back, and lies by the
kitchen-fire in his rags, and everybody mocks at him.
But at last he throws off his beggar rags and comes out
in his full glory. It is the sun rejoicing in his strength,

and throwing off the thick clouds which had enveloped it. These few instances are enough to illustrate the solar myth as found in Norse folk tales. The well-known stories are told over again with infinite humor, — the grim Teutonic humor: it is not so keen as the Keltic wit, but it is more kindly. In them all, the devil is spoken of in a manner very irreverent to our ideas. Mr. Dasent says, " The devil has taken small hold upon the mind of the Norsemen ; he constantly reappears in a pagan aspect, is simple, and easily outwitted." The Norse demons are really the old Norse gods, as we saw in our last chapter   They did not lose their power when Christianity was accepted, but became powerful for ill. This is very evident in the story of the Wild Huntsman.

" When the winds blew, and the clouds hurried along, it was no longer the stately procession of Odin and the Valkeyrie and the chosen heroes in triumphant progress, it was the Wild Huntsman followed by fiends. In Germany it is still Wodin, a demon ; in France, Le Grand Veneur ; in England, Herne the hunter, whom Falstaff met."

We must stop for a moment to speak about our ancestors brought a little nearer to us, — the Angles and Saxons, who invaded and conquered Britain, and drove the Kelts into the remotest corners of the island, — into Wales and the Highlands of Scotland. Our Anglo-Saxon fathers had ballads sung by wandering minstrels called Scops ; but they were mute indeed compared with their brethren in Norway and Iceland, who poured forth sagas for five hundred years, and wrote immortal works. There are three ballads and two fragments in

Anglo-Saxon which are known to be authentic, and the manuscript which contains them is the oldest original manuscript of all the Teutonic families. The poems are not as old as the Edda ; but the Edda was collected by Sæmund from different sources, — perhaps manuscripts, but more probably just from the very lips of people ; so the manuscript of that is not original. This manuscript of the Anglo-Saxon pagan ballads exists in Exeter Cathedral in England, and contains runic letters. The oldest one is the Complaint of Deor, a Scop : it has the simplest forms of the Anglo-Saxon language, and it introduces one important character who appears in all the Teutonic families. This is the first instance in which one literature has consciously copied the heroes of another, except the Latin literature, which frankly copied everything Greek. First, he describes the misfortunes of a bard : —

"He sitteth bereaved of joy, his breast laboring with care, and thinketh with himself that his portion of hardships is endless. Then may he reflect how the all-wise Lord worketh abundant changes throughout all the world, exhibiting to many among men honor and the fruit of prudence, to others the portion of woe. This I may affirm from my own experience. Once was I Scop to the high Dane, beloved by my lord. Deor was my name ; many winters had I an excellent following and a faithful chieftain, until a crafty foe deprived me of the freedom, the land right, which that glory of chieftains had bestowed upon me."

Next, he gives an account of the misfortunes of others, to console himself, and tells the same story about Weland the Smith which was in the Edda. Welend is Velende in the island of Ceylon, Hephaistos in Greek, Vulcan in Latin, Völund in Norse, and finally as Wayland the Smith comes into the folk-stories of England in the Middle Ages. The root is the verb *velen*, to burn; he it is who makes wonderful armor for the gods and heroes; and he means the fire, the flame. He is always lame and ugly: so flame comes from a little spark, puny at its birth, but strong and powerful afterwards. Völund is married to a Valkeyrie, who is a bright cloud; in Greek, Hephaistos married Aphrodite, the dawn; in Latin, Vulcan married Venus, the dawn: this typifies that the brightness of light is akin to the brightness of fire. This ballad and the Traveller's Song are of the seventh century, and both are pagan.

The third pagan ballad in Anglo-Saxon is Beowulf. It is a little later than the poetic Edda, written about the middle of the eighth century; the Edda and the Anglo-Saxon ballads being earlier than all the other sagas. It is not certain where Beowulf was composed. The manuscript is very old, but genuine, and was discovered in 1705. It may have been brought over from the Continent, or composed in England; but it shows the great intercourse between the branches of the Teutonic family. And the Anglo-Saxon pagans fill up the gap between the Norse and German pagans. Those who wandered to Britain were Christianized four centuries sooner than the Norsemen who wandered to Iceland, carrying the two Eddas with them; so Beowulf is Christianized, and therefore of much less value. However, there is only a very thin coating of Christianity, and the paganism shines through so plainly that the family likeness is very evident. It is of course very interesting that such a poem should exist at all; but it is still more interesting that it should be simply a counterpart of the other Aryan epics. The miraculous birth and death of a hero come in; but they are applied in this poem to the father of the chief hero. He is borne to the country floating in a boat, like Perseus in Greek. This child in a boat is always the sun resting on the water; but he does not appear in any other of the Teutonic families: the Anglo-Saxons were the only ones who preserved this primary myth. When the father died, they committed his body to a ship. We meet this ship of the dead in Arthur's romance, where the three queens bear him away. It has no oar, no rudder, no rigging; but it sails and sails, and reaches its destined haven: so sail the clouds.

" Then at his fated time Scyld the strenuous departed from amongst them to go into the protection of the Lord. They then, his beloved followers, carried him away to the sea-shore, as he himself bade, — he, the Scyldings' lord, while his words had power, the dear chief of the land. There at the harbor stood the ring-stemmed vessel, glittering like ice, and ready for the voyage, a prince's bark. Then they laid down their beloved prince, the ring-dispenser, in the bosom of the ship; by the mast they laid the famous one. Thereon was stored great store of treasures, of ornaments from afar. On his bosom lay a pile of treasures, which were to go far away with him into the possession of the flood. Yet more, they set up high over his head a golden ensign, and let the sea bear him away; they abandoned him to the ocean. Upon the sea and alone went Scyld; they mournfully gave the king and his treasure to the deep and solemn sea, to journey none knew whither."

Then comes the second part of the solar myth, — the hero fighting with a monster. The first one is Grendel, in human form, who comes to the palace hall at night, and drags out the sleepers, and sucks their blood, which is just the action of the vampires who come into Slavonic literature. Nothing can be more ghastly than this awful struggle in the dark hall. When, finally, Grendel is killed, his fearful mother, the devil's dam, came to avenge his death; the second struggle is but a repetition of the first. But there is a peculiarity of Beowulf of which we must take notice. After he has killed the two demons, the queen drinks his health, and the Scops in the hall sing his praises, and compare him to Sigmund the Waelsing. Now, this is a confusion between Sigmund and Sigurd the Volsung, his son, who slew the worm; but it proves that the Anglo-Saxon bards were acquainted with the ballads of the Edda. This is the second instance we have as yet found in which one nation was consciously influenced by another in its literature. If the same ideas reappear in other epics, it is wholly unconsciously and independently. The Scop also sang a ballad of the battle of Finnesham. It was not contained in Beowulf, but it has lately been discovered in a fragment of manuscript, so the episode could be introduced if thought best. Beowulf succeeds to the kingdom, and when he is full of years and honors another awful monster appears. Beowulf goes out to attack him and deliver his people, though all others falter. He says, "If I fall in the fight, send to Higelac that most beautiful coat-armor which guards my breast; it is the work of Weland."

Then comes the third, last struggle, in which Beowulf kills the dragon, but is himself stifled by the breath of the monster, and dies. Before he dies, however, he longs to look upon the gold which had belonged to the dragon, and he feasts his eyes on the treasure he had won for his people. So the sun gazes upon the gold and violet clouds which surround his setting. In the graceful mind of the Greeks, these violet-colored clouds become a lovely woman watching over the dying hero, as Iole watches over Herakles. " In the North it is not alone the barbaric splendor of gold and jewels which consoles the dying hero, but the thought that these treasures will benefit the people for whom he died." If this personification of a sunset is less beautiful, it is more noble than the Greek. When Beowulf is dead, his followers build a lofty funeral pile, covered with all things precious, and his body is burned upon it. It was in order that the smoke might carry up the soul; the ballad says, " The soul of Beowulf curled to the clouds."

There are those who think that Beowulf was a real person ; that he reigned over the Saxons in Northumbria : a lake is still called Grendelsmere. This may or may not be true. The Scop sang the traditions which were in the mind of the people. It is of little consequence whether he was true to fact or not; he certainly was true to the Aryan nature, and is one of the noblest characters of Aryan literature. Taine says of the poem : " The people are not selfish and tricky, like those of Homer. They are noble hearts, simple and strong. This Beowulf is a knight before the time of chivalry. The hero is truly heroic."

These three ballads may very properly be considered an Anglo-Saxon epic. They are written in alliterative poetry, full of comparisons. Beowulf's flesh is called

his " bone-house " and his " bone-locker." But for the
Norman conquest we should have used just such compound words; alliteration, instead of rhyme, in our
poetry; inflections in our grammar. Now we adopt a
French or Latin word to express our meaning; but an
Anglo-Saxon priest wrote the " Ayenbite of Inwyt"
to express the sting of conscience. He made up his
own word. It is a little irrelevant, but so interesting
that I must refer to the fact, that the Anglo-Saxon
grammar has some differences from ours. The Anglo-
Saxon adjectives, pronouns, and articles were declined.
It even had a definite and indefinite declension, like
the German ; and not only the qualifying words, but
the nouns themselves, were declined. Professor Whitney says that " English is stripped and shorn."

There is a Christian literature in Anglo-Saxon, and
although this is not its proper place in the mental
history of Europe, it seems convenient to include it
in the Anglo-Saxon chapter. Their monks were the
only ones in Europe who condescended to use the
native dialect of the people. They wrote the famous
Anglo-Saxon Chronicle, beginning at the invasion of
Britain, and coming down to the accession of Henry
II., 1154; also, a grammar of the language ; and these
are very valuable, being our only authorities for the
history and grammar. Cædmon, the Saxon, put parts
of the Bible into alliterative poetry. There is one
characteristic touch which shows the manners of the
time. The invading Danes would swoop down upon
defenceless England, and carry off the inhabitants;
and this was called harrowing a country. So one of
Cædmon's poems relates the triumphant entrance of

Christ into hell. It describes the rage of Lucifer, the dread of fiends, the joy of the ransomed, when Christ descended into hell, and led forth the redeemed in person. It was known in the Middle Ages as the "Harrowing of Hell," which sounds very irreverent to us, but not meant to be so. This literature is not valuable, because it was borrowed from monkish theology, not worked out from the native instincts of the pagan blood. But the energy and fierce defiance of the race come out, especially in Cædmon's conception of Satan. He wrote an account of the temptation in the garden, and the fall of man, which are most poetical and strong. The poem was translated into English, and published in 1685, a thousand years after; and it is quite possible that Milton may have seen it. The pagan fire had not quite burned out when the following lines were written. There is a fierce energy in them which is wonderful: the mind is unsubdued, though fetters load the limbs.

PART OF THE SPEECH OF SATAN.

Is this the hateful place (unlike indeed
The seats we once in heaven's high kingdom knew)
To which the conqueror chains me, — never more
(Expelled by him, the Almighty One) to gain
That realm ! How hath he wronged us of our right,
Who the dread flames of this infernal gulf
Pours full upon us, and denies us heaven !
That heaven, alas ! he destines to receive
The sons of men : 't is this that grieves me most,
That Adam, he, the earth-born, should possess
My glorious seat, — that he should live in joy
While we in hell's avenging horrors pine.
O that my hands were free ! that I might hence

But for a time, but for a winter's day !
Then with this host I — but that these knotted chains
Encompass, that these iron bands press on me.
Oh ! I am kingdomless ; hell's fetters cling
Hard on each limb ; above, beneath, the flame
Fierce rages ; sight more horrible mine eyes
Ne'er yet have witnessed. O'er these scorching deeps
The fire no respite knows ; the strong-forged chain,
With ever-biting links, forbids my course.

In order to understand the foundation of the German language, we must go back to a time long gone by, though mentioned in the preceding chapter. Of all the invading Teutons who left their Northern strongholds and swarmed over Europe, the Mœso-Goths approached nearest to Byzantium. Ulphilas became converted to Christianity (the Arian form), and was sent as Bishop to his countrymen. He must have been a man of thought and courage, for he " dared to translate the Bible into the language of the despised barbarians ; as if foreseeing, with prophetic eye, the destiny of those Teutonic tribes to become the lifespring of the Gospel, after Greek and Latin had died away." It is the only book in the Gothic language ; the language itself is dead. But the book was adopted by the Germans when they became converted ; and though the language is not German, it is the principal element of it, and helped to identify the Germans as Aryans. The Goths were the first Teutons to be converted, and Ulphilas anticipated the work of Luther by a thousand years, in giving them the Bible in their own tongue, in 355 A. D. He really is connected with the Byzantine civilization, in point of time ; but it seems better to include him among the Germans, in point of family.

We have heard the last echo of paganism in Beowulf, which was only half pagan. Now we must turn to the Germans. They have no sacred books; we must go to an outside source, for we know nothing more of their religion than Tacitus has told us: that they worshipped in groves, and offered human sacrifices, and had a god named Tuisco, and another named Tiu, or Zio, which are both forms of the name Dyaus, and have been traced. Max Müller says, "The Heaven-Father was invoked in the dark forests of Germany a thousand years. Then his old name was heard for the last time." Another god was called Wuotan, or Wodin, which is the same as Odin. Slight as this knowledge is, the philologist is grateful for it: these names identify the relationship between the Germans and the other Aryan families. The earliest sacred poem known in German is the Weissenbrun Hymn, probably of the eighth century, and therefore Christianized; for the Germans were converted in 755. It is not worth while to allude to the Christian literature of German. I only copy the Weissenbrun Hymn because the beginning of it is so much like the Edda.

> " This have I heard from men,
>   the chief of the elder sages,
>   that originally there existed
>   no heaven above,
>   nor tree, nor mountain,
>   nor was there .   .   .   .
>   nor any star.
>   No sun shone forth,
>   nor did the moon give her light ;
>   neither the vast sea.

Then there was naught
from end to end ;
but then existed the one
Almighty God,
most merciful to man,
and with him also were many
godlike spirits.
Holy God,
Almighty ! the heaven
and the earth thou hast wrought,
and for men
thou providest so many blessings.
Do thou bestow on me, in thy grace,
a right faith,
and a good will,
wisdom and good speed,
to withstand the craft of the devil,
and to eschew evil,   ˗
and thy will to work."

But if they have not gods like the many grand forms
of Norse mythology, they have heroes, whose names
and high deeds are duly set forth in ballads. The oldest is the Hildebrand Lied ; and this is only a mutilated fragment of what may once have been a German
epic. It is very simple and strong, like all the genuine
poetry of the people. It is as old as the eighth century,
— as Beowulf, for instance, — and it tells another of
the tales common to the Aryan race, gives another form
to the solar myth. Hildebrand, a brave warrior, left
behind him a wife and an infant son, and went off to
fight the Huns. After thirty years he returned, and
a brave young German warrior, thinking him to be a
Hun, challenged him to combat. But Hildebrand rec-

21

ognized his own son, declared himself, and offered his golden bracelets as a token. The son refused to believe him, saying that his father was dead, and insisted upon fighting. They fought; the son was conquered: both finally returned alive to the wife. This is the sun-light of one day struggling with the sun-light of the new day, and is the same myth which was so beautifully elaborated in Sohrab and Rustem, in Persia. Yet there could have been no influence exercised, for the Persians did not even know of the existence of the Germans, in their remote forests. The Hildebrand Lied is written in alliterative poetry. It is almost as majestic as the Edda. I quote part of Hildebrand's speech to his son, it is so simple and pathetic

> "Well-a-day now, governing God!
> Woe worth shall happen!
> Summers full sixty,
> and winters, I wander,
> ever called with the crowd
> of shooters of spears:
> nor in mine own household
> delayed, as the dead.
> Now shall the child of me
> smite me with sword,
> bite me with broad steel,
> or I be his slayer."

The figurative expressions, too, prove its kinship. Another of the old ballads tells of the horny Siegfried, a hero who was born covered with a coat of horn: and in the Maha Bharata occurs the same thing. The hero Karna has a coating, like shell, which he, however, puts on and off at pleasure. These were written in Old

High-German,, which is very much like Anglo-Saxon. But the most celebrated of the old ballads of the people is the Nibelungen Lied, or song of the children of the mist; Nibelung being from the same root as Niflheim and nebula. It was originally a series of ballads, springing up among the people, no one knows when or where; for the German bards did not write down their songs. Finally, these were collected and rewritten by one person, about the middle of the twelfth century, in the form which they now bear, in Middle High-German, which resembles modern High-German more than Chaucer's English resembles modern English, and can more easily be read without a translation; but they were lost for many years, and utterly forgotten. About a hundred years ago, in 1757, they were discovered in manuscript, in the library of an ancient noble family. Several other copies were found after diligent search, and all closed with the words, "Here endeth the Nibelungen Lied." It has been translated into modern German, and many foreign languages, and the Germans overflowed with pride at the thought that they too had a national epic. But on a close comparison with the Volsung Saga, which is included in the Eddas, and is the Norse epic, such a remarkable resemblance was found, that it is now acknowledged that the Nibelungen Lied is simply a reproduction of the Volsung Saga, but unconsciously so. This is perfectly natural, since the Norsemen and Germans are brothers, of the same Teutonic branch of the great Aryan race, and once may all have lived together on the shores of the Baltic Sea.

The story is just the same; the names, even, are but little changed; but the spirit is utterly different. The wild, strong, daring Norsemen — the men and the women of heroic proportions, tall and bright as gods and goddesses — have been converted into mild, church-going knights, who gain their ends by craft rather than by frankness and courage. So I think the Volsung Saga the finer of the two, as well as the more original. It is nearer to the primitive form of the solar myth ; thus the connection of the Teutonic with the other Aryan epics is more easily traced in it. William Morris has put the story into such lovely melody that his poem will be accepted as the standard version of the two Teutonic epics. There is no good poetical translation of the Nibelungen. I do not feel that it is needed since Morris's poem. An appreciative account of it was written by Mr. Carlyle, in the Westminster Review, 1831. But all these new discoveries in comparative mythology have been applied to the Nibelungen since then ; so his account is not enough, sympathetic as it is. As I related the story so fully in the last chapter, in speaking of the Volsung Saga, I shall only mention the differences.

The hero is Siegfried, or Sifrit. There were three parts in the Volsung Saga, and this is like Wagner's opera, where the first one tells the story of the hero's family and father. The Nibelungen begins at the second part. The hero himself, Siegfried, kills a dragon, and bathes in its blood, and thus becomes invincible ; but, while bathing, a leaf from a linden-tree fell between his shoulders, and stayed there, so that one little spot was not touched by the dragon's blood, and he can be wounded there, — like Achilleus vulnerable in one spot alone, the heel. Siegfried then gains the treasures of the dwarfs, and a cloud mantle or cloak, which gives him the strength of twelve men and makes him invisible. This is the same invisible garment which so many heroes have worn, — like Fortunatus's cap, for instance, — and is the mist or fog which hides the sun in the spring sometimes. All that lovely story about the awakening of Brynhild does not come into the Nibelungen. The Brünhilde of the Nibelungen has physical force; but she has not the wisdom and the spiritual power of the Brynhild in the Volsung Saga. Gunther, the king, desires to wed the strong woman, Brünhilde. She comes forth carrying a mighty spear, and hurls a stone which four men could not lift. But Siegfried wins the Brünhilde of the Nibelungen by throwing stones and spears, and by wrestling till this amazon is tripped and thrown to the ground. This is much less poetical, and also much less dangerous, than riding through the flickering fire. He does it under his invisible cloak, while Gunther, the king, stands by, and makes all the gestures; there is something undignified, almost laughable, in this. Siegfried takes off the ring and the girdle of Brünhilde, and gives them to his own wife. She is named Kriemhild in the Nibelungen; but she is the sister of the king, and corresponds to the Gudrun of the original story. The crisis is brought on, just as in the Volsung Saga, by the quarrels of the two queens. But the revenge is different. In the Volsung Saga it is prompted by the love and jealousy of Brynhild, and then, when the hero is dead, her heart breaks too. She forgives him, but she dies with him. The treasure is not thought of. In the Nibelungen Lied, Brünhilde does not love Siegfried; she is simply angry because he is a more distinguished man than her own husband, and lives on very comfortably after his death. We hear no more of her. Her anger prompts her to work upon the avarice of Hagen, whose name means prickly thorn; and he promises to kill Siegfried by strategy, because he desires to have the gold, the Nibelungen hoard. While they are on a hunting excursion, Siegfried stoops to drink at a spring of water, and Hagen, standing behind the mighty hero, pierces him with a spear just in that one spot between the shoulders where he is vulnerable. This is the manner of the death in Wagner's opera. So the thorn of winter kills the summer; the thorn of darkness kills the bright sun. There are many stories in which the death of the hero is connected with water. It means the setting sun sinking below the water. The second part of the Nibelungen is the revenge of Kriemhild, Siegfried's wife. It is the story which we met in the Volsung Saga. She marries a foreign king, entices her brethren to come to visit her, and then kills them all in that vast slaughter-hall. Little is said about the gold, the Nibelungen hoard, in the Volsung Saga; but it plays a very important part in the Nibelungen. In the Volsung Saga, the revenge of Gudrun was the real motive; the gold, only a bait held out to Gudrun's new husband: in the Nibelungen, Kriemhild cares quite as much for the gold as for revenging her slaughtered hero. But the ending is the same. The gold is drowned beneath the water; neither side can possess it.

In the Nibelungen Lied, the tale of the revenge is tedious, as well as sickening: thousands of warriors fall: new heroes are introduced only to be killed, and the agony is prolonged. One hero, Volker, is a harper.

This is like Phemios, the harper in the Odyssey. An effort has been made to give historical names to the characters, and prove that they really lived. Kriemhild's second husband, Etzel, is called Attila, king of the Huns; but his character is entirely different from that of the real Attila, and I think there is nothing to warrant such a supposition. The names and characters resemble those of the other epic poems far more than they do any living, actual people. It is only because there are mediæval manners and ideas in the Nibelungen Lied that such an explanation came up.

It is precisely this mediæval spirit which makes the Nibelungen Lied less beautiful than the Volsung Saga. It is near and real; the characters and the motives which actuate them might really be; the only supernaturalism, the invisible cloak, is found in a hundred mediæval tales. But the Volsung Saga is remote and shadowy and vast. The gods themselves come down and dwell with men, and no men ever lived so mighty as those heroes; even the swart, blue-clad Niflungs are great and grand to see. The women are beautiful and wise and loving as goddesses. The motives are bold and clear, the plot is simple and contains but few subordinate characters, and the very soul of poetry breathes through it all. It is as free and wild and daring as the Norsemen who gave it birth.

I will copy a passage I met after I had written this chapter. Matthew Arnold says: "There is a fire, a style, a distinction, in Icelandic poetry, which German poetry has not. The fatal humdrum and want of style of the Germans have marred their way of telling this magnificent tradition of the Nibelungen, and taken half its grandeur and power out of it; while in the Icelandic poems which deal with this tradition, its grandeur and power are much more fully visible." The dark, tragical element, "the sorrow after joy," which Carlyle felt, but could not understand, which runs through both poems, has been explained to us by the comparative mythologist. It comes from the perpetual warfare, the stern aspect, of the physical nature of the North. However beautiful the summer may be, there is always the consciousness that the darkness and cold will return. The Persian and the Teutonic epics end in gloom; the Indian and Grecian, in joy and triumph. Rama brings back Sita, stolen by dark powers; the Greeks carry back Helen and her gold; Odysseus lives in happiness with his beloved bride. Yet this was worked out unconsciously. Naturally and independently these different nations expressed the thought that was in them. They brought out different results from these same original germs. It is only lately, since all literatures have been traced back to their very origin, — the phenomena of nature, — that we have understood the deep undertone of melancholy, "the pathetic minor," which runs through every manifestation of the Teutonic mind, — its art, its music, as well as its literature. It is part of our inheritance.

CHAPTER XI.

MEDIÆVAL HYMNS, AND COMPARATIVE MYTHOLOGY
OF THE MEDIÆVAL BALLADS.

OUR subject is Mediæval Literature, — a most interesting one, for in its unformed condition lies
modern Christian Europe. The languages, as well as
the society, are in a chaotic condition; and yet this
apparent confusion can be made clear by reducing the
whole civilization of the period into two elements. All
literature was divided between minstrels and monks, —
two classes of people. It is very seldom that so sharp
a distinction can be made; but in the Middle Ages we
find the hopeless yearning of the monk, the rough joyousness of the minstrel: everything is decidedly subjective or objective.

We followed the classic pagan Latin till it died out
in Boëthius, 525 A. D. But, amidst the corruptions of
society, the gloomy thoughts and bombastic language
of the last classic Latin, a new spirit arose from an
unexpected source. The histories and commentaries
of the Fathers of the Church, the hymns of the Christians, are full of noble thoughts in a noble language —
what is called Mediæval Latin, as distinct from the
classic Latin. It is not the Latin of Cicero and Tacitus; but it became the language of the pulpit and the
school, and from it have proceeded our modern lan-

guages. It was used for all literature, which was composed by two distinct types of mind. The clear-headed, ambitious man of intellect saw in the church and the monastery his surest path to power, and wrote volumes of theological controversy. The enthusiast, to whom this world was but an abode lying in wicked-ness, and the heavenly city his home, sang in exulting strains of the New Jerusalem, the true home of the spirit. Or some gentle soul, wounded and wearied with the turmoil of Europe, where society was break-ing up, sought the shelter of the cloister. His sor-row, his hopeless yearning for earthly happiness, found voice in passionate hymns, which express the love of the heart for God. They were the outburst of souls which had resigned all earthly happiness, and loved God as other men loved their own families. Mat-thew Arnold says: "They are the masterpieces of spiritual work of the Aryan mind, taking pure religious sentiment as their basis. They clothed themselves in Middle-Age Latin, which is not the genuine native voice of any European nation," — but are characteristic, nevertheless. Another critic says: "Ten thousand years separate the monastic poets from the last poet of heathen Rome. He had no thought of individual, per-sonal goodness, or reformation; while the key-note of the monastic hymns is the overpowering sense of sin."

Gradually the monasteries absorbed all the learning: scholars, even if they felt no religious vocation, became monks, that they might enjoy the libraries of manu-scripts which were collected by the studious among the monks. Not only the learning, but the architec-ture, the art, the music, and the agriculture of the

period centred in the monastery. The monks copied and illuminated the manuscripts, sang the chants
of Ambrose and Gregory, erected beautiful buildings ;
and, more important still, they cultivated the ground,
they cut down the forests, and drained the swamps,
and raised acres of grain and fruit and flowers, while
everybody else was fighting, and the land had become
a desert. It is hard to over-estimate the rough, hard
work they did toward clearing the forests and rendering
productive the land. Villemain says : " The civilization of the Church is a kind of intermediate world between ancient and modern history." Montalembert
says, " The Church formed a kind of neutral ground
where Romans and barbarians could meet." You can
trace the progress of Christianity through Europe by
seeing the monks spring up in succession.

We must go back a little to speak of the Fathers of
the Church, though we can only allude to the greatest
of them. We must turn our minds, and see the rise
of another literary centre. I have alluded elsewhere
to the greatest names of Byzantium, — Ulphilas and
Tribonian. The civilization which had been trans-
planted from Rome to Byzantium was modified by the
Greek literature. The Fathers of the Eastern Church
admired and studied Plato and Demosthenes. St. John
(347–407), surnamed Chrysostom, the golden-mouthed,
because he was so eloquent, is as great among Christian
orators as Demosthenes among pagan. The Christian
literature of Byzantium is wholly theological. Such
questions were to Byzantium what politics are to us.
The partisans of Arius and Athanasius frequently came
to blows about the divinity of Christ and the nature of

the Virgin Mary. Surrounded by the Greek drama as they were, the Christians were inspired by its beautiful choruses. The echoing measures which had celebrated heathen deities were used to sound the praises of the God of the Christians. The Greek hymns are not so well known as the Latin, but are beautiful, especially " Art thou weary, art thou languid?"

HYMN BY ST. ANATOLIUS (A. D. 458),

FOR THOSE AT SEA.

Fierce was the wild billow,
  Dark was the night,
Oars labored heavily,
  Foam glimmered white ;
Mariners trembled,
  Peril was nigh ;
Then said the God of God,
  " Peace ! It is I."

Ridge of the mountain wave,
  Lower thy crest;
Wail of Euroklydon,
  Be thou at rest :
Peril can never be,
  Sorrow must fly,
Where saith the Light of Light,
  " Peace ! It is I."

Jesu, Deliverer,
  Come Thou to me ;
Soothe Thou my voyaging
  Over life's sea :
Thou, when the storm of death
  Roars, sweeping by,
Whisper, O Truth of Truth,
  " Peace ! It is I."

At the city of Milan, the Christians had become so powerful, that Ambrose, the bishop, (340–397,) even dared to rebuke the great Emperor Theodosius for ordering a massacre at Thessalonica. He forbade him to enter the church, telling him that his presence would pollute the holy building. Theodosius repented, did penance, and thanked St. Ambrose for his faithful boldness. Quarrels were constantly coming up, and a band of soldiers was finally sent to carry Ambrose to prison and to exile. He and his friends barricaded themselves in the church, and there remained all night; and, to rouse their enthusiasm and sustain their courage, they sang the Latin hymns which Ambrose had composed, in imitation of the Eastern Church. The soldiers were withdrawn, and he was allowed to remain and preach in Milan. We remember him, not for his sermons and commentaries, but for his hymns. The most famous are the Easter song, "This is the very day of God"; the evening song, "O God! creation's secret force"; the Christmas song, "Come, Redeemer of the nations"; and the hymn to the Trinity which Luther copied and translated. Indeed, they are the models which inspired Luther's hymns. Ambrose was the first in the Western, Latin Church to realize the immense power which might be exercised by music in subduing the barbarians, and spreading the conquests of the Church as an organization. He was the first to put sacred music into definite form. He introduced chanting; and his manner of singing the service is still called the Ambrosian chant. It is a lineal descendant of the antiphonal Greek chorus. We must remember that Ambrose's hymns are not written in rhyme.

HYMN FOR ADVENT.

Hark ! a thrilling voice is sounding :
"Christ is nigh," it seems to say ;
"Cast away the dreams of darkness,
O, ye children of the day !"
Wakened by the solemn warning,
Let the earth-born soul arise ;
Christ, her sun, all ill dispelling,
Shines upon the morning skies.
Lo ! the Lamb, so long expected,
Comes with pardon down from heaven :
Let us haste, with tears of sorrow,
One and all, to be forgiven,
That when next he comes with glory,
And the world is wrapped in fear,
With his mercy he may shield us,
And with words of love draw near.
Honor, glory, might, and blessing
To the Father and the Son,
With the everlasting Spirit,
While eternal ages run.   Amen.

To my mind, this is the most interesting, because the
most spiritual, of Ambrose's hymns.   Usually they are
doctrinal, putting some great doctrine into poetical
form.   They sound like a paraphrase of Scripture.
The theological thought contained seems to be enough
for Ambrose ; the resurrection to another life seems to
him matter enough for celebration ; and he does not
make a spiritual application of it to the soul of the
individual in this present life.

Prudentius was a layman, but has left most beautiful
hymns, full of an enthusiasm inspired by that certainty

f immortality which Christianity taught, and which was uch a contrast to paganism.

FUNERAL HYMN BY PRUDENTIUS.

(A. D. 348.)

Each sorrowful mourner, be silent !
Fond mothers, give over your weeping!
None grieve for these pledges as perished ;
This dying is life's reparation.
Now take him, O earth, to thy keeping,
And give him soft rest in thy bosom.
I lend thee the frame of a Christian,
I intrust thee the generous fragments,
Thou holily guard the deposit ;
He will well, He will surely require it,
Who, forming it, made its creation
The type of His image and likeness.
But until the resolvable body
Thou recallest, O God, and reformest,
What regions unknown to the mortal
Dost thou will the pure soul to inhabit ?
It shall rest upon Abraham's bosom,
As the spirit of blessed Eleazar,
Whom, afar in that Paradise, Dives
Beholds from the flames of his torments.
We follow thy saying, Redeemer,
Whereby, as on death thou wast trampling,
The thief, thy companion, thou willedst
To tread in thy footsteps and triumph.
To the faithful the bright way is open,
Henceforward, to Paradise leading ;
And to that blest grove we have access,
Whereof man was bereaved by the serpent.
Thou Leader and Guide of thy people,

Give command that the soul of thy servant
May have holy repose in the country
Whence exile and erring he wandered.
We will honor the place of his resting
With violets and garlands of flowers,
And will sprinkle inscription and marble
With odors of costliest fragrance :
For what mean the tombs that we quarry,
What the art that our monuments boast in,
But that this which we trust to their keeping
Is not dead, but reposing in slumber?

It is hard for us to realize that the northern coast of
Africa was once the seat of the highest civilization of
the period. Saint Augustine was born near Carthage,
A. D. 354. His mother, Monica, had been converted
to Christianity; but he was a pagan, and passed his
early life in dissipation first, in study afterwards. Finally he became a Christian, through the prayers of
his mother and the teachings of Ambrose, the brave
Bishop of Milan. He was made Bishop of Hippo, in
Africa, near Carthage, and is probably the greatest
theologian the world has ever seen. The doctrines
which we call Calvinism are found in his writings : but
the dry hard statements of Calvin lose their most repulsive features in the spiritual and eloquent expositions
of Augustine; for he united the passionate heart of
Africa to a clear and logical brain. His controversial
writings are not of universal interest; but two of his
works have been admired and loved for centuries, and
can never be forgotten. The first is his Confessions ;
the story of a soul wandering and confused, but coming
at length into peace and rest by knowing and loving
God. It is one of the few great devotional books of the

world. By Confessions, he means rather a different idea from that which we attach to the word. There is no long list of actual crimes : instead, it is an analysis of a soul and an intellect, which loved this world and its own opinions better than God. It is the confession of wrong thoughts and affections, not of wrong actions. Yet Saint Augustine was a very good man, according to the pagan standard ; but when he has once caught sight of God's purity, a crushing sense of sin overwhelms him. His self-abasement seems almost unnatural. But Augustine loves God so much that he longs to resemble -Him ; and his own nature looks dark to him, in comparison with that awful purity. The word acknowledgment would express our idea of the second thought of the book. It is an acknowledgment of God's incomparable beauty and goodness. Saint Augustine not only believes in God with his head, he loves him with his heart. He exclaims, "Not with doubting, but with assured consciousness, do I love Thee, O Lord ! " And he wishes to confess him before men. There is an absolute reality in the book. His spiritual life was his chief concern, — an actual, real thing to him. He knew God as clearly and as nearly as we know our living friends. And yet there is an exquisitely human touch in the beautiful description he gives of his last conversation with his mother, Monica, as they stopped at Ostia, on their return from Africa, and of her death. This is a small part of it : —

"It chanced that she and I stood alone, leaning in a certain window which looked into the garden of the house where we now lay, at Ostia ; where, removed from the din of men, we were recruiting from the fatigues of a long journey. We were discoursing then together alone, very sweetly : and forgetting those things which are behind, and reaching forth to those which are before, we were inquiring between ourselves, in the presence of the Truth which Thou art, of what sort the eternal life of the saints was to be. Scarce five days after, she fell sick of a fever. Looking on me and my brother, standing by her, 'There,' said she, 'shall you bury your mother.' I held my peace and refrained weeping, but my brother spake something ; wishing for her, as the happier lot, that she might die, not in a strange place, but in her own land. Whereat she with anxious look, checking him with her eyes, for that he still savored such things ; and then looking upon me, 'Behold what he saith'; and soon after to us both, 'Lay,' she saith, 'this body anywhere, let not the care for that anyway disquiet you ; this only I request, that you would remember me at the Lord's altar, wherever you be.' But I, considering Thy gifts, Thou unseen God, which Thou instillest into the hearts of Thy faithful ones, whence wondrous fruits do spring, did rejoice and give thanks to Thee, recalling what I knew before, — how careful and anxious she had ever been, as to her place of burial, which she provided and prepared for herself, by the body of her husband."

Lovers of music in church will be glad to know what St. Augustine thought about that.

"Sometimes I err in too great strictness, and to that degree as to wish the whole melody of sweet music which is used to David's Psalter banished from my ears, and the Church's too. And yet, again, when I remember the tears I shed at the psalmody of Thy Church, in the beginning of my recovered faith, and how at this time I am moved, not with the singing, but the things sung, when they are sung with a clear voice and modulation most suitable, I acknowledge the use of this institution. Thus I fluctuate between peril of pleasure and approved wholesomeness ; inclined the rather, though not pronouncing an irrevocable opinion, to approve of the usage of singing in church, that so by the delight of the ears the weaker minds may rise to the feeling of devotion."

St. Augustine's other popular work is called "The City of God." It is the Christian model of a city, as compared with Plato's model state of society. It has twenty-two books: the first ten confute pagan religion and practices; the last twelve set forth Christian doctrine, under the form of two cities, — the city of the world and the city of God; and it prophesies the future triumphs of the gospel, in exulting strains. One critic says, "The world has set the City of God among the few greatest books of all time." It has abstract thought in popular language. It deserves to be classed among the great epics of the world; yet, grand as it is, it has not that personal feeling which makes the Confessions so unrivalled.

With the death of Boëthius, 525, and the great king of the Ostro-Goths, Theodoric, open the Middle Ages. He learned to read, and invited learned men to his court, and embraced the Arian form of Christianity. (The Mœso-Goths had already been converted, in 355, under Byzantine influence.) The next Teutons to embrace Christianity were the Franks. Radegonda, the Christian wife of a Frankish king, obtained permission from her husband to found a convent at Poitiers, in the country which is now France. The Abbess Agnes and herself passed their time in literary conversation and writing poetry. They were visited by a learned Italian, Venantius Fortunatus, 530–609. This is the same Fortunatus who met Welsh bards at the court of the Frankish kings. He first put hymns into rhyme; they have been preserved till this day. One of them is the Vexilla Regis, "The royal banners forward go," which deserves to live, it is so musical. This is the only cultivated society we read of in the interval of utter darkness from Theodoric to Alfred. We must seek another country; yet not quite another, for the Latin language and the monasteries gave unity to Europe in this period.

The busy monks kept a Latin diary of the events of every day. From these chronicles we obtain the facts of mediæval history. To these narrow-minded monks there was no proportion in events. The visit of a foreign brother to their monastery, or the earliest fruit of the season upon their table, was as important to them as the death of some powerful king, and are all jumbled together on one page of a chronicle. The proverb says, "dull as a monkish chronicle"; but they are sometimes interesting from their very *naïveté*. These monkish chronicles were lent, and copied, from the monasteries of Britain to those of Rome. The earliest of them are found among the Kelts inhabiting Britain, who had been converted to Christianity in the first century by the Romans, as we saw in the Keltic chapter. Gildas at Dumbarton in Scotland, and Nennius at Bangor in Wales, in the sixth century wrote Latin histories of the Britons. These Keltic monks seem the most poetical and interesting. Their ardent natures embraced Christianity with enthusiasm.

"St. Cadoc made all his scholars learn Virgil by heart, and once he began to weep at the thought that Virgil, whom he loved so much, might even then be in hell. St. Cadoc doubted if he were; but his friend Gildas was sure that Virgil was damned. St. Cadoc fell asleep, and heard a voice saying,

'Pray for me! pray for me! never be weary of praying for me.
I shall yet sing eternally the mercy of the Lord.'   So St.
Cadoc was consoled."

Then St. Brandan, a Welsh monk, felt pity for
perishing souls, and he set sail for Ireland to found
a monastery there.   All the bees from the Welsh
monastery followed; so he turned back, but the bees
turned also.   Then he started again for Ireland, and
the bees swarmed in his ship, and would not leave it.
So he took that blessing to Ireland, where they had
been before unknown.   When the good St. Brandan
had founded many monasteries, then he sailed again
into the ocean to seek new souls to convert.   But he
was carried to the earthly paradise, which was an island
distinctly visible from the west coast of Ireland, and he
returned no more.   Now these delightful creatures are
living figures.   But a cold recital of actual facts tells
us that really Ireland was in the seventh century the
most cultivated country in Western Europe : three thousand students attended the school at Armagh.   War
and religion were the two passions of the Irish.   Ireland swarmed with monks, who were at first the clans
reorganized under a religious form, and some monasteries had a bard attached to them.   The reader will
remember that Ireland and Scotland had incessant intercourse; so he will not be surprised that St. Columba
went from Ireland to Iona in Scotland.   He and his
followers converted the Angles north of the Tees ; and
finally, coming from Iona to Lindisfarne and Whitby,
they assisted in bringing Christianity to the Anglo-
Saxons in England.   So the Kelts returned good for
evil to the Saxons who had driven them away.

The Anglo-Saxon monks had their chronicles written in Latin. The most famous of them is the "History of the Anglo-Saxon Church, by the Venerable Bede," which is really a first-class book. "He was the first barbarian to win a place among the Fathers of the Church." (672–735.) In another chapter I spoke of their writings in their native tongue. They were the only monks in Europe who condescended to use their vernacular. The great and good King Alfred endeavored to form a literary society. He learned to read, and himself translated Bede's history into Anglo-Saxon.

We find another of the human links which bind society in examining the rise of the German monks. The restless Angles and Saxons who had invaded England had gone unconsciously to meet their destiny. When converted, they thought of their brethren in Germany, and the brave Boniface went over and converted the Saxons who had remained at home, 755 A. D. They translated the Gospels and Psalms into German, and adopted the Bible of Bishop Ulphilas, 355 A. D., which was sufficiently near their language to answer every purpose. Their Latin literature is not worth alluding to. They have left nothing to compare with the admirable chronicles of Keltic and Anglo-Saxon monks, or the theological and mystical and poetical works of the French monks.

Then comes the great Charlemagne, 742–814. His friend and tutor, "the learned Alcuin, that large-browed clerk," was a Saxon monk; for Charlemagne brought back Christianity from his wars with the Saxons. He himself composed the hymn Veni Creator Spiritus, "Come, Holy Ghost, Creator, come, In-

spire these souls of thine," which is so very familiar
to all.   He founded schools called *scholæ*, — our word
scholasticism comes from it, — and gave the teaching
into the hands of the monks.   These French monks are
the lineal descendants of Augustine ; they are remarkable for their theological writings and their scholastic
philosophy, which ruled Europe from the eighth to the
fifteenth century.   There was no other serious study in
Europe, — no science, no political economy ; the clergy
absorbed everything, partly because they alone had
time for study.   There was but one learned layman in
Europe for six centuries ; and he was a Kelt, John
Scotus Erigena.   He went from Ireland to France to
study, and wrote in Latin of course.   Mr. Lecky says :
" His thoughts were far in advance of his age : even
modern thinkers have not gone much beyond him."
He was persecuted by the Church, and his works condemned as pantheistic.   He denied the Romish doctrine of transubstantiation, and taught what Protestants
believe, — that the Lord's supper is simply a commem-
orative rite ; so naturally he would be persecuted.

The extraordinary empire of scholasticism over the
minds of men was based upon the writings of Aristotle.
These were received into Europe in two ways.   I allude
particularly to these as showing how curiously nations
are connected.   His works on logic — that is, on the
proper way to reason — had been translated into Latin
by Boëthius, in the sixth century, and so had circulated
from one monastery to another.   His works upon science had been translated from Greek into the Syriac language, in the fifth century, by the Nestorian Christians
who fled from Byzantium into Persia.   In the seventh

century Persia was conquered by the Mohammedan Arabians. They were so much pleased with Aristotle that they translated his writings into Arabic, and carried them to Spain. They furnished the Mohammedans in Spain with part of their knowledge of science, and from Spain they easily spread through Europe. From the Arabic they were made into a very poor translation in Latin ; after so many different bodies, but little of their original spirit could have been left. I hope this explanation will not seem unnecessary. In the next chapter the reader will understand why it was made ; and Aristotle, mangled and ill understood as he was, became the absolute authority in all matters of reasoning and of science, as the Bible was in all matters of faith. It was an intellectual despotism. The services to humanity of the first monks scarcely counterbalance the follies of scholasticism. It is hardly worth while to discuss their opinions, forgotten now : we will only speak of the most interesting topic they discussed, and the two most interesting personages, — Abelard, 1079–1142, and St. Bernard of Clairvaux, 1071–1153, — the two names which stand out to represent the period.

Abelard has been called the " patriarch of modern rationalism." He marks a new epoch in thought. He, first, undertook to apply logic to theology, — to bring logic as an independent power to aid in proving the truths of religion. That is, he sought to prove the dogmas of the Church by reason, instead of blindly accepting them through faith. He uttered the opinion, then very audacious, that all theological dogmas should be presented in such a way as to appeal to the reason. He did not question their truth, but he wished that they should be examined and tested by reasoning. Mr. Lewes says, " Logic played like lambent flame around the most sacred subjects, under the plausible aspect of seeking for truth." ˋAbelard represents the spirit of free inquiry, and was therefore the forerunner of Luther and Protestantism. His brilliant eloquence and his innumerable hearers awoke all the thunders of the Church, and St. Bernard of Clairvaux, a stern controversialist, came to the rescue. With great ability he asserted the doctrine of the Church ; which is, that faith is the source of all light, — of all science, metaphysics, and human knowledge, — and that this faith is taught by the Church alone. The Church is the supreme authority in matters of science, as well as of religion. Abelard was overwhelmed, and recanted his ideas.

These theological discussions may seem very dull to us ; but they did not, evidently, to the people of that time, for thirty thousand attended the lectures of one man alone. I only dwell upon these names to show how barren was the mind of those days ; to emphasize the fact, that all serious literature took a theological impress. Yet man's spiritual nature can never be utterly crushed down ; and as a reaction from the endless discussions of Abelard and St. Bernard rose up, from an unknown source, the most devotional of all books, — the mystic writings called by the name of Thomas à Kempis. Some gentle monk, shut out by his own choice from the activities of this present world, lost himself in contemplating the future life, and annihilated his own existence in the Divine existence. This mysticism we have found in India and Persia, and shall find in Germany, in the fourteenth century, in Tauler, a monk. It is common to the Aryan families. It teaches the nothingness of all creation, in comparison with the love of God, and the joy of communion with him. It expressed itself also in poetry; hymns appeared again in great number. In this second period, Latin hymns reached their perfection. They were always long; so that, in translating, we divide them into several different hymns. The four which are the most celebrated, because the greatest, express the mental phases of the epoch. The awful Dies Iræ, " Day of Wrath," (thirteenth century,) paints the final judgment, which the Church suspended over the guilty sinner, and thus wielded a tremendous power over men's fears and terrors. The pathetic Stabat Mater (thirteenth century), —

> " By the cross her station keeping
> Stood the mournful mother, weeping," —

appealed to their tenderest emotions of love and pity, at the sight of one dying for them. The triumphant Jerusalem the Golden (twelfth century) offered consolation for the sufferings of this world.

> " Brief life is here our portion,
> Brief toil, unending care," —

has been made into a separate hymn in our translation; and thus the unity of Bernard of Cluny's thought has been destroyed. The four hymns marked 490, 491, 492, 493, should be read as one. Finally, the personal experience of the individual soul was expressed in the passionate Jesu Dulcis Memoria : —

> " Jesus, the very thought of thee
> With sweetness fills my breast."

It was the stern controversialist, Bernard of Clairvaux, who wrote this most mystic and subjective of all
the Latin hymns (twelfth century). This one is less
known : —

HEAVEN.

By Hildebert, Archbishop of Tours (1057–1134).

Mine be Zion's habitation,
Zion, David's sure foundation ;
Formed of old by light's Creator,
Reached by Him, the Mediator.
An apostle guards the portal,
Habited by forms immortal:
On a jasper pavement builded,
By its Monarch's radiance gilded,
Peace there dwelleth uninvaded,
Spring perpetual, light unfaded :
Odors rise with airy lightness;
Harpers strike their harps of brightness :
None one sigh for pleasure sendeth ;
None can err, and none offendeth ;
All, partakers of one nature,
Grow in Christ to equal stature.
Home celestial !   Home eternal !
Home upreared by power supernal !
Home no change nor loss that fearest !
From afar my soul thou cheerest ;
But the gladness of thy nation,
But their fulness of salvation,
Vainly mortals strive to show it :
They, and they alone, can know it, —
They, redeemed from sin and peril,
They who walk thy streets of beryl !
Grant me, Saviour, with thy blessed,
Of thy rest to be possessed !

Mediæval Latin hymns are a genuine production, and deserve to stand on their own merits. (The mediæval Latin prose is not so good.) In them the form is as beautiful as the thought. Rhyme was a new element of poetry. The Latin hymns invented it, introduced fixed laws for it, and finally, after six centuries, it reached the perfection of the following lines, which are certainly perfect music in themselves. They are quite as worthy to be praised and copied as the Greek unrhymed metres.

> "Stant Sion atria conjubilantia, martyre plena,
> Cive micantia, Principe stantia, luce serena :
> Est ibi pascua mitibus afflua, praestita sanctis,
> Regis ibi thronus, agminis et sonus est epulantis.
> Gens duce splendida, concio candida vestibus altis,
> Sunt sine fletibus in Sion ædibus, ædibus almis ;
> Sunt sine crimine, sunt sine turbine, sunt sine lite
> In Sion ædibus editoribus Israelitæ."

"They stand, those walls of Sion," is the equivalent. Here is another, with a rhyme in the middle of the line : —

> "Felix Anna, ex te manna
> Mundo datur, quo poscatur
> In deserto populus :
> Hoc dulcore, hoc sapore
> Sustentatur, procreatur,
> Ex manna vermiculus."

The English monks exercised but little influence compared with the French monks, whose scholasticism ruled Europe for several centuries ; but they have left some good Latin chronicles. Geoffrey of Monmouth tells the story of Arthur ; and William of Malmesbury wrote a history of the English kings, from the Norman conquest, 1066, to 1142. His book has been translated; it is most delightful, — so gossiping and *naïve* and full of wonders and miracles. It is well to read it and learn how William Rufus was shot; how Henry and Stephen quarrelled with their barons; how the great bishop, Roger le Poer, built cathedrals and castles. So here, in these monkish chronicles of all lands, history begins.

If the monk, in his two forms, either a keen logician or a devout mystic, is the representative of the Middle Ages, there was another type which could no longer be repressed. The men who lived and loved and fought in this present world, and cared little about the next, began to assert themselves. To please them, the monks took an important step. It is to the latter we owe what, at first glance, seems very remote from them, — the drama. The whole modern drama can be distinctly traced to the Miracle plays, which the clergy used to represent in the churches. The fathers of the Church had extinguished the theatres everywhere; but in Byzantium the Greek love of the drama persistently lingered. The Bishop of Constantinople composed plays on Christ's passion, to supersede the dramas of Sophokles and Euripides. They were first performed in Constantinople, and the returning Crusaders brought them back. These plays were first acted in Latin, probably in the twelfth century; afterwards they were written in the dialect of the country, whether Italy, France, Germany, or England. They gave scenes from the life of the Saviour, or the lives of the saints: the action took place on a middle stage; below, devils were writhing in flames; above, God the Father on the judgment seat was sitting. Later came the Morality plays, where the vices and virtues were represented as human beings. Only the clergy were allowed to act in these dramas, which formed the book of the common people, in those days. Certainly, they seem very shocking and irreverent to us; but where else were the poor, ignorant people to learn about Mary and Joseph and Herod, — about Abraham, and Isaac's sacrifice, — and all the other characters of the Bible? There was one other source; the statues on the porches, the painted glass in the windows of cathedrals. This poem was written later, but it so describes the spirit of this period that it may come in here. It is very lovely.

PRAYER TO THE VIRGIN,

BY FRANÇOIS VILLON, A TROUVÈRE (14TH CENTURY).

Queen of the skies, and Regent of the earth,
　　Empress of all that dwells beneath!
Receive me, poor and low, of little worth,
　　Among thy chosen after death.
Nothing I bring with me, nothing I have;
　　But yet thy mercy, Lady, is as great
As all my sum of sins.' Beyond the grave,
　　Without thy mercy, none can ask of fate
To enter heaven; and without guile or lie
　　I in thy faith will faithful live and die.
Only a woman, humble, poor, and old;
　　Letters I read not, nothing know,
But see in church, with painted flames of gold,
　　That Hell where all the wicked go;
And, joyous with glad harps, God's Paradise.
　　One fills my heart with fear, one with delight;

For sinners all may turn repentant eyes
To thee, O Lady, merciful and bright,
With faith down laden : — without guile or lie
I in thy faith will faithful live and die.

But the minstrels, who represent the objective side
of Europe, had been constantly gaining ground. They
were numerous and powerful, and constantly waged
war upon the monks. So these latter took another
step to gain the favor of the laity, and endeavored to
reach a higher class of people. They wrote tales which
they called *gesta*, from a Latin word which means actions. These monkish gesta are a curious mixture of
legends from the lives of the saints, from classic history,
done into a barbarous, mixed Latin. They would be
read aloud in the long winter evenings, when the monk
and his guests would be seated around the refectory
fire. From some returned Crusader, some wandering
minstrel, these stories must have derived their lay
element.

For the power of the minstrels could no longer be
checked. Popular poetry, crushed under scholastic
theology, lived in the hearts of the people. Low-born
minstrels, called Jongleurs, — our word juggler comes
from this, — wandered from castle to castle of the ignorant nobles (who did nothing but fight), and sang those
ballads which afterwards expanded into the literature
of modern Europe. The languages which they used
were as chaotic as the thoughts, — a compound of the
native dialect of Kelt and Teuton with the monkish
Latin, different in each different country. These innumerable ballads may be grouped into four divisions,
which literary men call cycles. We have already seen

two of these cycles arise; for the same cycles were carried into each different country of Europe by the Jongleurs. The first cycle to arise was the Keltic, — that
of Arthur and the round-table knights; to it was afterwards added their search for the Holy Grail, which was
originally a separate story. The next cycle to take
form and spread were the ballads of the Gothic, Frankish, and Burgundian pagans, that is the Nibelungen
Lied. These warriors all belonged to the Teutonic family. Charlemagne was German at heart: in his Saxon
wars he collected these old ballads; they were sung
probably at his court, and there received their Christian
modifications, — there the wild Norse sea-rovers were
tamed into Christian knights. They are not mystic
and spiritual, so that we know they were untouched
by the religious spirit which transformed the Keltic
cycle. The third cycle was that of Charlemagne and
his twelve peers, and with this is connected the Spanish
cycle of the Cid: all these heroes fight against the
Saracens. It was not composed, of course, until one
or two centuries had elapsed, and allowed Charlemagne
and Roland to assume heroic proportions. This is the
cycle which is typical of the Middle Ages.

It is now known from what source the chivalric spirit
came into the mind of Europe. It was in a curious,
roundabout way. Nationalities had become so mixed
and fused together that a perfectly distinct type — like
Arthur among the Kelts, Siegfried among the Teutons
— could hardly be reproduced. The mixed nations
could not have a genuine native voice; still, their tone
of mind was the same, — it was chivalric. And this
they adopted from a new people. The reader will

remember how Aristotle came into Europe. The Mohammedan Arabs conquered the Persians; adopted
from them the science of Aristotle, the figures which
we use, the game of chess (the Persians took these two
from the Hindus) ; also, the chivalric tone of mind.
They carried them to the Mohammedans living in
Spain, called Moors; and the latter taught them to
the Spaniards. The Spanish cycle of the Cid caught
the precise tone of the event it described, which was the
perpetual fight of the Christians with the Pagans in
Spain ; but the lofty courtesy of the Moors gave manners to this warfare which made it quite unlike the
brutal fights of Romans and Barbarians elsewhere.
The earlier wars in Europe had been merely for ag-
grandizement of territory and power ; but these barbarians, once Christianized, fought for a religious motive,
and therefore the typical hero of the Middle Ages is
a Christian fighting with a Saracen. Long before the
Crusades the holy war began, — first in Spain. Here
it took on the chivalric manners of the gallant and
graceful Moors, which soon spread over Europe. The
Spanish ballads of the Cid are purely chivalric. This
is owing to their passing through Moorish influence,
which took out the wonderful or supernatural in them.
So I shall not dwell upon them, fine and stirring as
they are.

The " Song of Roland," which is the finest of the
Charlemagne cycle, on the contrary, has a very large
share of the supernatural, thus proving its Aryan origin : it is not purely chivalric. This is why it is so
beautiful: it unites a childlike faith in the marvellous
to the most noble and manly traits of character. Ro-

23

land is the true knight of the Middle Ages. He has an exalted respect for woman, an honor towards his foe; a spirit of patriotic self-sacrifice towards his country, but also a devout faith in Christianity. He is armed by faith and love of God. These sentiments must have found a response in the hearts of old feudal France, among its original people, for the ballads grew up spontaneously; their author is unknown, but they breathe the perfume of reality. The French may well be proud of them; " The Song of Roland" ought to be their national epic. It was sung at the battle of Hastings, when the Normans conquered England, in 1066. It was written in the old Frankish dialect, translated into Latin by the monks, then back again into the old French in which we now have it, which is easier to understand than old English, — Chaucer's, for instance. It has lately been put into modern French. You will find a new tone in the story, very unlike that of the other epics; no paganism is here. The Moorish king of Spain, who was a Mohammedan, sends to Charlemagne to ask for peace, after Charlemagne had been fighting against him for seven years. Ganelon, the traitor, tells Charlemagne that the Moorish king will submit, if Charlemagne will withdraw his army, and march out of Spain. So Charlemagne marches away, leaving the rear-guard of the French army under command of Roland. There are but twenty thousand men, and the false Moor falls upon them while they are passing through the mountain pass of Roncevaux, or Roncesvalles in Spanish. His friends beg Roland to sound his horn, knowing that Charlemagne will at once return if he hears this cry of distress. But Roland scornfully

refuses. The Saracens attack the French, and finally
kill every man of the twenty thousand, except Roland.
He has been performing prodigies of valor, and slaying
hundreds of men with his own arm and his own sword,
Durandal. Finally his head splits open at the temple,
and he feels that his death is near. So he sounds the
horn at last, to call Charlemagne, though too late.
Then, at the last moment, four hundred Saracens attack him at once. His body does not receive the least
scratch, but his head splits more and more; yet he
repulses the four hundred till they flee. Then he stag-
gers to a rock rising out of the plain, and strikes his
sword Durandal against it. He wishes to break Durandal, so that no paynim Saracen may get possession of
it; but the good sword will not break. Now I will
give a literal translation. He says : —

"O Durandal, my darling, thou art shining and white;
　All the rays of the sun are reflected by thee.
　One day the king was in the valley of Mauriveine,
　When an angel came to him from the Lord,
　And told him to give thee to a brave and valiant knight.
　Then Charles the Great girded thee on my side.
　Go die, good sword, and do not fall into the hands of any
　　paynim.
　May God save France from any such dishonor! "

"On a dark rock he struck the sword with fury, and he made
an enormous breach in the side of the rock. The blade sprang
back, and sparkled in the air. The Count saw that nothing
could break his sword, and with a dying voice he repeated his
complaint : ' My beloved Durandal, as beautiful as you are
holy, your golden hilt contains relics of great value : a lock of
hair of St. Denis, the blood of St. Basil, a tooth of St. Peter,

a piece of the Virgin Mary's dress. Such an arm is not made for paynims. No, no ! you must have a Christian master.' Then, feeling death nearer and nearer, he lies down under a pine-tree, and he hides his horn and his sword under his body. He turns his face towards the host of the infidels. He wishes, glorious Count, that Charles and his army, returning, shall find him here, and declare that he died victorious. He confesses all the sins he can remember, then he offers his glove to God. [This was the sign of submission from a vassal to a feudal lord.] 'True Father,' said he, 'who never liest to anybody, through whom the dead Lazarus opened his eyes in heaven, and who didst know how to preserve Daniel from the lions, save me from danger, and pardon my soul from the punishments which thy justice might claim.' Saying this, he held out his right-hand glove. The angel Gabriel received it from his hand. Then God sent Michael, and the two carried the soul of the Count to paradise."

There are a simplicity and faith in this which are the best characteristics of the Middle Ages. Roland is not the type which afterwards was fastened upon Arthur and Galahad, the Christian monk. He is a man in this world fighting a brave fight; but a Christian still, and hoping for paradise. He reminds one of Rustem in the Shah Nameh, constantly; and, like his, Roland's name is attached to the valley in Spain where he died. But the supernatural traits of Roland show him to be more than a mere picture of the manners and thoughts of his age. Roland has the characteristics of the solar myth. True, he may have really lived; but no real man, no real weapon, could ever have performed the prodigies of valor which Roland and his good sword did. The sword, too, was brought to him in a miraculous way. It is not the pagan way in which Perseus and Sigurd got their swords.   It is the Christian way, which performed all the other miracles of the Middle Ages.   And the Song of Roland is so delightful because it has this new tone, and because it sustains this tone so perfectly throughout; all the prodigies are impressed with it. Still they are prodigies, not natural acts.   No hero could, single-handed, kill four hundred men at a stroke, after his skull was split open.   But if you look at Roland as a solar hero, the work would be easy indeed for the irresistible power of the sun.   Roland's death, too, is supernatural.   He has not one scratch on his body, though his armor is pierced with a thousand darts.   His skull splits open from excessive toil; his brains ooze slowly out.   With his death his sword must go too. No other can wield it.   With the death of the sun, its rays no longer shoot across the sky.   Roland has another characteristic of the solar myth.   He had been betrothed to a lovely princess, named Aude, when he went forth to fight for others.   When the great king came back, Aude asked news of her hero.   When they told her that he was dead, " she cried not, nor uttered sound; the color faded from her face, and straightway she fell dead at the king's feet.   God is kind : he takes the broken-hearted home."

Another hero of the Charlemagne cycle is Olger the Dane, the national hero of Denmark ; and he represents many other features of the solar myth.   In the first place, he is one of the fatal children who kill their mother, the dawn.   There is a little touch about his birth which is too beautiful to be overlooked.   " There appeared about the bed of the new-born babe six fairies, whose beauty was so wonderful and awful that none but a child might gaze upon them without fear." Olger grows up beautiful and strong, but is sent as a hostage to the court of Charlemagne. Here he labors for others, like the other solar heroes, and fights for beings meaner than himself, under the following circumstances. There is a delicious confusion in the geography, which could only be found in the Middle Ages. These were the places familiar to its mind. A messenger appears at court, and says: " The Sultan and the Grand Turk, and Carahcu, Emperor of India, have taken Rome by assault. The Pope and the cardinals and the legates have fled ; the churches are destroyed ; the holy relics lost, — all save the body of St. Peter; and the Christians are put to the sword! Wherefore the Holy Father charges you as a Christian king to march to the succor of the Church." Olger does most of the fighting ; he engages with Carahcu, Emperor of India, in single combat, and conquers him: Carahcu and his bride are baptized in Rome, and return as Christians to rule over India. Then a Saracen giant appears, and Olger kills him. Then the emperor does him a wrong ; and his anger, like the wrath of Achilleus and of Rustem, makes itself felt. He goes out into the world as a wanderer, and travels far and wide, like Odysseus. Finally, he longs to see his land again, and sets sail ; but the ship is wrecked. The waves bear him to a strange land, where a stately palace stands. This is like the palace on Kirke's enchanted isle. At morning he finds himself in a flowery vale ; and Morgan le Fay comes to him, and welcomes him to Avalon, and takes him to the palace, where he finds Arthur healed of his wound. Then Morgan gives him a wreath of forgetful-

ness for his forehead, and an enchanted ring for his
hand ; while he wears these, he never grows old. By
and by the wreath slips from his forehead, and he remembers Charlemagne, and longs to go back and fight
the Saracen. So he reappears, like the Seven Sleepers
of Ephesus, or Rip Van Winkle. That is, the sun
comes back, after being carried away by the darkness.
Morgan le Fay had given him a torch, which is the
measure of his days, like the firebrand of Meleagros in
Greek. While it burns, he can never die. He fights
as bravely as before, though the world has changed ;
for hundreds of years have gone by while he was gone
in Avalon. When he is about to wed the Empress of
France, Morgan le Fay appears, and bears him away.
But the torch is still burning in an abbey crypt, and
therefore he is expected to return ; like Sebastian of
Portugal, and Frederick Barbarossa, and Arthur of
Brittany. When Denmark is in danger, then the Danish peasants are sure that Holger Danske will return.

This is substantially the story told in Germany,
later, of Tannhäuser. Venus carries him away into the
middle of a hill, called Hörselberg. There he lives in
forgetfulness ; but he longs at length to return to a life
of virtue, and goes out of the hill. He meets a priest
and confesses his sin ; but the horror-stricken priest
tells him that his own oaken staff may as soon bud and
blossom into roses as his sin be absolved. So the poor
Tannhäuser goes back to the enchantress. Eight days
after, the staff does bud and blossom into roses ; and
all the people expect Tannhäuser to reappear. In Scotland, exactly the same story is told of True Thomas of
Ercildoune, carried into a hill by the Fairy Queen, com-

ing back to the world; then again carried away. Both are the same enchantress who carried away Odysseus; wherever she carries away mortal men to dwell with unseen beings beneath the earth, she is the darkness carrying away the sun.

The Charlemagne cycle arose before the Crusades; we have it in its primitive form. It prepared the mind for the Crusades. To the bold baron who had listened in his own hall, to the jongleur who sang the strife between the Pagan and the Christian in Spain and France, the next step would be to seek the paynim on his own territory. In the Crusades he sought the Saracen one step farther away, that was all. The fourth cycle has been hard to explain, — the classical ballads. Europe was full of them: the jongleur sang of Alexander, and the tale of Troy, as often as of Arthur, Siegfried, and Roland. It has often been wondered whence Shakespeare drew his classical knowledge. From these classical ballads: the Greeks and the Trojans in Troilus and Cressida seem like knights of the Middle Ages. But they did not arise until after the Crusades; they were, therefore, brought back by the returning Crusaders. And they must have learned them from the Saracens whom they met in the intervals of fighting. One step more takes us back to Persia; for the Arabs learned them from that story of Iskander which formed part of the Shah Nameh. The tale of Troy the Crusaders must have learned in Constantinople, as they passed through. So all the nations are linked together. The Crusader brought back, too, much of the supernatural element in the Middle Ages, when the supernatural was all in all. Saints were Christian: heroes were Aryan:

good and evil spirits, genii and divs, marvellous birds
called griffins, were Persian.   It is interesting to separate the other features of the stories.   A tame lion,
following about a hero like a pet dog, is Keltic, —
from the Mabinogeon; a sea-fight is Teutonic; and
so on.

There were fictions of a later age, made up consciously
by writers, instead of being the genuine growth of popular tradition.   I will take Guy of Warwick as the
type of these later fictions, because the spirit of the period is so artlessly and touchingly expressed.   It will
explain all the other stories of pilgrims to the Holy
Land, and show how the solar myth takes on a local
coloring.   In Guy of Warwick, the sun appears as a
hero slaying monsters; afterwards as a wanderer.   He
is born poor, the son of a servant; but he dares to love
the princess, Felice.   So he goes out into the world to
do great deeds that he may win her.   He kills many
bad gentlemen, who are false knights; he sets free distressed damsels; finally, he goes to the Crusades.   An
emperor gives him his daughter in marriage; at the
very altar Guy remembers his early love, and turns
away (like the sun wedding other brides).   He sees a
lion and a dragon in fight; he kills this dragon, and the
grateful lion follows him about like a pet dog.   Then
he comes back to England and slays his second dragon,
— the black-winged one which was devastating Northumberland, and is still spoken of there.   The Percy
family claim to be descended from Guy; the fight between him and the dragon is sculptured on Warwick
Castle.   After all this, the proud Felice becomes his.
But the doom of the wanderer is upon him.   Forty

days after they were wed he said to his wife, "How many men I have slain, how many battles I have fought, all for a woman's love, and not one single deed done for my God! I will go on a pilgrimage for the sake of the Holy Cross." So he wended his way to Jerusalem. (Are you not reminded of Odysseus?) There he shrived him of his sins: then he travelled many years as a pilgrim, and slew a fierce Ethiopian giant, who was oppressing pilgrims. There is again delightful confusion in geography. Guy visits Spain and Constantinople within a few hours' time. The Saracens themselves are said to have stolen away his son. How the Saracens got into England, and reached Warwick Castle in Northumberland, is another of those charming inconsistencies with which the land of romance abounds. Years went by: like Odysseus, Guy still wandered. The king of England was besieged by a Danish army who had a Danish giant for their champion. Old and worn, Sir Guy came back in the robes of a palmer from the Holy Land, like Odysseus in his beggar-robes. He said he would fight for "the need of a people beset with enemies." He conquered the Danish giant, but no one knew that he was the great Sir Guy. He went to his own castle hall, and there his wife was feeding the beggars, and nursing the sick and weary travellers, and she bathed his feet and said, "Holy palmer, in all your travels, have you seen my lord, Sir Guy?" But he feared to break in upon her holy life, and went and lived in a cell near there. Here comes in the spirit of monasticism and asceticism which prevailed, and would not allow him to live happily with this Penelope of the Middle Ages. And when his end drew near, he sent his ring to Felice, and she came to him, and soothed his dying hours. The weary wanderer had found his rest, — the sun had sunk. But the twilight could not linger long behind. "Fifteen weary days Felice lingered sore in grief; then God's angel came and closed her eyes." Like Roland and Aude; like Lord Nann and his wife.

But the myth has appeared in another form, also, in England. After the Norman conquest, the cowed and trembling Saxons fled to the marshes and the greenwood, and there they sang of the bold spirits who showed a remnant of the old Norse courage. There is a ballad cycle, familiar to every child who loves to pore over these splendid old songs. It tells of the brave Robin Hood, — the Cid of England, the hero of the people. The foes are no longer the distant Saracens; they are the usurping Normans, with their laws against killing the red deer; with their haughty priests, who wring the last penny from the poor peasants. Robin Hood's foes are the sheriff of Nottingham, watching over the deer, or the Archbishop upon his palfrey. To the poor and helpless he is ever kind and noble, and he devoutly worships the Virgin Mary. Here the Christian spirit comes in. For however much substratum of historical truth lies beneath these marvellous deeds of Robin Hood, the solar myth must claim a large share of the credit. A grateful country has placed him among its heroes, but the unerring bow, and the arrows which never miss their mark, show plainly enough that the real man has been covered by the early mythology. The latest authorities agree in saying that he is the same unerring archer whom we found in the other mythologies; that he was brought over by the invading Angles, Saxons, and Danes; for in Yorkshire as many mighty fabulous actions are attributed to him as to King Arthur in Cornwall. We may accept this, because outside of the Robin Hood cycle is another fine old ballad, called "Adam Bell, Clym of the Clough, and William of Cloudeslee," which tells the familiar story of an apple shot from the head of a blooming youth. We found it in the Norse story of Egil. If the one was imported, why not the other? William says:—

> "I have a sonne, seven years old,
> Hee is to me full deare :
> I will tye him to a stake,—
> All shall see him that be here,—
> And lay an apple upon his head
> And goe six paces him froe,
> And I myself with a broad arrowe
> Shall cleave the apple in towe."

We cannot leave these delightful Middle Ages without explaining one more of their original thoughts. This one is an instinct which belongs to several Aryan families; especially the Hindus and Teutons. It prompted the beast epic. Reynard the Fox is the longest beast story in existence. Grimm says: "Side by side with those books which tell the relations of man to man appeared, from the earliest times, those which tell the relations of animals to animals. The poetry which treats of them is neither sarcastic nor didactic, originally, but is simply intensely natural. It is an epic, springing out of that deep love of nature, and observation of animals, which belong to an early and simple state of society." Reynard the Fox first appeared among the Franks in the fourth or fifth century, and was rewritten by the Germans, about the tenth century. But in this first form of the story, the animals appear in their own proper character, each one is true to the beast nature, and therefore very charming and interesting. That beast story, where the animals are turned into human beings disguised as beasts, with all the characters of human nature, is a much later form, — a state of degeneracy and decay, such as we find in the Fables of Æsop the Greek, of La Fontaine the Frenchman; but such as we do not find among the nature-loving, kindly Aryans, of a primitive age.

CHAPTER XII.

COMPARATIVE MYTHOLOGY OF SLAVONIC LITERATURE.

WE must turn aside from the continuous development of literature in Europe, where each branch of the race has brought something to modern thought, to speak of a family which contributed nothing to the gathering current until very lately. The Slavs are an interruption, wherever we may introduce them in the history of literature ; but since the new sciences of comparative philology and comparative mythology have crystallized, they have gained a value to the world which they never had before. The information about them was scanty and inaccessible, till recent events made the Slav the bugbear of Europe ; but the dream of a Panslavic empire has at least served the useful purpose of turning the labors of the Slavonic *savants* upon their own philology, and their own scientific position as members of the Aryan family ; and the results of their investigations have been published and translated.

It is not known when the Slavs entered Europe, or how. They came last of all the Aryan families, and sat down behind the Teutons. They have never consolidated into a powerful and influential family for several reasons. First, they preserved the original Aryan form of government for an unusually long period : the several tribes were bound together by language, cus-

toms, and traditions; but they had no political unity.
Courrière says: " The predominance of the patriarchal
and family rule prevented these tribes from ever reaching federation, and forming a powerful state. They
were subdued by more compact peoples." Had they
occupied a remote and inaccessible corner of Europe,
they might have found rest and peace, and therefore
time for consolidation. But they never pushed beyond
the frontier: exposed to every inroad of an invading
foe, they had scarcely time to take breath after one
attack, before another was upon them. Christianity,
which united other pagan families, only served to divide them. It was brought in from Byzantium in the
ninth century, by Cyril, a second Ulphilas. He translated the Bible into Slavon, their most important dialect; invented an alphabet, called the Cyrillic; and
taught the faith and ceremonies of the Greek Church.
This alphabet and Slavon language are used to-day by
sixty millions of people, either Mohammedans, or belonging to the Greek Catholic Church. It is an ecclesiastical language, like Latin among us; it is learned by
every educated Slav at the present time, and it was the
language used for high literature until the eighteenth
century.

In the ninth century, the Slavs were homogeneous;
but a portion of them adopted the Roman Catholic
form of Christianity, and the Latin language and alphabet, which divided them more and more, and by the
fourteenth century the separation was complete. Different nations had arisen, each with a dialect of its own,
and political unity was no longer possible. Nineteen
millions of Slavs use the Latin language and alphabet

at the present time, and belong to the Roman Catholic or Protestant Church. We need scarcely wonder, therefore, that they have made themselves so little felt. The Slavs occupy the space enclosed between the Elbe, the Alps, and the Adriatic Sea, on the west; the Ægean and Black Seas, on the south; the mouths of the Dnieper and the sources of the Don, on the east; Lake Ilmen and the Baltic Sea, on the north. They form the small independent nationality of Montenegro; the predominating element of the Russian empire; and are so intermingled with the Turkish and Austrian empires, that it is hopeless to try to disentangle them, or define their ever varying political status. They are certainly a very picturesque people, and we know that they are our brothers, first, by their language. Fire is *agni* in Sanskrit, *ignis* in Latin, *agon* in Russ. Family names are very similar; as, *malka*, mother; *sestra*, sister; *brat*, brother; *syn*, son. The parts of the body, as *nos*, nose; the actions of people, as *sidiet*, to sit; the farm implements, as *ploug*, plough; parts of dwellings, as *dom*, house, *dvor*, court-yard, — resemble each other in the Slavonic languages, and resemble all Aryan words.

A second proof of the identity of the Slavs is to be found in their literatures, which have developed without reciprocal influence. As the comparative mythology is what we are seeking, I shall describe only the pagan and semi-pagan literatures; and shall not speak of the modern literatures which have grown up since the Slavon was confined to ecclesiastical purposes. For instance, Poland has a brilliant literature, but it is altogether modern, reflecting Latin, French, and German thought. Poor Bohemia, on the contrary, tortured by Jesuits and Germans, watered by the martyr blood of Huss, has a delightful pagan past, but nothing of general interest in modern literature. Still, we must not for a moment imagine that the Slavonic poetry can bear any comparison with the spiritual and beautiful poems of the Rig Veda, or with the vague, grand hints of the older Edda; it is heroic, not religious. But it is fortunate that it should exist at all, and we must be thankful for its incidental references to Slav beliefs.

Through all the literatures runs the same mythology; but there is very little information to be gathered from them all combined. We discover that the Slavs worshipped, first, their dead ancestors; next, the powers of nature, like the other Aryan peoples. They offered sacrifices under an oak, and at first there were no temples nor priests; the head of the family was his own priest. The forms of their deities are very indistinct and shadowy. The Slavs kept always very near to nature; they remained in that early stage of mythology whose traces are found in the Rig Veda, but which had already past by when that was collected. They never emerged even into the clear personifications of the Rig Veda, much less into the anthropomorphism of the Greeks. This gives their mythology an interest of its own, since it has preserved better than any other of the Aryan literatures a certain stage of thought, — that earliest poetic naturalism, where rivers and mountains, the grass and the earth, are personified, but without being as yet worshipped as gods. This will be particularly evident in the Russian literature.

Still the Slavs did pass on to the next stage; they

24

evolved a chief deity called Bog: our words *bogy* and *puck* come from the same root. He was also called Swarog: the name has been traced to a root meaning the all-surrounding sky, like Varuna. He has children: the sun, called Dazh-Bog, the day god; Stri-Bog, the god of the winds; Ogon, the fire. But all these gradually fell into neglect, and Perun, the thunder god, took their power, and most of their characteristics. That the Slavs paid great attention to agriculture is evident to whoever reads their poetry; the peasants always say the " sacred corn "; so Perun, who had the rain under his control, soon became the god most important to them, and he was worshipped by each Slavonic nation. He is the only deity who has a distinct form; the traditions describe him as tall and well shaped, with a long golden beard. He rides in a flaming car, and grasps in his left hand a quiver full of arrows; in his right, a fiery bow. In the spring he goes forth in this fiery car, and crushes with his arrows the demons whose blood streams forth. This is the counterpart of Indra's work: the lightning piercing the dark clouds, and causing them to send forth rain. Sometimes Perun's arrow becomes a golden key, with which he unlocks a cave, and brings gems and hidden treasures to light. That is the lightning, which rends open the frozen winter earth, and brings back the light and warmth of summer, and lets loose the frozen brooks; then he takes the characteristics of the sun in other mythologies. The Slavs thought that the lightning could see; at that flash of summer lightning, gone before one can catch its gleam, they cried out that Perun was winking. The oak-tree was sacred to him; even when the Slavs accepted

Christianity, and gave up their idols, they would not allow their sacred oaks to be cut down. Lada is the goddess of spring, and of love; the counterpart of Freyia in the Norse mythology; the word means luxuriance, union, harmony.

The Slavs never had that spiritual instinct which told them of a future state where " wickedness should be punished, virtue rewarded, wrongs redressed, and griefs assuaged." They had only that idea of another world which is found among children and childlike peoples. That the dead are living still, but that their life is simply a continuance of the one they have left behind, is always the first conception of immortality. The chieftain remains a chieftain; the slave, a slave. Therefore they gave to the dead everything that he would need in another life,— horses, armor, even a partner for eternity. If a man died unmarried, they killed some woman upon his grave, so dreary would his lot be without a wife. It is a decided fact, that, as late as one thousand years ago only, widows killed themselves among the Slavs to accompany their dead husbands; the rite of Sati, burning on a funeral pile, prevailed there, as in India. It is undecided whether the Slavs had invariably burned or buried their dead; but it is certain that they never sent them afloat on an actual ocean like the Norsemen. They believed in a road which led to the other world; it was both the rainbow and the milky way; and, since the journey was long, they put in boots, (for it was made on foot,) and coins to pay the ferrying across a wide sea: this suggests Charon in Greek. There is a tradition which suggests the dogs of Yama in Sanskrit: as soon as a man died in Ruthenia, a hole was made in the roof; a black dog was passed through it, that he might free the soul from the body. The abode of the dead was the home of the sun, a warm fertile land, the isle Buyan. There were collected all the forms of tempest also; "there lies the lightning-snake, and broods the tempest-bird [the raven] ; there swarm the thunder-bees, who bless the longing earth with the honey of rain." This expression is one of the primitive Aryan thoughts : in the period before the Rig Veda was written down, every good and pleasant thing was called honey ; they prayed, " Bless us with the honey of sleep," in India.

It is possible that we may soon be able to make an important addition to our knowledge of Slavonic mythology. It is an accepted fact that the Bulgarians were originally Turanians. They were called into Europe by the Huns : having spread terror through the Eastern lands, they finally settled at the foot of the Balkan Mountains, conquered the Slavonic tribes whom they found there, and in the ninth century they embraced Greek Christianity and the Cyrillic alphabet. This completed the fusion of the races ; they adopted the Slavonic customs, and are practically Slavs at this time. Obeying the impulse given to Slavonic studies, *savants* have collected their popular poetry. Within the last few years, M. Verkovicz, living at Serres, near Salonica, published in 1874 the most remarkable of these collections. He gave it the pretentious title of the Veda Slovena, " Slavonic Veda." It contains the songs of Mt. Rhodope : these songs were floating about among the Mohammedan Bulgarians, but M. Verkovicz claims to have traced them to an ancient monastery on Mt. Rhodope in Thrace. A great outcry has been made : some Slavonic *savants* consider them genuine ; others, a forgery.

If the Veda Slovena be a forgery, Bohemia possesses the primitive poetry of the Slavonic family. In 1818 was found in the library of the castle of Zelenchora an ancient · manuscript, which is proved to be authentic. It contains '' The Judgment of Libussa, the Wise.'' The events described took place at the beginning of the eighth century, and the poem is exceedingly valuable as showing the manners and ideas of the time. Patri- archal government still prevailed, but the hatred be- tween Slav and German had even then arisen. The wise Libussa is a grand figure gleaming through the mists of centuries, — a heroine who would do honor to any nation. Prophetess and Vala though she be, she proves herself to be also a woman. It is impossible to find the whole legend, but its fragments are enough to make us long for more. When the king of Bohemia died, the kingdom was given to his youngest daughter, Libussa ; for she was skilled in all knowledge, and had the gift of reading the future. Hearing of her wisdom, two brothers came to ask her what should be done with their father's kingdom. So the wise Libussa appointed a day when she would give judgment, and convoked a tribunal of the nobles of the land in her great castle hall. They came by classes ; and a list is given, like Homer's catalogue of the Greeks.

" When all were seated, the wise Libussa entered the hall, clothed in white raiment, and sat down on her father's throne. Beside her stood two young girls skilful in divination : one of them held the tables of the law ; the other, the sword which dispensed justice. Before them was the fire which witnesses the truth ; at their feet, the miraculous water."

These must have been the symbols of the ordeal by fire and by water, which belongs to each Aryan family; they are called in the poem the "judgment of God." Libussa divided the kingdom between the two sons, according to the Slav custom.

" Then Crondoch, from the shores of winding Ottava, arises; anger has entire possession of him ; all his limbs tremble with rage ; he brandishes his fist, and roars like a bull : ' Woe to the brood where the serpent penetrates ! Woe to the man governed by a woman ! It is for a man to rule over men. It is to the oldest that the inheritance must be given !' Libussa rises from her throne and says: ' Kmets, Lekhs, and Vladykas, you hear how I am insulted; judge yourselves what the law may be. Henceforth I will no longer judge your quarrels. Choose a man, one of your equals, who shall govern with a sceptre of iron : the hand of a virgin is too feeble.'"

Then another of the nobles arises, and declares that Libussa's decision is right, and according to the Slav customs.

" Here every one is master of his family : the men work in the field ; the women make the clothing; when the head of the family dies, all the children possess his property in common : they choose a vladyka from the family ; he goes to the glorious assembly for the good of the people, and walks with the three ranks into the hall."

So Libussa's judgment is accepted, and the Germanizing tendency put down. Soon after, a peasant comes to consult Libussa. She reads in the future that he is to become her husband ; but when he comes the next day for her answer, the awkwardness of the situation impels her to tell him that he must come again, till she is sure that she has read the future aright. Then she

marries him, for her foresight has taught her that he is
the worthiest man in her kingdom; and their dynasty
rule Bohemia for five centuries. It is a simple and
stately poem.

The second manuscript is called that of Kralove-
Dvor (the queen's court), and contains six hero ballads
and eight lyric poems. It was found in a monastery
in 1817, is much later than the Judgment of Libussa,
and extends from the ninth to the fourteenth century.
The first poem is the most interesting, as showing how
the Bohemians struggled against Christianity; how they
regarded what we consider an unmixed blessing; and
also what was the worship they paid to their heathen
divinities. Zaboï, who commands half the Bohemians,
consults Slavoï, who commands the other half. They
summon their armies to the secret recesses of the forests, and sing them the following inspiring song : —

> " Brave men, and brothers with fiery glances,
>   I sing to you from the lowest valley :
>   This song takes rise in my heart,
>   My heart plunged in dark sadness.
>   The father has gone to rejoin his father:
>   He left his children and his companions an inheritance,
>   And to no one did he say,
>   ' Brother, address brotherly words to them ! '
>   But the stranger has come by force into the inheritance,
>   And commands in foreign words
>   That which is practised in foreign countries :
>   Our wives and children must do it ; .
>   And we can have only one wife
>   Through all our life, from youth till death.
>   They have driven all the hawks from the forest ;
>   And those gods which the strangers possess,

We must adore them, and make offerings to them.
We dare no longer prostrate ourselves before our gods,
Nor give them food at twilight.
. There, where our fathers brought food to them
And went to sing their praises,
The strangers have cut down all the trees.
O Zaboï, you sing from the heart to the heart
A song full of sadness.
Like Luimir, whose words fired all the country,
So hast thou touched us, me and my brethren.
The gods love the noble bard.
Sing! they have given thee power to touch our hearts."

Finally Zaboï and Ludiek, the chief of the German invaders, settle the question by the original Aryan mode, — single combat. The fight is described in a most animated manner, and Ludiek is slain; then Zaboï sings a triumphant song of victory. The souls of the dead were disposed of in the following way by the pagan Bohemians. "The blood came out from the strong hero, and ran across the grass into the damp ground; his soul came out from his warm lips, fluttered from tree to tree, here and there, until his corpse was burned."

The other ballads are later, and gradually become Christianized, till they cease to have any especial interest for us; although they are fine hero ballads, and furnish material for a Bohemian epic.

The Russian literature is peculiarly rich in certain directions, and the Russians themselves are the most important members of their family. The constant intercourse between Scandinavia and Byzantium, by way of Russia, brought about a definite result. Rurik, the chief of a band of Varangians, on his way to Byzantium paused, conquered the Slavonic tribes whom he met, and founded a kingdom at Kieff. Some of the band went on, embraced Greek Christianity, and brought back the faith and worship of the Greek Catholic Church, which they forced upon the Norsemen and Slavs at Kieff, in the ninth century. Christianity existed under sufferance; finally, it was made the state religion by Vladimir, the Charlemagne of Russia, who ascended the throne about 980 A. D. He himself overthrew the statue of Perun, which had a golden beard; founded monasteries, churches, and schools; used Cyril's translation of the Bible into Slavon, and the Cyrillic alphabet; and proved himself to be a great and wise ruler. He took the name of Wassily at his baptism, and has been turned into St. Basil by the Russo-Greek Church. A whole cycle of hero-ballads has collected about him, just as about Charlemagne; all the old pagan beliefs can be traced in these ballads, which must have wandered long on the Russian soil before they took shape under the fostering care of the great Vladimir. They tell us part of what we know definitely about the Russian mythology, for there are no sacred books. A few ritual songs have been preserved by the peasantry, which celebrate the agricultural changes of the seasons; but they have been so frowned upon by the priests, that they preserve little of their original meaning. The death of winter is still celebrated: the peasants build a bonfire, dance around it, and sing songs to Lada, the goddess of spring and fertility, and for a week the children shoot with bows and arrows. The priests have transferred this festival to Butter Week, the Russian carnival, and it takes place if the weather be cold or warm. The burial of Kupalo, the summer, is celebrated in the autumn : a straw figure is actually buried, a bonfire is made, and a Kolo is danced by the young men and women. These can be nothing less than the survival of the pagan mythology. Perun was the god who received the chief worship of the Russians. But in hero ballads Russia has developed unexpected richness and variety ; for until the beginning of this century no one imagined that she could boast a national epic. These ballads have been gathered together with the greatest difficulty. In 1859 M. Ruibnikoff began a series of long and dangerous journeys, with the object of collecting them : he went into distant provinces of the empire, and lived among the peasants, at the actual risk of his life. His account of his adventures is really thrilling ; and from the lips of the peasant reciters he took down the bylinas, which have been recently published in Russ. They have been analyzed and described in French by M. Rambaud, but not translated. No account of them has been given in English, though Mr. Ralston has promised a volume upon them.

There are two classes of these bylinas or hero ballads ; the first, legendary, which descended by oral tradition from the eleventh century, the time of Vladimir ; the second historical, which have been preserved in writing. I shall speak first of those most interesting and valuable for our purpose, the legendary ballads, which are much more ancient, and take us back to an epoch when the genius of the common people was not only strong, but still predominant. We see the very beginnings of pagan Russia, and watch the Russian imagination struggling to give its own impress to those hero types and those demigods who are universal to the Aryan race. These last are but slightly sketched, though they have gigantic stature and superhuman powers, and scarcely emerge from the natural forces which they typify : they are Titans who cannot direct themselves. The first of them is Volga. A mortal maiden was his mother, a serpent his father ; as soon as born, his voice resounded like thunder, and he grew to boy's stature in a few months. Volga is like Proteus in Greek, in his power of changing himself into different forms, such as a bird. a mouse, or an ermine : the last animal gives a local coloring to the myth, which shows the variableness of nature, and means the sun covered by clouds of different shape. A soothsayer told him that he would be killed by his horse. So he ordered the animal to be slaughtered, and long after he mounted its fleshless skeleton. But a serpent came out of its whitened skull, and stung the hero to death : this is quite a new form of the miraculous death and the serpent of darkness. Sviatogor reminds one immediately of the Norse mythology : he is the strong man whom mother earth can scarcely bear up, but crumbles beneath him. He is wearied and burdened with his own weight : he cannot walk on the plains of Russia ; only on the mountains and massive rocks. Utterly wearied out, he finally pauses on one mountain, and there remains till this day. He is a delightful and novel addition to the family of giants.

So now the world is ready for its heroes, and they first appear grouped around Vladimir as he holds high revel in the halls of Kieff. There are many of them ; but we have time only for one, although each presents

some feature of the solar myth. Ilia de Mourom is a
first-class hero, and he takes his place worthily beside
Rustem, Achilleus, Sigurd, or Roland. The early bylinas which tell of him are semi-pagan ; and much the
more satisfactory, for the personifications are nearer to
nature. The monsters which oppose him are vague
and formless, hardly to be separated from the cloud or
fog which they typify. The world is still primeval :
the gods, the heroes, the animals, live on the most
familiar terms ; the rivers become persons ; serpents,
horses, and birds talk. Vladimir is not yet a tzar : he
is only a feudal monarch. There are no guards, no
courtiers : he is simply the father of his people, who
enter without restraint into the hall where he sits to
give audience to admiring strangers, or listen to foreign
minstrels. In the later bylinas, Ilia de Mourom becomes a Christian knight, who founds churches ; the
celestial mountains, which were only clouds, the celestial sea, which was only the vast blue sky, become real
mountains, real seas ; the dragon monsters, which were
only storm clouds, become real Tartars. And these
events settle upon an historical personage, who attended
the court of an historical king. In all the bylinas,
however, just as Achilleus is subject to Agamemnon,
Olger the Dane to Charlemagne, so the great hero Ilia
de Mourom is subject to King Vladimir, — Fair Sun, as
he is always called ; and when the need of the people is
sorest, it is Ilia who toils for them. Unlike any other
epic, the Russian shows that it arose from the people,
by choosing its hero from among them ; Ilia is the son
of a peasant. Until he is thirty years old, he is paralyzed and useless ; then two divine beings come to him,

bring him the water of life, and he is immediately endowed with enormous strength. They say to him:
" Ilia, you will be a great hero; you will never die in
battle. Give battle, then, to all heroes or heroines;
but take care not to attack Volga: it is not his
strength which renders him invincible, it is his cunning.
Do not attack Sviatogor; damp mother earth herself
can scarcely support his weight." The first use which
Ilia makes of his new strength shows the feature which
the Russians have added to the type. He cultivates
the soil of " holy Russia"; while his parents sleep, the
good son does their agricultural work. They had been
striving to cut down a forest; with one turn of his
hand he tears up all the oaks, and throws them into
the river. Then he departs to kill dragons, robbers,
and heathen: he is a free peasant, who seizes the
sword to rid his native land of every foe. He gets
himself a magic steed, which is at first dark-colored
and stupid; but for three nights Ilia bathes him in the
dew: then he becomes powerful and light-colored; he
clears lakes, rivers, and forests at a bound, as Ilia
prances along to the halls of Vladimir, Fair Sun. On
his way he meets the brigand Soloveï, — a new variety
of the inevitable monster, who is a gigantic bird, called
the nightingale. He had built his nest on seven oaks,
and his claws extended for seven versts over the country, which he had infested for thirty years. He roared
like a wild beast, howled like a dog, whistled like a
nightingale. At this awful whistling Ilia's horse fell on
his knees with fear; but Ilia scornfully reproved him,
dragged him up, and let fly an arrow, which hit Soloveï
in the right eye. He fell from his lofty nest; Ilia

attached him to the saddle, and rode off. Then the wife and children of Soloveï followed after, and talked to Ilia, offering him three cups full of gold, silver, and pearls. Unlike the greedy heroes who seek the Nibelung hoard, the disinterested Ilia refuses the treasure, and hastens on that he may reach the court of Vladimir, Fair Sun, at Easter. The prince welcomes him: "Art thou a tzar, or the son of a tzar?" The peasant makes no disguise, but declares his name and condition, and presents his prize. Vladimir requests Soloveï to roar, howl, and whistle; but he declines. "I do not eat your bread; I am not your servant; it is not you whom I will obey." (A very feudal touch.) Ilia then orders him to roar, howl, and whistle with half his strength only. The gracious prince pours out with his own hand a cup of wine holding fifteen pints. The mischievous Soloveï drains it at a draft, then roars, howls, and whistles with all his fury. The roof of the palace falls off; the courtiers drop dead with fear; Ilia puts the prince under one arm, the princess under the other, to protect them. This reminds us of the fun when Herakles the Greek brought the dog Kerberos to King Eurystheus. Ilia, indignant, cuts the bird Soloveï into little pieces, which he scatters over the fields. Then, of course, he enters the service of Vladimir, Fair Sun, to fight against the foes of his country. One day arrives a polenitza, a powerful amazon on horseback: Ilia fights with her, conquers her; but she refuses to tell her name. She turns out to be his own daughter, whose mother was a polenitza also, conquered and abandoned by Ilia. This is the story of Sohrab and Rustem in Persian, Hildebrand and Hadubrand in German, and well understood by this time. Ilia never blusters nor boasts : he protects the weak ; he frees his prison- ers without any ransom ; he spares a defenceless enemy ; he thinks sadly of all the blood he has been obliged to shed ; he is gentle, and even full of humor. When brigands attack him, he tries to get rid of them by a little mild sarcasm : " What ! forty brigands against an old fellow like me ! My caftan is not worth sixty rou- bles ; my arrows, five ; I may have forty roubles of ready money about me." The brigands are delighted at such an innocent : they attack him ; with one arrow he splits an oak into splinters, and they lie motionless with fright for five hours. The peasant hero never forgets his class : like all peasants in Russia, Ilia is a great drinker ; after one battle he drank so much that he slept for twelve days. On his awaking, he entered the palace hall, and found Vladimir surrounded by nobles only. He rebuked the king, who threw him into a dungeon, where he lay for three years, unfed by Vladimir. Kieff was assailed by Tartars, and Vladimir was in despair. Trembling, he sent down to the dungeon, expecting to find only a skeleton ; but the king's daughter had sent him food every day for three years, — like Olger the Dane, fed by a princess. Vladimir threw himself at his feet, and begged his assistance. He forgave more readily than Achilleus and Olger, and immediately went out to fight for " holy Russia." Rambaud says, " Ilia can bear a favorable comparison with the noblest pala- din of the Middle Ages."

M. Rambaud also says : " There must always be a prodigious catastrophe when all the demigods and he- roes disappear at one fell swoop. In the Roman legends it is the battle of Lake Regillus; in the Odyssey, Volsung Saga, and Nibelungen, the slaughter-hall; in the Song of Roland, the valley of Roncevaux." So all the heroes and heroines grouped around Vladimir follow the same law. They had just annihilated an army of Tartars; filled with pride, they cried out, "Our shoulders are not wearied, our swords are not hacked; let a supernatural army oppose itself to us: we could conquer an army which was not of this world." Immediately two unknown warriors appeared. Alexis charged them, cut them in two: at once four heroes began to fight; Alexis cut them all in two, and the eight began to fight; then the sixteen whom Alexis had created. Then Ilia came to the rescue, but the same process went on: all day long the heroes fought against an army which doubled at every stroke. At last, terrified, they fled towards a cave in the mountains, where they were all changed into rocks. A precisely similar tradition exists in Sanskrit, and is a very agreeable variety of the inevitable event.

Students of mythology can easily decipher the career of Ilia. He is paralyzed and immovable during the winter; two strangers, passing clouds, bring the spring rain, which awakens the energies of nature, and Ilia arises just in the spring at Easter time. The monster has infested the country just thirty years, as long as the sun, Ilia, had slept. And his whistling, howling, roaring, are the best descriptions we meet anywhere of the noise of the tempest. In the nest of Soloveï Ilia finds treasures, just as under the worm Fafnir; light and warmth they are. And Ilia cuts up the bird that his blood may fatten the fields: the sun scatters the clouds that the rain may fertilize the earth. The polenitza is the sun of yesterday; her mother is the dawn, whom Ilia leaves behind; the forty brigands are clouds; they fall to the ground, and the oak is splintered, after a gleam of sunlight. The dungeon into which Ilia is plunged is the darkness, or night, from which he emerges into another day. Finally, if he be turned to stone at his death, it is because winter imprisons the summer in stony slumber.

The women of the Russian bylinas offer excellent examples of the hero-woman. They are not valas, prophetesses with something sacred about them, like the wise Libussa; they are amazons, like Gurd Afrid in the Shah Nameh, Brünhilde in the Nibelungen Lied, Atalanta in Greek; and they all lose their power when they are married, and become humble and submissive. One day Dobryna was riding along, when he met a polenitza, and gave her a blow on the back of her head: she did not even turn her head. "It must be that I have lost my usual strength," said the hero to himself. With his club he struck an enormous oak which flew into splinters. Reassured, he returned and gave another terrible blow to the polenitza, with the same result. The hero doubted his strength, and tried it on a rock, which flew into splinters also. At the third blow, the polenitza turned around and said, "I thought some gnats were stinging me, and lo, it is a Russian hero who moves his hands." She seized him by his blond curls, and put him into her pocket, on horseback as he was. Her own giant horse trembled, and spoke out to complain of the increased load. So Nastasia said, "If the nobleman is old, I will cut off his head; if he is young, I will keep him a prisoner: if he suits my fancy,

25

I will marry him." She drew him out of her pocket, married him, and became an affectionate and dutiful wife. Afterwards she became almost a Russian Penelope, and awaited his return from abroad for twelve years. Then she consented to marry another, but Dobryna returned in season, and upbraided her, saying, " I do not wonder that you have fallen ; women have long hair, and short wit."

We come now into another atmosphere, and reach the historical epic. Russia has a true national epic, more correct historically than most of the other epics of the world. The " Song of Igor " was written in the twelfth century, shortly after the events it celebrates, which took place in 1185 A. D. The manuscript is of the fourteenth or fifteenth century, and was discovered in a monastery in 1795. Igor, a prince of Novgorod, his son, brother, and nephew, make an expedition against a nomad tribe of mixed Finns and Tartars. The account is written by one poet whose name is unknown to us, but who was evidently an educated man, trained in the learning of Byzantium : poetry has ceased to be, therefore, of and for the people ; the Song of Igor was written down for an aristocratic class. The legendary world is left behind : no more demigods and heroes walk the earth, embodying the ancient pagan divinities, in slightly varied forms ; the personages of the Song of Igor are simple mortals, — princes and nobles and soldiers. The ancient divinities are introduced from a respectable distance. The Russians are the posterity of Dazh-Bog ; the poets, children of Volos ; the winds, sons of Stri-Bog ; just as we speak of Apollo and the Muses as part of the furniture of an epic, but not with the simple confidence in their actual presence of an earlier age. The goddess Discord is introduced; but she is evidently borrowed from the Greek epics, which the poet might have studied at Constantinople. The poem is Christian; but, as not more than two centuries had gone by, Christianity had not struck root very deeply. M. Rambaud says, " It is a recognized law that the chief gods in a destroyed religion are sooner forgotten than the secondary ones, — those which are interwoven with the daily life and old associations." This is very evident in the folk-songs; and it comes out in the Song of Igor, in that poetic naturalism which I spoke of as the chief characteristic of Slavonic poetry. The Song of Igor shows, not only a passionate love of nature, but an intimate sympathy between it and mankind : nature responds to his external conditions, as well as to his feelings. Igor leads his warriors in person : an eclipse of the sun takes place on the first day, and the earth trembles beneath the tread of his army. It is his mother earth, who tries to warn him. But Igor persists; he crosses the vast steppes, and plunges into the river. " Land of Russia," he cries, " you are far away, you have hidden yourself behind the mounds." (These are the tumuli which break the monotony of the plains of Russia.) Meantime his wife is left behind.

" The Jaroslavna (daughter of Jaroslaf) laments on the city wall at morning : you would say it was the lament of the cuckoo. 'O wind, terrible wind! why, my lord, blow so hard ? Why, on your light wings, do you carry the arrows of the Khan against the warriors of my hero ? Is it not enough for you to blow up there in the clouds? to rock the vessels on the blue sea ? Why, my lord, do you throw my joy down on the grass of the steppe?' The Jaroslavna laments at morning on the city wall: 'O haughty Dnieper! you break a path for yourself between the rocky mountains of the Polovtzi's country! You lulled on your waves the barks of Sviatoslof when he buckled on his armor against the warriors of Kobak. O my lord! bring back my spouse to me. No longer let me send him my tears every morning, by my messenger, the sea.' The Jaroslavna at morning laments on the city wall: 'Brilliant sun! trebly brilliant, you warm us all, you shine for all! Why, my lord, dart your burning rays on the warriors of my spouse? Why do you dry up their bows in their hands, in that desert without water? Why do you add weight to the quivers on their shoulders by the torments of thirst?'"

In all pagan literature there is no more lovely example of that early stage of personification. Far away, Igor fights for three days; then he is defeated and taken prisoner because he nobly refuses to fly and abandon his people. At length he makes up his mind to escape; not for his own sake, but that he may preserve his people at home, who are a prey to wandering tribes. His friends at home had been endeavoring to arouse the other princes to go to his rescue; and they promise to unite in this holy war against the invading Tartar. Then the poet breaks out in a lament over the lack of national feeling at the time he is writing, and urges the princes to form a united Russia, solid against the Tartar tribes, like the princes of the earlier day, and to forget their fratricidal wars. The Tartar is now to Russia what the Moor was to the Cid, the Saracen to Roland; the principle of evil fighting against good, of light fighting against darkness. When Igor tries to escape, pitfalls open under his feet; it is the soil of the enemy trying to hold him back, and the grass whispers it to every passer-by; but he at last reaches the friendly shores of the river Donetz; he talks with it, and complains of the cruel Stronga which broke his ships, and drowned the young prince, Ivan, his friend: the river answers him with kindly greetings, and wafts him gently over to his own shore. The poet intended to write the history of Russia, but gives us only one episode: yet this disastrous story is but a type of the misfortunes which overwhelmed all Russia, kept her for two centuries crushed under the rule of the Tartars, and prevented all intellectual development.

The Russian folk-songs have been translated by Ralston, but are not especially interesting in themselves, or as furnishing material for comparative study; but the folk-tales are both extremely charming and valuable. Ralston has given us a critical and reliable collection, translated from many volumes. They are told in a very animated and dramatic manner; they are considered to take the next place to the Hindu folk-lore; the Slavonic peasant is tenacious, and the primitive, patriarchal life and thoughts have lingered in his memory. The early stage of naturalism to which I have alluded is delightfully expressed in the following tale.

VAZUZA AND VOLGA.

Vazuza and Volga had a long dispute as to which was the wiser, the stronger, and the more worthy of high respect. They wrangled and wrangled, but neither could gain the mastery in the dispute, so they decided upon the following course.

" Let us lie down together to sleep," they said, "and whichever of us is the first to rise, and the quickest to reach the Caspian Sea, she shall be held the wiser of the two, and the stronger, and the worthier of respect."

So Volga lay down to sleep ; down lay Vazuza also. But during the night, Vazuza rose silently, fled away from Volga, chose the nearest and straightest line, and flowed away. When Volga arose she set off, neither slowly nor hurriedly, but with just befitting speed. At Zubtsof she came up with Vazuza. So threatening was her mien that Vazuza was frightened, declared herself to be Volga's younger sister, and besought Volga to take her in her arms, and bear her to the Caspian Sea. And so to this day Vazuza is the first to awake in the spring, and then she arouses Volga from her wintry sleep.

The evil beings, the dark powers of Slavonic mythology, are better depicted in the Russian folk-tales than in any branch of Slavonic literature. The peasant still preserves these awful creatures, and gives us the usual form, and some new varieties. Of course, darkness is still the many-headed snake ; and here comes in the destined hero. "Once there was an old couple who had three sons. Two of them had their wits about them, but the third, Ivan, was a simpleton. Now in the land in which Ivan lived there was never any day, but always night. This was a snake's doing. Well, Ivan undertook to kill that snake." Then came a third snake with twelve heads. Ivan killed it, and destroyed the heads ; and immediately there was bright light throughout the whole land. The myth is pushed on, and there is also the monster who devours maidens, called a "Norka" ; and Perun takes the work of Indra and Saint George, enters the castle (dark clouds), and rescues her. But the dark power takes a distinctive Russian appearance, in the awful figure of Koshchei, the deathless, — a fleshless skeleton who squeezes heroes to death in his bony arms. He carries off a princess ;

after seven years (the winter months) the hero reaches
his under-ground palace and is hidden; but Koshchei
returns and cries out, "No Russian bone can the ear
hear, or the eye see; but there is a smell of Russia here,"
— like the giant "Fee, faw, fo, fum," terror of our childhood. He really typifies the winter; the name means
to make hard as a bone, a figurative expression for
to freeze. There is a frightful witch, called the Baba
Yaga, who flies over land and sea, doing all the mischief
she can, but always stops at her own cottage, on the
edge of a forest. She is plainly the wind, which ceases
blowing when it comes to a thick forest. And there
are the usual secondary evil spirits, who live in the
waters or the woods. The Rousalka is a female water
spirit: she has long green hair; if it becomes dry, she
will die; so she never travels from home without her
comb. By passing this through her locks, she can produce a flood; which explains the comb of all mermaids.
Besides all these dreadful beings to be avoided, each
man's ill-luck is personified.

WOE.

Woe followed a merchant persistently, till his patience was
quite gone. So the merchant said, "Let us go into the yard
and play at hide and seek." Woe liked the idea immensely.
Out they went into the yard, and the merchant hid himself.
Woe found him immediately; then it was his turn to hide.
"Now, then," said Woe, "you won't find me in a hurry.
There isn't a chink I can't get into." "Get along with you,"
answered the merchant; "you could not creep into that wheel
there, and yet you talk about chinks." "Couldn't I creep
into that wheel there? You'll see!" So Woe stepped into
the wheel. The merchant caught up the wedge, and drove it

into the axle-box from the other side. Then he seized the wheel, and flung it, with Woe in it, into the river. Woe was drowned, and the merchant lived happily again, as he had been used to.

The Werewolf appears in great force in Russian tales: but the Vampire is the most repulsive form of the evil power, and he is original in Slavonic thought. In him, the evil spirit enters into a corpse, revisits " the glimpses of the moon," kills the living, and sucks the blood of the dead. The horrible Glam in the Norse tale of Grettir the Strong belongs to this family ; the modern Greek word for vampire is of Slavonic origin. He can be killed by chopping off his head by a grave-digger's shovel. Even modern legends teach that the body of a suicide will be taken possession of by the fiend, and turned into a vampire. The Slavonian peasants, therefore, drive an ashen stake once through the heart of every suicide : even in England the law insisted up-on this until 4 George IV. *c.* 52. Until this is done, the poor vampire must wander uneasily about. His victims can be recognized by a small wound directly over the heart. There can be no doubt that the vam-pire is a nature myth ; sucking the blood of the sleepers, or of the dead, is drawing rain from the storm clouds ; or it may be setting free the frozen brooks and rivers, killed by the cold of winter.

In ancient times, all pagans believed that any person could offer up a prayer which should affect the weather ; next, they came to think that only certain persons had this power ; and these people, like the Norse Valas, were regarded with the greatest reverence. But Chris-tianity turned them into evil beings, and they then became the witches and wizards whom we find in the modern folk-lore : they inherited terror and horror, instead of the reverence originally paid them, as representatives of the deities they invoked.

All these witch stories have lately been looked at in a new way, and explained by a new theory, which we may accept or not, — it is not fixed, — but which is more agreeable than to believe, as Tylor's "Primitive Culture" tells us, that witchcraft is part of every savage life, and that we once shared such beliefs ourselves. Comparative mythologists try to account for them, by considering them as survivals of the ancient thoughts of the Aryans about nature. These witches and wizards now perform the acts attributed to the forces of nature themselves at first ; and by slow degrees, which we have just traced, they arrived at this power. Let us examine their acts, and see what they do. They look into the future with clear and piercing eyes, just as Athene does in Greek, or the Vala in Norse ; which is always the gift of the dawn-light. Their most important work, however, is to control the weather. They steal and hide away the moon and the stars, which is of small consequence ; but they also steal the rain and the dew, and this cannot be overlooked or pardoned. They hoard the dew and rain, and give it forth at their own caprices. " Not long ago, in Russia, one of them hid away so much rain in her cottage, that not a drop fell all summer long. One day she went out, and gave strict orders to the servant girl in charge, not to meddle with the pitcher which stood in the corner. But no sooner had she got out of sight, than the maid lifted the cover of the pitcher and looked in. Nothing was to be seen ; but

a voice from inside said, 'Now there will be rain.'
The girl, frightened out of her wits, ran to the door,
and the rain was coming down, 'just as if it were rushing out of a tub.' The witch came running home,
covered up the pitcher, and the rain ceased. If the
pitcher had stood uncovered a little longer, all the village would have been drowned." The witch also can
direct the whirlwind, which is attributed to the wild
dancing of the devil, who is celebrating his marriage
with a witch: this is only another interpretation of the
stately procession of Odin sweeping over the sky, or of
the phantom armies of Brittany and Scotland, which
appear in their ballads. The witches themselves fly
through the air on shovels or brooms, — articles connected with fire and the domestic hearth, — and they
hold meetings on hill-tops. But they make themselves
especially obnoxious by milking the cows of others,
even from any distance; a witch just sticks a knife into
a plough, or a post, and the milk trickles along the edge
of it, till the cow is dry. The witches are either old
hags, or young maidens, but always clothed in loose
floating garments; the wizards wear long white beards.
Now could any description better apply to the actions
and appearances of the clouds? They are blown by the
whirlwind; they hover near the earth, and glide over its
surface; they spin and weave varying outlines; they
cluster on the tops of mountains; they draw up the dew;
they pour down the rain, that is, (the Rig Veda says,)
they milk the cows. It seems hardly possible to doubt
that, as these actions were once attributed to unseen
persons, they should at last have been fastened upon
actual, living people.

To protect themselves, the Russian peasants make use of spells. They belong to the same category as the runes of Norse mythology; and were at first uttered in a loud, clear voice, but now are whispered. These Russian spells are full of poetry, and expand into much greater dimensions than the simple Norse runes. They are addressed to the powers of nature, either in their elementary forms, or personified in a thousand different characters; and we must believe that they are but the survival of those prayers with which our far-off ancestors sought protection in the cradle of their race, in their common home in Asia. How are the mighty fallen!

A SPELL

AGAINST GRIEF AT PARTING FROM A DEARLY BELOVED CHILD.

I have sobbed away the day, — I, his own mother, the servant of God, — in the lofty parental terem [upper chamber], from the red morning dawn looking out into the open field toward the setting of my red sun, my never-enough-to-be-gazed-on child. There I remained sitting till the late evening glow, till the damp dews, in longing and in woe. But at length I grew weary of grieving; so I considered by what spells I could charm away that evil, funereal grief.

I went out into the open field, I carried with me the marriage cup, I took out the betrothal taper, I fetched the wedding kerchief, I drew water from the well beyond the mountains, I stood in the midst of a thick forest, I traced an unseen line, and I began to cry with a piercing voice : —

"I charm my never-enough-to-be-gazed-on child, over the marriage cup, over the fresh water, over the nuptial kerchief, over the betrothal taper. I bathe my child's pure face with the nuptial kerchief. I wipe his sweet lips, his bright eyes, his thoughtful brow, his rosy cheeks. With the betrothal taper I light up his long kaftan, his sable cap, his figured girdle, his stitched shoes, his ruddy curls, his youthful face, his rapid gait.

"Be thou, my never-enough-to-be-gazed-on child, brighter than the brilliant sun, softer than a spring day, clearer than fountain water, whiter than virgin wax, firmer than the fiery stone Alatnir.

"I avert from thee the terrible devil, I drive away the fierce whirlwind, I keep away from thee the one-eyed Lyeshy [wood demon], the stranger Domovoy, the Vodyany [water demon], the witch of Kieff, the beckoning Rusalka, the thrice-accursed Baba Yaga, and the flying fiery snake. I wave away from thee the prophetic raven and the croaking crow. I screen thee from Koshchei the deathless, from the spell-weaving wizard, from the daring magician, from the blind soothsayer, from the hoary witch.

"And thou, my child, at night and at midnight, through all hours and half-hours, on the highway and the byway, when sleeping and waking, be thou concealed by my abiding words from hostile powers and from unclean spirits, preserved from untimely death and from misfortune and from woe, saved from drowning on the water, and kept from burning when amid the flames.

"And should the hour of death arrive, do thou, my child, remember our caressing love, our unsparing bread and salt, and turn towards thy well-beloved birthplace, bend thy brow to the ground before it, with seven times seven salutations take leave of thy kith and kin, and fall into a sweet, unbroken slumber.

"And may my words be stronger than water, higher than the mountains, heavier than gold, firmer than the fiery stone, more powerful than heroes.

"And may he who tries to beguile or to cast a spell over my child, — may he be shut up beyond the mountains of Ararat, in the lowest gulfs of hell, in boiling pitch and burning flame! And may his spells be for him no spells, his deceit be no deceit, and his guile no beguiling!"

There are great tenderness and pathos in this, and a native poetry. One's blood quite runs cold at the catalogue of evil spirits and possible dangers. There is still another spell, — that for raising the dead, who almost always come back for a friendly purpose, — to assist a relative or child in distress. Ad is the Russian name for the dark, under-ground world, "where evil spirits and sinful souls dwell." This is evidently the Greek Hades, and has been brought in by Christianity; the pagan conception was different, and the pagans sometimes taught that the dead were living in their tombs or coffins. We find this idea in the Hindu folktale of Punchkin, and the German Ashenputtel.

SONG TO CALL BACK THE DEAD.

From the side of the East
Have risen the wild winds,
With the roaring thunders
And the fiery lightnings.
All on my father's grave
A star has fallen, — has fallen from heaven.
Split open, O dart of the thunder,
The moist Mother Earth !
Do thou fall to pieces, O Mother Earth,
On all four sides !
Split open, O coffin planks !
Unfold, O white shroud !
Fall away, O white hands,
From over the bold heart !
And do ye become parted, O ye sweet lips !
Turn thyself, O my own father,
Into a bright, a swift-winged falcon !
Fly away to the blue sea, —

To the blue sea, the Caspian.
Wash off, my own father,
From thy white face the mould ;
Come flying, O my father,
To thy own home, to the lofty terem !
Listen, O my father,
To our songs of sadness !

From this feeling that the dead returned and watched over their children, there was a belief that the souls of dead ancestors were always present ; that they were not only worshipped by the sacred fire which burned on the hearth, but were actually present in it. This worship, which belonged to every Aryan family and culminated in the majestic service of the Roman Vesta, has survived to the present day with the Russian peasant. Agni is now the Domovoy, or household spirit. The customs connected with him are so numerous and striking, that I shall select him to describe, rather than the Robin Goodfellow or Brownie of English folk-lore.

The Domovoy of Russia now lives in the stove. He comes out every night, and eats the food which the family takes care to provide for him ; for he is very angry if he fancies himself neglected. The customs connected with building a new house are especially curious : it is supposed that whichever member of the family enters the new house first will be the first to die ; so some animal is killed, and laid in one corner. In that corner will be placed the table where the family eats its daily meal, because the dead ancestors, including even little children who have died, are supposed to be present at the meal. Their images once stood in the corner ; but since Christianity was introduced, an ikon, or sacred picture, has taken their place. When the house is finished, and the family wish to remove into it, everything movable is taken away from the old house. Then the oldest woman lights a fire in the stove for the last time, and waits until mid-day. Precisely at mid-day she rakes the burning embers into a clean jar, covers them with a new, white napkin, throws open the house door, and says, " Welcome, grandfather, to our new home!" She then carries the jar containing the fire to the court-yard of the new dwelling ; there she finds the master and mistress, who have come to offer bread and salt to the Domovoy. The old woman strikes the door-posts, saying, "Are the visitors welcome?" The master and mistress reply, " Welcome, grandfather, to the new spot!" After that the old woman enters the house, the master preceding with bread and salt, places the jar on the stove, takes off the napkin, shakes it to the four corners, and then empties the burning embers into the new stove. The jar is broken ; its fragments are buried under the sacred corner of the house. If the distance is too great when the peasant may be emigrating to a new country, a fire shovel and all the fire implements are taken. Such is the present representative of the sacred fire which the haughty Roman colonist carried to every new city. Yet we must not despise the degraded form ; for without the one, we might not have known how to understand the other. The Domovoys of different families sometimes quarrel with each other; and when a death is near, the poor Domovoy is heard lamenting, like the Keltic Banshee.

We are apt to forget that the riddles which are child's

play to us were once supposed to be oracular utterances, made by superhuman beings, and worthy of the most serious attention. Oidipous gained a throne by guessing a riddle, and through these Russian enigmas gleam nature myths, more carefully preserved than in more pretentious forms. "A fair maiden went roaming through the forest, and dropped her keys. The moon saw them, but said nothing; the sun saw them, and lifted them up." The keys are the dew; the maiden the dawn. "A golden ship sails across the heavenly sea; it breaks into fragments, which neither princes nor people can put together again." The moon breaking up into the stars.

Christianity could not destroy these beliefs, interwoven into the peasants' innermost fibres. It could only direct them somewhat. The traits of the Slav deities were transferred to the saints of the Russo-Greek Church. Perun, the thunder god, took the name of the prophet Elijah, and is turned into Ilya. He is said to destroy the devils with stone hammers, like Thor; or with lances, like Indra. On Ilya's day the peasants offer him a roasted animal, which is cut up, and scattered over the fields. St. George becomes Yegory the Brave, and is accompanied by a wolf, the characteristic animal of Russia.

But the most peculiar personification is that of the days of the week. Wednesday, Friday, and Sunday are stately women, who were worshipped in pagan times. Friday takes its name from an ancient Slavonic goddess corresponding to Freyia and Venus, from whom the French got Vendredi. Mother Friday wanders about from house to house, and is offended if certain work is going on. She dislikes spinning and weaving in a woman, twining cord or platting shoes in a man, because the dust gets into her eyes. So any work done on that day is sure to be unlucky. Wednesday shares the same feelings. I copy this story because it is more prettily told than the Friday story.

WEDNESDAY.

A young housewife was spinning late one evening. It was during the night between a Tuesday and a Wednesday. She had been left alone for a long time ; and after midnight, when the first cock crew, she began to think about going to bed, only she would have liked to finish spinning what she had in hand. "Well," thinks she, "I'll get up a bit earlier in the morning, but just now I want to go to sleep." So she laid down her hatchel, but without crossing herself, and said, "Now then, Mother Wednesday, lend me thy aid, that I may get up early in the morning, and finish my spinning." And then she went to sleep.

Wednesday, very early in the morning, before it was light, she heard some one moving, bustling about the room. She opened her eyes, and looked. The room was lighted up. A splinter of fir was burning in the cresset, and the fire was lighted in the stove. A woman no longer young, wearing a white towel by way of head-dress, was moving about in the cottage, going to and fro, supplying the stove with firewood, getting everything ready. Presently she came up to the young woman and roused her, saying, "Get up."

The young woman, full of wonder, got up, and said, "But who art thou? What hast thou come here for?"

"I am she on whom thou didst call. I have come to thy aid."

"But who art thou? On whom did I call?"

"I am Wednesday. On Wednesday surely thou didst call.
26

See! I have spun thy linen, and woven thy web: now let us bleach it, and set it in the oven. The oven is heated, and the irons are ready. Do thou go down to the brook, and draw water."

The woman was frightened, and thought, "How can that be?" But Wednesday glared at her angrily: her eyes just did sparkle!

So the woman took a couple of pails, and went for water. As soon as she was outside the door, she thought, "May n't something terrible happen to me? I'd better go to my neighbors', instead of fetching the water." So she set off. The night was dark. In the village all were still asleep. She reached a neighbor's house, and rapped away at the window until at last she made herself heard. An aged woman let her in.

"Why, child," said the old crone, "whatever hast thou got up so early for? What's the matter?"

"O granny, this is how it is! Wednesday has come to me, and has sent me for water to buck my linen with."

"That does n't look well," said the old woman. "On that linen she will either strangle thee or scald thee."

The old woman was evidently well acquainted with Wednesday's ways.

"What am I to do?" said the young woman. "How can I escape from this danger?"

"Well, this is what thou must do. Go and beat thy pails together in front of the house, and cry out, 'Wednesday's children have been burnt at sea!' She will run out of the house, and do thou be sure to seize the opportunity to get into it before she comes back, and immediately slam the door to, and make the sign of the cross over it. Then don't let her in, however much she may threaten you or implore you; but sign a cross with your hands, and draw one with a piece of chalk, and utter a prayer. The unclean spirit will have to disappear."

Well, the young woman ran home, beat the pails together, and cried out before the window, "Wednesday's children have been burnt at sea!"

Wednesday rushed out of the house, and ran to look ; and the woman sprang inside, shut the door, and marked a cross on it. Wednesday came running back, and cried out, "Let me in, my dear! I have spun thy linen ; now I will bleach it." But the woman would not listen to her, so Wednesday went on knocking at the door until cock-crow. As soon as the cocks crew, she uttered a shrill cry, and disappeared. But the linen remained where it was.

Mother Sunday rules the animals, and she collects her subjects together by playing on a magic flute. A Hindu story exactly reverses the Russian myth, where Mother Sunday is to be dreaded. The former warns all from touching a certain tree, for misfortune abides in it ; but on Sunday it may be touched, for then Lakshmi, Good Luck, inhabits the tree.

The Servians are of pure Slavonic blood ; in the tenth century they embraced Greek Christianity, the Cyrillic alphabet, and the Slavon language, which was also their literary language. The Turks entered Europe, 1355, fought with the Servians in many battles, and finally, through treachery, conquered at the battle of Kossovo, 1389. The unfortunate Serbs who refused to embrace Mohammedanism were reduced to the level of mere peasants, their laws and liberties overthrown. Nothing remained but their popular poetry, which was history of the past and inspiration for the future to the Serbs, and has prevented them from ever sinking so low as the Bulgarians have done. Their pure blood kept the poetic instincts of their race alive in them : for Servia is called the " nightingale of the Slavonic race." It alone has more popular poetry than all the other Slavonic nations put together. The songs are heroic and domestic, not religious. One date is burned into their brain, — the defeat of Kossovo, 1389 ; and the most beautiful of their poems is the heroic poem of the battle of Kossovo. It describes the marriage of Tzar Lazar ; the challenge of Sultan Mourad ; the departure of the Servian army for the field ; the exploit of Milosch, who penetrates into the tent of Sultan Mourad, and puts him to death ; the treachery of Vouk, who went over to the enemy on the field of battle ; the defeat ; and the glorification of Tzar Lazar. It is very spirited, and pathetic also ; what makes one charm is the intermingling of Turkish with Christian customs and titles. As the poem is Christian, it does not come within our subject. But there is another poem which we may describe ; since it tells of Marko, the national hero. He is a compound of Roland and Rustem. He has a talking horse, who lived a hundred and fifty years. He himself lived three hundred years ; finally he took refuge from the Turk in a cavern, where he still sleeps ; but he will return, like Arthur, or Frederick Barbarossa, or Holger Danske, when his country needs him most.

Montenegro was peopled by Serbs flying from the defeat at Kossovo. These glorious people have been three times invaded by the Turks since then, but never conquered. Their national hero is named Ivo : he too is now sleeping in a grotto, but he will awaken when the Turk is to be finally conquered. Soon be the day when the poetic Slavs may take their place among the foremost peoples of the earth !

CHAPTER XIII.

THE MODERN POETRY OF EUROPE.

WE have followed the Teutonic and Latin languages till they broke up into their modern forms ; and in this chapter we shall trace their seven contemporary literatures, and thus understand the spirit of modern Europe, the action and reaction which one language and literature have exercised over the others. Of course, with such a plan, I can speak only of the greatest names ; but, by treating them as contemporaries, we shall obtain a much clearer idea of the development of the human mind, the real growth of thought, than by taking one literature at a time.

Modern literature arises with the modern languages, and the glory of heading it belongs to France, in the eleventh century. We saw in the preceding chapters its formless beginnings ; but ballads, fresh, vigorous, and charming as they are, do not constitute a literature. Poetry is always the first branch to arise, springing from the universal heart of humanity and the simple strength of the people ; and therefore Provençal poetry is the beginning of the modern literature of Europe.

The earliest popular dialect to crystallize into form was the French in its two forms. The " Langue d'Oc," where " yes " was expressed by " oc," was spoken in Provence, a district of Southern France. It spread to

Southern Spain and Northern Italy, and gives the present name Languedoc to the country which was formerly Provence. It was used by minstrels called Troubadours, so called from *trobar*, to find. No longer poor and wandering jongleurs, these Troubadour minstrels were sometimes kings, — Richard Cœur de Lion was one of them, — and always rose to be honored and powerful, even if they had been born among the people : thus they were the first to assert the dignity of intellect. They sang of love and ladies, and the beauties of nature, — nothing more ; and if these songs seem monotonous to us, we must remember that they express the spirit of the age. Besides, they are beautiful in themselves. They sprang into being with a perfection of language, of rhyme and melody, which is amazing to us, but was derived from the Latin hymns. These Troubadours introduced curious customs, which prevailed over Europe, and were even carried to the camp of the Crusader. One of these was a Court of Love, in which questions were argued and decided such as these : "Does every lover grow pale at the sight of the beloved one?" "Is love never the same? is it always increasing or else diminishing?" "Can one woman be loved by two men?" These were all decided in the affirmative, and every Troubadour was bound to accept these decisions as final. There were also floral games, at which each Troubadour wore the flower of his lady love and sang. The victor was rewarded with a golden violet. Every Troubadour was obliged to select some one lady, whose beauty and virtues he celebrated. She was never his wife ; but sometimes some powerful queen, his friend and patron. It was therefore a love which could not end in marriage. And their songs express just such a hopeless and imaginary passion, defined by the absence of the beloved one: it was the love of the rose for the nightingale, of the low-born minstrel for the noble *châtelaine*, of the lonely monk for the stately Queen of Heaven. For this Troubadour poetry, apparently such a new creation, was in reality only a degradation, — an application to actual people of that same sentiment which inspired the Latin hymns. Thus each age inherits from the past, and nothing stands disconnected. In spite of its follies and abuses, the Provençal poetry rendered a service to humanity, because it lifted woman from the degraded position she had held among the Latin families, where she was little better than a slave. The songs were adapted for different occasions: our word *serenade* comes from the Troubadour's evening song; and he had also *aubades*, or morning songs. This lovely poetry was a brief blaze of glory. It was utterly crushed out in the religious persecutions of the Roman Church. It died, and left no following.

In the north of France, where the Keltic Gauls had been conquered by Teutonic Franks and Norsemen, a stronger dialect arose, called the " Langue d'Oïl," because " yes " was expressed by " oïl." Its minstrels were called Trouvères, from *trouver*, to find. They sang of love and war; but they used those ballads which they inherited from the Middle Ages, and did not originate a literature at first. They sang of Arthur and the Holy Grail, which they impressed with a mystic tone; of Roland and the Cid fighting against the Saracens, warlike and chivalrous ballads; of Alexander, and the tale of Troy, classical ballads ; — all of which we examined in the mediæval chapter. But the Trouvères were far from understanding what we ourselves have just learned, — that these ballad stories which they inherited were personifications of the powers of nature ; and as they grew away from the simplicity of the Middle Ages, the stories seemed to them absurd : so they put a hidden meaning into them. The living spring of poetry which existed in the Middle Ages was turned into dull allegories, like the Romance of the Rose, where virtues and vices were personified. Or knowledge of the world brought satire ; and the Trouvères took the simple beast epic of Germany, Reynard the Fox, and turned it into a satire upon the clergy : it spread all over Europe, and is the origin of modern satirical poetry. Finally they wrote little stories, called Fabliaux, which satirized the customs of society : these are the most original work of the Trouvères, and they give us the daily life of the common people. The Trouvères went everywhere, — to the second and third crusades, to the courts of Constantinople and England ; and this early influence of France is far more creditable than that she afterwards exerted. It is only within a few years that we have understood this first blossoming, — have realized that these Trouvère ballads are the source of the modern poetry of Europe, and also the true glory of French literature. The " Langue d'Oïl " was rough, but strong. It was much less beautiful than the " Langue d'Oc," spoken by the Troubadours ; but it lived, and is the foundation of the French of to-day. The last Trouvères were Charles, Duke of Orleans, a royal prince, and Villon, the son of a shoe-

maker, who has been withdrawn from obscurity by the
pre-Raphaelite artists and poets of England lately.

In the twelfth century, the Minnesingers arose in
Germany, inspired by Provençal poetry. They sang not
only of love and ladies, but also of green fields and
singing birds, — of nature. Walther von der Vogelweide is their greatest name ; but Tannhäuser, the hero
of Wagner's opera, was also a Minnesinger. In the
following century, the thirteenth, they copied the ballads of the Trouvères : their poem Parseval, to be the
libretto of Wagner's future opera, is simply copied from
the Arthurian cycle. Max Müller says, " The Minnesingers had an ideal element, an aspiration, a vague
melancholy, sorrow after joy," in their poetry. They
were thus quite different from the joyousness and healthy
objectivity of the Trouvères ; but we know where this
Teutonic spirit came from. In the fourteenth century
poetry passed from the nobles to the homes of burghers
and artisans, and the Meistersingers arose in Germany.
Each trade had a guild, or association of its members,
who chose a chief singer ; and the chief singers of the
different guilds used to meet in poetical contests. The
victor would be rewarded by wearing a silver chain and
wreath, the property of the guild. The Meistersingers
flourished and wrote for two hundred years continuously. They are characteristic of the sturdy middle
classes of the Teutonic race. They express that grim
humor which we found breaking out in the Edda, which
comes out also in the architecture ; as inborn an element as the vague melancholy and the ideality of the
Minnesingers.

The second great burst of original poetry was in

Italy. Italian literature proper begins with Dante (1235–1321) and the fourteenth century. The Troubadours and Trouvères are the natural result of the hymns and ballads of the preceding ages. Dante is singularly uninfluenced by them. He is rather the product of the drama of the Middle Ages; for his great poem in its form resembles the miracle plays. It is divided into three parts, Inferno, Purgatorio, and Paradiso; and he called it a comedy, because it has a cheerful ending; also because it was written in the dialect of the people, — less dignified than the language for tragedy, the Latin. Later, the people called it the "Divine," and gave to Dante the supreme name of poet. No Christian had borne the title before.

Dante visits the Inferno and the Purgatorio under the guidance of Virgil, who was immensely admired and studied, and symbolizes human learning and wisdom. Dante's knowlege of him is owing to the fact, that the profane Latin literature had been revived in the twelfth century; and Dante also knew Aristotle through the Latin translation. Dante describes the persons and the scenes in the Inferno with a terrific realism; but the glories and splendors of the Paradiso are just as strongly depicted by his boundless imagination. The very exactness of these descriptions shows more imagination than a vague suggestion would. Few persons get beyond the Inferno, in reading Dante; but the whole Paradiso is a blaze of light and glory, and uplifts one to its own heights. I should advise all readers to begin with the Paradiso, where the mystic religion of mediævalism paints the final beatitude of the good. Dante's deeply religious nature revealed the spiritual worlds more clearly

to him than to any other human being. He seems to
rise so far above all other poets, as to be more than
human. Taine places him among the four immortals,
— Shakespeare, Michael Angelo, and Beethoven being
the others. And I do not hesitate to consider the Divina
Commedia as the greatest poem which has ever been
written by mortal man.

The Inferno is not only horrible, but hopeless : in
the Purgatorio, a ray of hope lights up the gloom ; puri-
fication through pain is its key-note ; in the Paradiso,
completed victory brings exultation too great to be
expressed in words. Light, music, and motion make
up the Paradiso. What we call angels, Dante calls
lights ; and describes them as spiritual bodies, penetrated through and through with light. They move in
vast circles to the sound of music, so sweet that it
cannot be described.

> "And I beheld the glorious wheel move round,
>   And render voice to voice, in modulation
>   And sweetness that cannot be comprehended
>   Excepting there where joy is made eternal."

As increase of happiness is expressed on earth by a
smile, it is expressed in Paradise by an increase of
light : —

> " Through joy, effulgence is acquired above,
>   As here a smile ; but down below, the shade
>   Outwardly darkens, as the mind is sad."

As the angels increase in goodness they approach
nearer to God, and move continually faster, spurred
on through burning love. In the highest point of all,
Dante's dazzled eyes are opened by prayer, and he sees

the form of a vast white rose. Its leaves are made up
by row upon row of bright beings, who are men redeemed from sin. In the centre is a point of light; as
Dante gazes upon it, he sees it unfold into a triple rainbow. Upon the second bow is impressed an image
like a human form, — the union of the human and
divine in Christ. And then he sees no more; he has
reached the limit of human capacity to see or to describe. His guide through Paradiso had been the spirit
of Beatrice, — a woman whom he had loved on earth:
no other poem has ever placed woman so high.

Dante's life helps to explain his poem, though it does
not account for its superhuman ability. The love for
Beatrice was his earliest inspiration; she was only nine
years old when he saw her first. She died young, and
married to another; but he wrote a poem to her, though
he married a noble lady of his own city. Then he
plunged into politics and civil war: exiled and poor,
he passed years in wandering; a burning patriotism
glowed in his heart, and made another inspiration for
him. The abuses and encroachments of the Roman
Church filled him with indignation; and his satire is
directed against the foes of a pure Christianity, as well
as against the foes of his country. He was singularly
progressive in this, — far in advance of his age.

But these motives were secondary. He was a great
preacher; he wanted to make men better; and with
this end in view, when he was old, he told them his
theory of life. It is not only the story of a single soul
that he gives, it is the elevation of humanity that he
strives for. He wishes to show that there is a God;
that he judges all men; that this world is but a prepa-

ration for the next; that the spiritual world is just as real as this; that it completes and explains this. He puts into the Inferno men who were still alive upon this earth. It was because he knew the truth of the Apostle's words, "He that liveth in pleasure is dead while he liveth." If the soul had died, to Dante's pure vision, the man had died too, even if his body remained living. Finally, he says that both these worlds are parts of one whole. It is to make them both real, that he puts in such a mass of detail: all the art, science, politics, theology, society, of the period, are expressed; but they are the illustrations, not the main idea, — that is, to turn men from their sins by holding up God's judgments. It is a plan, vast in its idea, comprehensive in its detail, and carried out without failure, — great in design and execution. Dante's words are most musical and well selected, and he fixed the forms of the Italian language, which was an unsettled dialect until he came.

Petrarca (1304–1374) is the second great Italian poet. His sonnets to Laura ring every change of a lover's heart. He prided himself on his Latin poems; but is remembered only by those sonnets and canzone, written in a very finished and scholarly Italian, full of Latin words, not so musical nor expressive as the popular Italian of Dante. He wrote nearly three hundred love poems; and, for four hundred years after, all love poems were only repetitions of his. The best, because simplest, of the Canzone is " Clear, fresh, and dulcet streams " (XIV.), which has been charmingly translated by Leigh Hunt. And the best of the sonnets are numbers LXIX., CXXVI., XXIV., LII., to my taste. He may be called the last of the Troubadours; for we must throw ourselves into the spirit of the age before we can understand how Petrarca expended all this devotion upon a hopeless love : also how a perfectly estimable married woman could allow herself to encourage it; which is just the Troubadour spirit. In reading Petrarca to-day he seems to have more imagination and flow of language than real passion. He does not wring the heart, like poor Tasso. The affection that he paints is almost Platonic; a love of the beautiful, rather than of one individual.

And now arises, in the same great century, — the fourteenth, — the third great modern poet. In England Geoffrey Chaucer was born (1328 – 1400). No visions of heavenly splendor, like Dante's, no lover's wasting melancholy, like Petrarca's, are his. Healthy, happy external life, the pomp of courts, the stimulus of travel, the activity of a successful politician, filled up his outward life, and are reflected in his verse. Yet these are so clearly and heartily given back, that his pictures of contemporary life will never be forgotten nor obsolete. He was a master spirit of his own kind. The Anglo-Saxon ballads of Robin Hood lived among the people in England, and the Norman-French ballads of the Trouvères, at court. Chaucer is, at first, the last of the Trouvères; for his earliest writings are merely translations from these ballads. " Troilus and Cressida " is from a classical ballad ; " The Romance of the Rose," " The Flower and the Leaf," from the Trouvère allegories of the same name, — and are all too full of allegory to be satisfactory. The legend of Griselda he found in Italy, where it was read to him by Petrarca.

Think what the meeting of these two poets must have been !

But at sixty years of age, after a long and eventful life, he wrote what he himself had observed, and painted about thirty distinct figures, all pilgrims, who are bound to Canterbury, and tell tales as they wend on their way. It is true that this is all objective : he does not portray character, nor motives of action ; but he makes us feel the beauty of nature, and see the appearance of the people of the period, so well that we cannot but be delighted. His language is interesting, as being the first English, — the resultant of Kelt, Angle, Saxon, and Norman, — but very different from our English, while Dante and Petrarca are like modern Italian. Chaucer is a nominal son of the Church, though not a very spiritual or devout one. These three great poets are pre-eminently Christian ; the faith of the Middle Ages still clung to them. They believed and worshipped God, and the Virgin Mary, and the saints, with sincerity and earnestness. But their splendid burst of poetry had no immediate results : for more than one hundred years there was not one great poet in Europe. When poetry blossomed again, it was under new conditions.

We must go forward to Italy, to the Renaissance ; that is, — to the revival of classical languages, literature, art, and philosophy, — to the admiration for everything Greek, the contempt for everything mediæval, — for Dante's poetry and for Gothic architecture. This spirit impressed itself upon Europe : for Italy became its centre, — the school to which every young nobleman from France, England, Spain, eagerly pressed at the close of the fifteenth century. In 1453, the Turks conquered Constantinople and threw open its libraries. The banished Greeks fled to Italy with the writings of Greek authors, which were eagerly welcomed, studied, and adopted. It is not so much one poet we think of now, but rather a whole society of authors, artists, architects, and philosophers, and a new tone of thought. The princely houses of the Estes at Ferrara, the Medici at Florence, and Pope Leo X. at Rome, vied with each other in encouraging art and literature. The greatest of them was Lorenzo de' Medici (1448 – 1492), who wrote poetry himself, and quite good poetry too, for a prince.

The second poet of the Renaissance was Ariosto (1474 – 1533). He lived at Ferrara, and wrote the Orlando Furioso. This is our old friend Roland of the ballads, who reappears with Charlemagne and Christian knights fighting against the Moors of Africa and Spain. The name comes from the story that Roland has been driven insane by love of the beautiful Angelica, who marries a private soldier, after refusing Roland and many other celebrated knights. But the real hero of the poem is Rogero, the ancestor of the house of Este; and Ariosto probably chose this subject to glorify his patron, the Duke of Ferrara. Everything in Ariosto is borrowed; first, from the old ballads of the Trouvères; then, from the Greek and Latin epics; then, from contemporary poetry. So he begins in the middle of the story; he introduces many characters, and jumps from one to another so often that it is impossible to keep the different plots distinct. Each knight has adventures with giants and pagans, so that the poem never halts for want of action; but the same adventures become tiresome at last, as they happen to all the knights. For instance, two distressed damsels are tied to rocks, and rescued by knights on flying horses. The influence of the Renaissance is shown in the sorceress Alcina and her beasts, borrowed from Kirke's enchanted island in the Odyssey: the two amazons, Bradamante the Christian, and Marphisa the pagan, copied from Virgil's Camilla. It is the most elaborate setting forth of the grand old ballads, but it utterly lacks their simplicity and freshness. Pretending to be a chivalric poem, it should contain nothing but love, war, and religion; and in Ariosto the most important element is utterly lacking. It is, technically speaking, a Christian poem, because the subject is Christian; but there is nothing in it of that genuine love of God, and simple faith, which entered into the characters, and therefore the poems, of the Middle Ages. The Orlando Furioso is too long and too disconnected; the personages are not noble, and the poem is coarse. Yet there must be something to account for its reputation, and that something may be found in the grace of the style, and the overflowing vitality which pervades it. You feel that Ariosto was unexhausted; he might easily have written forty-six cantos more.

The most original part of the poem is that where Astolpho visits the moon, and sees there all things which have been lost on earth; such as time spent in pleasure, lover's sighs, wishes. Among these he finds Orlando's lost reason, and carries it back to him. He had been deprived of it as a punishment for loving a pagan maid. He found also the Decretals of Charlemagne; these were the titles which gave certain privileges to the Popes, but which he shrewdly suspected to

27

have existed only in the mind of the Popes, and to have been falsely claimed as presents from the great Emperor. This sly sarcasm is the product of the age. It was not the lofty religious earnestness of Dante, but the mocking spirit of the Renaissance, which prompted Ariosto.

Yet he is a poet, and a greater one than the next Italian singer of the Renaissance, — Torquato Tasso (1544 – 1595). We do not find in him the robustness of Ariosto, but if we knew nothing of his life we could recognize his delicate and beautiful nature from reading his poem. He took for his subject the last days of the first Crusade, — Jerusalem delivered from the pagans; and this is the same idea which runs through the mediæval ballads, — the struggle of Christianity with Paganism, of light with darkness. In Tasso's day another Crusade was actually talked of, for the Turk was then the bugbear of Europe : so the subject was well timed, although at first sight it does not appear so to us. It certainly was an eminently poetical one ; it admitted of strange adventures, as well as of warlike contests, in that far-off, romantic land ; and through them all ran the motive which sanctified every effort, — the freeing of Christ's sepulchre from the paynims, — so that every requisite of a chivalric poem was there. Tasso has hardly equalled his theme ; but it is a Christian poem in its spirit, as well as its plot. The characters are very noble, especially that of the general in chief, Godfrey of Bouillon. And it is pleasant to know that history agrees with the poet in his estimate of Godfrey. When the other Crusaders fall into sin, they repent and do better: they pray to God for guidance, and are possessed with an enthusiasm for their cause. Tasso-shows the taint of the Renaissance in the form of his poem. It begins like the Æneid : it has an amazon, borrowed from Camilla ; a sorceress, Armida, borrowed from Kirke, — a fury, Alecto, who rouses hatred and revenge, — an enchanted forest, where the trees bleed and speak when broken, — all three copied from the Greek. We are rid of Mars, and Mercury, and the other classic deities ; it is the devil who aids the Pagans, Saint Michael the Christians, and God who rules both ; but this very mixture gives an unreality and a made-up effect to its Christianity. The poem is complete, the action is confined to a few days, the episodes are connected with the plot, unlike Ariosto's rambling stories. But the real greatness of Tasso is in the transcendent power with which he paints his lovers and their conflicts of feeling. It is not in battles nor in prayers that he reaches the height of his abilities. It is in the analysis of feeling, in sentiment, tenderness, delicacy. There are three love stories, which are most delicately and naturally told : so in the poem feeling predominates over action. He is pre-eminently the poet of love, and from his temperament we can understand his life, and that unfortunate love for the Princess Lenore d' Este, which made him pine for years in a dungeon, while Europe was ringing with the Jerusalem Delivered. Gondoliers in Venice still sing its strains as they row.

Tasso wrote one very perfect love poem, Aminta, a pastoral, which was copied from Theokritos and Virgil. It is not read, as the Jerusalem Delivered still continues to be, and its importance is not understood. It set that fashion for pastoral poetry which raged in

Europe for three centuries. Although every poet considered it indispensable that he should write a pastoral in imitation of Theokritos, he got his inspiration at second-hand, through Italy and Tasso's Aminta.

In this brilliant Italian society many women were prominent; but the best as well as greatest of them was Vittoria Colonna (1490–1547). She was a princess, married at seventeen to a husband whom she adored. He died from wounds in battle; he was the Marquis of Pescara, commander-in-chief at the battle of Pavia: and she devoted the rest of her life to writing sonnets and religious poems, which are really beautiful. In addition to her own beauty and rank, and genius and devotion, she has another claim to our interest. She was the friend of Michael Angelo (1475–1564). Nothing more than friend, yet the inspirer of some of his best sonnets. For that wonderful genius deserves to be classed among the poets of the Renaissance, though he wrote but little.

In France the Renaissance opened half a century later than in Italy, — at the beginning of the sixteenth century; and we associate a powerful prince with it there also. Francis I. (1515), — a picturesque figure himself, and a real lover of learning, — established the Collège de France, with chairs for Greek, Latin, and Hebrew, and invited learned foreigners to his court. But no great poet gilds his reign.

Even poor little Portugal surpassed her; for, inspired by the activity of the age, she produced one poet who will live, — her only poet, Camoens (1524–1579). He wrote beautiful sonnets and elegies; but his great work is an epic poem, the Lusiads. He wished to be the

Homer and Virgil of Portugal, to recount the achievements of its great men : so there are numerous episodes which tell about the different heroes. But the thread which binds them together is the voyage of Vasco da Gama. Other poets had written of the voyages of Ulysses and Æneas. In Camoens's eyes Vasco da Gama was as great as they ; and he was quite right. A new route to India was the dream of Europe ; it was that which urged Columbus on his weary way. The Portuguese were the nation most distinguished in Europe for their maritime discoveries : Diaz in 1487 discovered the Cape of Good Hope, which he called the " cape tormented by storms " ; and in 1497 Vasco da Gama passed around and beyond this cape into unknown oceans, and sailed on until he reached India. It was one of those commercial victories which are nobler than the greatest triumphs of war ; its interest extends far beyond Portugal, and Camoens very justly considered it the most brilliant event in Portuguese history.

The charm of this truly beautiful poem lies not only in its noble sentiments, but in its style. That is always simple and natural ; sometimes most pathetic and true, as in the farewells between the men who accompany Vasco and the friends they leave behind them, and in the episode of Inez da Castro ; sometimes very poetical, as in the description of the spirit of the stormy cape, the giant Adamastor ; and every heart must respond to the self-sacrificing patriotism and lofty generosity which Vasco expresses. The poem is not too long, and the episodes are perfectly connected with the main story. It was written in India, after Ariosto, but

before Tasso ; he borrowed the eight-line stanza of the
Italians, and he settled the Portuguese language into
its present forms.

But Camoens could not escape the influence of the
Renaissance. There is an odd mixture in the poem of
Portuguese Christians and Latin gods and goddesses,
Jupiter, Bacchus, and Venus. To spread the Christian religion is one motive of the expedition to India ;
and Vasco offers up prayers to Providence, which are
answered by Venus. The Portuguese are protected by
Venus, and opposed by Bacchus ; first, because they
are a temperate people ; and, second, because they are
trying to conquer India, his native country. Of the
four poets developed by the Renaissance, I should put
Camoens unquestionably first. He has outgrown the
age of chivalry ; yet he has its vigor and heroism and
patriotism, added to the luxuriance of Ariosto and
Spenser, and the sentiment of Tasso, — a strong and
many-sided nature.

The poet himself led a very adventurous and unfortunate life. He went to India, and was shipwrecked in
a fearful storm. He swam ashore, holding his precious
poem, which was all that he saved. His name became
known throughout Portugal and Spain ; but a faithful
slave, who had accompanied him from India, begged in
the streets of Lisbon his master's daily bread. Camoens died in a hospital ; his very winding-sheet was
given him by charity. Ungrateful Portugal !

And now we pass to England, where the Renaissance
opened half a century later than France, a whole century later than Italy, in the middle of the sixteenth
century. Its splendid day was heralded by Surrey

(1516–1547) and Sidney (1554–1586), two brilliant
noblemen and soldiers who had studied in Italy. English Petrarchs they might both be called, since they
wrote sonnets, and were the first in England to do so.
Then come a crowd of poets, grouped around a reigning
sovereign, for Elizabeth belongs to the Renaissance in
England : I have no time to mention even their names.
The exuberant vitality of the time overflowed into a
thousand channels ; and poetry, which had been repressed since Chaucer, one hundred and fifty years before, shared the new life.

Edmund Spenser (1533–1599), the second great poet
of England, would have been sufficient of himself to
form an era. Chaucer had copied the Trouvères, and
Spenser copied Chaucer in using the form of allegory,
which was the fashionable form for all poetry, except
the sonnet. Spenser's first poem was " The Shepherd's
Calendar," in which the gentlemen of the court were
transformed into artless shepherds ; and this poem was
undoubtedly inspired by Tasso's Aminta, quite as much
as by Virgil, which had only just been translated by
Surrey. In his second poem, " The Faerie Queene," the
men who surrounded Spenser were turned into knights
of the age of chivalry. But, as bare tales of chivalry
had long ago ceased to satisfy the mind, a hidden moral
was put into every character. The allegory was to
have been explained in the twelfth book : but, as Spenser only wrote eight books, he was forced to explain it
in a prose preface, which is a great defect in the art of
the poem.

Prince Arthur falls in love with the Faerie Queene,
and sets out to seek her in Faerie Land. She is hold-

ing an annual feast for twelve days, during which twelve adventures are achieved by twelve knights, who represent different virtues. The Red-cross Knight is Holiness; Sir Guyon is Temperance; Britomart, a lady knight, is Chastity; and so on. The object of the allegory is to " fashion a gentleman in virtuous and gentle discipline"; in plainer words, to make a perfect character. The unity of the poem is therefore allegorical; it is the unity of a character: these virtues and vices are but parts of it; the completed character is the perfect whole. Life, according to Spenser, is a battle-field, — a perpetual struggle between a man's virtues and vices, a fight against all that is mean and base in himself and others. Its final aim is — a character. I think we may claim that Spenser has nobly expressed this noble conception; for, with all the faults of the poem, such a spirit breathes through it that we are both shamed and inspired as we read. We long to reach such a standard ourselves; it seems impossible to do anything unworthy or low after we have known the Red-cross Knight and the faire Una.

Mr. Church says, " The power of ordering a long and complicated plan was not one of Spenser's gifts." If he did not wholly succeed, it was that he was embarrassed by his own richness. The allegory is plain for a time; but it is soon lost in a crowd of new characters. It was so easy for Spenser to invent them, that he surrendered himself to his own boundless imagination. The poem is too long: it is finally tiresome and confusing, amid the cloying richness of its beautiful descriptions. His verse, which he himself invented, is most musical. The language was unsettled, and he bent spelling and pronunciation to his own metre. There is a courtly stateliness about the stanza of nine lines, which is typical of the courtly age for which he wrote.

Spenser borrowed immensely: he is steeped in Ariosto and Tasso; from Ariosto he imbibes his coarseness, quite as much as from Chaucer. Through Ariosto and Tasso he gets two personages of classical mythology: his enchantress, with her bower of bliss, and his amazon Britomart. The adventures can be traced back to mediæval ballads, through Chaucer, for we recognize the material we are accustomed to: the distressed damsel, the many-headed dragon slain by a brave knight, whom we found first in India. The shield of Prince Arthur, which slays all who gaze upon it, we have seen in the hands of Pallas Athene, the dawn, and of Perseus, the sun: it is the light. The trees which bleed and speak when broken came from Greece, through Tasso: we have indicated their first appearing in India.

But Spenser has his own poetic gift, and this was to paint pictures of the scenery and the bodies which his mind's eye has perceived. He does not analyze motives nor feelings; there are no characters which live and move, but all the bodies are alive. The virtues and the vices — Faith, Hope, and Charity, Despair, Envy, and Avarice — might be put upon canvas: more wonderful even are the figures which symbolize the months and the seasons. And he creates so many different bodies that one is lost in wonder: he has truly the imagination of the poet. Nothing can be farther from every-day life than the Faerie Queene: it has been called " the poem for poets," and people now-a-days complain that it is long and dull. But it will ever remain a gallery of pictures and a lofty ideal of character.

The drama is undoubtedly the most characteristic expression of the Renaissance. Gradually companies of laymen usurped the privilege of acting. As early as 1400, the Brotherhood of the Passion bought land in Paris, and built a theatre, where they acted the mystery of the Passion, and also some morality plays. Later, Les Enfants-sans-Souci played farces; and the same circumstances existed all over Europe. We do not find the name of any great author, though there are single plays which are very good. From this confusion England was the first to emerge. The drama expressed itself there with such vigor and splendor that it never has been equalled in any country, or any age of the world. It forms a literary epoch greater than those of Greece or Italy.

Everybody wrote a play, either a tragedy or a comedy: among the writers are many names, which singly were great enough to have thrown lustre over any country,— Beaumont and Fletcher, Ford and Massinger, "rare Ben Jonson." But they all pale before Shakespeare: they are so infinitely below him, that they hardly seem to belong to the same race. And yet this brilliant flower sprang into being all at once. There is no hidden growth long enough to account for such a perfect development. Like Provençal poetry in the eleventh, like Dante's poetry in the fourteenth century, it was born full grown. We have seen that Shakespeare drew his plots from the classic ballads and from old stories; but where did he learn to make so many characters, each one of whom would be sufficient for an ordinary writer, — to pierce the motives of every action, — to create living beings?

In Germany there is no Renaissance period. Something else arose there, equally a product of the Renaissance. The foundation of the Universities in Germany put education within the reach of the poorest; the rise of the commercial cities created a powerful and thoughtful middle class; finally, the vices and habits brought in by the Renaissance created such an impression upon the mind of Luther when he visited Italy, that "the Reformation was born side by side with the Renaissance." The power exercised by the hymns of Luther (1483–1546) and his followers cannot be ignored in a history of literature. His hymns were inspired by the Latin hymns of the Middle Ages; next him, the best hymnologist is Hans Sachs, the sturdy shoemaker of Nuremberg, the last of the Meistersingers. He was well educated, knew Petrarca and the Latin authors: he wandered about as a journeyman cobbler, and settled at Nuremberg when twenty-two years of age, and wrote over six thousand poems. The sturdy independence, the keen sarcasm, the grim humor, the moral earnestness of the Teutonic family, speak out in them. These noble and useful qualities atone for the lack of poetry and ideality in Hans Sachs, and at that period probably helped on the world more. That the Meistersinger poetry should have flourished so continuously and so long, shows that it expressed the mind of the people. And the Renaissance made not the slightest impression upon German poetry. There was but one style of poetry: everybody wrote hymns. The people suffered so frightfully by the Thirty Years' War, in the next cen-

tury, that religious poetry was their only consolation.
The German hymns are the only poetry that the nation
produced for five centuries; in fact, the first original poetry that she produced at all. From Walther
von der Vogelweide to Lessing, not one great poet arose
in Germany; though the hymn literature lingered as
long as the Meistersinger poetry had done. Hans
Sachs fairly represents the sixteenth century in Germany, while Ariosto, Tasso, Spenser, and Shakespeare
were the product of Italy and England.

But the Reformation had its poet, — one who united
the religious earnestness, the perception of moral beauty,
the close reasoning of the Reformation, to the exu-
berance and splendor and learning of the Renaissance.
John Milton in the seventeenth century (1608 – 1674)
had every advantage which the times could afford. His
education comprehended everything: his generous Pu-
ritan father gave him masters who taught him Greek,
Latin, and Italian, and the glorious poetry of his own
land, from which Spenser and Shakespeare had just
passed away. They taught him, too, Hebrew and theology and music. He travelled in Italy, where he was
taken for an Italian, because he spoke the language so
well, and wrote Latin and Italian prose and poetry.
His early writings show the influence of Italy and the
Renaissance. " L' Allegro," " Il Penseroso," and the
exquisite " Comus," which is his masterpiece, have a
perfection of form which must have been assisted by
the study of the Greek metres. His sonnets were
taught him by Italy.

Later on in life, religious and political controversies
absorbed him: he wrote prose, with occasionally some

noble sonnets.   In his old age, abandoned by the world, he tried to paint the glories of heaven ; but he gives us, instead, a theological treatise.   Milton was undeniably a great poet, but his imagination is limited as compared with Dante, or Shakespeare, or Spenser.   He does not create heavenly splendors like Dante, nor souls like Shakespeare, nor bodies like Spenser ; he describes theological thoughts.   His genius is lyric, not dramatic ; his verse rolls on with a mighty music and a lofty enthusiasm.   His language is the very pomp of poetry, sublime or beautiful as suits the theme, and stately always.   But all his personages argue and reason, from the Heavenly Father down to the lowest fiend : and this is both unpoetical and unspiritual.   His Satan alone is a creation, magnificently drawn, but strikingly like the Satan of Cædmon the Saxon.   His wars of the angels are grand and stirring ; but they are not spiritual. His services to freedom and his powerful prose can never be too much praised.   No writer ever summed up in himself a more perfect picture of the time.   Taine says, "The exuberant, poetic England dies in him ; the liberty-loving England is predicted and foreshadowed by him."

But more than a century had to pass by before Milton's legitimate ideas were expressed again in poetry : a long, dark period had to be passed through, — that included in the Queen Anne period.   To understand this, we must go to other countries, — first, to Spain. Spain is one of the four nations which have an original drama, — India, Greece, England, being the other three. When we read the Spanish drama, we find all the plots and situations which we have met in Italian opera, or

French comedy ever since. It was not influenced by
the Renaissance, but remained mediæval and Romantic.
Lope de Vega (1562 – 1631) wrote amusing and thoroughly national comedies, which describe the manners
and dress of the period, and therefore are called
plays of "cloak and sword." They are poetical, but
one is exactly like another, and there are fifteen hundred
of them. Part of them have been collected, and fill
twenty-three large volumes.

The greatest play-writer, Calderon (1600–1681),
was first a soldier, then a priest. He wrote one hundred and twenty profane plays, both tragedies and
comedies ; one hundred autos, which were preceded by
long prologues ; so that the quantity he wrote was simply enormous. They are founded upon history, Greek
mythology, and daily life, being then "plays of cloak
and sword" ; thus the field he covered was wide. In
Calderon we do not find thought, profound philosophy,
development of character, as in Shakespeare. The plot
is everything, and the people are but single passions
embodied, not characters slowly evolving ; so that in his
plays we see the surface of life, not its moving springs.
His comedies are very elegant and amusing, his tragedies terrific ; but they are so from the situations, not
the personages.

But the autos are the most original and peculiar of
his plays, — those by which we distinguish him from
all other play-writers. They are strangely beautiful
always, with a mixture of ghastly terror in their poetry
and charm. They were written to be acted upon the
festivals of the Church ; they are, therefore, religious
and moral allegories, like the miracle plays of the Mid-

dle Ages. Undoubtedly they are the most finished form
of those plays ; and we can at once be transported into
the spirit of the Middle Ages by surrendering ourselves
to the enchantment of Calderon's exquisite poetry. In
" The Sorceries of Sin," the old story of Odysseus and
Kirke is used. The senses are put into human form :
they leave the man and follow Sin, till they are turned
into beasts, and come upon the stage in that shape.
The man hesitates long, but finally yields, and follows
Sin. He is brought back by the Understanding and
Penance, actually embodied. All the *dramatis personæ*
are carried away from the island, in a ship which is
the Church, the symbolism being preserved throughout.
The most popular auto is "The Wonder-working Magician." Cyprian sells his soul to the devil, in order that
he may marry Justina. The devil tries to bring her to
him in person, but has no power over her, because she
is a Christian, and calls on God to help her. Cyprian
then becomes a Christian, and both are martyred at
Antioch, A. D. 290. This is a form of the mediæval
legend of Faust. In these plays Calderon rises to be a
Christian in its broad sense, as portraying man over-
coming sin by divine help : usually he is merely a
Roman Catholic, and merits the title he has received,
"the poet of the Inquisition." The play, "The Devotion of the Cross," shows him in his worst light;
a murderer and villain is immediately pardoned, by
kneeling before the cross. "The Purgatory of Saint
Patrick" contains very fine poetry, and was much admired by Shelley. "The Steadfast Prince" is most
touching. The Infante of Portugal is taken prisoner by
the Moors of Africa : he dies a slave rather than sur-

render to the Mohammedans the city of Ceuta, which is his ransom. We shrink from criticising the patient, suffering hero.

The principal importance of the Spanish drama in the growth of literature is that it influenced Corneille, the father of French tragedy (1606–1684). At one bound Corneille outstepped all his predecessors. His first great work was the romantic drama of the Cid. The subject was taken from Spanish history, and the play is not only a fine one, it is really interesting. The Cid kills the father of his lady-love so that the situation of Chimène is trying as well as dramatic, and the struggles of her mind are expressed with the greatest naturalness. The plot is so ingenious that she can at length justify herself, in our eyes and her own, in doing what she wishes, — marrying the Cid. But the critics reproached him, although the play was a masterpiece; so he studied Greek and Latin authors, and originated the French classic drama. The plays were written in rhyming couplets of twelve feet each; no action was seen upon the stage, but long speeches were addressed to a confidant. It was not an actual reproduction of the Greek drama; for there was no chorus to come between author and audience and illustrate the situation; "it was composed according to a set of arbitrary rules founded upon a misconception of a passage in Aristotle." Generally speaking, it had not the religious meaning of the Greek drama, although in two plays there is an attempt to put a Christian spirit into the Greek form, — the "Polyeucte" of Corneille and the "Athalie" of Racine. In the latter is a chorus, which enforces the religious lesson of the play, in perfect versification. I admire Corneille. It is true that his characters are somewhat unreal, that his verse is somewhat rough; but he is very noble and strong. It is not life that he gives us; it is some virtue or some passion incorporated in a human form. But he lifts one into a lofty ideal world, which was yet a real world to him. His native vigor frets against the rules of classical tyranny; but Racine (1639–1699) willingly accepted them.

He showed no traces of Spain; he wrote one comedy like the early French farces. His characters are meant to be perfectly copied from antique models. They are really French courtiers of the pompous and artificial court of Louis XIV. The subject was called Greek: it was really but the court intrigues of an idle nobility. The verse is exquisitely smooth, but nothing can be duller than Racine's tragedies. Heine says that the great French *noblesse* are punished in hell by being obliged to listen to them. Rachel's genius revived them for a time; but they will always remain the most artificial product of the most artificial age of the world, — the period of Louis XIV. Towards the close of his life Racine became very religious, and wrote only on sacred themes. He composed "Esther" and "Athalie," which latter the French consider the masterpiece of their drama. He really was religious; yet he died of a broken heart because the king, while passing through the throng of courtiers, did not speak to him.

But the age produced one great and original dramatist, Molière (1622–1673). At first he was much influenced by Spain, and also showed the Renaissance spirit by occasionally imitating Terence and Plautus, although he never satirized government as they did. Very soon

28

he stood on his own feet, and copied no man. It is contemporary society that he gives us, its vices and follies that he paints. Yet "L'Avare" will always remain a type of the miser; "Le Tartuffe," of the hypocrite; "Le Misantrope," of the cynic: these are as old and as new as human nature itself. His language is wonderfully true, — elegant or boorish, as the character demands; his wit and naturalness are inimitable. He has left us several distinct types, yet none that are very lovable or noble. There is no description of nature in his plays, and no poetic spirit.

The Renaissance culminated in this stately literature of the age of Louis XIV. Its spirit was called Christian: for it was an attempt to imbue Greek form with such a spirit. Its poets were Boileau, who was not in the least a poet, and La Fontaine, who was truly such, although he wrote only fables. His Renaissance studies gave him only the framework. He is really pervaded by the spirit of the French mediæval writers: Æsop's fables seem very simple compared with the dramatic action, the character-painting, the delicate satire, and the delicious style of La Fontaine. Within the limits of one short fable, he will give distinct and life-like characters, — the great lord and lady, the rich parvenu, the poor peasant (a mere beast of burden), — with a good-natured hit at their faults and follies, and such a feeling for nature that it is brought before us in all its freshness. No other French author brings nature so near to us. His style is absolutely untranslatable, for every word is full of subtle meanings, which could only be translated by using several words, and its grace hides its power. Although La Fontaine describes the habits of his animals with such loving fidelity, they are not real beasts at all : they are human beings, — *le grand monde* veiled under the beast form, and playfully satirized.   It must be acknowledged that his morality is not elevated : good-sense, wit, and success are his gods : and he is never earnest.   But he exemplifies the best traits of French literature : nobody but a Frenchman could have written these inimitable fables.

Boileau (1636–1711) has no charm ; but he wrote very correct poetry, according to the rules of Horace, whose Ars Poetica he translated.   He was the great critic of his era, and established rules for poetry, and exercised an influence which we find it hard to understand.   He was, however, a high-minded man when everybody else was a fawning courtier.   He introduced into poetry the heroic measure, which was universally adopted in Europe for a hundred years after, where two lines rhyme, like Virgil ; and his arbitrary rules took away all freshness and spontaneity from French poetry.

Not French poetry alone was injured by him ; for, France being the model of the seventeenth century, his rules were strictly followed in England, where this period extended, and is called the Queen Anne period. Strictly speaking, it began before her, and followed after her ; but, broadly, it should be embraced under her name.   If we now go back to England, we shall understand the situation there.   With the restoration of the Stuarts, 1660, came back French morals and manners and poetry.   Graceful, witty, wicked courtiers mocked at old, blind Milton, and wrote light love-songs. John Dryden (1630–1700) is confessedly the strongest writer of the period ; yet everything is imitated, except his "Ode for St. Cecilia's Day," which is really splendid, full of poetry and inspiration. He translated the Æneid into the heroic measure taught by Boileau, and put Chaucer into stilted English ; but these are forgotten, as well as his political and satirical poetry.

We find a crowd of poets : everybody wrote poetry, even the great prose-writers, Swift, Addison, Johnson, and Goldsmith. They called it poetry : it does not seem so to us, for all sounds as if ground from a machine, the rhymes are so true, the number of feet so correct, the antitheses so well balanced ; but there is no imagination, no soul.

All these poets so called culminated in Alexander Pope (1688–1744). He lacked the poetic fire of "glorious John" Dryden ; but he carried the heroic verse to its greatest perfection, and usually wrote the second line of a couplet before the first. He translated the Iliad into pompous lines, utterly unlike the simplicity of the Homeric poems. His "Messiah" would sound grand to us, if we could for a moment feel that he felt it himself, or forget that it was copied from Virgil's Pollio.

Gray's Odes (1716–1771) have a stately swing to their measures, which comes nearer to Pindar than any other poetry. He is the most successful copyist of the Greek metres, and he never fails to stir us by the mere power of style.

In the Queen Anne drama, immoral and vulgar dramatists are a disgrace to the nation. They were innumerable, but they are deservedly forgotten. The tragedies are slavish copies of French models. Dryden,

Addison, and Johnson wrote dull tragedies. But there are three exceptions. Otway wrote a pathetic romantic drama, " Venice Preserved." which was severely blamed by the critics. Dear old Goldsmith (1728–1774) painted English contemporary society in a charming comedy, " She Stoops to Conquer." Sheridan (1751–1816), who lived somewhat later, but belongs to the period, tried to copy Molière in " The School for Scandal." It seems vulgar beside " Le Misantrope."

The true successor of Molière was found in Italy in the eighteenth century, — Goldoni (1707–1793). He is almost as fertile a writer as Lope de Vega. It is character comedy that he gives, — few incidents, no nature, no poetical spirit, but lively conversations and amusing situations. And the opera, which had been born in Italy (1579), was continued by Metastasio (1782), who wrote innumerable libretti.

But great ideas were fermenting in France. In the early part of the eighteenth century, Voltaire (1694–1778) visited England. He studied the metaphysics of Hobbes and Locke, the physics of Newton, and introduced them into France. Then England became, in the eighteenth century, the literary centre of Europe. Voltaire is the very sceptic of all sceptics in this most irreligious century; yet he is the greatest French poet of the age. He wrote dramas, poems, and an epic, but we remember him by his metaphysics. Voltaire's epic, " La Henriade," is simply ridiculous. The time of Henry IV. is so near our own that the supernatural machinery seems utterly absurd. But Voltaire's dramas have a merit of their own; they touch the feelings. They belong to an age of decadence: they are neither classic, like Racine, nor romantic, like Victor Hugo; they have a mixed style. Like Euripides in Greek, they attempt to unite the merits of two opposite schools. The princes preach the most extreme doctrines of liberty, equality, and fraternity; and the heroines have a liberty of conduct which was never allowed in the Greek or French classic drama. The effect produced on the mind is confusing : they lack the unity of a perfect work of art. Yet they are interesting, especially Zaïre ; and are written in beautiful French. His "Poésies Légères" are models of grace and lightness.

Beaumarchais (1732–1799) wrote two very amusing comedies, " The Barber of Seville," and " The Marriage of Figaro," suggested by Molière, which exposed the wickedness and frivolity of the great nobles. There was never a time when literary men exercised such power. It is not too much to say that Beaumarchais's comedies, Rousseau's novels, and English thought as interpreted by the French philosophers, brought about the French Revolution, 1789.

The French Revolution has a touching and noble figure connected with it, — the young poet, André Chénier (1762–1794). He was the first to turn away from the arbitrary rules established by Boileau ; and he broke out into a lyric measure of his own, full of music, and behind it fresh and pathetic thoughts. His "Young Captive" is truly beautiful and poetic ; it expresses the feelings of a young girl, his fellow-prisoner, dragged away to die. He had been thrown into prison through his generous endeavors to save his brother ; and might have lived had he disclosed the mistake. He died on the scaffold, two days before the close of Robespierre's

reign of terror. One of his fellow-sufferers cried out,
" You, virtuous youth ! are they taking you to death,
bright with genius and hope?" " I have done nothing
for posterity," sighed Chénier : then, touching his forehead, he said, " Yet I had something there ! "

Germany also felt the influence of England : first,
they studied Shakespeare with enthusiasm and intelligence ; next, the ballads of the Edda, lately discovered
at Copenhagen, and of the Nibelungen Lied, discovered
in Germany. A literary movement arose, called the
Romantic school. It had two branches : one historical,
which wrote ballads about the Middle Ages, or dramas
from German history ; the other philosophical, which
described feelings, analyzed motives, depicted daily
life, or wrote about the effect produced on the soul by
external nature. But there was something more than
mere choice of subjects in this new school of thought.
A critic says, " The writings of the Romantic school
mark a transition, not so much from the pagan to the
mediæval ideal, as from a lower to a higher degree of
passion in literature."

The drama was the first to awake. Lessing (1729–
1778) was the first to write national drama. He discovered that the men about him were as interesting as
those of Greece and Rome ; and he wrote tragedies and
comedies based upon English models. " Emilia Galotti "
is a powerful tragedy ; " Nathan the Wise," a lesson of
religious toleration ; " Minna von Barnhelm," an amusing
picture of daily life. Bayard Taylor says, " Criticism
was Lessing's true work ; his poems and plays are
wanting in that warm imaginative element which welds
thought and passion into one inseparable body."

Then came Schiller (1759–1805) in the Romantic drama: he and Lessing wrote it from conviction; Goethe (1749–1831), from the fancy of the moment. Schiller was truly patriotic, and his " Wallenstein " is a noble monument of German poetry. His ballads, too, are very full of the modern spirit. They honor woman, and domestic life, and labor; and if they copy Greek subjects, they put a Christian tone into them. In the "Cranes of Ibycus," he shows that the Greek Nemesis is our own conscience; "that a man's moral destiny is the result and evolution of his own character."

The first great poets in Germany, — the only poets for five centuries, — were these three, at the very close of the eighteenth century, and who were not understood till the nineteenth. Germany's blossoming was late, but glorious: in the nineteenth century she rules Europe. For I suppose nobody will deny that Goethe is the greatest poet since Dante, — one of the few great poets of the world. As a man, we cannot admire Goethe; he resolutely shut himself out from the tremendous political and patriotic questions of the day, and retired to his study to imitate Persian poetry. He wrote everything, — lyric poems, ballads, dramas, romances. I wish to speak of him in this chapter especially in connection with the Classic and Romantic schools. For no other poet ever succeeded as he did in both these forms; and he was equally successful in the difficult and peculiar metre of modern Persian poetry. It is perhaps a moral deficiency that he was so; it may show a lack of convictions, — of a genuine outgrowth from an inner development.

His mastery of two opposite forms is most strikingly

shown in the three episodes of the second part of Faust, which are so disconnected from the main story that they may be treated separately. They are symbolic of the growth of Goethe's mind, which began. as we saw, by adhering to the Romantic school. The first episode is purely Romantic in its character, therefore. A carnival masquerade gives, in an allegory, a picture of the classes which compose society, — a picture of human life. Then Goethe visited Italy, and was intoxicated by Greek art. Matthew Arnold says : "His admiration of style caused the immense importance to him of the productions of Greek and Latin genius, where style so eminently manifests its power. With his fine critical perception, he saw the power of style, and the lack of it in the literature of his own country." The second episode is called the classical "Walpurgis Night." Mr. Bayard Taylor says : "Through it blows a breeze of poetry fresh from the mountains and seas and isles of Greece ; it is full of Tritons and Sirens, Fates and Furies, Greek philosophers and gods. It symbolizes ideal beauty." The third episode, the "Helena," is a perfect poem in itself; it was published as such in 1827, though written in 1800. Its meaning is very plain : it seeks to reconcile, and fuse into one, the Classic and Romantic schools of thought. It is symbolic ; Faust being the type of the romantic, Helena of the classic spirit. They marry, and their child, Euphorbion, symbolizes poetry ; Goethe thus proclaiming his belief, that the highest and newest poetry is the product of all the past, — is beyond the narrow bounds of race or period, — unites human life to ideal beauty, fuses them into one.

Even without its symbolism, the " Helena " is a fine

poem. The first part of it is in classic form, with a chorus; then the scene changes to a castle of the Middle Ages, with knights and banners; and the metre of the poem changes also, from the Greek unrhymed measure to the mediæval rhyming measure. In the dialogue, Helena uses the Greek, Faust the mediæval metre. The episodes of the second part of Faust are not really necessary to the poem, and they seem to be written from the very fulness of Goethe's powers. He takes delight in his command over words. Their interest is purely literary, and to us the contest between the Classic and Romantic schools of writing seems hardly a sufficient subject to expend so much exuberant poetry upon: it appears far away from the realities of life; thus the episodes possess perfect language, but not much feeling.

Everybody is sufficiently familiar with Goethe's works to separate them into their own schools. There is no question about Faust. It is written in the form of a drama, but really should be classed among epic poems. It is essentially the epic of this subjective nineteenth century, because it shows the struggle of a soul against inward temptations, where older epics paint the struggle of a body against external circumstances. It may be called a Christian epic, not only from its spirit, but from its form, which is that of the miracle play. It is thoroughly Romantic, — a perfect picture of the life and belief of the Middle Ages. The heavenly characters are treated as in the miracle plays; that is, they are real persons, walking about and talking; and this means nothing irreverent, although it strikes us so unpleasantly when we read it. Faust is uninteresting as

an individual, and only becomes so when we regard
him as the type of humanity. In the first part, we
have simply the life of an obscure person who longs for
the good things of this life ; and since he has not obtained them, he has an intelligible motive of discontent.

In the second part of Faust, we find a far higher
style of character. The poem is not so universally
known, but is a very grand one ; most noble in its
plan, crowded with beautiful detail, and overflowing
with wonderful poetry. In reading it for the first time,
we feel overwhelmed with the mass of material. The
overflowing creative power of the author lavishes itself
in a poetic richness of thought and language which
amazes us, and the unity of the work is hard to trace
among the bewildering details. Innumerable characters are introduced, who express themselves in most
appropriate language, whether it is keen sarcasm or
beautiful poetry. They are not only perfect in form,
but they have a hidden meaning lying under them :
they symbolize some individual, or some idea of Goethe's own about society, science, and art, and there
are symbols within symbols, also. There is a mis-
taken idea that it was written in Goethe's old age. On
the contrary, Mr. Bayard Taylor says, " It was the
conception of Goethe's prime, entirely planned and
partly written before the appearance of the first part."
It was sketched in 1800, the fifth act written then ; the
gaps were filled up, and the whole concluded in 1831,
his eighty-second year. This will account for the differences of style and of thought which constantly annoy
us in the poem. Some parts are prosaic, others wonderfully poetical. Mr. Taylor says, " The acquisitions

of thirty years formed a crust over the lambent poetical element in his nature; but it broke through clearly and joyously." The second part of Faust is composed of two distinct allegories; one of which is contained in the three episodes, which are very slightly connected with the story itself.

The main story exhibits the struggle of man towards immortality, — the development of character to a higher plane through temptations. The first part was a life of the senses; the second begins with the life of the intellect. Faust awakens to a new sense of existence: he forgets the past and Margaret, and goes on to new adventures. He still keeps his compact with Mephistopheles, who gets him a place at court. But, wearied with politics, he turns to the pursuit of the beautiful, who is symbolized by Helena the Greek. Faust's love for her symbolizes the love of the artist or poet for his ideal, — the yearning for the beautiful. But even this at length becomes unsatisfactory. Then he is attracted by the war of the elements against man; and he determines to enter into conflict with nature, and bend it to the human will. He devotes himself to a great industrial undertaking, but solely from intelligent human ambition. The king whom he had served gives him a wide waste of land on the sea-shore; he resolves to redeem it from the destruction of the ocean. Mephistopheles derides all such hard, honest work, and proposes to Faust to build a splendid palace, with every appliance for pleasure and luxury, instead of dams and sluices. But Faust scorns him, and labors on despite sneers and scoffs. He succeeds; and, as he gazes on his completed work, a higher thought comes to him.

His clearer spiritual vision sees that it is to become a
blessing to his race. On this rescued soil his prophetic
eye beholds a free people blessed with good government. He experiences one moment of supreme bliss ;
he calls upon time to stay. But his compact with
Mephistopheles is thus fulfilled, and he must die. He
reached his moment of happiness in spite of the fiend ;
yet not through the senses, nor the pure love of the
beautiful ; not through political power nor congenial
labor, but through unselfish working for the good of
others.

If the episodes of the story are perfect Greek, the
close is purely romantic : it is more, it is filled with a
lofty spirit of the purest Christianity. Again, Goethe
adopts the machinery of a miracle play. On the stage
the jaws of hell are open, and demons are seen to
arise from them. But also angels descend from above
to claim the soul of Faust. The Eternal Love sends
them : they bear it aloft, and sing : —

> " Rescued is the noble member
> Of the spirit world from evil :
> Who ever aspiring exerts himself,
> Him can we redeem."

Mephistopheles cannot comprehend that he has actually lost Faust ; that a soul can be redeemed through
love of God and beneficent labor for others. He stands
stupidly staring, while the angels gradually disappear,
carrying the rescued soul away with them. Then comes
a beatific vision of Paradise, where loving souls are ever
aspiring towards the Highest. Margaret appears as
the spiritual guide of Faust ; she leads him ever up-

ward through ranks of adoring intelligences, till he, pervaded with penitence and love, is permitted to reach the upper sphere. But the Highest is not visible to his eyes: the Virgin Mary is the only manifestation he sees.

The saint of the Middle Ages was a monk. Montalembert frankly says, "The monastic life is the perfection of Christian life": the saint of to-day goes out into the world and seeks to make it better, instead of flying from it. The hero of the Middle Ages was a soldier; the hero of the nineteenth century is a peaceful artisan, like Watt and Stephenson, who endeavors to help his fellow-men, instead of killing them; who labors to conquer nature and make it useful to the human race, rather than to conquer and degrade man. Great industrial works are the typical works of this century. Mr. Leckey says, "You cannot lay down a railway without creating an intellectual influence: it is probable that Watt and Stephenson will eventually modify the opinions of mankind quite as much as Luther or Voltaire." That Faust should have toiled in an industrial work, should have tried to give honest labor and good government to his fellow-beings, is pre-eminently the spirit of to-day; and that Goethe's prophetic mind felt this noble thought shows him to be a true prophet and guide. Goethe is usually a pagan; here he is not only Christian, but essentially modern.

The Romantic school was first followed in England. We must go back a little: in the stagnation at the close of the Queen Anne period a real poet appeared; his first volume was published in 1780. Even before the French Revolution had proclaimed aloud that idea which was stirring in the heart of the world, Robert Burns (1759–1796) had expressed it. Its essence was found in his first volume, however often literal critics may remind us that it was not until 1795 that he used the actual words,—

> "The rank is but the guinea's stamp,
> The man 's the gowd for a' that!"

And his songs appeal to the universal heart of humanity. Mankind is greater than a class; queens and nobles are but men and women; love and joy, sorrow and death, can never cease to be, — they are as real in the cottage as in the palace; and Burns sang of these, till every creature that was capable of feeling wept or smiled over his words. His life was sad, partly from himself, mostly from his surroundings. France was ripe for him, England was not; but his genius is more valued as time goes on.

Then comes another real poet, — poor Cowper (1731–1800). If Burns expresses the human passion, the courageous manliness, of the time, Cowper gives voice to its religious aspirations, its delicate sensibility, its nervous introspection. Human love made Burns a poet; a love of God as passionate as that of the Latin hymns made Cowper such. The anguish of his tortured soul, the joy of his reconciled heart, found vent in genuine poetry, which burst all arbitrary rules for versification. Cowper's simple and realistic poetry creates an epoch; his importance has not been properly acknowledged. It was he and Burns who founded the Romantic school. Both of them show a heart-felt love of nature, and a feeling for the charm of domestic life, which were unknown qualities in the poetry of England then. They brought back passion to poetry, and thus restored the period of Elizabeth.

But before the tone of thought was definitely adopted, foreign influences came in, — the French Revolution, then Germany. The historical branch of the school was eagerly welcomed and spontaneously adopted by Scott. When a boy he had loved and studied the wild and beautiful Border minstrelsy of his own country, and the German ballads and dramas were thoroughly congenial to him. It was a labor of love for him to translate them. But Southey followed the school consciously. Burns and Cowper had spontaneously expressed the philosophical branch of the school. It was adopted consciously by Coleridge, Wordsworth, Shelley, spontaneously by Byron.

In France the Romantic school was brought in by Madame de Staël's critical history of the literature of Germany. She introduced the two nations: they had never known each other, for France had always despised Germany. The Bourbons brought back English literature and ideas (1814). Philosophical poetry came with Goethe; historical, with Schiller and Scott. France eagerly seized these new ideas, and a tremendous literary revolution was accomplished. It was aided by a writer who is not, technically speaking, of the Romantic school, yet in a broad sense should be included in it, because he introduced into French poetry a new form, and a true love of liberty.

For one hundred years versification had been exactly what Boileau had made it, — rhyming couplets of twelve feet each: even André Chénier could not break it up.

Poetry was supposed to be confined to one form. Bé-ranger (1780–1857) began to write witty, pointed, graceful songs, first about his own life, then about poli-tics. He adored Napoleon, and detested the Bourbons ; he was imprisoned by them. Finally, "le petit bour-geois" woke up to find himself a political power, the best song-writer of his country ; one of her original, typical poets. His range is narrow, and his morality very low ; but his style is charming, and his love of the people is genuine.

The earliest Romantic writer was Lamartine (1790–1869), who represents the philosophical branch. The melody of his poetry is exquisite, and the thoughts are always noble and pure. He is at times sentimental beyond the point of healthiness ; but his best poems have an irresistible pathos. Nothing can be more touching than the lines on the death of his only child, a daughter. "L'Isolement" and "Le Lac" are exqui-sitely lovely. He has a wonderful feeling for nature, not only its beauty, but its soothing power over a suffer-ing soul. But life means something more than to feel, to suffer, to weep. His own life has had action, but his poetry has none. It is so much like our own poetry that we forget how very different it is from the French poetry, — what an immense advance it is upon the di-dactic, descriptive couplets, which are all we can find unless we go back to the witty or wicked Trouvères. His longest poem, "Jocelyn," was considered to be a protest against the celibacy of the clergy. Lamartine disavowed any such intention, in the second edition. He was not only a religious man, but he begun life as a royalist and an aristocrat, being born in that class.

29

A much greater writer, Victor Hugo (1802), showed precisely this spirit in his early writings; but both of these poets became true lovers of liberty and sincere friends of the people. Victor Hugo has faith in the future, as well as reverence for what is worthy in the past. Both branches of the school, therefore, meet in him; his historical novel, "Notre Dame de Paris," and his ballads, paint the Middle Ages with tremendous realism, the mind as well as the external life are given. He strips off the veil of enchantment, and shows their faults as well as their virtues: he looks at the past with the mind of to-day. In his novels of modern life he always takes the side of the oppressed, and strives to elevate and reform society. They are painful from their vivid descriptions of sinning and sorrowful human beings; but they are written with a purpose. Therefore he gives us types which are too absolutely noble to be natural, but which hold up before us the loftiest ideal of character. We find in his writings the strongest shadows, the highest lights, and too many antitheses: in the hand of an ordinary writer these would become tiresome; they only render Victor Hugo more powerful and poetical.

He is equally great as critic and dramatist: his prose preface to the drama of "Cromwell" (1829) gave the reasons and fixed the epoch of the Romantic school; and his grand dramas broke forever the chains of French classic drama. Everybody believes in him now; but he has worked an absolute revolution in French literature, and met with unstinted abuse at first.

His earliest writings are in verse, — odes and ballads, some of them written at sixteen years of age. Relatively they do not stand so high as his dramas, (which were his second productions,) or his novels. Yet his love-poems and .pictures of domestic life are very pure and sweet, and nobody has ever painted children more charmingly than he. Whether in prose or verse, Victor Hugo's children must live forever. His life has been as noble as his writings ; and the French may well be proud of Victor Hugo, the head of that romantic school under which we are living.

PARTIAL LIST OF BOOKS CONSULTED,

GIVING THE TRANSLATION ONLY WHERE
THERE ARE SEVERAL.

Chips from a German Workshop. Max Müller
Life and Growth of Language. Whitney.
Science of Language. Max Müller.
Oriental and Linguistic Studies. Whitney.
The Dawn of History. The Brothers Keary of the British
    Museum.
The Ancient City. Fustel de Coulanges.
The Mythology of the Aryan Nations. G. W. Cox.
Origin of Fairy Tales. J. Thackeray Bunce.
Myths and Mythmakers. John Fiske.
History of Architecture. Fergusson.
History of Sanskrit Literature. Max Müller.
Influence of India on Modern Thought. Sir Henry Maine.
Translation of the Rig Veda. H. H. Wilson.
    "   "   "   Max Müller.
    "   "   "   M. Langlois.
History of India. Vols. I., II., III. Talboys Wheeler.
Nala and Damayanti. Milman's Poetical Works. Vol. III.
The Iliad of the East. Miss Richardson.
Religious and Moral Texts from Sanskrit Writers. Muir.
Sacred Anthology. Conway.
Indian Wisdom. Monier Williams.
Bhagavad Gita. Thompson.
The Hindu Drama. Vols. I., II. H. H. Wilson.
The Origin and Growth of Religion as Illustrated by the Religion
    of India. 1878. Max Müller.
Sakoontala. Monier Williams.
Westminster Review. October, 1848.

Oriental Poetry. W. R. Alger.
The Light of Asia. Edwin Arnold.
Old Deccan Days. Miss Frere.
The Avesta. Bleeck, from Spiegel's German Translation.
The Shah Nameh. Atkinson.
La Poesie en Perse. M. Barbier.
Le Théâtre Moderne en Perse. M. Barbier.
Tales of Ancient Greece. G. W. Cox.
Studies in Greek Poetry. Symonds.
Pindare et la Poésie Lyrique. Villemain.
Aischylos. Preface to Translation. Plumptre.
Sophokles. Preface to Translation. Plumptre.
Study on Euripides. Mahaffy.
History of Philosophy. Lewes.
History of the Drama. Schlegel.
Origin of the Homeric Poems. Packard's Translation.
Translation of Plato's Phædo. Church.
History of Rome. Vol. I. Mommsen.
Preface to Lays of Ancient Rome. Macaulay.
Latin Literature. Thomas Arnold.
La Mythologie Gauloise. M. Lefloq.
Keltic Literature. Matthew Arnold.
Les Bardes Bretons au 6ème Siècle. De la Villemarque.
    "   "   "   12ème "   "   "
Translation of Breton Ballads. Tom Taylor.
The Mabinogeon. Lady Charlotte Guest.
Le Foyer Breton. M. Souvestre.
Tales of the West Highlands. Campbell.
Teutonic Mythology. Grimm.
Translation of the Edda. Thorpe.
Northern Mythology. Thorpe.
Yarl Hakon. Oehlenschläger.
Popular Tales from the Norse. Dasent.
Translation of the Heimskringla. Laing.
Sigurd the Volsung. William Morris.
Grettir the Strong. Morris and Magnüssen.
Gunnlaug the Worm-tongue. Morris and Magnüssen.
Burnt Njal. Dasent.
Tales from Teutonic Lands. Cox and Jones.

Frithiof the Bold. Anderson.
Anglo-Saxon Literature. Conybeare.
Beowulf. Late Prose Translation.
Studies in German Literature. Bayard Taylor.
Early English Writers. Morley.
Intellectual Development of Europe. Draper.
History of Rationalism. Lecky.
Les Pères de l'Eglise. Villemain.
Les Moines de l'Occident. Montalembert.
Translation of Latin Hymns. Neale.
Life of St. Bernard.
Popular Romances of the Middle Ages. G. W. Cox.
Middle Ages. Wright.
La Chanson de Roland. Republication of Old French form.
The Lytell Geste of Robyn Hood. Ballad Book.
Early French Poetry. Besant.
The Troubadours. John Rutherford.
Study on Dante. Church.
Study on Spenser. Church.
Translation of Calderon. McCarthy.
       "   "   "   Trench.
Study on Calderon. Lewes.
Loves of the Poets. Mrs. Jameson.
La Fontaine et ses Fables. Taine.
La Littérature Anglaise. Taine.
Curious Myths of the Middle Ages. Baring-Gould.
La Littérature chez les Slavs. Courrière.
La Littérature en Russie. Courrière.
Songs of Servia. Owen Meredith.
La Russie Epique. Alfred Rambaud.
La Littérature du Nord au Moyenâge. Eichoff.
Russian Folk Tales. Ralston.
Songs of the Russian People. Ralston.
The Ottoman Turks in Europe. Freeman.
Theology in the English Poets. Stopford Brooke.
German Thought. Karl Hillebrant.

INDEX.

30

[R

University Press : John Wilson & Son, Cambridge.